treacherous WATERS

treacherous
WATERS

STORIES OF *Sailors in*
the Clutch of the Sea

Tom Lochhaas

EDITOR

EPICS OF THE SEA

International Marine / McGraw-Hill

CAMDEN, MAINE ■ NEW YORK ■ CHICAGO ■ SAN FRANCISCO ■ LISBON ■
LONDON ■ MADRID ■ MEXICO CITY ■ MILAN ■ NEW DELHI ■ SAN JUAN ■
SEOUL ■ SINGAPORE ■ SYDNEY ■ TORONTO ■

The McGraw·Hill Companies

1 2 3 4 5 6 7 8 9 0 DOC DOC 0 9 8 7 6 5 4 3

Library of Congress Cataloging-in-Publication Data
Treacherous waters : stories of sailors in the clutch of the sea /
Tom Lochhaas, editor.
    p.   cm.
Includes bibliographical references.
ISBN 0-07-138884-2 (pbk. : alk. paper)
1. Shipwrecks. 2. Survival after airplane accidents, shipwrecks,
etc. I. Lochhaas, Thomas A.
G525.T666 2003
910.4´5—dc21   2003007293

For permission to use excerpts from copyrighted works, grateful acknowledgment is made
to the copyright holders, publishers, or representatives named on pages 348–50, which
constitute an extension of the copyright page.
Special thanks to the librarians at Newburyport Public Library for years of assistance with
interlibrary loans and other research.
Photo credits: pages ii, vii, 65, 66, 83, 107, Beagle Channel, Tierra del Fuego, Chile by
Colin Monteath/ImageState; pages 1, 2, 17, 33, 45 by Hal Roth; pages 123, 124, 135, 14,
166, 187 © Photodisc/Getty Images; pages 209, 210, 228, 248, Antarctica © Ben Osborne/
Getty Images; pages 271, 272, 282, 290, 304, 322, Pacific Ocean © Bryan Mulleanix/
PhotoDisc/Getty Images.

To Kate and Cassandra,
wife and daughter and sailors both,
for love and inspiration and everything
else it takes to stay afloat.

contents

introduction

Odysseus wasn't the world's first sailor, but the story of his adventure may be the oldest surviving sailing narrative. That epic began the literature of the sea and still captivates readers three millennia later. Sea stories are surprisingly unchanged after such a long history, perhaps because of their focus on fundamental themes. Countless generations have crossed oceans since Odysseus, still hearing the sea's siren call, still braving wind and waves, still seeking the middle ground between Scylla and Charybdis, exploring exotic lands, and making an inner voyage of discovery. Every generation has to sail off and do it themselves. Every sailor—and every reader—does as well.

The oceans are not always treacherous, but anyone who sails long enough and far enough will confront inevitable dangers. It doesn't matter how large your ship is: the waves can and will get larger, the wind more than the ship can take, reefs and shoals unavoidable. These dimensions are universal; what differs is how one responds, the human dimension. On some primal level readers can't help but be captivated by that man against nature theme. But there's much more to it than that: great sailing stories are far richer than, say, a simple confrontation between a man and a grizzly bear in a forest. The literature of sail is also about exploration—the outer and inner voyage—the quest that is intrinsic to heroic and epic literature.

Until a century ago most great sailing expeditions were voyages of exploration. Dias, da Gama, Columbus, Magellan, Cook, and Champlain are just a few of the sailors who shared Odysseus's drive to explore the world. More recently explorers like Ross, Amundsen, and Peary sailed to the polar regions, a new generation of explorers still hearing the sirens' call. The public read their stories with avid interest and excitement. At the same time the literature of sea fiction matured, exploring human realities now that the geographic realities were known. In the novels of Melville and Conrad, readers found the same adventures as in the journals of old salts: the same truths about the sea, the same fundamental confrontations.

With the twentieth century came historic changes that turned the literature of the sea in new directions. Two factors seem foremost. The world had been explored—all of it, every last little Pacific atoll and remote village—and while new generations of sailors still sought unspoiled paradises, they could no longer hope to be the first to arrive. The old theme of exploration gradually focused more on the sea itself, the ship, the human experience. Treacherous waters were no longer something you had to pass through to get where you were going—they *were* where you were going.

Almost coincident with that historic shift, and central to most of the stories in this book, sailboats were becoming smaller, allowing just one or two people to cruise the world. Even as steamships were ending the great age of sail—those tall ships that crossed oceans on commercial or military voyages—amateur middle-class sailors were experiencing for themselves in smaller craft what previously they could only read about. In 1895 Joshua Slocum finished rebuilding his 36-foot sloop *Spray* and left on a three-year voyage to become the first sailor to circumnavigate the globe singlehanded. His marvelous book about it sometimes seems as exotic as the *Odyssey*. In 1899, Howard Blackburn, a tavern owner in Gloucester, Massachusetts, crossed the Atlantic alone in a small sloop and proved that just about anyone could do it. With these historic shifts sailing became a personal matter. That people could go to sea not for a job but for all kinds of personal reasons led to huge changes in the world of sail and the literature born of that world.

As we see in these stories, people still sail for adventure, of course. Or to study nature, or escape the confines of civilization, or be alone with a loved one, or be the first or fastest—but it always involves *the sailing itself*. There is no exotic destination as the central focus, no commercial enterprise driving decisions, no enemy to do battle with, no need to get anywhere. The voyage is everything. You don't need much money or even maritime experience. You can be a farmer, a poet, a tavern keeper, a French teacher.

With so many different personalities going to sea, the literature of sail has exploded in a hundred fresh directions, but always it explores the human dimension of voyaging. What do you learn after weeks or months at sea, alone or in small company, experiencing the joys of fine weather, wallowing in the doldrums, suffering the horrors of severe weather on a sinking ship? What do you learn about nature, about the world, about humanity? About yourself? Many write of a clarifying vision that can be experienced only away from all the trappings of life ashore. Invariably we trip over meaning-of-life musings.

All this—and so much more—attracts us to sea stories. Distill the universe down to bare essentials—water, wind, sun, a small boat devoid of most comforts, and a human being or two—and you have a fascinating opportunity to see how things work. And never more so than when the sea becomes treacherous.

All the sailors whose stories are excerpted here, one way or another, encountered dangerous waters. But that's about all they have in common. How they respond as individuals is part of why we read them—the myriad thoughts, emotions, and actions of human beings similar to or different from ourselves. We read their stories and react with them. We may wonder how we would respond in those circumstances. No small number of readers go to sea themselves, some explicitly to find out.

I've tried to give some order to these stories by grouping them according to certain themes. It's only natural to make comparisons when we read, and juxtaposition seems a good way to appreciate variations on a theme. These categories are fluid, however—arbitrary and overlapping. The dangers of storms are winds and waves, and it is these that make Cape Horn or a lee shore treacherous as well. The particulars are always important but when it comes right down to it, how much does it matter whether your ship is holed by a reef, a killer whale, an iceberg, or a log just beneath the surface? Or whether the cabin of your small boat fills with water from a portlight blown out when a rogue wave tosses the boat on its beam ends or, having pitchpoled in 60-foot seas, the water simply explodes in everywhere? It's not the log or breaking glass we focus on, but the individual world of the sailor—the stuff of the best stories.

Many of these stories involve severe storms at sea, every sailor's nightmare. Richard Maury writes eloquently of battling a North Atlantic winter gale in his small schooner. Sailing a small open boat across the Pacific, Webb Chiles survives a capsize but carries on for days in his dinghy alongside his water-filled boat, thinking about death. Marlin Bree fights a hurricane-like storm on Lake Superior in a small boat he built himself. Kim Leighton describes the worst nightmare of all: the 1998 Sydney–Hobart race storm that destroyed seven boats and killed six men, while others struggled heroically to live.

The dangers are not always far out to sea, however. The stories by Ann Davison, Gordon Chaplin, and Gilbert Klingel all involve shipwreck on a reef or lee shore. Jonathan Hall barely escapes the rocks and ledges surrounding him when caught out alone in a small boat on a dark night. Three of the stories involve that most famous geographical danger—Cape Horn—where the winds and waves of the Southern Ocean rise to their greatest extremes. Alone approaching the Horn, Lisa Clayton's boat is knocked down repeatedly but manages to keep on going. John Guzzwell on the Smeetons' boat describes how they are pitchpoled and almost sunk, and how even with broken bones Beryl Smeeton swims back to the ruined boat through unbelievable seas and calmly gets out the bailing buckets. Réanne Hemingway-Douglass is also pitchpoled at the Horn, resulting in a fight for survival that goes on for days.

Polar oceans are another kind of treacherous water. In seeking the high northern and southern latitudes, Tristan Jones and Deborah Shapiro (with Rolf Bjelke) must escape crushing icebergs and endure having their ships frozen into pack ice. Crossing the Atlantic by the far northern route in an historic leather-hulled boat, Tim Severin and his crew battle an icefield in which even the smallest collision could sink their fragile craft.

Most of the sailors in these stories survive. In Faulkner's phrase, they do not merely endure, but ultimately prevail and keep on sailing. Yet these are not sailor-saints who succeed against all odds. These are real people, not mythic heroes, and not all of them reach happy endings. Lovers, spouses, even children sometimes die. John Rousmaniere tells the story of a father who takes his two sons on an early transatlantic race and drowns along with them. Jim Carrier describes how a hurricane takes an entire ship and its crew. Tami Oldham Ashcraft comes to after a knockdown and finds her fiancé simply vanished from the boat. Gordon

Chaplin loses hold of his lover's hand in the turmoil of a storm and cannot find her again. Louise Longo sees her daughter die in the life raft after their sailboat sinks. These are chilling realities and reminders of the fragility of life, especially at sea.

The individual stories in this collection were selected not only because they are powerful stories in their own right but also to represent the rich diversity of the literature of sail. Some were written decades ago, some yesterday. Some are meditative, others pure adventure, some are highly personal, others focused entirely on events. Some are humorous, some tragic. But they are all, ultimately, as timeless as the sea itself.

Treacherous Waters is one of the first two books in the *Epics of the Sea* series, along with *Intrepid Voyagers: Stories of the World's Most Adventurous Sailors.* Written mostly over the last half century, some of these stories have become classics, others remain more obscure. They were chosen both to introduce new readers to modern sea literature and to provide seasoned readers with some gems they may have missed. Unfortunately some of the original texts are out of print and known only to collectors and those who look for them. I hope by sharing these stories with a wider audience that these collections help preserve at least some part of the original works.

The true stories in *Intrepid Voyagers* involve less elemental violence than those in this book but perhaps more human drama. With Harry Pidgeon you'll cruise on a small boat around the world on a voyage of discovery, and discover how easily you could do it yourself. Seven decades later you'll do it again with a teenage girl alone on a 26-footer she only barely learned to operate before starting out. You'll cross the Atlantic in a rubber raft without food or water, then do it again through big seas in a boat only 6 feet long. With Bernard Moitessier you'll know what it feels like to leave civilization so far behind that, after circling the globe alone, you decide to keep on going. With the Smeetons and the Pardeys, famous cruising couples, you'll discover how to build a whole life at sea, but from Donald Crowhurst you'll learn how months alone at sea can literally drive you insane. You'll encounter gales and doldrums, adventure and comedy, fear and love. Some voyages pass through geography, some through the inner self, others into heaven or hell.

///

treacherous WATERS

FROM

the SAGA of CIMBA

BY
Richard Maury

In the cold of November 1933, Richard Maury, age twenty-three, sailed from Connecticut with a companion in his 35-foot schooner, *Cimba*. They were headed for Bermuda, the Caribbean, the Panama Canal, and finally the South Pacific to explore the then still unspoiled islands of Tahiti and Fiji.

Almost immediately they were engulfed in gale winds and high seas. The North Atlantic in early winter is seldom comfortable for small sailboats. The following selection begins a few days after their departure, still caught in the gale.

Later, after *Cimba* was wrecked on the reefs of Fiji, Maury went on to live a long, full life. One of the most powerful writers of the literature of sail, Maury is often compared to Conrad. Jonathan Raban calls *The Saga of Cimba* "irrepressibly buoyant in spirit" and "the most eloquent prose poem ever written to the exhilaration, the beauty, and the sheer joy of being at sea." Maury was eloquent even in the middle of a life-threatening storm; his words are as alive as the sea, as strong as the oak frames of his ship.

///

A schooner is usually hove to by securing the helm alee and furling all cloth but the foresail. Once hove to she should, unattended, creep to windward with the foresail, until the rudder has pinched the sail so close into wind that headway becomes lost, and, the vessel falling off, the foresail fills, the manoeuvre being repeated. This counter-balancing of sail and rudder, depending on the force of the wind-sea, should keep the vessel working slowly to windward, holding her own or else falling gradually to leeward.

The *Cimba*, usually a good heavy-weather craft, did not heave to especially well on the night after the calm. The seas were higher than they had been, and neither Dombey nor I could get her lying comfortably amid them. Either she would yaw widely or else pitch into the eye of the wind until we thought her rocking masts would snap their stays. And the fault was not hers, but very much my own. When the draught had been increased in Nova Scotia I was the one who felt that the small original rudder should be kept, that a larger one might part in a seaway. Under ordinary conditions the rudder worked well, but now, with waves high enough partially to blanket sail and lessen headway, it lacked sufficient surface to force the hull to the wind.

We tried righting this with more headway to give greater rudder action, taking the close reef out of the foresail and running it up single-reefed. But the sail, overpowering the rudder, sheared the schooner broadside to the first big sea. She slid into a trough. The double reef was quickly put back and a storm trysail set to the main, a combination successful once or twice before, but now throwing us into the eye of the wind, where another roller drove us stern first along its crest. Pulling up in a groove of sea, we stowed trysail and set about making a drag, or hold-water, out of wood and weighted tarpaulin. Easing it over the port quarter, we tried lying-to stern first. The drag was a failure, and the bows were put back to the wind.

It grew cold, the barometer took a rapid dip, and rain fell on the sea. Dombey and I, holding to backstays, watched the craft and tried to solve our problem. The weather looked severe, and, with all thought of Bermuda gone for the moment, we saw with concern the heavy building up of the seas. Nearly always it is the seas that threaten the small sailer, just as usually it is the wind that finds the vital point in large sailing-ships. Some craft have not enough forefoot, or displacement forward, to heave to. The *Cimba* had, and we had to get her to ride with it safely. Time and again the foresheet was trimmed to a nicety, the helm adjusted, and then readjusted in the dark. After each change we waited, watching the result. Dawn found us still on deck, gripping to stays, studying the lively schooner as we drank from tins of condensed milk. An eternity of seas rose and fell between us and an east that glowed a windy sepia. It blew harder with the expanding light, and as it did we hit upon the best press that could be shown to the wind—a reefed foresail and a blanket set in the weather main rigging.

We stirred the fire in the stove and warmed the cabin. The work of the night had not been hard, not so hard as had been the waiting and watching between moves. In a small craft there is seldom enough physical work to stimulate the circulation. There is much of footwork, a lot of holding on, but even in tight moments agile fingers are as valuable as strong arms.

At half-past eight in the morning the wind moderated, the barometer held its own, then once more fell very slowly. The *Cimba* moved restlessly; the ocean brooded on some first thought. Overhead a pale sea of clouds ran to leeward, joining the storm-wrack twisted over the horizons. Straight-edged horizons had disappeared, to be replaced by a moving ocean's edge lifting and falling, sometimes seen, more often hidden by the streaming, uplifting water about us. Perhaps once every three minutes a sea, higher than its neighbours, would heave us to a dragging grey top, allowing a quick glance, a bird's-eye view, over wide distances, before again we were descending blank walls of cold, shadowless water.

The wind came back at Force 11 of the Beaufort Scale, moving everything before it. Only the schooner offered resistance as the seas, under a scud illuminated by weird yellow gale lights, bore down, rolling, gigantic, a full quarter of a mile from crest to crest. She stood before them, rakish, tar-daubed, her defense awaiting the attack.

We didn't talk. A gale, as does a calm, induces silence. Often one of us would go up to watch the fight of the schooner, only to return to the cabin disappointed that there was nothing to do. They say that doing nothing is an art. If this is so, then the art must lie in overcoming the very hopelessness of the act. We cooked cracker hash, our last hot meal for some time, took turns at keeping vigil at the weather porthole, watched a whirling, telltale compass, and saw to it that spikes and sheath knives were handy. We broke silence to consider running off before the blow, deciding in the end that it was too dangerous, and under the conditions the last resort for a small craft.

> BOATSWAIN. *Heigh, my hearts! cheerly, cheerly, my hearts! yare, yare! Take in the topsail! Tend to the master's whistle. Blow, till thou burst thy wind, if room enough!*

It was half-past two. I was glancing at Act One of the very appropriate *Tempest* while drying out a last meagre ration of tobacco. Suddenly Dombey shouted from the port:

"Look at this sea!"

It must have been perpendicular! I felt the cabin lifting as though striving for some great altitude. A second later there was a thud, the deck slipped away beneath my feet, careened, and the craft dived to a trough, falling down, as though knocked beam-on along a great decline. The cabin revolved, and we were driven against the bulkheads as amid a deafening noise the hull went over, and we, together with a thousand articles, were flung through space to crash on the cabin-top, now upside-down. We fought our way out from under a heavy heap, to find the cabin in darkness, the ports under water. Looking up, I caught sight of the flooring over my head; one of the floorboards dropped as I did so. Although the companion and the hatch, now leading into the ocean, were closed, water came running in. Quite suddenly the cabin filled with smoke as the ship's stove, bolted to the floor and now overhead, emptied its coals and wood, to blaze on the cabin roof; a stream of water poured out of the stove from the submerged vent.

Why didn't she right herself? Not sure whether she had not foundered, we knew intuitively that the ton of iron on the keel, now up and down above us, was being offset by the weight of the masts, the bulk on the cabin carlings by the water that was filling her; and underneath the foresail was acting as a canvas fin, itself a keel of sorts.

We tried to stand up and handle the fires glowing in the semi-darkness, finding it difficult to keep a footing as we scooped water at the flames. The smoke increased, and we choked from the odours of kerosene, burning wood, and paper. There was the sound of another disturbance outside. We were hit again—thrown back to our knees. Once more the cabin swayed; we were tilted up against the bulkheads, pinned to them for a second, then dropped with a last stunning fall on to right-sided floorboards. The ocean is unbiased. A second wave had hit, causing the hull, which had gone over to port, to make a complete circle under water before coming up to starboard, to send the spars out of the sea and spinning back to windward.

We made the most of the chance. I groped about in the smoke, found a marline-spike, forced open the hatch, and reached the deck. All the gear stood; halyards and sheets trailed overside; but there was the foresail, still aloft, stiff and dripping wet. Waiting for a chance, I climbed aft and, while Dombey fought the fire, swung the *Cimba*, running her before it.

One look at the sea, and I knew that this was only the beginning, that the worst lay to windward, to the north-west. Presently I saw Dombey on deck furling the foresail. He came aft, shouted that the fire was out, and with hands on hips looked at the sea and gave a long whistle.

THE *CIMBA* stormed along in a south-easterly direction, away from Bermuda, wet to her very trucks, her glistening masts and rigging offering windage enough to drive her rapidly to leeward. She needed no sail, and no sail could be set. Astern a tall lifting of grey would build up, close in; the bows would drop as the after-sections climbed, fighting to the steep level of the wave. For a moment it would appear that instead of rushing ahead she was making sternway up a vast slope of oncoming water. When it seemed that she could no longer hold the severe angle without pitch-poling—drowning the bows and throwing counter and keel out of water—she would fight into the crest, to be attacked by grey-white water, broken, wild, to be sent skating, wedging over ocean for one hundred, two hundred, three hundred yards. Then the wave had gone, and she was falling again, falling under the steep shadow of the next sea.

For quarter of an hour Dombey and I, utterly silent, watched her every move. It was not as it had been before. We now sailed a ship that knew of defeat—a ship we had imagined undefeatable. We stood there fascinated by her spirited action, her effort, knowing, as we did, how much more courage is needed by the once defeated.

As she scudded we had to hold her directly behind the seas, which could be done only by facing aft into the blow, handling the tiller firmly, gingerly, never moving it much at any one time, although constantly shifting the rudder as though it were the tail of a fish. Steering on the slopes and in the troughs was not difficult, but when on a wave-top, with the hull surrounded by eddies shearing us first one way, then another, it was a different matter; then the helmsman dealt with two unseen forces, applying one, the invisible rudder, to offset the other, the invisible currents and roving counter-currents rushing the crest.

Atop the larger crests the hull would vibrate from keel to truck, as though a charge of dynamite had exploded close by, and at such times, with the rudder taking the brunt of the shock, it required not only two arms, but a strong back as well, to save the tiller from tearing free. In ordinary weather six-hour watches were held, and later we set what we called the "*Cimba* watch," a twelve-hour wheel trick. But now, running before it as we were, watches were shortened to an hour. Partial exhaustion came on after the first fifteen minutes, and, cold though it was, a perspiration with it. The watch over, we would climb down to a wrecked cabin that no longer had bunks, jam ourselves against the skin, and even while holding a nautical prescience that the worst still lay to windward sleep soundly through the free hour.

Coming below at midnight from another hour's wheel, I found the cabin still wet and damp, although nine hours had passed since the capsizing. Overhead charred areas stood out on the glistening paintwork. A swinging lamp with a cracked shade showed heaps of books, boxes, firewood, and bedding floating on the slop of the floorboards. I picked up *The Tempest*, soggy and dripping, then threw it back. The oven door banged open, and out flowed a small stream of water. Although my foot had gone through the frame, I saw the original *Cimba* still sailing on the bulkhead, and opposite Miss Landi looking down on the scene through tears of glistening sea-water.

After finding a tin of corned beef and opening it with an axe I began to consider our position. We were running before a long gale, now far from Bermuda, with no land between us and the African coast, with the water in one tank ruined, and that in the other tank almost gone. The blow was not moderating; not by any means. Yet we could not keep before it indefinitely, and on the first change for the better the craft must face it again.

She tore madly along a crest. The cabin vibrated with her thunder, and the lamp shadows dipped in swift, long arcs. She was labouring, trying hard to overcome defeat—the once beaten, striving out there in the dark to do so well in the cheerless gesture of just holding her own. Another unmuffled detonation about the hull; another. . . . I slept.

It seemed only a moment later when I was roused by the signal. One o'clock! I felt by the roll that it had grown worse. I had felt it in my sleep, as one is apt to do at sea.

For some unaccountable reason I opened the chronometer case bolted to the ship's skin. The chronometer, swinging in double gimbals, was ticking away as though nothing had happened, but, wonder of wonders, it was faced about so that the numeral "six," instead of "twelve," was at the top, a position that could be brought about only by the instrument simultaneously making two complete revolutions in the gimbals—a fore-and-aft one and an athwartships one. After taking a reading of the low barometer I went on deck.

"It's blowing up," said Dombey, through clenched teeth. Yes, there could be no doubt about it. On a convenient trough I took over the watch coat handed me, grasped the tiller, and, feeling Dombey's hand withdrawn from my back, knew that he had left for the cabin.

Into my face drove an eighty-mile wind, freezing and crying and sweeping down from the far-off ice-fields. The sky was naked, almost blue, and near its zenith a cold last-quarter moon shone light on to the crests of black waves, of waves travelling at high speed, now resembling tall cliffs, rather than mountains, cliffs formed by cutlass-like slashes of wind, ripped into storm patterns, now of a solid, ungiving black, now glowing in great fissures of infuriated silver, and sounding iron-like above the roaring wind.

My back was to most of the *Cimba*, to her bows, which were working every moment, to her bare masts resembling stunted arms raised against the night. I saw only that small area of after-deck, the paintwork beaded with frozen water picked out by the moon, the stiff parts of ropes, wet and shining on the narrow planking.

The waves built up in the moonlight, tightened, until the advancing slopes over which we had to rise became almost concave. Perhaps once a minute the schooner climbed a black slide of sea, once a minute fought a crest; then followed a brief breathing spell, of falling down a lee slope, of watching with fascination the growth of the next wave, majestic, mammoth, rolling rapidly out of a trough to swing mast-high, then more than mast-high. And in that pause I would wonder as to the climax of the gale, knowing that in its box of tricks there must be one supreme trick.

It is not true that a small craft can survive any weather, or that in storms she is always superior to a large ship. True, hers is the easier task in the average storm, for she rides atop waves the big ship labours through. Such waves, awe-inspiring as they are, have not the broken water at the apex to harm the smaller vessel; but there are others, waves an ocean cruiser may complete her life span without meeting, sufficient in broken water to confound any small craft, and in the end to over-whelm her illusive buoyancy—always her main defence. Fighters though they are, there is a foundering-point for all small craft.

At half-past one it became clear that the *Cimba* was nearing hers as a storm from polar regions blasted over the ocean, warm with an opposing current. She raced on, spreadeagled from sea to sea, while I awaited the climax, still to windward. We had done what we could for her—a consol-ing thought in those moments. She had been moving too fast for safety; she still was, but now the lengths of a pair of cables trailed over the stern to restrain her somewhat. Storm oil had been needed, and, having none, we remembered that the old-fashioned engine had a central lubricating system, that consequently the tanks held a small amount of oil along with the petrol. Three jumpers, their arms and necks frapped, were stuffed with oakum and held under fuel-jets until saturated. Pricking them once or twice with a needle, we fastened lanyards about them, and secured one over the stern and one to either quarter, to ease the schooner appreciably.

At a quarter to two the long-awaited-for appeared. The *Cimba* climbed a wave, and, looking far to windward, I saw a black shape reared from horizon to horizon. As we dropped down a slope I knew that we were fated to meet the greatest sea I had ever come upon.

We climbed again, and I caught sight of its long moving body, al-ready much nearer. This time as the schooner sank my heart sank with her. She was too small, too thin, for the purpose. I was minded to rouse Dombey, yet somehow did not do so. Instead I watched the inflexible purpose, the unfaltering purpose, of the wave, which now gleamed in one great moonlit plane, now darkened into heaving shadow, disap-peared, lifted again, and rolled on and down towards us.

When it was still some distance off I could hear the roar of its cap above the gale. It closed in, travelling at eighty miles an hour, with a potential strength of thousands of pounds' pressure per square foot. As its half-mile body lifted black towards the moon, ranging to almost twice the height of the spars, I hurried my last preparations. Locking the tiller in a groove, I beat my hands on the coaming, warming them, and rubbed my eyes vigorously, that they would be at their best. Knowing that we were at least to be boarded, I lashed the mainsheet about my waist. Finally, after bracing my feet in the small well, knocking my fists a last time, and taking up the tiller, I was ready.

As the shadow of the wave reared above we began the journey up the almost perpendicular face. The *Cimba* went up rapidly, the ascent becoming steeper every instant. In the wild light the slope inverted to appear as a cavity, as a cave of sea-water. The sea was as black as pitch, and on it the white schooner fought for altitude, at such an angle that a man not holding to deck would have fallen clear forward and off the hull. The counter tilted upward in the moonlight, while far below the bows strove to withstand the pressure bearing upon them.

There was a great scream of wind, and, like a bad dream, over that black sea loomed a charge of white water. The *Cimba* struggled for the crest as the broken lip began to tremble, the body of the great sea to stagger. Just then arose a quarter wave—a portion of the main wave diverted to come bursting in at an angle to the wave proper. It was but little ahead of the main crest. Two things could be done—slew off course, taking the quarter sea properly over the stern, and chance getting back in position to meet the main wave, or hold course, ship the quarter sea, and trust to holding in line with the main flow.

I chose the latter. The quarter wave curled our way, a single cap of fluid silver hovering overhead, breaking to sweep the unprotected side. We were going over, so I jammed the tiller in a notch to have the craft more or less in line with the main sea should she work clear. The wave struck with immense impact, broke, rushed aboard, and, my lashing holding, I was driven head first and upside-down, to be jammed at the bottom of the well. As I tried to free myself, hampered by coat and sea-boots, I was not sure whether we had foundered or not, as for the second time that day I lost a sense of balance. I escaped from the water-filled well, saw the cold moon filmed with scud, the vessel, fighting beneath it, caught in the main crest—a leaping glitter, dangerous, rolling, roaring, and packing in against the struggling hull.

There was another scream of wind as the gale literally hurled the heavy white water at the schooner. I took the helm out of the notch and tried to guide her, standing waist-high in water, bracing arms with back; but the tiller was useless, absolutely useless, and I might as well have been holding to a walking-stick. Fearing for the rudder as the full force of the sea struck, I slammed home the tiller in the midship notch. The wave picked us up and hurled us as though we were a match, so that I caught rapid visions of the moon, first on one quarter, then on the other.

The stern was sucked down; great areas of sea sought the vital decks. But the counter buoyed the surfaces, the bows fought as always they fought, and the stiff bilges underneath lifted and lifted. For three or four seconds I could not touch the tiller, during which her own buoyancy was all that could save the craft from being shattered, hove under.

The drive along the crumpling rim began. I freed the tiller, and as I put my weight against it felt the rudder-stock vibrating, the rudder quivering like a fin. Swinging through space from the altitude of the crest, I caught a glimpse of the surrounding ocean, far below, endless and empty, a distant heap of mounds, slow-rolling, cut by the great gleaming wind-slashes. The *Cimba* reeled in the flying wash, moving at utmost speed, while a wind as rare, as stinging, as that of a Himalayan gale blew against the thin wires of her rigging. With bow high, stern low, she planed, swinging with all her power in one long, exhilarating skid. Then suddenly the wave was beyond, and the *Cimba* was victoriously sinking to the trough. Glancing over my shoulder, I looked up to the receding form inclining in a tremendous slide of dragging foam to a crest, windy, shining. Already a quarter of a mile away, it made a freakish hinge towards the sky, tumbled, dropped in a smooth fall, and, with infinite majesty, glided into the oblivion to leeward.

Another sea struck at three o'clock. At four, while I was sleeping, a third wave rode us down. I awoke as the cabin reeled violently and the lamp blew out. Fearing for Dombey, I made for the hatch and looked out. But there he stood, bundled in the watch coat, the only silent form in all that confusion, composedly heaving on the tiller as though it were an oar and guiding the schooner safely down another slope.

At daylight it moderated, but only slightly, and for almost five hours more we were forced on under bare poles to an estimated position 165 miles west of Bermuda, blown completely off our only chart of the North Atlantic. At nine o'clock a consultation was held in the steering-well. Stores were low, water almost gone, and every hour that passed was taking us farther from the myth of land. The sea, still up-and-down, had fallen slightly. The time had come to attempt putting about and driving into the weather. One stood at the helm; the other double-reefed the mainsail. Timing it between two waves, we let the canvas press us around until, with jib and mainsail drawing, we headed to windward. The steep waves over which we had been sliding scenic-railway fashion now lunged at the bow, causing our motions to become sharp and rapid. With wet sails flattened in the wind the *Cimba* weaved and smashed a way into the white horses, travelling more like a submarine than a schooner. The wind appeared to be abating, causing the sea to loosen, until waves swelled in size, but waned in power. Then at nightfall the storm came back with much of its old strength, and after a quarter of an hour of futile fighting we went on the defensive and hove to.

"Again!" shouted Dombey.

"And again!" I echoed, furling the jib. And out of the night came a third echo, an ironic undertone of wind.

After much effort the stove was lighted, and a hot meal cooked, of ship-bread and corned beef mixed into a hash. Drinking-water was doled out with care. We had neither coffee nor tea, both ruined in the capsizing. There was no tobacco. The meal over, we began a watch-and-watch, and, slightly nauseated by an odour of kerosene, were only too glad to stay out in the weather, still cold and now accompanied by rain.

On the morning of the next day we again set canvas against the blow. The fisherman put her heart into the scheme, shattering a staggering, lumpy sea, wetting her sails in a blunt attempt at headway. Her gear strained as she swung up and into the drive of water, her masts over to leeward, while the gentle curved bows hammered into broken, streaming waves. For an hour she plunged west with trembling luffs, biting into sea after sea in a wet uphill hack. Then, in a rising Force 9 gale, for the eighth time since departure we hove her to, bringing the total number of hours in this position to over a hundred and thirty.

Through all of a day, in which ponderous ghosts of seas loomed from out of the rain-light to moan, burst, and disappear, endlessly, and through a night of flying rain the schooner lay with her head under her wing. We, her two attendants, took care of her few wants, standing vigil round the clock.

And then the morning and the totally unexpected—morning and a sun climbing a clear sky to warm a gleaming sea of blue. Sail was swung aloft to the gentle wind, and we ran a shining sea of the long-lost, straight-edged horizons. The sun warmed the decks, dried the sails, and the *Cimba*, her red paint cutting blue water, slid to the west.

Before noon course was altered to north—we considered ourselves once more on the chart—and again preparations were made for a land-fall. At twelve the phantom of a ship, an oil-tanker, the first vessel sighted since the liner, was seen far off on the horizon. There was a temptation to follow her. At least she was headed somewhere, while we—well, we were only searching. But Dombey had a hunch, the result of a handful of sights and good dead reckoning, and, I agreeing, we held our way, drop-ping the tanker out of sight.

Ever since taking departure the two of us had worked hand-to-hand in perfect co-ordination under the tension. The arrival of good weather did not lessen this tension, which until Bermuda was raised would even increase. So, sharing but one thought in common, we worked together on the weathered deck, flattening the salted sailcloth, setting up the rigging.

At four o'clock I climbed the mainmast and looked for land. Nothing was seen; not even a gull hovering over the calm ocean. It grew on to sun-set; the colours brightened in the west, paled on the sea; shadows grew longer, the light wind lighter. It was time for another consultation.

The way in which land is picked up from the deck or rigging of a small craft is always fascinating. The land does not slowly appear out of mist, nor does it come suddenly to stand boldly on the horizon. Rather, it first appears as a vision, as a happy portent arriving out of thin air, out of a vastness of space, to lie with utter humility upon the curved lip of the sea. First it is not there; then, at the flick of an eyelash, there it is, a flimsy mirage that may or may not be more than a low and wandering cloud.

Beneath the leaning mast the shadows became darker on the pear-shaped deck. There was Dombey in the cockpit, from time to time giving me an impatient glance. The schooner seemed to be moving easily, her way slowed by the falling wind. Beyond her some porpoises played on the pale water. Presently they were gone, and the ocean was empty. The wind drew off, and the schooner stopped in a silence broken by the clatter of her gear; then a slight breeze, the masts leaning, the hull beginning to murmur through water. In the west a cloud burst into sudden flame to flare over the immutable plane, now dark, outsweeping to the sky. And under the cloud, touching the sea, something appeared—another cloud, the slight blur, the low, unmoving vision! I came down the shrouds, and Dombey, jumping from the tiller, caught my hand. We were happy, demonstrative. And then, quite unexpectedly, there happened a very strange thing—Dombey and I in a dispute, in a dispute over some absurdly trivial matter. Bermuda had been raised, the tension snapped!

Before starlight the scents of distant earth were floating in the wind. Our difference had passed like an aimless squall, and together we watched the vision change shape and size, and, later, the shining lights flaring on the low body.

The wind was little more than a breath by the time St David's Head was abeam. We sailed up to a lighted ship, H.M.S. *Scarsborough*, anchored some way off-shore. There was only one figure on deck, a middy. We hailed him. Had he any tobacco? The sight of a lonely northern schooner appearing out of the night manned by a crew making such a request surprised him, to say the least. Without a word he ran below, returned, and, still silent, threw something into the mainsail. Tobacco and papers! We thanked him and headed on, leaving him still speechless upon the deck.

The chart of the approach to St George's Channel had been ruined in the capsize by tar, coal-dust, syrup, and cocoa, and to pilot the *Cimba* I had to fall back on a knowledge of the waters learned in boyhood.

Gliding into harbour, we found the town asleep in the dark armlike hills of cedar, and only one or two lights left burning above the water. A few drops of rain fell, but save for their beat and the creak of the gaffs aloft there was utter silence. The *Cimba* ghosted by Ordnance Island, and, bringing up at Market Wharf, closed her voyage.

The Square, except for a sleepy coloured boy, was deserted, the soft forms of its buildings appearing unreal, like the darkened scene of an ended play. The boy saw us, woke up, and ran into the White Horse

Tavern, just closing for the night. A stalwart figure came out by the lighted doorway, hurrying towards us.

"Is it the *Cimba*?" "Is it the *Cimba* turned up?"

Yes, she had turned up after half a month of sea adventure in weather that had sunk a forty-five-foot schooner, a sixty-five-foot ketch, and a four-masted schooner, all close by her. She had turned up after the officers of Bermuda-bound liners had held no hope for her in the December gales; to win after first losing, and in the end to make port under her own canvas, without a leak, without a strained spar, without a torn sail.

FROM
the OPEN BOAT

BY
Webb Chiles

In 1978 Webb Chiles, an accomplished long-distance sailor, decided to make a different sort of voyage and cross the Pacific in an 18-foot open sailboat. He rowed out of a San Diego marina in *Chidiock Tichborne*, which held enough provisions for sixty days. He and his gear and supplies were the boat's only ballast; at just 850 pounds *Chidiock* was more than merely vulnerable to storms at sea.

In 7,000 miles on the tiny craft Chiles survived gales, capsizes, and even shipwreck. When he made his first landfall in the Marquesas, a reporter told him how many people had placed bets that he wouldn't survive. Why did he do it? After completing his first solo circumnavigation in 1976, he had asked himself, "What does an obsessed man do when he has fulfilled his obsession?" *The Open Boat* is his answer, the voyage itself the reason for his voyaging.

This selection begins near the end of the voyage, after his fifth landfall at the island of Suva, in a chapter he titles "A Single Wave." That was all it took to pitchpole *Chidiock* and set into motion a series of events that would lead, days later, to philosophizing about death and the sea's indifference. . . .

///

BY midnight the light on Vatu Leile was well astern, and I knew that we had made more than sixty miles since noon. I was tired, and there was no reason for me to exhaust myself by steering through the night, so I hove to for a few hours' sleep.

At dawn the wind and waves were still high, the waves higher than those in the fifty-knot storm we had been in around Tahiti, perhaps as high as fifteen feet, though the wind was only thirty knots. I reached for the small water jug I keep lashed to the mizzen for daily use. It was not there. More irritated than alarmed, I crawled back to see if it had fallen beneath the inflatable dinghy lashed to the afterdeck. But it was gone. The passage to Port Moresby would probably take three or four weeks and I had debated carrying three or four of the five-gallon water containers, in addition to the small, one-gallon jug. Because *Chidiock* was a bit stern-heavy when loaded, I did fill a fourth container and lashed it to the bow cleat. Now as I glanced forward, I saw that it too was gone, leaving behind only its nicely secured handle. Overnight, twenty-one gallons of water had turned into fifteen—more than ample, but still distressing.

After eating a granola bar and drinking a cup of cold coffee, I tried to get us underway again. A wave caught *Chidiock* just as I was turning her and threw us sideways a couple of boat lengths; but once we completed the turn and the wind steadied on the port quarter, I was able to get her to steer herself as we sped westward at six knots.

Steadily throughout a day of fast if wet sailing, we made our way through the worst of the band of rough water off Viti Levu. The odd wave continued to break over us, but now they were in the six- to ten-foot range, and the wind had dropped to twenty to twenty-five knots. That second night I was able to let *Chidiock* continue sailing, although I slept very lightly, a part of my mind ever alert to an accidental jibe, which threatened every half hour or so. Usually I would awaken in time, but twice I was too late and we were hammered by the waves. I knew I was pushing *Chidiock* too hard, that it would be safer to heave to, but I also knew that every mile we made was carrying us out of the rough seas.

The next morning I found that the two buckets, one inside the other, that I use as the head, had washed away, leaving—as had the water container—their handles neatly lashed behind. I had one bucket left, but I began to wonder what would be next.

All that day, Friday, conditions improved, although I could not use the stove or get a sun sight, and that night we lost nothing except the last sliver of the dying moon, hidden by clouds.

Saturday, wind and waves dropped further to about eighteen knots and four to six feet respectively, and Saturday night I fell asleep at 8:00 P.M. in the belief that I would have my first real sleep since leaving Suva.

Just before 10:30—when I looked at my watch a few minutes later it read 10:33—*Chidiock* slid down a wave, hit something, and pitchpoled. It is difficult to separate what I have concluded upon reflection must have happened from my sensations at the time. One moment I was sleeping wrapped in the tarp on the port side of *Chidiock*'s cockpit, and the next I was flying through the air, catapulted like a pebble, as *Chidiock*'s stern came up. Dimly I recall a kind of clank, seemingly metal to metal, and then the stern rising behind me. In flight I was afraid it would come down on me, that I would be impaled on the mizzen. Then I was in the water. I struggled free from the tarp, choked as a wave passed, and swam the five yards back to *Chidiock*. I believe that given time she would have righted herself, but when I reached her, she was on her starboard side, her masts thirty degrees below the water. Worse than last time, I thought as I swam around the bow. But when I put my weight on the centerboard, she quickly came upright.

I flopped over the side, which was not too difficult. The gunwale was even with the sea: much worse than last time. I fumbled beneath the water for my glasses and found them still wedged in place by the bilge pump.

Chidiock felt as though she were sinking. Except for a few inches at the bow, she was completely below the water. With each wave, she dropped from beneath me and I thought that despite her flotation, she was gone. But each time she came back. The sails cracked in the wind. The pitchpole had been an explosive movement and the jib and main were ripped along their leach tapes. The mizzen support was broken, and the mizzen floated along the stern. I pulled it back inside the hull, though I don't know why I bothered. Inside, outside, the sea was the same.

Food bags, clothing bags, the bag with navigation tables, all were secured to a long line tied to the mainmast, and all were bobbing around the surface. An oar floated away, as did a bag I recognized as one con-

taining books. It was still within arm's reach and I could have saved it—
later I was to regret very much that I did not—but it did not seem important at the time. Among the books were several bought in California, including *Little Dorrit,* the only major Dickens novel I have never read and
apparently am meant never to read: I had also lost a copy in the first capsize between San Diego and the Marquesas.

A huge number of lines writhed like a nest of snakes. Where had
they all come from? I wondered as I searched beneath the sea for the jib-
furling line. We were lying beam on to the waves, the sails were trimmed
for a broad reach, and by the time I had furled the jib and found and released the main halyard, both sails were seriously damaged. The main
particularly so, with a tear from the chaffing patch at the head down to
and then along the reef points.

Another oar floated into the darkness. The cloud cover was complete, broken by not even a single star. Beneath the black sea *Chidiock* was
unfamiliar. Already everything had been tumbled about, and I could
only reach into the depths blindly, catch something, and pull it to my
face for identification. So far surprisingly little seemed to have been lost.
But I could not find the last bucket. The biggest thing left with which to
bail was a plastic bowl.

Gradually I began to gain confidence that *Chidiock* was not going to
sink. She is, as an aerospace-engineer friend of mine likes to say, an object for going out, rather than an object for going down. And had I been
able to clear the water from her within those first hours, we could have
resumed sailing not much the worse for wear. That I was not able to do
so was partially bad luck, but mostly bad management. I had swamped
her before and recovered, but never quite this badly. I had swamped her
before, but during daylight. I had swamped her before, but I had had a
bucket.

I had contemplated such a swamping and made preparations, but
despite my experience I had not foreseen the situation as being as
chaotic as was the reality. The problem was the centerboard slot. When
Chidiock is so swamped that this is below the water, it must be blocked before the cockpit can be bailed out. For such an eventuality I had cut two
pieces of wood to screw into place to close the slot, one for the top, one
for the forward edge. In more than 6,000 miles I had not used them.
When last seen they were in the forward starboard bin with the spare

anchor rode, now hopelessly twisted with the mainsheet, bags, oars, and pieces of sail, if they had not already floated away. I waded forward in gingerly fashion—with each movement *Chidiock* dropped away like an express elevator—but I could not find them. The screwdriver would have been in the tool kit in the flooded aft locker, the screws in another box. With the clarity of hindsight the solution was simple, and I cursed myself for not fixing the centerboard fully extended and blocking off the slot before leaving port. That was so obvious—now. With a sense of futility I gave up the search and returned aft and sat down in the waist-deep water and took my little bowl and began to bail. I did not think it would do any good, but I did not have any better way to spend the night.

Chidiock almost seemed to help me, to try and ride higher, though probably it was only that the waves decreased a bit without my noticing, and gradually I made some progress. Her gunwales were now, more often than not, an inch or two above the sea. I stopped bailing. I needed a break. I tore up one of my foam sleeping pads and stuffed it around the centerboard. It did not remain in place, so I tried some shirts. They too were carried away. The turbulence was too great, as though we were within a surf line, and I resumed bailing.

After another hour I permitted myself some hope. We had several inches of freeboard, the seats were usually clear, and the water was mostly confined to the cockpit well. Only four more inches and I would reach the top of the centerboard trunk. But it was not to be. For two more hours I struggled without gaining even a fraction of a fraction of an inch. The ocean and I had reached a point of equilibrium. Sometimes I would think I was gaining, but *Chidiock* was now able to heel a few degrees. In the next moment she would roll back and I would see that nothing had really changed. It may well have been that what gain we had made had come from her rolling the water out rather than from my bailing.

At 3:30 A.M. my back cramped. I was very tired. Perhaps the answer was to wait until dawn, jettison everything not absolutely essential, and try again.

Chidiock was too awash to permit any useful rest, so I managed to inflate the Boston Whaler dinghy, pumping largely by hand. When it was rigid, I secured it to *Chidiock* by two lines and fell inside, where, soaked to the skin beneath my foul-weather gear and no longer warmed by exertion, I lay shivering through the remaining hours of the night.

Six o'clock A.M. found me back aboard *Chidiock*, who was deeper in the water than when I left her, but not gunwale deep. I transferred the food bag and the two remaining water containers to the dinghy. One container held about a gallon and a half of slightly brackish but drinkable water; the other, a gallon. The third container had been punctured during the night. I also moved the navigation bag, the document bag, a Nikonos camera, two of *Chidiock*'s three compasses, the sextant, the solar still, the big tarp, and two bags of clothing. The clothes were not important in themselves, but I had already learned that even a small amount of water in the inflatable makes rest difficult, and I wanted the bags to lie upon.

Almost everything else I threw away: the spare rudder; a box of screws and bolts; my first new typewriter in fifteen years, bought just before I left Suva; the two new stoves; some camera equipment, which I had not kept in the safe Voyageur bags but had trusted to an allegedly watertight aluminum case; the RDF, the third since San Diego; one anchor; and the kerosene lamps. Once I had untied the main securing lines and opened the aft locker, other things I would have liked to keep, such as the medicine kit, a suit of brand-new sails, and an underwater flashlight, were washed away. I was like a cat holding down four mice, one with each paw, while a dozen more played around my nose.

Finally, one way or the other, *Chidiock* was stripped of all but her main anchor and rode, which I thought might be useful if we ever reached land.

Once again I settled in with my bowl and once again I made progress to the same level of four inches of water over the centerboard trunk, and once again, no matter how furiously I scooped, that, once again, was all.

Every hour my back cramp returned and I had to flop into the dinghy to rest. With such breaks I continued on throughout the day.

In late afternoon I accepted the inevitable and climbed into the Whaler, this time to stay. I sprawled on the clothes bags. Something hard dug into my leg. Too exhausted to sit up, I squirmed until it slipped to one side. I noticed that the sextant case was missing, but I did not care. The Voyageur navigation bag was beneath my head. I tried to envision the chart. Navigation had been by dead reckoning all the way from Suva. We were probably halfway between Fiji and the New Hebrides, 18 or 19 degrees south, 172 or 173 degrees East. Not very precise, but what did it matter? Three hundred miles from the nearest land.

The dinghy spun so that I could see *Chidiock*. Corners of torn sails snapped. The mizzen floated off the stern again. I should do something, I thought, but I did not move. I just lay there, thinking, as do all wounded, how much had changed and how quickly, in the passing of a single wave.

AT DAWN and dusk I looked for land, even though no land could be near. And during the day I looked for ships, even though we were far from shipping lanes. I do not pretend that I would not have welcomed rescue, but I was forced to live up to my admonition to save myself, to rely on no one. Yet for the present the wisest action was no action. Enforced passivity is one of the great facts of being adrift. Uncertainty about duration is another. At any moment a ship could appear; or I could drift for months, slowly dying.

On this morning, Tuesday, May 20, the tenth day of living in the nine foot Boston Whaler inflatable after *Chidiock*'s swamping, there were not even any good imitation cloud islands in sight. For more than an hour I sat on the side of the dinghy, more comfortable than when I was lying on the now saturated and rock-hard clothes bags in the bottom, which still was better than lying directly in the permanent pool of water beneath them. I had nothing new to look at, nothing new to think, nothing to read. The sun rose steadily; waves slopped over *Chidiock* 100 feet to windward; the wind blew at fifteen knots from the east-southeast; we continued to drift west-northwest at about one knot. Everything was as it had been the day before, and the day before that. Ironically, good weather had settled in two days after the swamping, and we were missing fine sailing. I knew that if this wind carried all the way to Port Moresby, *Chidiock* would have made her fastest passage ever, a succession of hundred-mile days. Two thousand miles in less than twenty days had been my ambition in the unreliable trade winds last year, and now we could have done it but for the accident of hitting something—and my faulty preparations.

I had had more than ample time to consider what we had struck and was reasonably certain that it was inanimate rather than animate. Great flukes towering above us would be a good but untrue story. No, it had been a log or a tree or, as I was inclined to believe, a container washed from a ship. *Chidiock*'s hull was unmarked, but with a draft of only ten inches that was to be expected. Only the centerboard had hit, and it had not sustained serious damage.

I glanced at my watch. Seven past nine. I could not wait any longer. Time for the big event of the day.

Sitting down on the yellow-plastic clothes bags, I studied the waves. They were only three feet high and rarely coming aboard, but I was acutely aware that whenever I opened the three layers of plastic bags protecting the ship's biscuits, I was risking a month of life. Quickly I grabbed a handful of crackers and the jar of raspberry jam, the joy of my existence.

Long ago the sea imposed on me the habit of eating too fast—a habit I only partially succeed in breaking when I am ashore. But drifting had effected a cure. Each crumb I chewed slowly, completely, and those big enough to dip into the jam, even more slowly and more completely. I loved that jam so much that I could not bring myself to ration it. When it was gone, it was gone—probably in ten more days.

The last biscuit crumbs had been eaten, but I could not resist one last finger full of jam. I licked my finger clean before reluctantly returning the jar to the food bag. I waited a few more minutes before lifting the water container for my two morning sips. Sips, not mouthfuls, though occasionally the dinghy would be jostled when the container was to my lips and I would swallow more than intended. I was angry when this happened. I did not want to cheat. Jam was one thing, water quite another. As never before, I realized that the problem with the world's resources is distribution. I had more than $1,000 in traveler's checks and couldn't buy a glass of water. A few too large sips meant a lost day of my exquisitely measured life. I might reach land in a few more days or weeks. A ship might appear at any minute. But even if not, I nevertheless fully intended to be alive for a long, if miserable, time. A minimum of sixty days, ninety or a hundred or more if I was able to catch rain. On May 17, the first day I made any notes after the pitchpole, I wrote, "I will be alive in July. But June is going to be a long month." No. Two sips of water and two sips only. Each held in the mouth, savored indecently, swished about, swallowed.

They were gone. The long day loomed before me.

I tied the water container down and covered it with the corner of the tarp. There were three quarts of water left in that container, rainwater I had caught by spreading the tarp between my feet and shoulders during a brief squall—a lovely few minutes.

We had not had much rain, and only that one squall was catchable, combining heavy rainfall with an absence of breaking waves that would spoil the water before I could scoop it up with the lid from an empty jar. In that squall I had caught almost a full gallon of fresh water, in addition to drinking my fill. Another change: when sailing, I used to dodge squalls; now I dreamed of them. I also dreamed of fountains and running-water faucets and iced tea and drinking from a hose on a hot summer's day, and worst of all, of the half-full pitcher of Chapman's I had left at the Royal Suva Yacht Club at my departure. I found that incredible. How could I possibly have committed such folly? I vowed I would never leave a drink undrunk again. And then I realized that I might never have the opportunity again.

When I left Suva on May 7, I had twenty-one gallons of water aboard *Chidiock*; when I settled into life aboard the inflatable on May 11, I had little more than two gallons of water. Six gallons had been lost the first night out, five gallons, on the night of the pitchpole. At a generous estimate, I drank a gallon and a half between the seventh and the eleventh. I could not help wondering at this extravagance: had I ever really used a half a gallon of water a day? That should have left eight and a half gallons of water. I did not even bother to calculate how long I could live with eight and a half gallons of water: for practical purposes, forever.

Despite my meager diet, food had not been a problem. I had not even been bothered much by hunger. I recalled a story by Franz Kafka entitled "The Hunger Artist," in which the main character performs fasts as a sideshow at a carnival. He too did not experience hunger pangs after the first few days. But water was life, and I did not have eight and a half gallons on May 11, I had two and a half gallons. With the rain, ten days later I still had two and a half gallons. But what had happened to the missing six gallons? Leakage? Evaporation? I did not know.

The solar still had been a disappointment. Out of curiosity I once successfully used such a still on my last boat, but I could not get this one to work. And when I finally caught rain, I threw the still away.

The sun was warm enough for me to strip off my clothes and air my body. I was wearing the foul-weather gear and the same shorts and shirt I had had on at the time of the pitchpole. Digging into the clothes bags for a change was pointless. Everything was wet and never really dried, but my skin felt better for having been exposed to the sun.

I had a very uneven tan. Hands, feet, and, I suppose, my face were dark brown; but most of the rest of my body was fish white—where it was not red with the saltwater boils covering my forearms, buttocks, calves, and feet. A couple of spots on my buttocks, both elbows, my left wrist where my watch had rubbed, and both feet were ulcerated, despite application of Desitin. The ointment helped, but I needed the miracle of being dry.

I looked over the side and tried to judge our speed: a knot? a half knot? The difference was significant: 168 miles a week or only 84. I no longer needed to check the two compasses I had brought over from *Chidiock* to know our course: 280° true, just north of the sun's path, and unvarying for ten days. I feared any wind shift. I realized that in some ways we had been lucky—if unlucky to have hit whatever we had hit, then lucky to have done so 300-miles east of the New Hebrides rather than west. And lucky to have had steady wind blowing us in the right direction, even though such a wind should be expected. And most of all, lucky to have had it all happen this year when I had a good dinghy. I could have stayed alive aboard *Chidiock*, but the effects of exposure would have been much worse.

A wave halfheartedly splashed aboard and soaked me, and I shifted to the other side of the dinghy to face the sun. From its height I knew it was nearly noon. I leaned over and opened the Voyageur navigation bag, took a vitamin pill from the bottle, and closed the bag. Of all the things lost, I most regretted losing my sextant. It had been nothing special, one of the World War II U.S. Navy models made by David White and only two years younger than I, but it had taken me around the world and I was fond of it. And everything else I needed to find our position was still safe in the navigation bag. In this, as in many other ways, the transition from yacht to dinghy had been easier for me than it would have been for someone aboard a conventional craft. I put the pill in my mouth, lifted the water container for a single sip, and swallowed. Lunch.

Tomorrow there would be more. The cans were rusting and would have to be used. The labels had come off all the cans, but by shaking them I could tell which were which. A half a can of fruit cocktail for lunch, with the other half for dinner, which meant the only water I would use would be the two sips in the morning.

My liquid supplies came from various sources.

> 2½ gallons of water
> 7 cans of fruit
> 3 cans of vegetables
> 10 small bottles of Coca-Cola

My liquid ration was less than one cup a day, six sips, or only five, depending on my self-discipline at noon. I considered the prospect of kidney damage, but so far my kidneys functioned. I remembered Bombard's book about his drinking seawater on his drift across the Atlantic, but I was not tempted to do so myself.

Each can of fruit or vegetables would provide liquid for a full day: ten days total. The water on hand would last at least forty days, and surely in these latitudes it would rain often. But I did not permit myself to count rain in my calculations. Rain was a gift. The Coca-Cola, which I considered more secure in bottles than the water in plastic containers, was to be used last. Ten bottles for seventeen days, two days each for the first eight bottles. And, I had decided, then I would drink the last two bottles in quick succession. Once before I died, if only for a few minutes, I was not going to be thirsty.

My food supply consisted of:

> 5 cans ravioli
> 4 cans beans
> 1 can hot dogs
> 3 cans tuna
> 4½ packages ship's biscuits
> 3 boxes breakfast cereal
> ½ jar jam
> 1 jar Marmite
> 10 packages freeze-dried dinners
> 4 packets powdered milk
> 1 jar dry-roasted unsalted peanuts
> 1 can peanut brittle
> 1 bottle vitamin pills

Each can made two dinners, and the hot dogs would make three. I could stay alive a long time just on the crackers and the cereal. The peanuts and peanut brittle would keep me going for weeks. And with caught rain, each freeze-dried dinner would last three days and each packet of milk, a week. Without rain, of course, the freeze-dried provisions were worthless. I have eaten freeze-dried food without cooking, and I tried to eat some without water. It simply cannot be done. You just pucker away. And probably it is counterproductive; liquid must be drawn from the body somehow.

At times I wondered if I was being too hard on myself, particularly toward the end of the first week, when my body most strongly protested the new regime. The odds were very good that I would come upon land within a month. And for a drift of only a month I would not have to ration much of anything. But if we did not come upon land, if the wind changed, or if we did see land but were unable to get ashore and had to continue to Australia, I was determined to last the course. I felt stronger today than I had a few days earlier. In fact, I felt that for each of the past three days I had made some gain, however small; that I had managed to reverse the inexorable slide toward death.

To escape the blinding heat Saturday afternoon, I had swum from the Whaler to *Chidiock*. Already I had lost weight and strength, particularly in my legs. Once aboard *Chidiock*, in boredom I made another search of her flooded interior and found treasure: two bottles of Coca-Cola, a knife, a tube of Desitin and one of Eclipse—a sunscreen ointment, a pair of shorts, a mismatched pair of thongs, a hammer, and a plate.

The knife had a bottle opener, and I immediately drank one of the Cokes. The other still put me two days of life ahead, and the warm, sweet liquid did me a world of good. I pulled the Whaler to *Chidiock* and transferred everything except the hammer and the plate.

Small fish, some bright blue, some almost transparent, swam inside *Chidiock*. Someday, I thought, I may have to come back and eat you.

The next day I again returned to *Chidiock*, this time to attempt to bail her out after fothering the tarp beneath the hull. The seas were calmer than they had been at any time since she had been swamped, but it took me most of the morning to tie the tarp securely in place, and my social secretary had to cancel several important appointments. The problem continued to be that of not having anything suitable for bailing. First I tried a plastic bag, which was worthless. I looked around, and my eye settled on the plate. As a scoop it proved very effective. I was able to move a considerable amount of water with it, but unfortunately not considerable enough.

Before untying the tarp and returning to the dinghy, I inserted *Chidiock*'s rudder and then sorted out the tangled mainsheet and halyard. When I raised the torn sail, *Chidiock* responded by gracefully rolling onto her side and sailing for the depths. Less gracefully, I jumped clear. She righted herself and I scrambled back aboard and was able to turn her downwind before she could repeat her new trick.

Grossly, very, very grossly, I was able to steer with great sweeping movements of the tiller. In an hour I might change our position by a hundred yards. But if we sighted land, even such limited control might make the difference. Inordinately pleased, I furled the sail and dropped the rudder back into *Chidiock*'s gaping aft locker before returning home.

From the beginning of the drift I had held on to the hope that I could save *Chidiock* as well as myself, though I knew the odds against her were very long. That was one of the reasons I had kept the boats tied together, even though the dinghy would drift faster by herself. I also thought that both boats together were more likely to be seen than either alone; and that however unpleasant, the swamped *Chidiock* was somewhere to go if the dinghy deflated, which, thankfully, it showed no signs of doing. Now the odds against *Chidiock* seemed slightly reduced.

By midafternoon the sun was hot, and I took the spare pair of shorts and dipped them in the sea and then put them on top of my head. I had already draped my foul-weather gear loosely about my shoulders for shade. Unwashed, unshaven, uncombed, covered with more boils than Job, and with a pair of shorts as a turban, unquestionably I looked absurd; but this was not a beauty contest.

I found myself speculating about other solo sailors who have been lost at sea: Slocum, Willis, Riving, Colas, Piver. The list could go on. I wondered if they had died quickly or slowly. There have been other times when I thought I was going to die at sea, but always death would be quick. Now I was on the edge not for a few minutes or hours, but weeks, months. Already my tongue was thick, my lips pasty, and I wondered what it would feel like to be thirsty and know not that there was water that should not be drunk, but that there was no water. It was not death I feared, but the suffering along the way.

My initial reaction to being adrift was one of apathy laced with depression. I did not care about the voyage or the challenge or the sea. Sailing had brought more pain than pleasure, and if I survived, I would go ashore and find a life with a little comfort—the old chimera: peace, rest, ease. Surely I had earned them.

But after a few days of this, I knew that if the sea did not kill me—and it had missed some pretty good opportunities in the past few years; perhaps it would again—and if it were possible, I would sail on. If *Chidiock* were lost, I would try to replace her. I would not, however, sail indefinitely from shipwreck to shipwreck, disposing of open boats like used tissues. At a certain point, and I would know when, such a voyage would become ludicrous rather than honorable.

There seemed to me to be two quite different yet equally valid attitudes toward death: Socrates' "Why should I fear death, for when I am, death is not; and when death is, I am not" and Dylan Thomas's "Rage, rage against the dying of the light." By temperament I favor Thomas, but while I was adrift Socrates prevailed. The sea is immune to curses.

The terrible thing about the sea is that it is not alive. All our pathetic adjectives are false. The sea is not cruel or angry or kind. The sea is insensate, a blind fragment of the universe, and kills us not in rage, but with indifference, as casual byproducts of its own unknowable harmony. Rage would be easier to understand and to accept.

Whenever I thought of death, and obviously I thought of it often, I also thought of Suzanne—not really an unflattering association. I was thirty-eight years old. No man in my family had lived to so ripe an age for several generations. I had accomplished some of what I wanted with my life—not all, but probably more than most men. And for me dying at sea had long been accepted as an occupational hazard. Of all that the shore offers—the places I had not seen, the friends with whom I would like to share some conversation and a bottle, the music, the books, the paintings—most of all, I would miss Suzanne. I had never loved her more than during these last days, when the contrast between the happiness we had shared and the bleak reality of the present was so great.

When I left Suva I had not realized that it was the very day on which four years earlier I had left Auckland to sail for Tahiti. I had not known then whether I would ever see Suzanne again, and now, for quite different reasons, I did not know if I would ever see her again. I was glad that I was not yet overdue, that she would have no reason yet to be worried.

Something on a nearby wave caught my eye, something brown and round now hidden in a trough. Then, there it was. It was going to drift past. Terribly excited, I dove over the side and started swimming.

When I had the coconut safely in the dinghy and held it to my ear, I heard the glorious sound of liquid. With the blade of my rigging knife, I cut away the husk, and with the fid, I punctured two of the eyes. Normally I am not fond of coconut, but the slightly sour liquid was ambrosia. I took two big swallows before draining the rest into a jar, almost two cups. And there would be more moisture in the meat. But how to get to it? I recalled the hammer on *Chidiock* and pulled us over. With three blows, the shell cracked apart: days and days of life.

A half hour before sunset, I ate my dinner consisting of the last half of a can of tuna, washed down with coconut milk. Despite the can's having been open for twenty-four hours, the fish did not smell bad. And of course I would have eaten it even if it had.

In the last light, I searched for land. There was none. I wrapped myself in the tarp and tried to settle in for the long night of broken sleep. My thoughts were the same as they had been the last night and the night before that. How many more long days and nights: four? forty? a hundred and four? And what was at the end: an island? a ship? death?

We drifted on.

FROM

WAKE of the
GREEN STORM

BY
Marlin Bree

It's not only oceans that generate treacherous waters; the Great Lakes also are known for storms and seas big enough to break or swallow ships as large as the famous *Edmund Fitzgerald* (over 700 feet long), which sank in Lake Superior in 30-foot waves in 1975.

In July 1999 an unexpected storm—"the storm of the century"—descended on Lake Superior, the largest freshwater lake in the world, with winds that reached speeds of 100 miles per hour. Marlin Bree, sailing his 20-foot wooden centerboard sloop *Persistence*, which he had built himself, left Grand Portage, Minnesota, in a thick fog on the first day of his planned cruise to Thunder Bay, Ontario. It was July 4th, a day forecast to be warm and clear. An experienced sailor, he was intimately familiar with the sudden squalls spawned by thunderstorms on Lake Superior. He also knew his cruising area well and knew there were many harbors of refuge among the islands he would be cruising through in case something blew up. He had no reason to anticipate that within hours he would encounter a storm that threatened to capsize and sink his small boat.

In the part of his story excerpted here, unlike many of the other selections in this book, Bree does not write about cruising technique or psycho-
logical subtleties. This is pure action and struggle, a fight to survive against
the elements, which have suddenly become overwhelming.

///

SUNDAY morning, the 4th of July. I shivered and

looked out my portlight. I wasn't going anywhere, not in this pea-soup
fog. The weird electrical storm of the night before hadn't cleaned up
the atmosphere at all.

Where was the bright, sunny, hot July 4th that had been forecast?

Discouraged, I stalked off the dock to see Sue and Kek at the marina,
and to mooch some of their coffee.

"It'll burn off. You'll be OK." They seemed unconcerned by the fog.

After a cup of coffee, I walked back to the dock and looked around
the harbor. Grand Portage Island was beginning to clear, its dark shape
visible, though the fog wrapped around it heavily. Across the bay, the
old fur fort was starting to emerge. I could see the sharp points of its
stockade.

But outside of the harbor, the fog hung like a thick gray blanket.
Cold. Sinister.

I returned to my boat to get ready. Inside the cabin, I pulled everything that had any weight or bulk out of the stern and the stem and secured it alongside the centerboard case. I clambered topside to take off the
ties to the jib furler and to remove the mainsail cover. I checked the mainsail; it was held securely in place on the boom with elastic shock cord.

I snapped my GPS into its holder and crossed my fingers. This
would be the first time I'd actually use my new GPS for open water navigation.

It was supposed to be the hottest day of the year, but I wore cotton
long johns under a pair of heavy sweatpants, an arctic pile pullover, and

a pile-lined nylon boating jacket. On my feet, I had wool socks and boating mocs.

Superior was not to be trusted, no matter what the forecast said.

Patchy fog lay outside the harbor as I nosed my way into the lake. I was crouched in my inside steering position, my nose about a foot from the plastic windshield. Though it was warmer in here than in the open cockpit, I could still feel the fog's clammy, cold touch.

"Security, security," I called out on my VHF to alert any vessels of my position. I didn't get an answer. Not too many boats would be dumb enough to be out in this pea-soup fog.

The big lake was as cold as a snowstorm, eerie in its formlessness and silence. The only sound was the gurgling of the water passing the hull and the muted growl of the outboard engine.

I was glad I had worn the warm clothing or I'd be shivering by now.

Fog or no fog, we were on our way at last.

Slowly, the morning brightened. I moved back into the cockpit, my hand firmly gripping the tiller.

Below me, the waters of the icy lake glistened down far into its depths. Gliding through the easy swells, we seemed to be flying upon translucent air. We were aloft on the world's greatest freshwater lake.

Beautiful, small islands began to glisten in the weak sunlight, while further out on the lake, the fog wreathed ethereally.

But on the hazy, high bluffs of the headland, the fog hadn't lifted. Its cap of blue-gray didn't look quite right.

I moved my head around, feeling for a breeze on my face. There was nothing worthwhile; this was an eerie day. There was a peculiar heaviness to the air I could not explain.

As I neared Victoria Island, I picked up my mike and called the Thunder Bay Coast Guard. I was now across the International Boundary, in Canadian waters.

I filed my Sail Plan, telling them where I was, my course heading, and where I was going. I gave them an estimated time of arrival (ETA) of 2:30 P.M. at Thompson Cove, one of the outermost islands guarding the mouth of Thunder Bay.

I shrugged. I'd do that easy.

Something made me look over my left shoulder. Behind me, the crown of dark, bluish fog was sweeping off the land and heading out to sea. It looked like another fog bank, or at worst, a rain cloud. Although it had grown bigger and darker, it was still a long way off.

But it definitely was heading in my direction.

I turned up my engine to half throttle, and with a healthy snarl, *Persistence* began moving faster.

We'd tuck into the cove on Thompson Island long before anything hit us.

The sky grew overcast, then dark and gray. The water turned the color of lead, and the air had a tomb-like chill.

Not good at all, I decided, so I moved back into my inside steering position and closed the flap behind me. If it rained, I'd be warm and dry inside my dodger.

Ahead lay Spar Island, after that, a line of reefs running northeast to Thompson Island, a little more than five miles away.

Where was the cove? I grabbed my cruising guidebook and my chart and began studying them. It'd be easy. All I had to do was cruise along the south side of Thompson until I came to a cove not far from the island's eastern tip.

The VHF came to life sounding a harsh, alternating tone, a warning of some kind. I did not know what it was, but I could make out "dangerous weather."

Above the static a few minutes later came the dread words, "*Mayday! mayday!*"

Somewhere north of me, a sailboat had capsized. People were struggling in the water. What was going on?

The sky grew darker. I felt very lonesome out here.

The first drops of rain felt like little bombs on my canvas dodger. They were cold and heavy, followed by gusts of wind that made my boat shake. I felt the mast heel a little, then recover.

I wasn't too worried. There are always a few gusts when some heavy weather hits, but these spend themselves quickly.

But the wind came from the northwest, out of the fog area, rushing down from the hills.

Something was back there. The wind was hitting my boat on its all-too-vulnerable portside beam.

I punched in a new course and the Autohelm hummed, directing the tiller to steer us downwind. I'd present my transom directly toward the wind—a classic storm tactic. A few minutes of this, the gusts would subside, and I'd resume course.

Suddenly, a wall of wind, powerful and unrelenting, screamed at me. It caught us in its grip and threw us forward, skittering, faster and faster, and suddenly we stopped, pitching down, beam to the onrushing windstorm.

I fell sideways, hard. From below came a crash. I saw my alarm clock and other gear fly from one side of the boat to another. Some of it landed atop me. Pain stabbed my right side, and I realized I was lying on my back, looking up.

The cold waters of Superior rushed up to fill the starboard portlight with an evil green color. Part of the cabin was underwater.

"*This is it,*" my brain warned. "*We're going over.*"

The boat teetered dangerously.

The wind screamed like a banshee. I saw water slosh up through the open centerboard case.

I could feel an icy chill in my heart. We were turning over, slowly, oh so slowly.

I braced myself. We were not coming back up.

From behind me the autopilot clacked noisily, over as far as it could go, and unable to make a course change. The engine was howling, the prop out of the water.

We were caught in the teeth of the storm. Out of control.

If the wind could get a grip on the high side of my hull, it could shove my boat over. We'd capsize all the way, rolling upside down, mast down, bottom up.

She'd never come up from that.

I'd be underneath.

My survival suit was under the portside bunk. No time to get to it. No time to do anything.

Somehow, I pulled myself up and tore out of the dodger, grabbing the high, windward lifelines. Rain pelted my face as I faced my enemy.

The lake was cold and gray, its surface scoured flat by the terrible wind. Long contrails of mist whipped across the water like icy whips.

I turned in time to see four heavy rubber fenders tear away from the cockpit and fly away.

My boat balanced on its side, reeling with every gust. The mast spreader dipped into the water, then rose a little unsteadily.

Hand over hand, I crawled back to the transom. I jammed my thumb down on the autopilot's red button, turning it off. My hand closed in a death grip on the tiller.

Another huge gust tore into us. I felt us go down farther.

No! I threw myself over the windward lifelines as far as I could, but the boat still was on its side and out of control. I could only hang on.

After what seemed like an eternity, we came upright with a mighty splash. The mast flew upward. The engine's racing stopped as the prop bit solid water. We picked up speed.

I jammed the tiller over, heading farther off the wind. Now we were taking the wild gusts on the transom instead of our vulnerable beam.

But we were rapidly heading away from the islands—and any chance of shelter—deeper into the raging lake.

THE ENGINE POPPED OUT of the water, racing madly. I leaned out, adding my weight to the windward side, and we fought our way upright with me hanging on for dear life.

The boat was unstable, like a teeter totter—heading out deeper into the lake.

The wind slammed into us again. Down went the mast, up came the water, and out I went, leaning over the edge. It occurred over and over again, in a maddening battle of knockdowns.

I was shivering uncontrollably. The billed cap I had pulled down low on my forehead kept some of the driving rain off, but my glasses were misted with water. I couldn't see too well.

I was in a world of hurt. I had no place to run to, no place to hide, and nobody to help me.

Another violent gust flattened us. As the boat laid over this time, to my horror, I heard a "ping" noise.

Something had snapped.

I saw the mainsail come loose from its shock cords. The wind's fingers began to shove it up the mast. The big sail reared a third of the way up, flapping, rattling, and catching the wind.

My heart pounded.

The boat was on the edge of capsizing. What would happen with some sail up?

I could not leave the tiller. The only answer was to run on with the wind, deeper into the lake, until something broke or the wind let up a little.

I clenched my teeth and tightened my grip on the tiller. I would not give up.

Finally, I sensed the wind letting up a little; at least the insane gusts were not shoving us over quite so far.

"Do it!" I steeled myself. Timing the gusts, I shoved the tiller over hard—and I hung on.

Persistence did a dangerous dip to leeward, hung down on her rail for a moment—and finally turned.

We were facing the wind. The sail rattled on the mast, and the boat felt terribly unstable underneath me.

One hand on the tiller, I reached back and gave the outboard full throttle and locked it there.

Power. I simply had to have more power in the teeth of the storm. The engine would just have to take it.

The little Nissan bellowed and dug in. The boat bounced up and down, careening sideways. Sometimes the prop was in the water; sometimes it was out. The engine revved unmercifully and screamed.

We were gaining.

Through my rain-soaked glasses, I could make out an island ahead. How could this be?

I had already passed Spar Island and had been abeam of the rock-shoals leading to Thompson.

Where was I?

It was a low, wind-swept rock. Not much shelter, it seemed to me, but as I came closer, I found that the bluffs were higher than I realized.

Where were the reefs? I could only hope that this side of the island was bold and deep up to its shoreline.

As I came into its lee, I throttled down. The wind was still howling, but the island was deflecting the main blasts.

To my starboard lay some rocky pinnacles, now awash in the storm.

In the distance, I could make out a larger island. I must have done a complete loop in the storm and doubled back to Spar Island.

Little comfort. There was no place for me to hide on this barren island.

My heart was pounding and my muscles were knotted tight. I was shivering uncontrollably and practically gasping in the cold rain as I shoved the tiller over and began to run alongside the sheltering island. Overhead, and out on the lake, the storm still raged.

I wiped my glasses with my fingers. Ahead lay a row of spectacular rocky pinnacles, slashed with waves and spray. They stretched from the northeastern edge of Spar out into the lake. In the distance, I could make out a gray headland.

It had to be Thompson Island.

I twisted the throttle, and we roared ahead. The boat again caught the brunt of the storm. *Persistence* staggered, her speed diminished, her rail dipping low into the water. Wind shrieked in the rigging, wrestling with the mast.

I edged out over my port side, my leg locked around the traveler beam, one arm around a winch. The tiller was in a death grip.

Small, rocky islets—spray everywhere—flew by. I was desperate to reach Thompson Cove.

I hoped my progress would not be interrupted by a reef.

I reached down for my chart and a cruising guidebook, which I had jammed to one side of the gas tank. Both were soaked; ink was running where I had marked my course. I dared not let the wind get these—my only guides to where I wanted to go.

I glanced at my dodger, its back cover flapping wildly in the gusts. Above it the partly-raised sail rattled and tore at the mast, but it did not seem to be going any higher.

I wished I could move forward to grab my GPS unit, programmed for the coordinates of Thompson Cove. But I dared not leave my steering.

I'd just have to find the harbor—somehow.

I was headed for a small cove on a small island. How tough could that be? I'd just run alongside Thompson on the leeward side, far enough out to avoid any reefs, but close enough to see the cove.

I checked my watch. I told the Coast Guard I'd be in harbor in 45 minutes.

All I had to do was maintain course and spot the cove.

I'd have time to spare.

As we came under the lee of Thompson, the island shouldered the wind off me. I breathed a sigh of relief and began watching the shoreline.

I slipped past a large cove—there was no entrance—then rapidly approached the end of the island.

If I ran all the way to the tip of Thompson, I'd have to come across the entry to the cove. Easy.

I glanced at my NOAA chart again. There was nothing officially designated as Thompson Cove. The name only appeared with a detail drawing in my cruising guide book. In the jouncing, rain-soaked cockpit, it was hard to read.

Scanning the shore, I saw a rocky cliff leading down to the water's edge, its crest topped with trees. Farther away, lashed by waves and spray, a small, round island stood its lonely sentinel.

Shivering in my cockpit, glasses blurred with rain and spray, I headed to the tip of the island.

Off in the distance, I saw a dark blue line etched on the water. It was moving—rushing toward me.

That much blue on the water meant only one thing: wind.

Tons of it.

With a howl, the wind raced across the channel between the islands. The storm had switched from the west, veering to catch me.

The lake wasn't done with me yet.

The first blasts shook my boat, screaming past my partly hoisted sail, grabbing it and making it hammer with a deadly resonance.

The tiller twisted in my hand as the boat bucked and took a dive to starboard.

We were back down on our side, cabin going partly under, mast spreaders dipping in the water. Icy waves climbed the side of my boat and splashed into the cockpit.

I leaned my weight out over the cockpit, but the boat simply couldn't stand up to this windstorm. She kept careening down at a terrifying angle, mast nearly underwater, as I wrestled with the useless tiller.

I cranked the throttle back up to maximum. With a deep snarl, the little engine leaped to full r.p.m.s. The boat smashed into the waves.

Where was the cove? I was shivering uncontrollably—wondering if I was courting hypothermia.

But all I could do was hang on—and pray.

We neared a dangerous place—a gap between the land and a small island. A wave tore at the rocks, flinging spray high into the air. As it raced on, I shuddered. A teeth of reefs lay just beneath the waves.

Beyond, a mile or so away, lay something green. Land—the island. And the cove.

Out of the stormy waters, another boat headed toward me. It shot the narrow gap, bouncing like a log in a mountain stream. It was a large sailboat, with a tall mast but no sail up, and running hard under power.

Why were they headed this way? I shook my head to clear it.

They had come from where I wanted to go.

Still, I persisted. As I fought my way upwind, they turned around the tip of the land, heading westerly. I lost sight of them.

I took a deep breath. Adrenalin surging, I charged the gap.

I had to make it to the island.

Suddenly, I lost control. In a heart-stopping moment, we careened dangerously toward the islet's foam-lashed reefs, black teeth showing ominously.

I swore, prayed, steered, and careened my weight. Finally, the boat came back up and obeyed me.

We circled back—to try again.

This time, I worked my way further east—behind the protection of the tiny islet, letting it take the blast of the waves and wind.

I braced myself and squeezed the throttle hard to be sure I had every last ounce of power the engine could give me. We charged, picking up speed.

We bounced, careened, splashed—and suddenly, we were through the gap.

On the other side, I was awestruck at the size of the waves. My speeding bow speared into the first oncoming tower. The impact shook my boat.

The bow disappeared. The water kept coming over the cabin top—and hit me in the chest.

I groaned at the impact and the chill of the icy water.

We climbed the wave, teetering at the top. For the first time, I could see what lay ahead.

I was facing huge, square rollers—the worst waves I'd fought all day. There was a sea of them out there, all headed toward me.

Something was terribly wrong. Ahead lay not a cove, but another island. A very big island.

It finally came to me. My stomach lurched with despair.

That big, distinctive island ahead of me was none other than Pie Island. Somehow, we had overshot our destination.

I had made a mistake—maybe a fatal error.

We could not live out here.

Desperately, I timed the waves, and on the back of one of the steep chargers, I turned the little boat around—and roared back to the dangerous gap.

We were flying now, nearly surfing the waves, almost out of control.

We were up on the crest, then down in the trough. Monsters reared behind me.

Ahead, the gap loomed, waves crashing on either side, the black teeth of reefs yawning.

We were through. I turned westward.

I tried to figure things out. The other sailboat had come through here and headed westward.

But where was it?

I was growing tired. My reactions were slowing; it was hard to think. I was thoroughly doused in icy water, shivering uncontrollably, cold through almost to my body core.

I roared at full throttle back up Thompson Island. Rocky slopes rushed past me, close by my speeding boat. Beyond one crag, I saw something shining. Up high, above the trees.

I squinted, trying to clear my focus.

Unmistakably, they were sailboat masts—just the tops of them.

The water widened. On one side was a high outcrop of rock, and on the other, a spruce-covered hill.

And in between, still, blue water.

The cove! Blessed, beautiful Thompson Cove.

FROM
a HARD
CHANCE

BY
Kim Leighton

The 1998 Sydney–Hobart race, in its fifty-fourth year, was the setting for one of the worst sailing disasters ever when hurricane-force winds slammed into the fleet of 115 boats. Weather forecasters were caught off guard, and the warnings they issued when the freak conditions began to develop did not sound severe enough to many of the sailors who heard them to convince them to give up the race. The waters of Bass Strait and the Tasman Sea can be treacherous even in good conditions; in the freak storm that developed they were nothing short of hellish, with 80-foot waves and 80-knot winds. In all, the storm destroyed seven boats, forced the rescue of more than fifty sailors, and killed six men.

Leighton's narrative weaves together the stories of sailboats caught in the worst of it, stories that separate and conjoin as the boats and sailors themselves did at sea. In scene after scene we see boats tossed like toys and broken by giant waves, leaving survivors to struggle with the resulting injuries, dismastings, dead engines, and dead communications, fighting to survive. The passage excerpted here occurs near the height of the storm, at the life-or-death turning point for many boats. Leighton

avoids the temptation to draw easy conclusions from the events he describes and makes no attempt to dramatize the story with heroic prose. He
allows the sailors to speak for themselves, letting readers follow the events
as they unfold, that is frightening enough.

With so many boats and so many people involved, we get to know the
individual sailors less well than in many of the other narratives in this collection, but that makes the story no less dramatic or involving. This is instead a story of a group of men and women, a larger humanity of sailors
caught simultaneously in the same situation. It is the collective nightmare
of every one of us who has ever experienced a storm at sea.

///

BY midmorning Sunday, a half dozen boats, including line-
honors favorites *Marchioness* and *Wild Thing*, had sustained disabling damage and were forced out of the race. Many others,
confronting the full fury of storm for the first time, were heading for the
shelter of Eden's Twofold Bay. At 10 A.M., the Hobart fleet was an average
of 25 miles from Eden.

Among the seven boats in the lead Sunday morning was *Team Jaguar*,
a 65-foot sloop out of Sydney's Cruising Yacht Club of Australia. Running
for the shelter of Eden was not an option. The 1989 Farr design was formerly named *Brindabella* and raced by George Snow to a line-honors victory in the 1991 Sydney to Hobart. The boat's current owner, prominent
Sydney lawyer Martin James, had had *Team Jaguar* in a top position in the
1997 Sydney to Hobart only to be thwarted by a broken mast.

James and his crew of 18, most of whom were seasoned offshore rac-
ers, left the 1998 starting line with the objective of finishing among the
top five, which is as hard to achieve as it is desirable. But James' hope for
a top finish was dashed late Sunday when, running well ahead of the
pack, *Team Jaguar* was knocked down by a huge wave, which weakened
her mast and washed crewman Tony Eggleton overboard. He was recovered an anxious three minutes later.

At the entrance to Bass Strait four hours later, *Team Jaguar*'s weakened mast was no match for the strait's storm winds. It snapped, and a line from the downed mast jammed the big sloop's propeller. Adrift and pushed north by the oncoming front, *Team Jaguar* was taking a terrible pounding when her radios failed and her deck began breaking up from the stress of the sea's incessant beating.

Melissa McCabe, a 16-year-old Sydney high school student was among the crew of *Team Jaguar*. She won her berth with a first-place yachting essay in a contest sponsored by skipper James and "Team Jag," as the pocket maxi is known by local yachtsmen.

In the January 2 edition of the *Sydney Morning Herald* Melissa recounted her experience during which *Team Jaguar* was dismasted for the second consecutive year and feared lost.

"Excitement bubbled in my stomach as I left behind the crowded deck at Rushcutters Bay [the location of the Cruising Yacht Club of Australia and *Team Jaguar*'s home] destined for my first Sydney to Hobart yacht race. The harbor was filled with a mosaic of sails, spectator boats and white water as we swept past other smaller boats to gain a better starting position.

"The strong northeaster was carrying the boat along like a dream, allowing us to set our spinnaker whilst rounding the Heads and cruise at an average speed of 18 knots. The whole crew was ecstatic. The brilliant conditions heightened our pleasure over our successful start.

"We were making excellent time and had passed Jervis Bay well before nightfall. Although I was still exuberant, we were beginning to see signs of a predicted black southerly change. The swell had been continuously rising, and by dusk dark clouds began to seep into the horizon, soon forming two thunderstorms that enveloped the boat from the east and the west. We removed the spinnaker.

"I had wrapped myself in my wet-weather gear and strapped on a safety harness. Waves were beginning to wash over the bow of the boat. From my position on the boat's rails spray washed over me.

"We started our watch system at this stage—two hours on deck, two hours on the rails to be called in if needed, two hours sleep. At 10 P.M. I clambered below deck and arose again at midnight to find the conditions worse.

"In the dark, the boat made a harsh slapping sound as it slammed down the front of the swell.

"During this watch we tacked unexpectedly. The two crew members on either side of me managed to clamber into the cockpit. I wasn't so lucky. Panic-stricken, I managed to grab hold of the rail as water rushed over the deck and began to rise around my waist. I shouted for help and my crew members grabbed me and hauled me into the cockpit.

"We then had to make it to the rails on the opposite side. Frantically I had to unattach my safety harness in order to reattach it to the other side of the boat. My fingers were too numb to function. Using two hands I managed to unclip my harness. I hated the terror I felt, knowing that for a time I was totally unprotected.

"At 4 A.M. my watch was up. Exhausted, I struggled below deck only to find seasick crew members bailing and pumping because the bilges had flooded some sections of the boat.

"At 6:30 A.M. my watch was greeted with daylight. The sun seemed to soak up the night's miseries. The wind had relented slightly, and Eden was in sight to our east. I felt so glad to be aboard the boat that morning, knowing that we had all those miles behind us.

"At 11:30 A.M. I was lying below deck when I heard the cry of 'All hands on deck.' The mast was beginning to break. It was too dangerous for me on deck so I could only peep out of the hatch and gasp at the mainsail lying limp in the water and the boom sagging. Hacksaws, hammers, screwdrivers were used to pry off rigging to save the boat.

"At the moment that the mast slipped into the sea, I looked around at crew faces full of fear and intensity and knew that my hopes of getting to Hobart had also been gobbled up by the sea. The race was now for safety.

"With the mast gone nothing was left but to motor the 50 nautical miles back to Eden. A huge bang sounded as a mass of water cracked the deck frame above me. I jumped up, knee-deep in water, wanting to escape. I kept having flashes of disaster voyages. It was almost surreal. I was told to get up on deck, and did so swiftly.

"As soon as we got on deck I saw two crew being pulled back on board after being washed off.

"It was worse on deck than below. For our own safety, another two females and I were ordered below.

"Below deck I heard that ropes had been swept overboard and had jammed the propeller. The skipper tried the radio and realized we could make no transmission. This was the moment that I was the most scared. I knew that no one knew that we were in trouble.

"When communication was finally established using our emergency aerial we were informed that a trawler called *Moira Elizabeth* was coming to tow us to Eden. The worst part about waiting was listening to the radio and hearing real people's horror stories and frantic Maydays, knowing you couldn't possibly help them, or even yourself.

"Finally, at 4 A.M., we were found. At 12:30 P.M. we pulled into Eden wharf. I had never felt so thankful for seeing so many caring faces. When you suffer a piece of hell everything in life shines brighter."

While it is crushing to watch a hard-won and favorable position evaporate two years in a row, the blows James suffered were primarily to his pride and pocketbook. Other boats in *Team Jaguar*'s vicinity were taking a similar pounding. And while some of their crews were getting beaten up, all were getting spooked.

Twenty miles east on a course nearly parallel to *Team Jaguar*, Stan Zemanek, the skipper of *Foxtel Titan Ford*, was giving serious consideration to the concept of death.

"We were just bare-poling [no sails up] and the boat was still leaning over on a big angle," he said. "The boat just hit a wave and flew straight up in the air and I went with it, nothing to hang on to. I hit my head and ribs on the galley, breaking two. I thought I was a goner."

A consummately skilled sailor with a 20-year maritime career and 21 Hobart finishes to his credit, Roger Hickman, the skipper of *Atara*, described Sunday morning's waves: "We were in a 43-foot boat. You'd go up the wave and look to the bottom. And I reckon that they were somewhere between 60 and 65 feet from the bottom to the top."

John Stanley, a crewman on the ill-fated cutter *Winston Churchill*, said he had been warned 16 years earlier that tempting fate and Bass Strait was playing with fire.

"I remember a speech back in 1982 when it was said that sometime in the next 100 years we would get some horrific conditions in Bass Strait. And it looked like we were in those conditions," he said.

It would only be a matter of a few hours before the storm—at its greatest intensity—would start tearing into the Hobart fleet with no holds barred.

VC Offshore Stand Aside was its first victim.

Skipper Jim Hallion and co-owner Laurie Hallion, both of Adelaide, South Australia, thought they had a good chance of finishing the Sydney to Hobart ahead of the other boats in *Stand Aside*'s division. Jim Hallion had skippered the 40-footer to a divisional first and several divisional placings in Cruising Yacht Club of South Australia inshore and offshore events. He was a veteran of two Sydney to Hobarts, but 1998 was *Stand Aside*'s first. The boat had proved particularly fast when running and reaching, sailing with the wind from her stern, the kind of winds initially forecast for the race. So Jim Hallion and his experienced crew of 11 had reason to be optimistic about a good finish.

And even though the storm shifted the winds 180 degrees on Saturday from north to south, *Stand Aside*, at her best when running, had beaten more than 200 miles to windward in 24 hours. Averaging 16 knots overnight in rough seas, *Stand Aside* was running hard at the entrance to Bass Strait by 1 P.M. on Sunday. With steady winds of 50 knots, her crew had gradually reduced sail until *Stand Aside* was running only a small storm jib. With the wind, the seas had built, so most of the crew stood watch on the pitching deck, on alert for rogue waves. Within an hour the winds had escalated to 60 knots, with gusts as high as 80 knots. With such wind it didn't take long for a rogue wave to find *Stand Aside*.

Crewman Simon Clark, a 28-year-old who had sailed since he was a boy, wasn't worried. He had seen only one "green wave," as he called the huge walls of water that were knocking down so many yachts in Bass Strait.

Suddenly, though, a rogue wave Clark described as a tennis court standing on end loomed astern *Stand Aside*, dwarfing the yacht.

"Bear away!" he yelled above the roar of the wind.

"All of a sudden the call came that there was a huge wave behind the boat," said Laurie Hallion, an experienced yachtsman. "The skipper tried to bear away but the wave came down on top of the port side of the boat, crashed the boom down on to the deck and rolled the yacht over."

Eight members of the crew, most tethered to the boat by harnesses, went with it.

"Underneath the boat it was just a mass of bodies struggling to get free of the ropes and the harnesses," Jim Hallion recalled. He remembers being under the water for one to two minutes, feeling other bodies struggling around him. It felt like longer.

"We must have been hit by an 80- to 90-foot wave," said crew member Charles Alsop, another experienced yachtsman. "It broke over the boat and we took a 360-degree turn."

Alsop, who was thrown overboard when *Stand Aside* was struck, said he nearly drowned as a result.

"As soon as you're underneath the water, ropes all over you, all tangled up, your first thought is: 'I've just got to get to the surface. I'm losing air.'"

Crew member John Culley, a sailor with three years experience taking part in his first Sydney to Hobart, was wearing neither a harness nor life jacket when the yacht keeled over. "I was sitting on the rail, I think I was the furthest forward, and I just heard somebody say 'wave' and then somebody said 'Oh, shit!'

"I had this sensation of a slow-motion roll into the sea. I opened my eyes and I could see the deck underneath the water and a few bodies floating around. When I surfaced, the boat seemed like it was a mile away but in fact it was probably only about 40 meters away. I had my waterproof boots on which were filling up with water.

"I thought, 'I'm not going to make it,'" Culley said.

But the waves and the wind pushed him back toward the boat and he was hauled back on board by strong hands.

By this time, the yacht's mast was gone and its cabin destroyed. The engine was under water, as were the batteries. The main communications system was gone, leaving only a small hand-held radio to send the Mayday call.

The boat was filling with water through a 7-foot gash in its cabin.

All the crew could do was bail water as they sent out a distress call and waited for help.

As the magnitude of the disaster unfolded, increasingly larger government agencies would take control of coordinating rescue services and dispatching increasing numbers of ships, planes and helicopters to the stricken yachts. But for the moment radio operator Lew Carter, a longtime race volunteer, was coordinating rescue efforts from his crowded space aboard *Young Endeavour*, the Australian Navy's brigantine that harked back to the days when sailing ships ruled the seas.

Gary Ticehurst, the pilot of an Australian Broadcasting Network helicopter, found himself in the dual role of on-site rescue coordinator and ABC pilot.

"We went straight for the position that was given us for the yacht *Stand Aside*," said Ticehurst. "What greeted us was just unbelievable.

Unbelievable circumstances. Help was on its way, but it was an hour away. We had just refueled so we were able to stay on station. We were aware of a smaller yacht. *Siena* passed within a couple hundred meters of us and *Stand Aside* but because of the big seas did not see either of us."

Siena, an older 38 foot sloop skippered by Iain Muray of Sydney, was heading for Eden under a storm sail with a crewman who had suffered broken ribs. She passed *Stand Aside* while both were in troughs on opposite sides of the same huge wave. Neither yacht saw the other. But *Siena*, whose crew included Dr. Stephen Grenville, the deputy governor of the Reserve Bank of Australia, responded immediately to a hail from the ABC helicopter. Apprised that *Stand Aside* was dismasted and off her port, *Siena* and her crew of seven came about to offer assistance.

Watching the slow and dangerous maneuver from several hundred feet above, Ticehurst said, "That took a lot of guts. That really took a lot of courage for them in that small boat to turn around in those conditions and assist *Stand Aside*."

With *Siena* tending and Ticehurst hovering the ABC helicopter overhead, the crew of *Stand Aside*, several of whom were badly injured, waited. Below decks the boat was awash in a nauseating cocktail of sea water, spilled food, toilet chemicals and engine fuel. On deck it was just as unpleasant as the boat pitched over each new wave and dropped to the trough far below, all the while bucking wildly at the mercy of the gale winds. Three hours later a civilian Helimed rescue helicopter equipped with a winch arrived, hovered 100 feet above the yachts and made radio contact with *Stand Aside*.

"*Stand Aside*, this is Helimed One. Do you have a motor?"

"No, the motor is not working."

"Can you let the life raft out a bit further [astern]?"

"Yes, we can."

Ticehurst, who had remained on the scene in the ABC helicopter, said: "The worst injured on *Stand Aside* were put in a life raft. The first rescue attempt was made with the rescue swimmer lowered out of the helicopter into the water. But the waves were huge and breaking. We could see the air crewman in the water disappear in a trough as the wave broke. Due to conditions it took some time for the first rescue to be completed, as the pilot was warming to his task. But after that it didn't take very long to rescue the rest of the crew."

Shortly after the Helimed helicopter arrived, a second rescue helicopter reached the scene to replace a Victorian police helicopter that had been diverted en route to another stricken Hobart yacht.

Helimed paramedic Peter Davidson returned to the water eight times until he was exhausted. The Helimed helicopter from which he had been working was running low on fuel. So the pilot wheeled it about and headed for the mainland with eight of *Stand Aside*'s crew of 12 aboard. The lives of the four remaining crewmen were in the hands of the crew of the second helicopter on the scene, SouthCare, a civilian air-ambulance service from Canberra, Australia's capital city. On board was Kristy McAlister, a 30-year-old fit and youthful paramedic. Although an experienced paramedic, she had only been working on helicopters for two months, and this was her first ocean rescue. As the helicopter's paramedic, McAlister was the designated "down the wire guy," as air crews refer to the position.

As McAlister hooked the winch cable to her harness and looked below, one of the victims was drifting quickly away from the life raft tethered to *Stand Aside*, which held three other victims. Hesitating momentarily, she inventoried her nightmarish surroundings from the lurching helicopter that was struggling to hold position in the buffeting winds. In the space of a few seconds two monster waves rolled beneath the helicopter, reaching up 60 feet to lick its underbelly. Glancing at the instrument panel, McAlister saw the altimeter gyrate wildly in response to the upreaching waves and their deep troughs. The wind screamed demented notes through the vents of her safety helmet as she gave the "ready" signal, leaned out the starboard door and jumped, rescue strop in hand.

Immediately after a hard landing in the roiling sea she was clutched by a huge breaking wave and driven deep beneath the surface. Her lungs burning for air, McAlister clawed for the surface and came up almost beside the victim. With some hurried instructions, she got the oval-shaped strop over the man's head and gave the thumb's up, the signal to winch them aboard. A second massive wave that McAlister had not seen dragged them both under for several long seconds. When they surfaced, the wire tightened and hoisted them to safety.

After a perfunctory check of her first victim's condition, McAlister was back in the churning ocean, landing near the life raft and its three hypothermic occupants. With the last man rescued and the ruined and abandoned *Stand Aside* passing beneath the helicopter as it headed for the mainland, McAlister could hold out no longer. She began vomiting sea water in a series of violent spasms that would last for 10 minutes.

It was a difficult rescue for McAlister and the rest of the helicopter crew. As one of the pilots remarked: "One minute we had 80 feet under the aircraft and the next minute 10 feet. It took all our training and effort to get these people out."

One of the major points of confusion in all of the 1998 Hobart helicopter rescues was communicating with victims. Many of the stricken boats had lost their radios, so pilots could not explain to those below the high risk of tangling the rescue cable in the boat's rigging or slamming the rescuer against the boat when attempting to pluck a victim from the deck of a yacht. Even novice sailors are trained to "stay with the boat" as long as possible. So leaping into the sea, especially a wild sea, is not a comfortable proposition for sailors. But it is almost always the safest position for the helicopter crew from which to rescue a person, rescue pilots agree unanimously.

The four crewmen of *Stand Aside* with the worst injuries—Mike Marshmon suffering a severed finger, Clark with tendon damage to one of his knees, one with broken ribs, and another with head injuries—were flown to Traralgon District Hospital.

Jim and Laurie Hallion, Andy Marriette, Bevan Thompson, Bob Briggs, Charles Alsop, Hayden Jones, John Culley, Mike Marshmon, Rod Hunter, Simon Clark and Trevor Conyers had survived a hard chance.

Like *Stand Aside*, *Solo Globe Challenger* was entering Bass Strait Sunday evening and was handling the mountainous seas well, according to her skipper Tony Mowbray. "Cliffs of water," as Mowbray called them, were hammering down on *Solo Globe Challenger* with the force of thunderclaps, one after another. When the big ones struck, all the topside crew could do was hang on and turn away as tons of water pummeled the boat, and she shuddered in response.

At 43, Mowbray, a laborer from the middle-class coal-mining seaport town of Newcastle, 70 miles north of Sydney, thought of the 1998 Sydney to Hobart as a shakedown cruise. He had mortgaged his house and drained his savings to buy and outfit 44-foot *Solo Globe Challenger*. The veteran sailor with 32 years experience planned to sail solo, non-stop and unassisted around the world to raise money for an Australian children's hospital. Mowbray entered the 1998 Sydney to Hobart, his 14th, to spotlight his charity venture and to spend time with his sailing buddies, including his mentor and veteran of 22 Hobarts, Bob Snape, before circumnavigating the globe 10 months later.

In addition to Mowbray and Snape, *Solo Globe Challenger*'s crew included David Cook, David Marshall, Glen Picasso, Keir Enderby, Keith Molloy and Tony Purkiss. Mowbray knew each of the crewmen, but with few exceptions the crewmen had not met each other before the race.

The yacht and crew withstood Sunday's battering until a 65-foot monster wave crashed on *Solo Globe Challenger*'s stern at about 4 P.M. The yacht yawed sharply to port and rolled on its side at 145 degrees with its mast and rigging in the water. Like a body surfer, the knocked-down boat was pushed before the wave for nearly 30 seconds before it slowed and righted itself. Water gushed into the cabin through a broken skylight.

"I hadn't been to bed since the start of the race," Mowbray recalled. "And so on Sunday afternoon I went down below to get some rest. Not long after, the first monster hit us and laid us over. Before I had a chance to recover, the second one threw us over further and put the mast in the water. It just snapped off like a twig. The huge volume of water that came through the cockpit area smashed out the windows and blew out all our navigational and radio gear. We had no communication at all."

Crewman David Cook, from Lake Macquarie, in New South Wales, was below decks with David Marshall when the giant wave struck. "The next thing I know, a great wall of water came through the hatch and I ended up on top of Dave [Marshall]," Cook said.

Cook, an experienced ocean racer sailing his first Sydney to Hobart, remembers finding his way up out of the hatch after the yacht had righted itself again and finding sail trimmer Tony Purkiss sitting there, stunned, on deck with a huge gash on his head and blood everywhere. Purkiss, taking part in his fifth Sydney to Hobart, had been hit on the head when the mast came down. And deck hatches had come down on his legs, fracturing his left leg below the knee.

"Glen Picasso was hanging over the side, dragged by his safety harness. [Tony Purkiss] had his leg pinned by the mast and was in a lot of agony and screaming out," said Mowbray.

Picasso managed to drag himself back aboard. Purkiss was so entangled in the fallen rigging that he had to be cut free. Both men suffered head injuries and broken ribs.

After the initial shock, Mowbray quickly realized that the mast, still connected to *Solo Globe Challenger* by the rigging, threatened the boat as much as the next wave did.

"The biggest danger was the mast puncturing the side of the yacht, which would sink us. We had to cut the mast away and get rid of it. So we sent 35,000 bucks worth of gear to the bottom of the sea," the skipper said.

The yacht was now completely disabled and adrift.

"We had no mast, no engine, no communications, no rig," Cook recalled.

After bailing out the cabin and activating two EPIRBs (emergency position indicating radio beacons), all the skipper could do was stay at the wheel and use what little steerage he had to avoid another rogue wave. Nearby, the racing yacht *Pippin*, which was en route to Eden with seriously injured crewmen, some of whom had seen the knockdown, made a hazardous turn to come to *Solo Globe Challenger*'s aid. Mowbray waved the yacht off, believing the sea was too dangerous for any rescue attempt by another boat. Also, *Pippin* had its own problems. *Pippin* continued on its course, but not before alerting the fleet's radio-relay ship that Mowbray and his crew were in trouble.

Two hours after the knockdown, two aircraft circled the stricken yacht within 30 minutes of each other. Shortly after that, a container ship slowed some 300 yards from *Solo Globe Challenger*, then resumed its course. Mowbray and his crew, unsure if they had been identified by the planes or the ship, fired a parachute flare, but the ship continued.

With two activated EPIRBs but no radios, *Solo Globe Challenger* headed into the maelstrom with the last of the gray sky turning to black.

The storm that was taking a terrible toll on the Sydney to Hobart fleet was to test the entrants to the absolute limits of their physical and mental endurance. In the process, it would also produce a number of heroes and heroines. One of them was 19-year-old Australian Elizabeth Wardley.

An experienced sailor at 19, Wardley had fallen in love with sailing big boats five years earlier. Disenchanted with school, she sailed on a big boat with an experienced skipper for the first time when she was 15. The skipper, she said, told her she should follow her love of sailing. Wardley took the advice and worked her way up to racing big yachts. After finishing high school, she began delivering yachts all over Australia. By the 1998 Sydney to Hobart race, Wardley had sailed the event once, she was ranked number two in the world in 16-foot catamaran racing and she had recently passed a difficult national test to become a charter-boat skipper.

At the Sydney to Hobart starting gun, Wardley was the skipper of the 40-foot sloop *Dixie Chicken*, which she and her father had bought a year earlier. She commanded a crew of seven men.

At the 2 P.M. radio sked, *Dixie Chicken* was 25 miles off Gabo Island, struggling to negotiate the huge seas and winds that were recorded two hours earlier at Wilson's Promontory in Bass Strait at a steady 80 knots. During one 10-minute interval the wind speed was a steady 92 knots—greater than 100 miles an hour.

It was in such conditions that skipper Alan Quick and the 10 crew of the Victorian yacht *Outlaw* was knocked down by an enormous wave and seriously damaged. It was Wardley's *Dixie Chicken*, five treacherous miles away, who came to Quick's aid.

After five hours of tending the 44-foot *Outlaw* as it struggled to Eden, Wardley pulled *Dixie Chicken* out of the race, believing she had lost too much time. One of Wardley's crew, Carl Sriber of Sydney, called his skipper's actions courageous. Even coming about in Sunday's conditions to go to *Outlaw*'s aid was a dangerous 30-minute maneuver, he said.

Wardley's self-sacrifice, courage and heroism would not be the last in the 1998 Sydney to Hobart.

After a day of "screaming down the coast," as her skipper described it, *Sword of Orion* was among the Hobart fleet's lead boats Sunday afternoon. She was running a close race with Roger Hickman's *Atara*, which was a half mile off *Sword of Orion*'s port bow and in the same Division B size class. *Yendys*, a smaller Division C yacht skippered by Cruising Yacht Club of Australia Director Geoff Ross, was beating to windward off *Sword of Orion*'s port just a large wave or two distant.

A Sydney-based boat with a new owner, *Sword of Orion* was on a major winning streak. Owner Rob Kothe had campaigned the 47-footer to a surprise victory in the prestigious Hamilton Island Race Week a short time earlier. Formerly the *Brighton Star*, which finished well in the difficult conditions of the 1997 Sydney to Hobart, *Sword of Orion* had been race tuned, including being refitted with a lighter, faster carbon keel. Signalling his intent to continue the winning streak, Kothe recruited several crew members with world-class racing talent. Among them were Admiral's Cup yachtsmen Steve Kulmur and Andrew Parkes, bowman Darren Senogles and helmsman Glyn Charles of Great Britain, who represented his country at the 1996 Olympics regatta in Savannah, Georgia. The Cruising Yacht Club of Australia listed *Sword of Orion* as "extremely competitive" and "a definite chance" in her class.

Kothe, like many skippers in the 1998 Hobart fleet, knew about the low-pressure system in Bass Strait. And like many skippers, the 52-year-old Sydney to Hobart veteran considered the forecast—a Force 9 gale—literally par for the course. But the conditions at the time of the 2 P.M. "sked," the radio roll call that fixed each boat's position, were far worse than anything Kothe had expected. Wind gusts greater than 90 miles an hour were piling up series of sharp waves that were crashing down on *Sword* from heights of 50 feet. Those on deck watch were getting thrashed about like rag dolls each time one of the monsters struck. All were wearing standard nylon-web safety harnesses clipped to lines secured to the deck. But the force of tons of green water moving at enormous speed was straining the safety lines to their limit.

Drenched and shaken by the repeated dousings, Kothe made his way gingerly down the companionway to the navigation station and the boat's high-frequency (HF) radio. The 2 P.M. skeds were about to begin. Right on schedule, radioman Lew Carter aboard the race escort ship *Young Endeavour* began taking the roll alphabetically. When hailed, each boat responded, gave its position and signed off, which is standard race protocol. Offering or requesting additional information is typically reserved for emergency situations, under which the boat is no longer racing. More commonly, racing boats offer less information than more. For example, although the practice is frowned upon by race officials, skippers sometimes feign radio difficulties during skeds to mask their positions from other boats. Kothe listened to this litany until it came to boats whose names began with the letter S. When *Sayonara* reported, there were nine more boats—45 seconds—before *Sword.* Kothe made a tough decision. Breaking with protocol and giving away what is considered top-secret tactical information, Kothe gave a weather report for the benefit of the many boats far astern.

"*Young Endeavor,* this is *Sword of Orion.* The forecast is for 40 to 55 knots. We are experiencing between 65 and 82. The weather is much stronger than forecast."

Radioman Carter, equally surprised by the wind speeds and Kothe's unusual disclosure, repeated the message to the Hobart fleet. Almost immediately, 20 percent of the fleet, some two dozen boats, headed for the shelter of Eden to weather the storm in retirement from the race or to continue racing after the storm abated. Among the boats that heeded Kothe's weather warning were Queensland yacht *Midnight Special* and *Polaris,* a New South Wales yacht whose owner and skipper John Quinn was washed overboard during the 1993 Sydney to Hobart then miraculously plucked from the ocean.

Kothe's call probably saved lives, but it spawned its own controversy. Because the storm was moving northeast toward the fleet in *Sword of Orion*'s wake and nearing its greatest intensity, scudding or close reaching to Eden was one of the most dangerous routes in the 1998 Hobart, as *Midnight Special* learned. *Polaris* laid over in Eden for 12 hours and then proceeded to Hobart, where she crossed the finish line in 30th place overall and in seventh place in her division. *Midnight Special* was in for a nightmare.

But Kothe's weather warning to the fleet, as unusual a procedure as it was, was not the first. Ninety minutes earlier, Gary Elliot, the skipper of *Doctel Rager,* had issued a similar report from his position at the head of the pack. Elliot, a lifelong sailor, had won the Plympton Cup in 1998, South Australia's oldest sailing trophy, and he had taken line honors in the race. In 1997, he had competed in the Sydney to Hobart with his son, who was 14 years old. When he issued his weather warning at 12:35 P.M., *Doctel Rager* was 15 miles west of *Sword of Orion* and closer to the building storm. Also, Elliot had his son and his 16-year-old daughter aboard. Elliot reported severe weather ahead with winds of 50 to 60 knots and gusts of 70-plus.

Fifteen minutes later, the yachts *Secret Mens Business, Wild One* and *She's Apples II* issued severe weather advisories over the single radio frequency used by the entire fleet. The three yachts were strung out for 45 miles behind *Doctel Rager*.

Within the hour, all three would head for Eden and shelter, along with the yachts *Sea Jay, Henry Kendall Akubra* and *Indian Pacific.*

After his radio report, Kothe went back on deck where the winds had suddenly dropped to 50 knots, conditions Kothe and fellow Hobart veterans consider a walk in the park. But it was a brief one. At 3:35 P.M., by Kothe's watch, a wall of wind he estimated at 80 miles an hour slammed into *Sword* without let-up. He ordered everyone below except young and nimble bowman Darren Senogles and Olympian Glyn Charles, who was at the helm. Next Kothe scrambled below and radioed *Young Endeavour* that *Sword of Orion* was withdrawing from the race and heading north, to the shelter of Eden's Twofold Bay.

Turning north for Eden was not an easy way out. It meant that *Sword* was sailing on a Force 11 following wind and the mountainous seas it was generating. Fifteen minutes after *Sword* changed course, Kothe, who was on the radio, felt the boat rising sharply up a huge wave. Without enough speed to top the monster, the 47-foot sloop was thrown backward. For two long seconds *Sword* was upside down and airborne before it slammed to the ocean with a horrible concussion. The boat somehow righted itself after several more seconds, and Kothe found himself face-down on the cabin deck covered in broken equipment. It was while staggering to his feet that Kothe heard Senogles' frantic wind-torn words from top side that all skippers dread: "Man overboard! Man overboard! Man overboard."

Almost as one, Kothe and the seven crewmen below deck scrambled up the companionway and onto the ruined deck, which had separated from the hull during the knockdown. Charles, 30 yards away, was encouraged with yells of "Swim! Swim!" Senogles, a close friend of Charles, tied himself to a rope and prepared to dive in. Charles, upwind and clearly dazed, raised an arm. A life ring was immediately tossed, but the wind blew it back on to the deck. Simultaneously, a second huge wave struck, knocking the crew down and tumbling them like bowling pins. When they recovered, Charles was doomed, 150 yards away.

"When the wave hit us we just rolled over with a great crashing roar as we fell down the face of the wave," Kothe recalled. "When the boat came back up Glyn Charles was in the water. There was a lot of yelling, a lot of anguish. One of the young guys was about to dive in the water and was restrained. It didn't make any sense. We didn't have a line that would go back 150 feet. We were all in danger of drowning. The boat was at enormous risk."

The struggling Englishman stayed in view for five minutes before he was lost from sight, forever.

Kothe went through a futile two hours of broadcasting urgent maydays. *Sword's* mast had snapped in five pieces when she plummeted off the monster wave. Atop the mast had been the boat's broadcast antenna.

Dangerously damaged and without radio communications, *Sword of Orion* was now adrift in huge seas with a shocked and disheartened crew, some of whom were injured, one with a broken leg. Less than an hour later they thought that their luck had changed.

Sword of Orion crewman Steve Kulmar and another crew member were on deck at about 4 P.M. when they spotted the *Margaret Rintoul II* sailing straight at them, about 500 yards away. One of the oldest yachts in the Hobart fleet, *Margaret Rintoul* shares the record with *Mark Twain* for the most Sydney to Hobarts. She and *Sword of Orion* both sail from the Cruising Yacht Club of Australia.

"We let off four or five flares and waved them," Kulmar said. "By the time we came up she was 150 to 200 metres dead to windward with a storm jib up only. We were somewhat amazed they didn't see us."

Richard Purcell, the skipper of *Margaret Rintoul*, did see them. "We had sailed past him *(Sword of Orion)* when we sighted him," Purcell said. "We saw one flare, for five seconds. I saw the flare, no one else saw it. I decided what we could and couldn't do for them.

"The total responsibility number one I have got is to my crew. All of them are married, except for two. All of them have children. I had to take responsibility."

Cruising Yacht Club of Australia Commodore Hugo van Kretschmar said, "There is an obligation on all the yachts to render all the assistance they can safely provide to a yacht in distress." The CYCA commodore, who competed in the 1998 Hobart and retired to the shelter of Eden, called failure to offer assistance gross misconduct. "It is not dissimilar to not stopping after a car accident," he said.

Sword of Orion's skipper Rob Kothe neither reported nor pursued the incident, hoping "it would just go away." But *Sword* crewman Steve Kulmar was angered by the snubbing.

"We were in a life-threatening position," he said. "We had no rig, no means of power. The boat had cracked open. We had a metre of water in the boat. Surely he had a duty just to stand by. He could have heaved to, dropped his sail and attempted to make some form of communication. We could have told him Glyn was overboard. He could have started the search. He could have contacted the radio relay vessel for us. There's a lot of things he could have done without physically endangering his boat or our boat."

Purcell insisted that by the time he spotted *Sword of Orion* and seen its flare, Charles had been overboard for several hours. "The English professional skipper was already dead. They saw him go under. He wasn't wearing a life jacket," he said.

When the two crews met in Hobart after the race, what is usually a jocular recounting of the race on New Year's Eve turned into a bar melee.

As this book was going to press, the Cruising Yacht Club of Australia was continuing its investigation of Purcell's actions during the race. He could be banned from ocean racing for life. Too, a coroner's inquiry into the death of Charles and others that was not concluded by press time could recommend its own sanctions.

The fact remained that *Sword of Orion* and her crew were left adrift in a Force 11 storm in a boat that was literally coming apart at the seams. At 7:30 P.M., halfway across Bass Strait, their distress beacon's signal was finally distinguished by rescue authorities, whose computer screens were lighting up like Christmas trees from 11 distress beacons all broadcasting on the same 121.5 megahertz frequency.

Thirty minutes earlier, faced with multiple knockdowns, retirements and Maydays, the Cruising Yacht Club of Australia let the fleet know that it was not going to call off the race. A message broadcast by *Young Endeavour* reminded skippers that the responsibility for and the decision to continue racing rested solely with them. Five minutes later, the Australian Maritime Safety Authority (AMSA) declared a Mayday for the entire Sydney to Hobart race course.

As soon as *Sword of Orion*'s EPIRB signal was distinguished from others, a search by a Navy Sea King helicopter with infrared night-vision equipment began. But it was nearly 12 hours later when *Sword of Orion* was spotted and her crew winched to safety aboard a rescue helicopter.

///

After a two-year legal battle Richard Purcell was cleared by the CYCA of the charge of gross misconduct. The coroner also found his actions in not returning to assist *Sword of Orion* were justified under the circumstances with his boat not having an operating engine.

///

cape horn

FROM

trekka
round the
WORLD

BY
John Guzzwell

In 1955 John Guzzwell set out from Victoria, British Columbia, to sail around the world in *Trekka*, a 20.5-foot wooden yawl he had built himself. He crossed the Pacific to Hawaii, swung south past Australia, across the Indian Ocean, and around the Cape of Storms, across the Atlantic, and through the Panama Canal back into the Pacific. He arrived home just over four years after departing. Like many long-distance voyagers who take their time, Guzzwell met a lot of interesting people, visited exotic ports, and had innumerable adventures aboard *Trekka*.

Perhaps his greatest adventure, however, occurred during an extended period he spent with two other Canadian sailors, Miles and Beryl Smeeton, aboard their 46-foot wooden ketch *Tzu Hang*. He volunteered to join them and stand a third watch on their voyage from Australia around Cape Horn and up to the Falkland Islands. He put his solo adventure on hold, put *Trekka* in storage, and joined their adventure.

That adventure, as *Tzu Hang* reached the enormous seas of the Roaring Forties on the approach to Cape Horn, has become one of the true modern classics of sail. The Smeetons wrote their version of it in *Once Is Enough*. Guzzwell's story, excerpted here, is not necessarily more dramatic than theirs but, as an objective account of the Smeetons, is perhaps a more revealing account of that most famous couple in sailing literature. With his "stiff upper lip" prose, you can use your imagination to fill in the details of that day as they approached the Horn.

///

EVER

since joining *Tzu Hang* I had been plagued with seasickness, being unable to adapt to her pitching in a seaway. Naturally this had caused me some concern as I wanted to be able to pull my weight as a crew member and I also wanted to enjoy the voyage. A friend in Melbourne had told us that in order for seasick pills to be effective you had to take them about four days before you went to sea. We had all done this and were delighted to find that this approach worked.

Tzu Hang seemed to know that we were off on a long passage, for she went along at top speed all that day, and by noon the next had run 168 miles on the log. We went through Banks Straits and then out into the Tasman Sea heading for the south of New Zealand. A strong blustery breeze drove us along over a rough sea and under grey skies. It seemed as though we were following a depression across the Tasman and moving along at about the same speed. It was wet uncomfortable sailing but the ship was going well, and nine days later we were between the Snares and the Auckland Islands, getting down to about the 50th parallel of latitude.

Then the weather changed and we were becalmed. The sea went down and the skies cleared; it was a welcome change from the grey days, and soon the deck was covered with bedding being aired while we attended to a few jobs that could be done in these pleasant conditions.

I had long decided that the two little doors in the aft end of the doghouse should be changed to washboards, so while the weather was good I made the alterations using some materials that B. had collected.

She never believed in throwing anything away and had little hiding places about the ship which, from time to time, Miles and I stumbled upon. They reminded me of secret bank accounts from which necessary withdrawals were sometimes made if the situation demanded it. On this occasion she parted with a nice piece of three-quarter-inch plywood which was just large enough to make the two washboards. The bottom one was made about ⅔ the size of the opening and had a small window in it; when installed with the hatch shut, it was possible to see the helmsman from down below without opening the hatch.

It was during this fine weather period that I had the first opportunity to get off in the dinghy and film *Tzu Hang* under sail. She looked so small, rolling along quietly under the twin staysails over that endless expanse of undulating westerly swells which were to accompany us constantly in the weeks ahead. There was something rather gallant about the way she carried herself, every line was clean and pleasing, she was a lady and a beautiful one at that. Looking through the view-finder as the camera ran gave me an intense feeling of satisfaction. I was very happy to be where I was, making a film of a unique voyage aboard a fine ship with a couple of people I had come to love dearly. What more could a young man want?

"We've got to have some scenes of big seas," I said as the dinghy pulled alongside *Tzu Hang*. "Come and see her from the dinghy, B.," I called. "She really looks great but you have to be away from her to see how much motion there is." I passed up the camera to Miles and scrambled aboard quickly as a swell lifted the dinghy almost level with the rail for an instant. B. jumped in smartly and Miles and I watched as she rowed away, sometimes disappearing out of sight behind a crest. I wondered how many other women had rowed a dinghy in those latitudes. None, I decided.

When the wind came back, it was from the northeast and we held on to the port tack, going south of east. This weather seemed unusual to us as we had been expecting steady westerlies, rather as we'd had across the Tasman Sea.

We drove on until we were down south of latitude 50 and inside the red line on the weather chart which indicated that ice extends that far north. It was a sobering thought, and rather than go farther south we decided to wait for a shift in the wind.

Slowly we made our way across the vast expanse of ocean, sometimes with fair winds, sometimes with foul. There were the constant sail changes to suit the particular conditions of the moment, being awakened from a warm bunk to put on wet rain gear and boots, climbing out of the hatchway into the blackness of a squall, clipping on your lifeline as you went forward to let go a halyard—the scenes and sounds of our little world as the low clouds raced across a sky lit only by starlight; the hiss of an approaching sea, the movement of the deck, the automatic grabbing of familiar handholds as we made our way back aft to a figure in the cockpit crouched over the binnacle holding the course by its flickering light; the satisfaction of knowing that the rest of the world was going about its business beyond the discomforts of yours and that you wouldn't trade any of this for it.

We were on watch at the same hours every day and got used to our own personal routines. Miles and I each did three three-hour watches during the 24 hours and B. was on for two, as she did all the cooking. This meant that we each got six hours off during the hours of darkness, which was usually enough, but could be supplemented during the day if necessary.

Apart from reading during my off-watch hours, I had other interests—photography or making various little projects from some of the materials that B. guarded so zealously. I found myself thinking more and more about taking *Trekka* on round the world when this present voyage was done, and passed many pleasant hours sketching on paper the various alterations I planned to make to the little boat.

The days and weeks slipped by, and we got used to the ever-changing weather systems, the highs and the lows, the great long swells which were always with us, and the magnificent southern albatross that were our only other companions. On watch at night, I could picture the old windbags loaded full of grain, running the easting down in these latitudes half a century before; now only their ghosts, the birds, and a 46-foot ketch were going down the old route to the Horn.

We were almost halfway across the Southern Ocean to South America before the winds steadied in the westerly quarter. I had thought that the wind was always westerly in these latitudes, but it was not. It moved about as each depression came along and sometimes blew from the east, leaving us to decide which tack was the best one.

Early on the morning of 14 February I was on watch from 3 A.M. to 6 A.M. *Tzu Hang* was running fast under twin-staysails and steering herself, but the wind was increasing and I heard the tops of the sails fluttering, which they did when it was blowing quite hard.

Miles came up from down below to check on the weather and we decided to take in the twins and run along under bare poles for a while. B. came on deck and took the helm while Miles and I went forward to get the twins down. Each sail was set on its own stay and could be lowered one at a time if need be. We let both come down together, unhanked the sails and bundled them down the forehatch, then snapped the twin poles to the lifelines.

We made our way aft along the wet side decks to the cockpit where B. had already untied the sheets from the tiller. After coiling them they, too, were put below out of the way.

"How's she steering?" asked Miles, sitting down and putting an arm around her.

"She seems to steer all right," B. replied, eyes still on the compass.

"I think we'll let the stern line go anyway," he said, getting up again. "It may help some."

I gave him a hand to pay out the stiff 3-inch hawser which was made fast to the mooring bitts on the starboard quarter, then hauled in the log spinner so that it would not get all twisted up with the trailing hawser.

There was still an hour to go on my watch, but Miles was well awake by now; as he was on watch next, he decided to take over now instead of waiting until six. B. and I went below, pulling the companionway hatch shut after us, and I got undressed and climbed in to my bunk which was the quarter berth I had built on the starboard side alongside the cockpit. It was a dry comfortable bunk and I was soon asleep.

I was awakened by Miles tapping on the side of the cockpit, which was the usual way B. called me on watch to take over from her. I was reluctant to leave the warmth of the bunk and wondered if he wanted a hot drink of cocoa or something. I slid the hatch back and saw that it was light outside.

"What do you want, Miles?" I asked rather sleepily, hoping it would be something easy so that I could go back to sleep again.

"You should see some of these seas now, John. They are really quite impressive and the biggest I have seen so far. How about filming some with your movie camera?"

I thought of getting back into wet oilskins and going out into the cold and part of me rebelled. "No, Man, the sea never comes out and besides the light is not very good," I said hopefully.

But then Miles was looking aft, and he turned to me and said, "Look at this one coming along now. You've never seen a sea like that before. Get the camera, you may never have a chance to get a shot like that again."

When I looked at the scene I saw what he meant. The sea looked different from the weather we'd had the last fifty days. There was a feeling of suppressed power about it, almost as though it were awakening after a long sleep. I saw another sea a quarter of a mile away roll up astern, higher and higher; then *Tzu Hang* began to climb the slope until the crest passed beneath her and she sank into the trough behind. Miles was right, I had never seen the sea look like this before.

"Wait a bit," I said, now more awake, "I'll have to get dressed and see if I can rig the camera up."

A few minutes later, with the camera inside a plastic bag to prevent it from getting wet, and only the lens exposed, I got some shots of a worried-looking Miles steering before that dangerous-looking scene. Abreast of us the wind was blowing the crests off the big seas, flinging the spray to leeward.

"I'll shoot more later on, Miles, when B. is on watch, the light will be better then and I'd like to have some shots of her steering."

The exposed film I put in a plastic bag, and as the tins I had been using were full, I put the bag in Clio's school locker. I was pleased later that I had done so.

B. tumbled out of her bunk at seven o'clock and started making breakfast. I ate mine and then went on deck to take the helm while Miles had his breakfast. He was soon back again at the helm and said to me, "Before I called you up to film the sea, two quite large seas broke over the stern and washed me right up to the doghouse. You can see how they burst the canvas dodger."

I thought that he could not have been dead before the sea because during the few minutes I was steering, while Miles had his breakfast, I had been quite impressed at the ease with which the boat steered and rode those enormous seas.

"Goodness, just look at those seas!" exclaimed B. when she came on watch at nine o'clock. "You should be happy now, John, surely. You've been asking for big seas ever since we started for your film. I hope you're satisfied with these."

"Yes, they ought to look good on the screen, even though the sea always looks flat on film," I replied.

I went below to get the camera and noticed that Miles was in his bunk reading. Pwe was sitting on his chest purring. I went on deck again and shot more film and finished the roll with a scene of B. steering.

"I must just go and put another film in the camera, B.," I said and slid the hatch back to go below.

I got a roll of film out of the locker and went aft to my bunk to load the camera. I sat on the seat by my bunk and opened the camera. The exposed film I laid on the bunk, then I started to thread the new film into the spool.

Tzu Hang gave a violent lurch to port and I put my hand out to grab the fuel tank opposite. I had a sudden feeling that something terrible was happening. Then everything was blackness and solid water hit me. I was conscious of a roaring sound and that we were already very deep. "She's been hit by an enormous sea and is full of water. She is already sinking. I must get out." These were the thoughts that flashed through my mind. I knew I had to go forward, then up out of the doghouse hatch and I started to fight my way against solid water. Suddenly I was looking at a large blue square. "What on earth is that?" I wondered. Then I heard Miles's anguished voice, "Where's B.? Where's B.? Oh God, where's B.?" and still dazed I watched him climb into the blue square. I realised that I was laying on my back in the galley and looking at the sky through the opening in the deck where the doghouse had been.

I scrambled out on to the deck and almost immediately saw B. in the water about thirty yards away. It is a picture I will never forget. She was wearing a bright yellow oilskin, the sea was almost white with spume and overhead the sky was a hard blue. B.'s face was covered with blood and for a crazy moment I thought, "Oh, what a shot for color film."

B. raised her hand and shouted, "I'm all right, I'm all right." While she started to swim toward us I looked about me and saw that both masts were in the water and all smashed into short lengths as though they had exploded apart. The doghouse had been wiped off at deck level and I noticed that both dinghies had gone. The side skylights were both smashed and the lids were gone too. I looked up and saw another monster of a sea approaching and I thought, "What a bloody shame! No one will ever know what happened to us."

"Hang on," I shouted to no one in particular, and *Tzu Hang* lifted sluggishly to meet the crest; she had a slow hopeless feel about her and I watched more water pour down the great hole in the deck.

Miles called to me to give a hand at getting B. aboard. I looked at the ruin everywhere and thought, "I might as well jump in alongside her."

B. had something the matter with her arm, for when we hauled her aboard she thought I was kneeling on it.

"Well, this is it, Miles," I said, knowing that we had come to the end of the trail.

He nodded. "Yes, it looks like it, John."

"Hang on!" I cried as another big sea came along. *Tzu Hang* again made a tremendous effort, but she lifted and I felt a spark of hope. "We've got a chance," I cried. And just then B. said, "I know where the buckets are."

The two of us climbed down into the waist-deep water that was splashing backwards and forwards in what a few seconds before had been our comfortable little home. My main thought was to prevent more water getting below and that meant we had to cover the doghouse opening with sails or something. I climbed into the forecabin and started pulling the twin-staysails aft; they would help.

For bearers to cover the opening, I took the rods from Miles's canvas bunk and the door off his hanging locker. My tools were still intact and the box was jammed on top of the galley sink. By some extraordinary luck the galvanized nails were still in the paint locker though everything else had gone. It was difficult working on deck for there was nothing to hold on to, everything had been wiped bare except part of the aft end of the doghouse, the winches, and the mainsheet horse. Miles gave me a hand to cover up the doghouse opening and we spread the Terylene genoa over the bearers I had nailed across, but soon I was able to carry on alone and he went to help B. with the Herculean task of bailing out a few thousand gallons of water from *Tzu Hang*'s bilges.

I let go all the rigging-screws except the forestays in the hope that the wreckage of the masts and sails would act as a sea anchor and hold us head to sea. For a few seconds she came around into the wind, but then she broke free and fell back with the wind on her beam.

I transferred the warp trailing from aft to the bow and secured the jib to it in the hope it would act as a sea anchor, but there was not enough drag to it and we continued to lie with the seas on our beam.

Just inside the forehatch there were two gallons of fish oil together with the canvas bags it was supposed to be used with. I thought I'd never have a better opportunity to try oil on breaking seas, so I punctured both cans and emptied the lot over the side; there was no time to fill the bags. I felt that even a few minutes respite would help. I also emptied four gallons of engine oil over the side. There was no sign of either on the water and it did not have the slightest effect.

The one thought that gave me hope was that I knew the barometer had started to rise again just before the smash, which indicated that the center of the depression had passed. If we could keep *Tzu Hang* afloat for a few hours we stood a reasonable chance of getting out of this mess.

Miles and B. were bailing out of one of the side skylights.

I covered the other with the red storm-jib, lashing it down as best I could. I could hear B.'s steady call, "Right," as she handed another bucket of water up to Miles who emptied it over the side. I got a bucket and bailed out of the forecabin skylight, my feet spread wide on each bunk as I bailed. At first I could easily reach the water bending down with the bucket, but as we slowly made progress it was necessary to climb down to fill the bucket then step up onto the bunks to empty it out on deck.

By dark we had got most of the water out of *Tzu Hang*. But what a pitiful condition she was in! The bilge was full of wreckage—hundreds of cans of food, most of them now without labels, clothing, broken glass jars, books, coal and eggs, parts of the stove, and miles of B.'s colored wool that had somehow tied everything together in a most infuriating way. B. had been wearing a pair of my sea boots when she went overboard and had kicked them off while in the water. For hours she had stumbled about in the wreckage below with only thick socks on her feet; that night she noticed that one foot was badly sprained.

Miles and I were still vague as to what had happened but B. was able to give us a fairly good idea. She said that she had been steering *Tzu Hang* down wind and had met each of the big following seas stern on, but when she looked over her shoulder again she had a brief glimpse of an enormous wall of water bearing down on *Tzu Hang*. Water appeared to be running down the face of it and she could see no white crests. She could not see how *Tzu Hang* could possibly rise to it but knew that she was dead stern on. There was a feeling of being pressed down into the cockpit, then she was in the water and thinking she had been left behind. She looked around and saw *Tzu Hang* very low in the water and dismasted.

I managed to get one of the Primus stoves working and heated up some soup. Miles had a little, but B. did not want any.

We dozed that night only to be brought wide awake as big seas hit the boat and water trickled below through the cover over the great hole where the doghouse had been. I thought about how to make it pretty watertight if I got the chance. It was an awful night, everything was soaking wet, and now that we were not bailing or covering up the openings, we had time to realise the serious position we were in—a thousand miles from the nearest land, and that was the inhospitable coast of Patagonia, and no hope of a passing ship picking us up.

With the masts and booms gone, there was not much left to make a jury-rig from either. If we got out of this one all right it would have to be on our own efforts and with a good helping of luck. In the morning the sea had gone down quite a bit, but it was still running a good thirty feet high and the wind was about 35 knots. We bailed the rest of the water out of the bilges, then after we'd had a snack of ship's biscuits and cheese, I set about making a better job of the doghouse opening. I nailed the two-inch square bearers from Miles's bunk round the edge of the hole to form a sill so that water running along the deck did not get below quite so easily; the hanging locker door, a piece of cockpit coaming, and some plywood from B.'s secret stash made quite a strong roof. And when the Terylene genoa was folded several times and laid over, then nailed to the deck through battens, surprisingly little water came below.

Miles went below to start the awful job of cleaning out all the mess in the bilges and trying to find the parts for the cabin stove. Pwe, the cat, was in a bad way; she had been soaked and neglected during the time we were bailing and her distressing cries from somewhere way forward had grown weaker as we fought to stay afloat. We did find her later and she recovered from her ordeal. Fortunately, Miles found the missing stove parts, and although the chimney on deck was gone, he and B. were able to coax some wet wood to burn after dousing it with kerosene. Without the chimney the stove smoked badly, and as all the deck openings were now sealed up there was insufficient draft to allow it adequate air. We worked away steadily, Miles sorting out the ruin below, B. getting the galley into working order, and I doing my best to stop any water from getting below. I sealed *Tzu Hang* up tight and the smoke from the stove below swirled across the cabin making our eyes smart. Slowly we made progress. There were no worries about going ashore for a few weeks so we decided to make the boat as comfortable as possible meanwhile.

MILES CAME BELOW a couple of days after the smash and announced that the rudder had gone. I went up to have a look and saw that although the top of the stock was there and still moving, the rudder itself had been torn off and the 2⅜-inch diameter bronze stock had been snapped off just where it emerged from the trunk.

Three days after the smash I began work making a jury-mast out of two broken booms, one a twin-staysail pole and the other a spare staysail club.

When these two were fished together we had a spar 15-feet 6-inches long. We stepped this spar using jib bridles for shrouds and the old mizzen shrouds for a forestay and backstay. The only sail on the boat that was small enough to use was a raffee that B. had made and which had long been regarded as useless. It now became the best sail we had.

The jury-mast bent badly when we hoisted the tiny sail so we took it down and screwed two splints alongside the mast to strengthen it. When the sail was set again, it did not bend so alarmingly and we noticed to our delight that we were slowly moving along at about two knots. *Tzu Hang* was on the wrong tack, however, she was still headed on a course for Cape Horn and we wanted to go northeast so as to make for a Chilean port. Miles and I struggled with sheets and paddled frantically with the dinghy oars and finally got her round on to the other tack. We returned below feeling pleased that we were at least pointing in the right direction and moving along slowly.

Miles got some sights that day and to my amazement I found that my radio was still working. We checked the chronometer and noticed that its rate had not altered. Miles's sights put us at 51 degrees seventeen minutes south latitude and 98 degrees west longitude, just under a thousand miles due west of the entrance of the Straits of Magellan.

During the night *Tzu Hang* went about on the other tack so we
dropped the sail and waited for daylight before trying to get her round
again. In the morning we tried just about everything to get her on the
other tack, and just got madder and madder. We paddled until our arms
ached, we tried towing a drag from the quarter and juggling with the
sheets, all to no avail. Miles and I went below, sick at heart, and B.
cheered us up by making a cup of tea.

Miles was for trying out some new scheme and I was for making a
steering oar.

"Out of what, though?" asked B.

"Well, there is a lot of material here that I could use," I said. "The
bulkheads are all tongue-and-groove boards and the door frames are
quite solid."

"Well, you make the steering-oar," she decided. After tea I started.

Poor *Tzu Hang*. I removed door frames and any pieces that were not
vital to the boat, and after a couple of days work had the most crazy-look-
ing oar imaginable. It was about sixteen feet long and was made up of
short lengths all scarfed and screwed together. The blade was a locker
door. We took this contraption on deck and screwed it together again.
Then I put it over the stern with a rope grommet to hold it in position.
Miles set the raffee, and once we were moving, I gradually exerted pressure on the oar. *Tzu Hang* slowly responded, and to our delight gybed
over on to the other tack. We hauled the oar aboard and altered the
sheets of the raffee before returning below, very smug with ourselves.
The only compass we had was a small one by Miles's bunk, the main compass on deck had gone overboard with all the other gear. I saw Miles
looking puzzled as he looked at the small compass and went over to have
a look. Evidently during the two days I had been making the oar, the
wind had changed direction and we had just put *Tzu Hang* on to the
wrong tack toward Cape Horn again. We went on deck again and put her
about again. Then we saw that we were now heading northeast.

B. had been below all this time, for her foot was in a bad way. Huge
blood blisters were breaking out on her skin, and though I urged her to
pop them she was wise to leave them alone. B. had been knocked about
worse than we thought. The wound on her head had looked most spectacular, though it proved to be just a deep cut, but her shoulder was very
painful and Miles and I thought she had broken a collar-bone. She sat by

the stove most of the time trying to coax the scraps of teak into flame. The stove smoked horribly, and with everything battened down tight, there was no fresh air below. When Miles and I could stand it no longer, we'd go on deck for a breath of fresh air. When we looked aft, we could see smoke emerging from the rudder trunk. Nothing ever seemed to come out of the chimney.

When we returned below the smoke seemed worse than ever, and it was difficult to see from one side of the boat to the other. The figure of B. crouched by the stove, her long hair unkempt and her face soot-streaked, slowly stirring a steaming pot as the cat sat on her lap, gave the impression of a witch's cellar in a Walt Disney movie.

The days passed quickly and *Tzu Hang* slowly crept northwards out of the "Screaming Fifties" and into the "Roaring Forties." One of the nice things about this kind of sailing was that, with no rudder, no one had to steer and we all slept in at night.

I would go on deck sometimes and watch *Tzu Hang* limping along. It tore at my heart to see her reduced to such a sorry sight, no more the loftiness of her masts or the delicate upward tilt of her bowsprit, instead just a battered hull and scarred deck. But they were honorable scars, and though she was limping she was still proud. I swore that if she brought us to port safely, I'd help heal her wounds so that she'd sail the ocean swell again.

The smoky saloon and forecabin were hives of industry these days. I was making a twenty-foot box-section mast out of the stump of the old mainmast and bulkhead material. Miles was splicing up wire rope for the shrouds of the new mast, and B. was unpicking the new Terylene mainsail so that we could make a lugsail out of it. Meanwhile *Tzu Hang* kept moving along slowly but surely, gradually reducing the distance to Talcahuano, the port we hoped to make in Chile.

Miles was hoping that we might be able to sail to windward, if the need arose, with the aid of the sail that B. was altering. When it was ready and I had completed the gaff, we took the new mast on deck and screwed it together, and then stepped it next to the small one. The little mast we set up aft as a mizzen.

We decided to try the new rig right away and hoisted the Terylene sail and its gaff. It looked as though we needed something set for a mizzen, so we set a tiny jib-topsail as a mizzen with a dinghy oar as a boom. *Tzu Hang* immediately started to come up into the wind but I was watching the mast when it suddenly broke in half and collapsed.

I went below and Miles passed me the two pieces and I began repairing it. Next day it was stepped again and had two extra pieces fastened halfway up to stiffen it. We decided to leave the big sail until the wind fell lighter. Meanwhile we had quite a bit of sail up considering what we had before with the little mast. The jib I had used as a sea anchor had split across the center. This was now set upside down as a mainsail, with the raffee as a kind of balloon-jib. The tiny mizzen helped make us point a little higher.

We had done just about half the distance to Talcahuano under the tiny raffee alone and with the extra sail set we seemed to be moving along very well. *Tzu Hang* was knocking out some wonderful runs considering the rags she had up and the fact that she was steering herself without a rudder. Our best day's run on the log was 77 miles in 24 hours. There were other days when the total was over seventy and we really felt we were coming along very well. The ocean current was giving us another 10 miles a day, too.

About two weeks after the smash, B. came on deck for the first time since she had bailed below amidst all the ruin. She had acquired quite a tan from the cabin stove, and though I had seen her looking better, it was encouraging to see her on deck and getting about again. The cockpit drains had become plugged with pieces of coke and Miles and I tried to unblock them using bits of wire. It took B.'s persistence finally to clear them and let the water drain back into the sea instead of slopping about in the cockpit.

As we crept farther north the weather became warmer, and the sea seemed almost calm after two and a half months of the Roaring Forties. The wind had swung more to the south and we realised that we were coming into the influence of the South Pacific High. All our charts had been lost in the crash except a National Geographic Magazine map of the Pacific which was printed on cloth, and a chart of the South Atlantic which showed just a little bit of the Chilean coast where we were heading. Miles was drawing a map using the little information from them and consulting the Pilot Book. From the look of it, Talcahuano was no good for a landfall as we would have to beat our way into the bay. The best place to head for was the little port of Coronel, some 40 miles south of

Talcahuano. It was easy to enter and we could perhaps arrange a tow once we got there.

We had plenty of food aboard, but there were a few items that we missed. Sugar was one of them. The sugar sack had been kept in a bin which formed the seat by my quarter berth. It was quite a large bin and as the sack of sugar took only half the space, there were a few other things stowed with it. B. had a pair of climbing boots there and I kept my photographs and magazines there too.

B. gave Miles and me a surprise one day by producing some fudge she had made while the two of us were on deck.

"Why that's wonderful, B.," exclaimed Miles. "May I have another piece?"

"Yes, there's plenty more. Help yourself," said B.

Now when B. gave away precious stuff like fudge generously, I became a little suspicious.

"Where did you get the sugar from, B.," I asked, quite innocently.

"Oh, I found some," she answered. "Here, have another piece."

Then suddenly I knew what she'd done. I went aft and lifted the lid of the sugar bin; it was half full of thick brown treacle, and submerged in it was the sugar sack, the remains of my magazines and photos and B.'s climbing-boots.

"You surely didn't use that?" I said unnecessarily, for I knew she had. "Why, your climbing boots are floating around in it."

"So what?" she said, quite unperturbed. "They're quite clean, and you said you liked the fudge, didn't you."

There was a wonderful feeling of comradeship between the three of us. We all realised that without the other two we would never have survived; though we all wanted to get into Coronel, I think we also realised that we would never be this close again.

Thirty-four days after the smash, B. sighted the top of Mocha Island early in the morning. We began to realise that the long journey was almost over.

As we went farther up the coast, we encountered thick fog. This was nerve-racking as we knew that it took us nearly a quarter of a mile to get *Tzu Hang* from one tack on to the other. If land loomed up suddenly out of the fog we might lose the ship.

Three days later the fog was just as thick but Miles had been able to get sights farther offshore where the fog was patchy, so he was reasonably sure of his position. We went on steadily through the fog, and we took turns at the bow peering through the whiteness. Then suddenly we emerged into sunshine and left the blanket of fog behind. Miles had got us right on course and the little town of Coronel was dead ahead.

All that day we crept toward it, *Tzu Hang* still steering herself. The sun was low in the sky when we anchored near the wharf, 87 days from Melbourne, having brought our crippled ship into port by our own efforts.

Three days later *Tzu Hang* was towed to the Chilean Naval Base at Talcahuano where she was lifted out of the water by a gigantic floating crane and set down on the ground near the sea wall where we hoped to repair her.

FROM
CAPE HORN:
one MAN'S dream,
one WOMAN'S
nightmare

BY
Réanne Hemingway-Douglass

In 1974 Réanne Hemingway-Douglass and her husband Don Douglass sailed out of Los Angeles for a two-year circumnavigation in their 42-foot wooden ketch. With them were their three teenage sons and a teenage friend. The trip didn't work out as well as the boys had hoped, and they jumped ship in Mexico, leaving Réanne and Don to press on alone for Cape Horn. Réanne was less than happy, telling Don, "I'm not in love with sailing like you are, and Cape Horn isn't my choice. What I wanted out of this trip in the first place was to see new countries and meet new people—not spend all my time at sea in extreme conditions." Unfortu–nately, extreme conditions were exactly what they found as they approached the Horn, pitchpoled in heavy weather, and had to struggle for survival for weeks thereafter.

In the preface to her book Réanne explains why it took her two decades to write her story and how she wanted to bring to it her honesty and candor as a woman, something she had seldom seen in sailing narratives. She writes that "the sea has traditionally been a male-dominated world. Because it takes *machismo* to sail around the world—self-confidence that verges on arrogance; a love of risk, of pitting oneself against nature; an ability to endure pain and privation. Did the sailors who wrote their adventure also chronicle their emotional ups and downs—even if they took a female partner? No! They wrote about hourly sail and course adjustments, about storms that carried away rigging, about seas that sent their boat on beam ends."

Her story chronicles the voyage of both their boat and their relationship, both of which are nearly torn apart in the Southern Ocean. To her Don is driven and sometimes maniacal, yet she will not leave him; completing the voyage becomes her own quest to endure the most frightening seas on the globe and to survive a pitchpole, the near-worst thing the sea can do to a small boat, turning it into a barely floating disaster in a place where there is no hope of rescue.

Twenty years later, she concludes, "What had I learned about myself? I had learned from our sailing nightmare that the will to survive is the strongest instinct I have—that when my life depended on it I could push myself far beyond what I'd ever believed possible. But that I had no desire to keep testing life 'for adventure,' as Don had—life was too fragile." Though motivated by different impulses, Réanne and Don, now in their seventies, are still adventuring and cruising the Northwest and the Alaskan wilderness in their own boat.

Réanne is related to Ernest Hemingway and writes just as well. But instead of E. Hemingway's macho view of the sea, she has a warmer, distinctly human perspective developed over the two decades it took for her to come to grips with what happened and then write the story. This is not just a woman's story, it's a great drama of all the forces involved in a human relationship tested by a near-death experience and followed by a protracted battle of self-sufficiency.

///

FEBRUARY 26, morning. "One week to Cape Horn!" Don said with enthusiasm as we gulped down our morning cocoa. "Just think! We're now south of New Zealand, Australia, and Africa—everything except Cape Horn."

My mind belched sarcastic thoughts. *God, enthusiasm is a disease with him. The more miserable it gets, the happier he is.*

His enthusiasm was short-lived. "Do you hear that clunking sound? There's something wrong with the motion of the boat." He glanced quickly at the inside compass. "The steering vane's not holding its course. I'll have a look." I watched from the partially opened hatch while he examined the steering vane. "Get your foul weather gear on, and come up and look at this."

I suited up and went above.

"Come back here," Don said, looking down over the transom. "Hang on tight to the mizzen boom gallows, and look straight down the steering vane shaft . . . What do you see?"

Hanging onto the gallows as if it were a chinning bar, I knelt and peered over the stern. I could see that the shaft was badly bent.

"It's not much good now," Don said. "It's bent at least fifteen degrees."

Not much good now . . . I knew what that meant—full-time watches in an open cockpit, around the clock, and one of us at the helm no matter what the weather—if we wanted to get to our next port on schedule.

The steering vane had been so trustworthy that we hadn't practiced much with the inside control lines Don had rigged when he thought he'd be singlehandling. When we tried them a week earlier, they had worked well, but the steering vane wasn't damaged at that time.

"I want to do one experiment before we give up on it. Let's see if we can get it to work from below." He went below, stationed himself on the middle step of the companionway ladder, and pulled alternately on the two nylon lines. Although the boat turned from one tack to the other, it wouldn't hold a straight course.

"Well, that's it, babe. You know what this means, don't you?" I nodded. I didn't have to say anything; he knew I understood. "This may change our plans," Don said.

After our last contact with John on the *Hero*, we had talked about what fun it would be to make a brief stop at Ushuaia on the Beagle

Channel, to visit the *Hero* and its crew before heading north to Punta Arenas. I didn't ask what he meant about changing plans. I was too discouraged to think rationally. It terrified me to see what the power of water could do to a 2½-inch-diameter stainless steel shaft—just twist it, like I would a disposable aluminum cake pan.

Afternoon. Don's noon sextant reading put us just over the 50th parallel, 800 miles west northwest of Cape Horn. We have logged nearly a thousand miles since leaving Easter Island, February 2.

I volunteered to take afternoon watch so Don could snooze. The storm was building to a full gale, like the one we'd had two days before, and I knew he would need his strength for the heavy stuff to come.

An albatross that had been following us for the past twenty-four hours had now disappeared. I wondered where it went. It would have a thousand miles to go before it found land.

At noon we had doused the jib and staysail, and we were running under bare poles again. Even without sail, I had to fight to control the helm. Waves crashed continuously across the port quarter, slapping the boat at a forty-five-degree angle, dumping gallons of water into the cockpit. As I looked up from the trough of each wave I was sure we would be engulfed.

Sleet mixed with salt spray stung my eyes and found its way through my muffler and down my neck. I shivered and looked astern. The sea was a battlefield of white. Rollers moved forward like tanks; geysers piled up and exploded. White froth curled and tumbled for a thousand yards before crashing into bottomless holes. Overhead, dark clouds churned, meeting the edge of a western horizon that glowed yellow with the intensity of an uncontrolled forest fire. It was the "old familiar white arch, the terror of Cape Horn" that Joshua Slocum had described—the sign, we now knew, of hurricane force winds that made the hair on our necks stand up—this was it.

I thought of Moitessier sitting under his little turret post, inside the steel-hulled *Joshua*, instructing Françoise how to handle the wheel in seas like this.

> *See that wave coming . . . the wind's dead behind so* Joshua *keeps up speed and the helm [can] respond. . . . Now I turn the helm, we heel, the stern lifts up and just when it begins to settle, I turn the wheel to the*

other side. . . . If the helm resists when the wave passes under the boat,
and if you don't let it go . . . you'll [put us] broadside without any speed.

I tried to do what Bernard had taught Françoise. What had she been thinking? Was she afraid? His descriptions of her made her seem imperturbable.

Don pulled open the hatch cover and climbed up into the cockpit. "You go below now. It's getting so bad I'm going to lash the helm." I unsnapped my safety harness from the mizzen mast traveler. "I'll be back down in a second," he said.

I climbed below and took off my foul weather gear. The wind hitting the rigging sounded like jet engines revving up. The mast shuddered and reverberated. How long could it hold up against winds like these?

I watched the barograph needle as the small brass penpoint inked its way violently down the graph paper, like a plunge on the seismograph. *It'll be off the paper if it goes any lower,* I thought. At home, atmospheric pressure followed an uncreative line, varying little over the course of a year. But at this latitude the pressure had dropped a full inch to 29.1 in the last twenty-four hours.

Don came below and lit the kerosene lamps. "This looks like a full-blown storm—the worst I've ever seen. I've lashed the wheel to starboard; everything's pretty secure. Not much more we can do, except lie ahull." He slid behind the galley table and lay down to rest on the galley settee, his head aft next to the radio locker.

The flames of the kerosene lamps cast an amber glow on the white bulkheads, the shadows flickering as the boat heaved and rolled. The gimballed table and stove swung back and forth, each in their own tempo, tolling bass tones as they hit against the bulkhead.

Aside from the violent motion, the noise of the wind and waves, and "waterfalls" through the center hatch when a wave broke over the cabin roof, the interior seemed shipshape and safe. Above, except for the kids' surfboard and the dinghy, lashed to the cabin with nylon rope and three-inch seat-belt webbing, the deck was clear.

I kept reviewing what we'd done since we left Easter Island, wondering what more we could possibly do to make the boat safer. We had moved the heaviest gear to the salon—the lowest point in the boat—to keep the center of gravity low and the motion less erratic. Our four anchors and the toolboxes were lashed either to the frames or to floor beams in the salon (wrapped three times with one-inch tubular nylon webbing). Heavy canned goods were stowed in the bilge. Unneeded sails were crammed into their bags and stowed in the forepeak. Anchor lines were neatly coiled and stacked in lockers under the galley seat. The bungee cords I'd installed across the face of the drawers and the string nets across the bookshelves had done their trick so far. The radio locker at the foot of the companionway ladder was protected by the canvas cover I'd made. Don's work on the engine had apparently put it in shape—we hadn't had any problems since February 21.

Was there anything more we could do? I made mental lists continuously.

The last half of the banana squash from the Ika's garden thumped and banged in the bottom of the sink whenever a wave slapped us to starboard. The thumping annoyed me, but there was nowhere else I could put the squash—it was too big.

Cooking had become a pain. I couldn't battle the galley. I asked Don if he would settle for Cup of Soup.

"Sure. Then fill the thermos with boiling water, will you? It's going to be a long night!"

We had tried to make contact with Tex and Big John earlier in the day, but there was too much interference, and we hadn't been able to rouse Palmer Station in Antarctica either.

"If I can rouse the South Pacific Net later tonight," Don said, "they may be able to get a message through to the States to let people know we're okay."

I pictured the kids standing next to Tex in the radio room. "K6KWS, K6KWS, this is W6PXQ. Do you read?" How many times had they shown up and not been able to talk to us? We hadn't talked to anyone at home in a week, and I knew Mother and Daddy would conjure up all sorts of horrible thoughts as our estimated approach to Cape Horn drew near.

Don shined the flashlight on the barograph to take a reading. He flicked his finger gently against the glass case. The needle didn't budge. It read the same as it had earlier.

"The bottom's fallen out of the barometer!" he said.

"Let's discuss emergency procedures again," I said, feeling uneasy.

The abandon-ship locker not only held our survival gear, but had been built to strengthen the cockpit just aft of the companionway. We could release its safety latch from below by pulling out a heavy stainless steel pin, but to open the locker we had to stand on the top step of the ladder with the hatch cover open, or completely exit and stand in the cockpit.

The cover itself weighed almost forty pounds and was a struggle for me to open. How fast could I execute the maneuver in an emergency? And could I pull up the Avon which weighed more than eighty pounds? Lashed by its own ripcord to an eye bolt inside the locker, the life raft was supposed to self-inflate when you threw it overboard. This wasn't something you practiced before you needed it. You prayed that the manufacturers were reliable.

"You remember the life raft procedures, don't you?" Don asked.

Yes. I had memorized the script: Release the pin, snap your safety harness onto the lifeline on deck. Pull up the locker top and secure it to the mizzen mast traveler. Put on your life jacket. Pull the life raft out of its locker and throw it overboard, making sure you leave its line tied to the mizzen mast until it's time to abandon ship. First mate goes into the Avon, then the captain releases the snap hook, or if the pressure is too great, he cuts the line with the attached knife and jumps in.

I thought again about our phone patch with the Durants early in the month. "*In case you don't hear from us, we have an eight-man Avon life raft with forty-five days' supplies.*" We never voiced it, but Don knew, and I knew, that with air and water temperatures in the thirties or forties and freezing seas washing over the life raft, we'd die of hypothermia, if the waves didn't get us first. No Coast Guard in the Great Southern Ocean, no helicopter patrols, no search planes. We were on our own.

Don climbed up the ladder, sliding the hatch cover open just enough to poke his head out. Clinging to the starboard handle at the top of the ladder to keep from being hurled down and across the galley, he studied the conditions. "It looks as bad as ever. Hand me the anemometer again, and take down the readings as I call them out." He called out the numbers at five-second intervals for three minutes: 55, 52, 40, 42, 48, 32, 51, 38, 46 . . . "Damn, those last ones pegged the meter at 65! Quick, total the figures and do an average."

Excited now, he climbed down and shut the hatch. "Wow, this qualifies as a Violent Storm with gusts at hurricane force! These are the worst conditions we've seen yet!" I was struck by Don's tone of wonder—he was truly amazed by what he'd just seen. "And don't forget we're drifting several knots down-wind and the current is with us—so add another 5 to 10 knots for the actual wind speed."

"Pass me Robb's book," I said. "I want to reread the section on survival before I go to bed."

Wedging myself into a corner on the floor below the sink, I opened the book and scanned a few chapters. I preferred Robb's book, *Handling Small Boats in Heavy Weather*, to any other sea survival book. It was short— about a hundred and thirty pages—and concise. A skipper with forty-five years of experience, most of it off the coast of South Africa, Robb was opinionated and "told it like it is."

He called what we were doing now—lying ahull—the sailor's last-ditch effort. With the helm lashed we were letting the boat assume her own position in response to the wind and waves, both of which were coming from astern. According to Robb, in these conditions it was easy to underestimate the velocity of the wind. I turned to the Beaufort Scale on page 40, ran my finger down the column of "Mean Wind Speed" to 52 knots (Storm), 60 (Violent Storm), 65 (Hurricane Force), then across to the description of sea conditions. I read the descriptions aloud.

"Which would you say?" I asked Don.

"I'd say Violent Storm matches what we're having right now. It'll be Hurricane Force if it gets any worse."

Every few pages a photograph showed either a huge cresting wave, a gigantic "geyser," or an avalanche of white water moving toward a ship. (One of the photos was the same I'd seen used in the Smeetons' book as an example of the kind of wave that had hit them.) I had opened the book to reassure myself, but kept coming across descriptions of "the exceptional" that horrified me.

I stopped reading for a moment to think about *le Dauphin*'s safety features: Water tanks bolted to the oak frames. The six batteries secured with stainless steel rods. The 3-inch-diameter stainless pole at the foot of the companionway running from the galley sole to the doghouse ceiling, strengthening the cabin. In the salon, the small emergency dome light wired independently to its own series fuse in case we lost house electricity. I hadn't appreciated the value of these touches when we were rebuilding the boat and said a silent "thank you" to Don and Al Ryan.

I turned back to the book.

Study the accounts of small boats that have been damaged or come to grief in heavy weather at sea and you will find that in a surprising number of cases if the crew had simply gone to sleep and left the boat to her own devices she would have ridden the gale unharmed.

Good, I thought, *we're doing the right things.*

I had purposely tried to avoid Chapter 7, "The Ultimate Wave." But like people who read about air disasters before climbing aboard their flight, I was compelled to read on.

The occasional freak sea, the abnormal wave, the catastrophic sea—the blame for many a lost-without-trace tragedy can be laid on them. . . . Once have I seen such a wave. . . . It rose far out, perceptibly higher than the surrounding seas, but what caught the eye was not so much the height but the shape, for the forward face of the wave appeared to be a vertical wall of water . . . falling continuously, so that it seemed like some white waterfall sweeping across the ocean at—maybe—30 knots? The speculation is inevitable—what happens to a small boat lying relatively stationary when it meets a vertical wall of water moving at 30 knots? . . . It goes against the grain to believe that a condition can exist in which no amount of skill, courage, vigilance or equipment can save a small vessel from catastrophe.

I closed the book. "I wish I hadn't read that."

"Not exactly a bedtime story, is it?"

"How about getting some sleep now?" Don said. "The boat will look after herself. No reason for you to stay up. I'll wait another hour till I can check into the Maritime Mobile Net. Besides, I'll have to get up every hour or so to check things above, so I'll just doze here on the settee. If I need help later, I'll wake you."

I did a quick alcohol swab of my face, climbed up into our berth without taking off my clothes, and made a diary entry:

I thought the gales yesterday and the day before were bad. Nothing compared to this! It's bitterly cold, rainy, sleeting, and miserable. Fortunately the sun shone this noon and Don was able to plot our position. We're now lying ahull facing east, taking a terrible pounding on the port quarter.

Do we really have enough to survive in a life raft for forty-five days? Could we survive in these seas, these temperatures? Of course we couldn't, and the life raft would cartwheel across the top of the grey-beards before finally being crushed under a wall of water.

I don't want to think about it. I am uneasy. No, more than that. I'm frightened. Fright has been such a big part of my adventurous life with Don. But I have to remember that I am here because I chose to be with him. He didn't force me. I made the decision myself. I have been miserable and have hated parts of this trip, but this is no time to complain—conditions are too critical.

I feel I have become a partner. I've done what I can to prepare for whatever comes next. I am afraid, but there's nothing more I can do. Neither of us has any power over the conditions, and the only thing we can do is work together and hope for a break in the weather.

I threw my diary into the hammock above our berth and wedged myself crosswise at the foot of the bed, my feet flat against the washboard to prevent being thrown out, but I couldn't fall asleep. I couldn't even begin to relax. Tense and jumpy, I felt every motion, as *le Dauphin* fought, shuddered, groaned, leapt, and then softened as if she had no more strength and could only submit to the waves.

An hour after I lay down, I heard Don make a brief contact with Palmer Station, Antarctica. The radio operator told him he had relayed the message to the port captain in Punta Arenas giving our new ETA. When Don signed off from Palmer Station, he checked into the Maritime Mobile Net in American Samoa. Bob, the usual operator, was not on the air. His boat had been tossed aground and damaged during a hurricane the night before. Don told his alternate: "Looks like maybe we're getting the same stuff that hit you. We're riding out a Force 10 to 11 storm, and it's pretty miserable, but we don't seem to be in any immediate danger. I'll check in again tomorrow night at this same time."

I fell asleep as soon as he completed the transmission.

February 26, night–February 27. I was dreaming that I couldn't move. I was being pushed against a bulkhead and couldn't shove away from it. My stomach was pressing against my lungs, my throat. I was doing loops and figure-eights, experiencing negative Gs, nausea? Was I in a small plane? *Oh no, I'm having the nightmare again.*

Now I was floating around the berth. There was a thunderous crash and a deafening noise, as if the lurching boat were being torn apart. Every timber groaned. I was flung out of the berth and across the salon. My shoulder hit the edge of the port pilot berth. The boat pitched and rolled. Metal, glass, and books shot through the salon. Icy water poured in from all directions. *Oh God, this is real!*

"We're going down!" I screamed.

The kerosene lamps blew out. Then, total blackness.

I heard Don. "Sweetheart, where are you? Are you okay?"

The boat plunged, gyrated, then rolled on her side. Water gushed through the cabin. I struggled to grab hold of something and stand up.

"Okay, baby, I think we've pitchpoled." Don's voice was shot with adrenaline. "This is it—a fight for survival."

Suddenly there was silence. *Oh God, it's all over. We're totally submerged!* Without a sound, the boat reeled, tumbled, twisted, and turned over. "We're upside down, we're sinking, we're sinking," I moaned. *We're spiraling to the bottom of the sea. I don't want to die this way.*

"It's okay, it's okay," I heard Don say. "Turn on the light and get pumping . . . Get to the gusher pump!"

Water poured over me again. The boat stumbled, heeled to starboard, shuddered—then held. Abruptly, the roar of the wind screaming and waves smashing against the hull began again.

"She's righting herself, she's righting herself," Don said. "The keel must have held, we're not under water now."

"I can't see anything," I whimpered.

"Turn on the emergency light, dammit!"

Dazed, drenched, oblivious, I felt for the light above the captain's berth and flicked on the switch; it crackled, arced, and fizzled.

"No, not that one!" Don shouted. "Turn it off so we don't have a fire."

He shoved me aside, reached above my head, turned on the emergency light, and grabbed me. "It's okay, we're going be okay, sweetheart." He held his face against mine, kissing me, stroking my hair. His face was wet and tasted like blood.

We're going to die, I thought. *No one will ever know.*

"It's okay, baby. Get pumping. Pump for your life. Pump!"

I crawled across a mountain of floating debris, silently repeating, *Don't let us go down this way without a trace. Don't let us go down.*

"Try the radio. Please try the radio," I urged.

I squatted in water at the foot of the radio locker. Diesel and kerosene mixed with the water. Wind rushed through the cabin—it was freezing.

Don reached over my head to grab the microphone on the transmitter. "Mayday. May . . ." he said. There was a flash. The transmitter sizzled and blew. "Shit! We could have an explosion." He jumped across the galley, reached down in the water, and turned off the master battery switch. "Okay, baby. This is it. We're really on our own, the radio's gone."

I ran my right hand along the side of the locker to locate the pump handle. It was no longer in its clip. The boat lifted and took a deep lurch to starboard. A wave hit the port quarter and rolled across the cabin top. Water poured in on both of us.

A momentary shaft of moonlight cut through the hatch, revealing chaos everywhere. "Oh no! The hatch is open," Don said. "I've got to close it."

In the brief rays of moonlight I could see the companionway ladder hanging askew at a forty-five-degree angle, its brass hinges twisted forward. Don pulled himself up, poked his head out the hatch, and looked forward across the top of the cabin.

"Oh God! The dinghy's gone. It looks like the main boom sheered off. But the masts are still standing! I can't believe it." His voice registered amazement.

I thought, *Even when he's about to die he sees the wonder in things.*

"I can't see anything out there but white foam," he said. "There's nothing but white foam. The dinghy's out there somewhere, but I can't see it."

A wave washed over the boat, knocking us abeam. Water cascaded through the hatch over Don, over me. The impact sent me face first into the edge of the radio shelf. Water gushed up the starboard bulkhead, soaking my front. My forehead stung, and I could feel blood dripping down my cheek.

"No, not again, please don't turn over again," I moaned. "Don, I can't find the pump handle."

"Oh Jesus, look for it!" he said, finally jamming the hatch in place. "I've got to find something to bail with."

How could I find anything in this mess? The pump handle could have been thrown out of the hatchway.

"Here! Here," he said. "Can you believe it! The handle's in the sink . . . with the chamber pot!"

I reached across the galley for the pump handle.

"Oh no, your face is bloody," Don said, pulling me toward him. He wiped his hand gently over my face so tenderly I wanted to sob.

I wedged myself into the space next to the pump and sat on a mattress. Water soaked into my pants. "Pump slow and easy, baby, slow and easy," he instructed.

I felt for the slot, inserted the handle, and began pulling and pushing for all I was worth. Water, diesel, kerosene sloshed over my legs—over everything piled on the galley sole.

"Slow down, sweetheart, you'll wear yourself out. Slow and easy, you're going to be pumping for a long time . . . I'm going to check for leaks first. Then I'll start bailing."

Steadily, slowly, like a robot, I pumped. I was stunned, in a trance, an abandoned child searching for her parents. *Please just let me see my family again. Don't let us vanish . . . where is my diary?* If I could just find it, put it in a waterproof bag, someone might find it floating somewhere. Then a part of us would remain.

The boat lifted, teetered, did a deep roll to starboard. A wave crashed over the cabin, and water poured over me again. I screamed. "Don! We're going over again, we're going over."

"No we're not. No we're not! Shut up and keep pumping!"

Don's sharpness made no impression. I was too petrified, too cold and wet. *I've got to keep pumping, got to keep pumping,* I told myself with each stroke.

"I love you, Réanne."

I looked over as he made his way toward me along the starboard bulkhead, checking the hull. The side of his face was covered with blood, too. "Don, your face . . ."

"It's okay, sweetheart. Don't worry about it now. I've got to find out if the water is rising or not."

I pushed, pulled, and counted—122, 123, 124—then wondered why I was counting.

The emergency light cast a grey pall throughout the cabin. I stared numbly at the chaos. Everywhere I looked lockers had emptied. The upper locker doors in the galley swung back and forth—the plates and bowls were gone.

I looked up. A jagged piece of ketchup bottle had lodged in the galley deckhead. The carving knife—embedded in a crack above my head—quivered with every jerk of the boat. Pots, pans, spices, broken mayonnaise and mustard jars were strewn everywhere. Galley floorboards lay upside down on top of mattresses and cushions. The bilge had regurgitated its contents: anchor chain, food tins, hardware, motor oil, grease cans, spools of wire. Wet sawdust, yellow squash, and ketchup were splattered all over the deckhead. The radios and barograph were missing from the forward shelf of the galley.

I watched Don lift and throw things out of his way, checking the hull for damage. Quickly, carefully—a physician probing for broken bones—he inched his way through the icy, oily water into empty lockers, worming his body into drawer spaces, running his fingers along the hull at the mast step, in the forepeak, the head, the salon, the galley, the aft quarters, giving me constant feedback as he moved. "Goddam, the water's above my knees in the salon here . . ." Lying down on top of debris in the salon, his arms and shoulders under the water, he felt for the keel bolts. "I think the keel's okay. The bolts feel secure. I can't feel any water coming in . . . That's good, that's good! The hull feels smooth here in the salon, I think it's holding! I think the keel's holding."

The boat lurched to starboard, knocking me into the locker. "Oh no, not again. Not again." Water poured over me. "Oh God, not again, please stop!" I screamed.

"It's okay. It's okay, baby, we're gonna survive. We're gonna survive. As long as the keel holds we'll be okay. Keep pumping. We've got to get this water out of here. I'm almost finished checking."

Back and forth, back and forth—256, 257, 258. With each stroke I thought about our families, our friends. *The kids? They'll recover; they're young. Mother and Daddy? It'll kill them if we disappear. Oh God, they'll never know a thing. No diaries. Nothing. "Vanished without a trace,"* the newspapers *will say.*

Water flooded over my head. "Don! Make it stop. Make it stop." Despite three layers of wool against my skin, I was beginning to shiver uncontrollably and was losing my senses. "I just want to get to land, see my family and friends. *Just get me to land!*"

"It's okay, sweetheart, it's okay. That wave was one in ten thousand. It won't happen again. I've checked as much of the hull as I can get to. It seems to be okay. I'm sure the keel's okay."

One in ten thousand . . . I wanted to believe him, but I couldn't. The waves just kept knocking us over. I looked at Don. Was the water rising? Was it over his knees? I couldn't tell. *Got to keep pumping.*

Don began bailing with the chamber pot, frantically dumping water into the sink. He began mumbling to himself, "I'm afraid it's gaining on us: The water's gaining . . . Those vibrations when the boat heels to starboard—what are they? The rigging? Keel coming loose? How can it take a pounding like this and stay fastened to the frames? I wonder if the hull's opened at the first strake? Maybe I should try to clear this junk away . . . stuff something in the crack . . . Hell no. There's no way I can see anything with water this high." He was getting panicky.

"Slow down, sweetheart," I repeated his words. "Don't panic—you'll be bailing for a long time."

"You're right. We've both got to fight panic. Smeeton was right—there's nothing like a drowning man to bail with vigor."

The boat lunged to starboard. Don looked at me and stopped bailing. "Good Lord. No wonder you're shivering. The cabin deck seam above you separated, and the portlight's blown away—that's why water keeps pouring in. Hang on and keep pumping. I'll see if can find the emergency board to nail over the port."

I heard him mumbling, "Jesus, I told her to shut up, and she's never stopped pumping. Sitting there with water pouring over her.

"These portlights are our Achilles' heel," he said, "even sturdy as they are. If I can find a hammer and the plywood, I'll plug that hole. The stuff should be here in the battery box."

The cover to the battery locker was a pain to open; we'd always complained about it. But it was the only one in the galley that had held.

The hammer was still tied to the bulkhead on the inside of the locker, and the boards wedged between the batteries hadn't budged. A box of 3-inch nails that had been wedged along the bottom of the batteries had spewed its contents, but Don was able to fish out enough to do the job.

"Jesus, with the force of that wave the stainless rod holding the batteries moved forward more than a half-inch. . . . Keep pumping, sweetheart . . . I'll go above and cover the hole." He opened the hatch enough to put his head through to look out and gauge conditions. "Not too bad right this minute. Now's my chance."

He pulled himself out and closed the hatch. I could see the board being flattened across the porthole and hear him trying to hammer. *My God,* I thought, *he's up there without a harness!* I quit pumping and yanked open the hatch, shrieking into the wind, "Get down here now!"

Shocked, he climbed down. "Sonovobitch. How stupid . . . I must be panicking . . . All I could do was hit my fingers—I couldn't get the damn nails started. I couldn't even hold them, my hands are so numb. I have to get these nails started where I can see what I'm doing."

He swept debris off the galley counter, laid the plywood board over it and drove in eight nails. "Shit! I overdid it. Nailed the goddam board to the counter." He pried it loose and started for the hatch again.

"Open the abandon-ship locker and get out the extra harnesses."

"I don't want to open it right now. It's too damn risky."

"You're not going back above without a harness!" I yelled. "Find *something*, dammit . . . I think I saw a line over there somewhere." I pointed to the salon.

"Come on. There's no way I can find anything in this mess . . . By God, you're right. There's the bitter end of something . . . probably a jib sheet."

He tugged on the line. A thirty-foot length came loose. He tied a bowline around his waist, threw a couple of half-hitches around the top step of the ladder, leaving fifteen feet of slack, and opened the hatch. He paused. "The mast is flinging back and forth wildly. Especially to port. I'll have to deal with that later." He climbed out and closed the hatch.

I heard nails being pounded into the side of the doghouse. The boat lurched, hit by another wave. Water flowed over the cabin, through the seam. The hammering stopped. *Oh, God, make him hang on. That line could break. Like the dinghy webbing did.* The hammering began again. *He's okay! He's okay.*

The boat righted herself. The hatch flung open; Don jumped back down. "I nearly lost it!" he raved. "I wrapped my arms and legs around the boom gallows stanchion to hold on . . . You should see that stanchion—it's bent forward, bad."

Grabbing the potty, he started bailing again. "I think the water's emptying overboard all right," he said, although much later he would tell me he'd been sure it was rising.

"I love you, sweetheart. We're gonna make it," he said.

I shook uncontrollably. *I'm so cold, so cold. The wind. I wish the wind would stop.* But it just kept on and on, shrieking in the rigging. *The noise is awful. God, I'm cold . . . Got to keep pumping . . . keep pumping.*

Suddenly I thought about my diary again. Where was it? I had to find it. If we went down, it would be the only thing left to tell our story. With each stroke of the pump I became more obsessed with finding it. If only daylight would come so I could search.

Don dumped potty after potty of water into the sink. "We're doing all we can. The water's holding steady."

"I hope so," I stuttered.

"It's time to get out some emergency supplies. Let me get the abandon-ship locker opened. Then I'll take over the pumping."

He climbed the ladder and clung to it with his legs, quickly opened the hatch, released the stainless pin, and opened the locker. "Here, catch this bag," he said.

I opened a moldy nylon ditty bag and rifled through its contents for Hershey's Tropical Chocolate bars. I dug out a handful and stared at them. The wrappers were blue with mold.

"Come on, babe. Eat one. You need some calories." Closing the hatch, he crawled down the ladder and took over at the pump.

I tore off one of the wrappers with my teeth and stuck the bar in my mouth. I couldn't swallow any of it. The pieces stuck to my molars. I had no saliva to wash them down my throat.

Watching Don's power strokes I suddenly realized how tired I was, and how slow I'd become. When I tried to stand up pain surged through my body. Soaked, cold, and cramped from crouching so long in cold water, I could barely unwind. How long had I been pumping? I looked down at my feet—I couldn't feel them. "The water's going down," I said expressionless. "It's at my ankles now."

"Yeah, by God, we're gaining! Give me a chocolate bar, sweetie, and try to find something dry to put on."

I crawled aft to the port quarter berth. "The *moai's* still here!" I said. "It hasn't budged."

"Good. That baby could have crushed one of us. But find some dry clothes, for godsake."

The two large duffels I'd stuffed with emergency clothing and army blankets were still at the foot of the berth. The quarter berths were like small caverns and the duffels had flown round and round inside. I unzipped one of them and pawed through its contents. I found sweaters, an army blanket, and a couple of pairs of wool air force pants my brother Tom had given us. *Tom. We haven't talked to him for so long . . . Please, Tom, help Mother and Daddy survive if we don't.* I pushed the duffels aside and lay down. It felt so good to rest that I started to doze.

"What the hell are you doing back there?"

I shook myself. "Lying down . . ."

"Dammit. Take off your wet stuff and put on some dry clothes—now! You're going hypothermic."

I unpeeled the wet layers, in slow motion. Every movement seemed to take forever. *It feels so good to get out of these wet things, put something dry on . . . If only it would get light. It's horrid not to be able to see.* Two dry wool sweaters, fishnet long johns, air force pants, hiking socks. I crawled out of the berth, warmer.

Don was still pumping strongly. I didn't know how he could keep going at such a pace.

"I'll take over again if you want me to."

"Not yet. See if you can find your foul weather gear and put that over your dry clothes. You'll need everything you can find."

I crawled across the galley. My dry socks immediately soaked up water from the soggy mattresses and cushions piled on the floor. Such an unbelievable mess! Every locker, bookshelf, and drawer in the salon had emptied. The drawers I'd secured with ⅜-inch bungee cord had shot out, dumped their contents, and resettled halfway back. They swung up and down, cracking each time a wave hit the boat. I shoved, pushed, closed. They were badly splintered and chipped.

Clothes were strewn about in soggy lumps. The small down pillow I'd used as a child was a clump of wet feathers. I picked it up by a corner and looked at it. Mother had found it as she was cleaning out cupboards and had sent it to me, knowing I didn't like heavy pillows. It would have to be chucked.

Waterlogged paperbacks and charts clung to the mattresses. I peeled off one of the charts. My diary was underneath.

My diary! The pages were soaked and stuck together, the ink was smeared and hardly legible, but I didn't care. *I've rescued our story,* I thought. The waterproof pouch with the ship's papers lay nearby. I stuffed the diary in with them. In my daze I didn't consider that the pouch might circle Antarctica for months, years, or decades, and my diary would finally disintegrate, unseen and unread.

"I can see the floorboards now," Don said slowly. "The gusher just started sucking air . . . I think we'd better rest now. Till dawn, when it's light. Then we'll figure out what to do next."

Tired, cold, our forces totally spent, we lay down on the crumple of sailbags and mattresses in the salon. I wrapped the wet army blanket around us, thankful for the wool. Each time a wave crashed over the doghouse roof, the boat heeled to starboard and water poured through the leaky skylight above us.

"Please make it stop. Please!" I whimpered, my teeth chattering. Don tugged at a cushion and pulled it over us. It was heavy with saltwater, but at least it would insulate us.

We clung to each other, Don stroking my face, my hair. "We've done all we can for now, sweetheart."

There was nothing more we could do but wait—wait through the dreadful darkness till dawn.

February 28(?). Last known position: 49° 52´ S, 89° 01´ W. Impossible to sleep. Waves continued to pound the boat, to knock her on her starboard beam. The mast reverberated like a body in convulsions, shaking from its head, fifty-five feet above, to its foot in the mast step next to us. Would it hold?

Please, I pleaded silently. *Let it get light.*

To whom was I pleading? I didn't know. I don't pray, but perhaps I was praying. I thought of the childhood bedtime prayer: *Now I lay me down to sleep* . . . I was exhausted, but fought falling asleep. Not being able to see, not knowing what it was like outside, was the worst part. *If I should die before I wake* . . .

"We're going over again, Don! We're going over!" I screamed.

He tightened his arms around me. "We'll be all right. I told you, that wave was one in ten thousand. Get a hold of yourself."

One in ten thousand. How many waves had knocked us on our beam since the Big One? Fifteen? Twenty?

"Ten percent chance of Force 10 winds" . . . *Don in Mexico, so casual, assuring Jeff and me, "Only ten percent . . ."*

Suddenly angry. Angry with Don for telling me to get hold of myself, for lying to me about conditions down here. Angry with myself for losing control. I snapped at him, "Look, just hold me. I'll be all right as soon as it's light. I'll be strong then. Just hold me now and let me be a baby."

Like the vibrating mast, Don shivered uncontrollably, his shoulders and torso trembling, his legs jerking. *Hypothermia. He has hypothermia,* I thought. *Wet, cold, wind-chilled. Numbness . . . that's why he couldn't hit the nails! Now the shivering. He was so concerned about my putting on dry clothes, but he's still wearing his wet ones. People die of hypothermia. "Exposure," say the headlines. "Exposed to the elements." Got to keep holding each other. Don't fall asleep. Don't let Don fall asleep. He might not wake up—hypothermia does that.*

I listened carefully to his breathing. He wasn't sleeping. "Animal stalkers," he'd once told me, "hold their breath and breathe shallowly through their mouth so they can hear better." His grip on me tightened with every quiver of his body. I knew that like a stalker Don was alert to every sound. I could almost hear him thinking: *That clunking noise when the boat rolls to starboard—what is it? Are the keel bolts loose? No. Maybe it's something inside a locker hitting a cross beam . . . No. It's hitting the hull . . .* But caught in my own terror, I didn't break this silence.

Dawn. Grey, dismal light filled the cabin. A war zone was revealed. *How will I ever find anything? Like people poking through embers after their house has burned. How can I even begin? There's too much to do.* Water sloshed heavily against the inside hull—like a siren warning us to man the gusher pump. I leapt up, terrified.

Don yanked on the hatch, pulled it partially open to check conditions, and stared at the seas. Sleet stung his face. The waves were still violent and heaping, skyscraper waves. "I've never seen anything like this . . . We'd better stay up—it's light enough now. I'm going up to see how bad the damage is on deck."

"Change into some dry clothes first," I urged.

I pawed frantically through the emergency duffel. I remembered how I'd complained about all the extra gear and clothing Don insisted on bringing for emergencies. "We don't have room," I'd said about each extra item he brought aboard. "We'll never find a place for all this junk—there's not even room for six *people*!" I would never complain again about what he had brought along. If only we could find more.

I insisted Don open the abandon-ship locker and get out the extra harnesses.

"You're not going anywhere unless you're snapped on." I pulled myself up to look in the locker. It was organized, reassuring. I grabbed the supplies I'd loaded the night before—pouches of cocoa and tea, foil packets of freeze-dried food, the first aid kit, waterproof matches, three hospital blankets, a waterproof flashlight, an extra rotor and line for the recording log. I put in the waterproof pouch that held the ship's papers and my diary. We hadn't found the logbook yet.

Grim. It was grim. Assessing damages, searching for missing gear. Was it last night I had sat on the galley sole reading Robb and discussing survival techniques with Don? The sole had gleamed under the light of the kerosene lamp. Now everything was grim and disorienting. I didn't know where to begin.

Don made a quick observation tour of the deck. As he'd suspected, the main boom had sheered off and was held only by the mainsail. The main and mizzen masts were cracked along the lines of lamination but were still standing.

"Well, we can't use the main, and I don't know what kind of load the mizzen mast will be able to carry under these conditions," he said.

The mizzen and staysail booms were fractured, but still attached. The main mast starboard spreader had been carried away, along with the deck light. All the mast tangs—where the shrouds attached—were twisted. Their through-bolts had held, but they had been shoved downward about three inches, badly tearing the wood of the mast. "I can't believe the mast could sustain this much damage without being carried away. We must have been dropped upside down, nearly vertically," Don said. The main and mizzen boom gallows were bent forward. Gone were one of the light-boards and the radio antenna. Also gone was the man-overboard pole with its attached xenon light. The deck had been swept clean. Hours earlier, we had realized that the dinghy was missing, but now we knew what that meant—even if we did get to land, we would have no way to get off the boat.

The warp line that was attached to the car tire ready to use as a drogue to slow the boat down had wrapped itself around the mizzen boom. Like a hangman's noose, the tire swung over the cockpit on two feet of loose warp.

Below, the damage seemed worse than above. Even with all my preparations—nothing, nothing had stayed in place. The anchors, the dinghy motor, lines, sheet—they were all down there in the salon somewhere. Someplace under the mess. Thank God we had stowed them below.

I stood dazed. Everything I needed was missing. Where were the stove elements? How could they have come unscrewed like that? The kerosene lamps were upside down, askew—mantels and globes missing, even their elements had come unscrewed. Radios, barograph—missing, too.

The galley sole was layered with cushions and mattresses, so heavy with water, kerosene, and diesel I couldn't budge them.

It seemed as if we were in an arctic elevator, riding up the face of each wave, down the back. Never stopping, never slowing.

Don's first thoughts were to put the boat in better shape, to help her cope with the punishing seas. He shoved the hatch open and peered down at me. "In a strange way it's good to be on deck again," he said. "I don't feel good below. At least up here I can see what's going on. I'm going to stay at the helm and drive us east with bare poles. I don't dare leave the boat to herself any longer."

Later, he wrote:

First thing was to stabilize the gyrating mast. The starboard spreader, sheared off at both ends, dangled overboard, held only by the nylon signal halyards. The upper shroud was so loose it didn't restrain the top of the mast.

Using two lengths of nylon webbing I made a tourniquet of sorts between the upper shroud, two lower stays, and the mast itself. With the spreader stub, I twisted the tourniquet over and over until I could get all possible tension into the upper shroud. This partially cuts down the gyration of the mast and the awful vibrations of the hull. I'm so happy to have both masts standing, to have a fighting chance to save ourselves. Completing this small task, in this wild environment, is deeply gratifying.

With the major safety items secured, I went to the helm, turned the boat from beam to the waves, to a course due east. Straight down the greybeards toward land.

I want to get near land as quickly as possible. The Horn and the lee channels to Ushuaia are about 750 miles to the southeast. Cabo Pilar and the entrance to the Strait of Magellan are about 600 miles east southeast. The rugged coast of Patagonia, the closest land, lies about 500 miles due east, and Valparaiso is more than 1,000 miles, clear across the Roaring Forties to the northeast. Until we can determine the boat's damage and weigh our options, the only thing to do is sail due east as fast as possible.

The more I think about it, the more convinced I am—no more lying ahull. No more staying below, wondering and worrying. We will drive this boat with all we have. As long as we have it.

I worried about Don in the cockpit. Could he keep his body core temperature high enough, with the icy seas breaking over the cockpit and cabin continuously? I kept shoving chocolate bars to him out the hatch. I had always snubbed them on backpacking trips—they were so dry I could barely digest them. *It's funny what you complain about at home,* I thought. I promised myself not to complain anymore.

FROM at the
MERCY
of the SEA

BY
Lisa Clayton

In 1990 Lisa Clayton was working on a charter boat in the Mediterranean and dreaming of more distant sailing adventures when she was inspired by reading Naomi James's account of her solo circumnavigation. James had meant to do it nonstop but was forced to stop twice for repairs. Clayton realized she could be the first woman to circumnavigate the globe alone and nonstop.

It took years for the fundraising and preparation of her boat from an unfinished 38-foot hull, but in September 1994, at age thirty-five, she had *Spirit of Birmingham* ready to depart. It would take her 285 days to complete the voyage.

As this selection begins, she has been at sea almost six months and is approaching Cape Horn. At the same time two BOC Challenge Race sailors are in the same area. She has suffered gales, equipment failures, injuries, stress, depression, apathy, and anxiety, all of which she writes about openly and honestly in a book based on her log and journal. Thanks to modern electronics she is in frequent communication with friends and family back in England by satellite fax. As she encounters terrifying heavy weather nearing the Horn, much of the story is told by these faxes, which are preserved here in their original form, complete with the typing errors that reveal her stress and often icy fingers. Hers is a story told not in a calmer retrospective voice but in the midst of emotional reality of actual events as they unfold.

/ / /

28 **FEBRUARY** (**DAY** **165**). Weather mostly force 8–10 so we're under storm jib, but I actually feel quite happy. *Spirit* seems to be enjoying it and the motion below is not too bad.

I have been wondering whether to ask Peter for details of how to contact the guys from the BOC single-handed race but I don't think I really want to. They go so much faster than me, I bet they are almost at Rio by now. No, I think it will just depress me. Some of their boats surf at 25 knots and average 16—I don't think I am quite in their league somehow. However, I would like to meet them one day. We must have something in common, us single-handers.

Peter has sent all the available information on icebergs, which gives details of some near to the Islas Diego Ramirez south of the Horn and also some by the Falklands, but they can't give details of anything smaller. Still, not long to go now till I shall be by the Horn—YIPPEE!

1 MARCH (**DAY** **166**). The weather hasn't so far turned out as bad as forecast and in fact at times has been quite pleasant.

After getting some decent sleep last night I felt relaxed this morning and decided that since there was nothing to worry about with the weather I would spoil myself and have a lazyish sort of day. Having had coffee and checked everything on deck I decided to take my book *Wheelbarrow Across the Sahara* and read for a while in bed, which felt all the nicer for that little tinge of guilt that I wasn't really tired and didn't need to be there. Or so I thought! I woke up five hours later still with the book in my hand. All was OK though, and the wind had dropped even more so I put some more sail out and did nothing for the rest of the day. I feel much better for it and am now very keen to get some more sleep in. It's made me realise just how tired I was. I feel very chirpy and very very content with everything.

I am also excited that I am now heading further south to round the Horn. Apparently there aren't any icebergs around till I get to the Falklands so unless there is some floating ice it shouldn't be a bad run down. I don't know why it suddenly seems as though I am now on my way home—maybe it is because I am at last making this final leg south before I go north again—but it's a lovely feeling. I feel really great at the moment. Still, I am not going to relax my vigilance. I'm growing rather superstitious about feeling too good, it seems to have been the portent to things going horribly wrong—so fingers crossed!

2 MARCH (DAY 167)

02 MAR   FROM: BT INMARSAT-C FAX   TO: PETER HARDING

Good morning,

Just a quickie as I have only this minute come down off deck and am not yet happy with things.

Speak soon.

02 MAR   FROM: BT INMARSAT-C FAX   TO: PETER HARDING

Hi,

Well, I suppose I should have let you sleep on—I wasn't quite sure what to do.

Things here are bad: force 10–11, just the storm jib up—couldn't haul the boom in even with all the sail down! Impossible to stand up on deck. Not quite sure what is the best thing. Still sort of sailing at the moment but not happy with it.

Anyway, I am OK but not likely to get too much sleep though I will try once I feel relatively happy—which isn't just yet!

02 MAR 08:47   FROM: BT INMARSAT-C FAX   TO: SARA SIMPSON

Hi Sara,

Happy birthday!

You must think yourself quite lucky, as I started a poem to you, but yesterday we hit a bad storm and conditions here are horrendous. Although I have tried I can't quite find the right words to finish it off!

In fact to type at all is a minor form of torture. The only place to be is in bed so I hope you won't mind that this is a short fax but the wishes to you are full of love and I hope today is a really great day for you.

All my love, Sara.

xxxxxxxxxxxxxxxxxx

02 MAR 15:30   FAX TO LISA   FROM: PETER HARDING

Hi Lisa,

Sorry things are not good. If I can do anything or if you just want to talk let me know. To be honest I am shattered so am going home but please know I am there for you if you need me.

Take great care,
Peter.

02 MAR 16:58   FROM: BT INMARSAT-C FAX   TO: PETER HARDING

Hi Peter,

Thanks for your two messages.

Conditions here are horrendous—the wind is even stronger now. I eventually managed to get warm but only by getting up and heating a hot-water bottle and snuggling up inside two sleeping bags. Luckily I was facing the hull, as all the books which were so tightly jammed on the shelves (and are held in by curtain wire) flew out and landed heavily on me—I was buried in them. Unless it is screwed or strapped down nothing is staying in its place.

It is quite simply bloody awful and to write this is taking an age. The only sensible thing I can do is go back to bed. I could try and sheet the storm jib flat or take it down but I think it would be more dangerous and to be honest if I get caught out with one of those waves I don't suppose that even my safety harness would be of much use—so basically I am hiding down here. At least here I have the best chance of staying with the boat! Anyway, can't write any more but we are OK.

02 MAR 17:55   FROM: BT INMARSAT-C FAX   TO: PETER HARDING

I need to talk to you—please tell me you are there.

02 MAR 18:11   FROM: BT INMARSAT-C FAX   TO: PETER HARDING

No, I'm not OK—well, I am still alive, but only just. God, I am so scared. I went on deck to try and sheet the storm jib flat but saw that all hell was let loose. The big sail that is strapped to the deck was over the side and dragging through the water so I went forward to bring it in. I tied my long safety line to the stay. The next thing I knew I was through the guard rails and in the sea. I felt myself totally submerged, couldn't breathe and really thought I had seen the end. I just remember thinking "Crikey, just like that, it's all over. I thought I was meant to make it." Then somehow I got yanked back.

I came below and then the boat screamed forward and now the sail is backed, the self steering has snapped in two and I know I have to go back up—but I am too scared.

---

02 MAR 18:15   FAX TO LISA   FROM: PETER HARDING

Lisa,

Thank God you are OK. Are you safe down below? Is there anything I can do? Talk to me, I am here and going nowhere.

BE CAREFUL!

---

02 MAR 18:19   FROM: BT INMARSAT-C FAX   TO: PETER HARDING

God, I hope I make it—it doesn't seem possible at the moment.

---

02 MAR 18:23   FROM: BT INMARSAT-C FAX   TO: PETER HARDING

had just decided to go on deck to tkae the storm jib down. Thank goodness I saw your message coming through—we have just capszied, I woudl have been ovr the side.IT was jst like being in a violent car crashh, the impact was tremmensous. I've still got to go up but I am nto sure it is safe. I wish i felt sure about what is hte best thing to do

I wish I wasn't so scared

---

02 MAR 18:32   FROM: BT INMARSAT-C FAX   TO: PETER HARDING

no there is not point alerting anybody—no one can do aything—apart from the fact it would take days it would endanger other lives as well. No the only thing to do is sit tight. I have just been on deck and managed to lash the rudder so hopefully that will be saved. The spray-dodgers were pracitically off—I have tied them as best I can but won't be surprised if we lose them and I have managed to get all the ropes back in. I as going to get the sial down but I couldn't as it suddenly got worse. Might try again in a minute—capsize again since we last spoke Thanks again but

nono point in alertin gnayboyd—nothing nayone could do—believe me I know

---

02 MAR 19:03   FROM: BT INMARSAT-C FAX   TO: PETER HARDING

Just to let you know I have got the storm jib down

---

02 MAR 19:10   FROM: BT INMARSAT-C FAX   TO: PETER HARDING

Just capsized again God this is frightening

02 MAR 19:25   FROM: BT INMARSAT-C FAX   TO: PETER HARDING

and again

02 MAR 19:30   FAX TO LISA   FROM: PETER HARDING

Lisa,

Do you want me to get help?

02 MAR 19:40   FROM: BT INMARSAT-C FAX   TO: PETER HARDING

No I am not considreing giving up yet. I will obviously wait until thi-ings have got a little better and then try and see the state of things.

If everything is reaonsable then I shall be able to continue—but I dont know for now—obviously I have to just keep my fingers crossed that I survive this and then sial on—stopping for repairs if necessary. It's not as if there is any decision to make about abandoning hsip—I couldn't even if there wer helicopters and ships around—it would be pracitcally impossible.

No I have to just hope that it pass es soon—though if anything it feels as htough it is getting worse not better.

I think I will lay my head down here at the chart table and then see hwo I feel.

Thanks for everything.

No need for you to not go to bedd—f I need you y ou wil hear the phone.

02 MAR 19:45   FAX TO LISA   FROM: PETER HARDING

Lisa,

Of course I am not going to go to bed. I shan't sleep till I know you are OK and sailing again. Talk to me all you want. I'm here for you.

Peter.

02 MAR 19:59   FROM: BT INMARSAT-C FAX   TO: PETER HARDING

Please will you do me a favour. If you kow Peter Berry's number phone him and ask him to say a prayer for me or else phone Peter Chippendale at Lickey Vicarage and ask him to—I don't think I am going to make htis.

God I am so sorry

02 MAR 20:20   FROM: BT INMARSAT-C FAX   TO: PETER HARDING

Hi t hannks—it's good to know.

We must have juust done a compllete 360. I was waitting for the flick back up but we jjust keept goiing rouund. Everything endd up on the ceiiling. Thank God I ws strappped in my chair. My hair was hannging up and I felt he blood rushhing to my head.

All everything is everyjwerer iif it weren't so tragic it would be funny. Even the floor board accesses have ended up stuck to the roof and the bilge pumps are oout of action but I dont think that is too bad as we haven't taken on too much water. I have just triied to clear all the saucepans and everything round the corner. I have a few cuts but nothing serious but he boat is a disaster—no way am I going on edeck = If Ihad been up there then I would have been derowned. Please just keep talking—I am sorryi you are tired by I need you desperately.

If i get htrough this I shan't care about carring on I shall just be glad to e alive.

Please keep talking al the time—don't stop.

02 MAR 22:45   FROM: BT INMARSAT-C FAX   TO: PETER HARDING

Yes I am cold but I don't thnk I can go to bed—at least i my chair I amheld in place—all the cushions are all over the palce. ther are broken pots all over the palce saucepans stuck everwhre, there is blood and = god knows what else spalttered over te h computer hte ceiling everyhing nad yet I don't seem to be bleeding muhc. No I think I will have to stay here. I don't knowo hwere the wind is anymre because the mast head unit is obviously broken.

02 MAR 23:34   FAX TO LISA   FROM: DAN AND GWEN CLAYTON

Hello sweetheart,
We hear you are in trouble. Everybody is praying for you.

All our love, Mum and Dad.

xxxxxxxxxxxxxxxxxxxxxxxxxx

3 MARCH (DAY 168)

03 MAR 00:33   FROM: BT INMARSAT-C FAX   TO: PETER HARDING

Peter

Its amzing but we are stll OK. Gow willing we'll beO K.

03 MAR 03:20   FROM: BT INMARSAT-C FAX   TO: PETER HARDING

sTill capszing but still heeere.

03 MAR 10:15   FAX TO LISA   FROM: PETER HARDING

LISA, PLEASE LET ME KNOW YOU ARE OK. HAVE SENT OVER TWENTY FAXES BUT HAVE NOT HEARD FROM YOU SINCE 0405 HRS—OVER SIX HOURS AGO. PLEASE PLEASE PLEASE GET BACK TO ME.

PETER.

03 MAR 13:10   FAX TO LISA   FROM: PETER HARDING

LISA—PLEASE PLEASE TELL ME YOU ARE ALIVE! GOD, LISA, PLEASE BE OK—HAVEN'T HEARD ANYTHING FOR OVER NINE HOURS!

03 MAR 13.45   TO: YACHT *SPIRIT OF BIRMINGHAM*

FAX to Lisa Clayton from Falmouth MRCC
Dear Lisa
Your Project Director Peter Harding informs me that he has received no response from you for nine and a half hours. Could you please advise this office if you are OK. Do you require assistance?

Mike Collier,
Falmouth Marine Rescue Co-ordination Centre.

03 MAR 13:36   FROM: BT INMARSAT-C FAX   TO: PETER HARDING

Peter, I am OK—sending to office and flat. Will speak again immediately when sent message to MRCC Falmouth.

03 MAR 14:45   FROM: BT INMARSAT-C FAX   TO: PETER HARDING

Yes I am OK—I remember being jolted with the capszie then hitting the ceiling and having all the tins and everything come up to hit me. I reckon I knocked my head and it put me out. I've gt the most cracking headache. Sorry about that, I really thought it was only a few minutes since I last wrote. I have notified MRCC at Falmouth.

the boat looks a wreck but I t hink it is mostly superificial. Impossible to walk below becaue of teh debris and I can't get anywehre near the engine room to check anything in there. I have just pulled all the ropes back in again.

I am so sorry to have caused all this wrorry—do I need to contact my parents?

Yes I am happy tooo—I prayed to God last night to let m e live guess he must have heard!

God what a mess, everywehre is complete chaos.

---

03 MAR 15:00   TO: YACHT *SPIRIT OF BIRMINGHAM*

FAX to Lisa Clayton from Falmouth MRCC

Lisa,

Glad to hear you are OK. Could you please advise us of your condition and exact position. We have received a distress signal from a BOC boat *Henry Hornblower*, and have been unable to make contact with the skipper Harry Mitchell. Also distress messages have been received from the Japanese contender of the race. The Chilean Navy are co-ordinating the rescue. We think you are approximately 300 miles from *Henry Hornblower* and 200 from the Japanese yacht. Please give an idea of the weather conditions, sea state, etc. and possibilities of assisting.

Mike Collier,

Falmouth Marine Rescue Co-ordination Centre.

---

03 MAR 15:45   FROM: BT INMARSAT-C FAX   TO: PETER HARDING

I must say my nerves are hsot to peices but apart from total chaso I think we can sail eventually though conditions are still bad.

About the BOC guys I need to know where they are and what there problems are—ASAP, will stand by for that—I also need to know fi they have inmarsat. If so how do I contact them direct—if not details of the frequencies on SSB if they can communicate.

I need details urgently

will wait to hear

---

03 MAR 16:30   FROM:BT INMARSAT-C FAX   TO: PETER HARDING

OK got your message about *Hornblower*—will wait for more ino. What about the Japanese yacht?

So sorry for all of this—bet you've been to hell and back. Let's just hope the wind doesn't keep rising as I am nto sure we have seen the end of it yet. I am just concentrating on tidying up—too much wind to sail yet and anyway I dont' know hwich way I am supposed to be headed.

I remember seven capsizes and two rollovers—so very glad to be alive.

03 MAR 16:50   FROM: BT INMARSAT-C FAX   TO: PETER HARDING

I am OK-obviously badly shaken but OK. I am trying to clear up some of the debris whist I wait to hear about the BOC boats. weather is stil not good—I am not sure it isn't getting up again—got about 45–50 knots at the moment

03 MAR   FROM: BT INMARSAT-C FAX   TO: PETER HARDING

Got your message—but I can't possibly sail off in the opposite direction if he might still be alive. I couldn't bear to do that.

Is someone polling me ont he inmarsat? I can see by the lights that something iss sending or retreiving signals on a regular basis.

Will wait to hear back from you. Have managed Have managed to clear th eengine room—nothing too dreastic and I ahve the engine running now to top up the batteris as they were flat—so at least hat is working.

03 MAR 17:01   FROM: BT INMARSAT-C FAX   TO: PETER HARDING

Peter

Yes Falmouth have suggetsed that I am not in the bst position to help and so carry on BUT I CAN'T unless I am sure someone clsc is better placed. I know it's not waht you want to hear but hope you understand. The record means nothing now and I might be Harry's only chance

Lisa

03 MAR 17:19   FROM: BT INMARSAT-C FAX   TO: GWEN AND DAN CLAYTON

Hi Mum and Dad

I know you know I am OK = this is just to say Hi. Things still aren't good but at least whilst there is absolute chaos everywhere what I can see appears to be superficial damage rather than anything else. Feel rather shaken up but so glad to be alive and thankful that *Spirit* is so strong.

I am still not sailing—is still a force 9 or so, which is nothing compared to what it was but it will take some time to organise things enough to get going, and I shall obviously wait to hear about the two boats in trouble in case I can help there. Anyway, thanks for your two messages yesterday—it helped a lot—I was so scared.

I love you both very much—send my love to everyone else too

xxxxxxxxxxxxxxxxxxxxxxxxxxxxxxxxxx

03 MAR 23:45   FROM: BT INMARSAT-C FAX   TO: PETER HARDING

Hi Peter

No nothing more than cuts and bruises. My head is the worst but is better for the Nurofen—must have really cracked it!

Yes I am continuing to tidy up bit by bit,t he weathaer is squally, lots of violent hailstorms but I am hoping that it is generally getting better—I am not sure.

Barometer has risen a lot but the wind is still very strong. Feeling rather knackered to be completely honest but I guess that isn't surprising.

I will do a bit more tidying up and then see what the situation is. God I really feel for poor Harry Mitchell—I wonder if he is still alive. How luck I am.

4 MARCH (DAY 169)

04 MAR 03:30   FROM BT INMARSAT-C FAX   TO: PETER HARDING

the bloddy rudder is bent on the self steering but no way I can fix in this will try and sail anyway

04 MAR 05:44   FROM: BT INMARSAT-C FAX   TO: PETER HARDING

No I am not heading for Harry. Yes I am trying to get sialing but I've got a few more problems than I realised

04 MAR 11:45   FAX TO LISA   FROM: DAN CLAYTON

Hi sweetheart,

So so relieved to learn you were still there. I'm sure things are pretty horrendous but both you and *Spirit* have proved you can survive.

I know you must be scared and frightened but if you can come through something like this then you have the ability to make it.

We are both just glad that you are still there to talk to, and hope and pray that whatever problems you have to face, you will come through in the end. Our thoughts are with you all the time and we look forward to seeing you safely back home.

All our love, Sweetie,
Mum, Dad et al.

---

04 MAR   FAX TO LISA   FROM: SARA SIMPSON

Lisa darling,

Thank goodness you are alive and OK.

I had a feeling there was something wrong when I woke up this morning and it was confirmed when you signed yourself using my name! But I believe you will be OK now. I can't tell you how I just know it inside. You're going to make it, Lisa.

I am sure conditions must be pretty horrendous and I am sure you are frightened but you have come through the worst. Just remain calm and have faith in yourself.

We all pray for you every day.
We love you, Lisa.
Sara, Anthony, James, Adrian and Richard.

---

04 MAR 15:00   FROM: BT INMARSAT-CFAX   TO: PETER HARDING

Peter

I am sailing slowly becuase I am nervous but I am sailing and heading for the Horn

---

04 MAR   FROM: BT INMARSAT-C FAX   TO: PETER HARDING

Yes I am fine—still shaky and a bit unsure of yself but we are sailing, though finding it difficult to keep course. I'm not even sure what course e are making at presentas I can't get the compass to agree with the GPS satellite fax.

I have backed the staysail to try and help us steer against the bent rudder but it is all rather nerve-racking.

I have managed to find the top of the cooker, and all the gas lines appear to be OK so have been able to make a hot drink, in the only mug I can seem to find at the moment.

I have responded to MRCC Falmouth and told them I am carrying on as suggested.

I have salvaged what I could from the First Aid kit and managed to disinfect my cuts etc and bandage myself up—not very well but at least I can use my hands without bleeding all over the place.

04 MAR	FROM: BT INMARSAT-C FAX	TO: PETER HARDING

Peter if that is you sending it didn't come through

04 MAR	FROM: BT INMARSAT-C FAX	TO: PETER HARDING

Peter are you trying to contact me

04 MAR	FROM: BT INMARSAT-C FAX	TO: PETER HARDING

I am not receiving any text, leave it a while and try again later.

Ironically, although terribly tired I'm unable to sleep for long. There's too much going through my mind. I get a surge of panic with every wave that surfs us along or breaks on the boat. It might be my imagination but the wind seems to howl in the rigging in a particularly eerie way.

Every time I shut my eyes all I can think of is Harry Mitchell and his boat *Henry Hornblower*. Are they still there or are they smashed to pieces? Tears keep welling up inside and I've got a lump in my throat. Oh please God let him be alive.

Since I can't sleep I've tried to keep myself busy tidying up more. It's pathetic really, being so tired I seem to be working in slow motion, but anything achieved is better than nothing. One of the worst things is that everything is horribly wet, even my chair won't dry out. There's water constantly dripping from the roof lining and running on to the computer and all the other instruments. All the cushions are sopping wet, and my sleeping bag's soggy.

I'm really worried about the self steering but know I can't fix it till conditions are calmer. I can't attempt to switch to the autopilot as the charging system for the batteries isn't working and the batteries are practically flat. I'm having to manage without instruments. I know the windvane must have gone from up the mast along with the aerials for the VHF but hopefully the SSB radio will still work.

On deck both the life raft and EPIRB distress beacon were dislodged and almost out. Carefully I managed to untangle the ropes around them and get them both resecured.

Some of the stanchions had been bent right over and were preventing easy use of the winches. I managed to straighten them a bit but will replace them when I get the opportunity. The sprayhood's completely flattened and distorted. I'd found that out the first time I tried to go on deck—I couldn't shift it. It would have been easier to take it off altogether but instead I managed to bend it back a little so that it would give a bit of protection although it did mean that it was difficult to use all the rope controls and winches beneath it.

I can't do any more, I just have no energy left. It's so terribly depressing looking at the mess, that it's making me feel even more drained. I know I ought to get something to eat to give me some much-needed energy but I don't know where to start digging around for all the necessary things to make an easy meal. So I've settled for a couple of Mars bars and a large glucose drink.

Oh God, what a horrible mess.

///

Clayton's wind-speed indicator was broken during the gales she experienced, but boats nearby in the 1994–95 BOC Challenge Race reported near-hurricane winds—over 70 miles per hour. Harry Mitchell on the *Henry Hornblower*, the 70-year-old British BOC sailor for whom Clayton was so concerned, was lost at sea in the storm. The Japanese BOC yacht to which she refers was *Shuten-Dohji II*, sailed by Minoru Saito; he lost all power during the storm and could not communicate, but he came through relatively undamaged and finished that leg of the race. A third BOC boat, in lighter winds farther away from the storm, was dismasted, forcing Alan Nebauer to limp around the Horn under jury rig. He tells his story in *Against All Odds*.

///

FROM
LAST
VOYAGE

BY
Ann Davison

Those who have never sailed out into the ocean often speculate that the greatest fear sailors face occurs far offshore amid mountainous waves, hurricane-force winds, and the terror of being so far from land and help in an emergency. The ocean sailor's greatest nightmare, however, is just the opposite—the shore. Except in the rare case where a protected harbor easily entered in a storm is a possibility, offshore sailors dread being caught on a lee shore—where the wind pushes a boat inexorably toward the rocks—and more disasters occur here than in deep water offshore.

In 1947 Ann and her husband Frank bought the *Reliance*, a 60+-foot wooden schooner built in 1903. The boat was a shambles, so with the last of their money they restored her as best they could. They were trying to escape postwar England and sail to a new life. They were also literally escaping creditors who sought them along the wharves, and the time came when they had to leave, whether or not the boat—and they—were ready.

Last Voyage ends with the following account of how the *Reliance* is caught off the coast of England with a troublesome engine. The storm has raged for days, with wind and tide pushing them repeatedly back against the coast, and they are exhausted when in this last scene they are thrown against the cliffs at Portland Bill.

///

INEVITABLY the wind eased off: we bucketed slowly away from the shore, out of green into gray water, up toward Portland Bill. If only we could clear one of the horns of this bay and get into mid-channel again. If only this infernal wind would blow from another direction.

In a melancholy mood I waited in the saloon for a weather report from the radio. The sky had been still full of wind at dawn, and I hoped to hear that the sky was a liar. The radio bleated a song popular in my early flying days, "There's a Small Hotel," evoking a host of memories. Was life really so gay, so carefree? It had changed to "Put your Shoes on, Lucy" when Frank came in and we giggled at it foolishly.

We listened to a gale warning and Frank said, "We'd better fix the engine in that case." He seemed quite brisk and cheerful. I picked a book at random from the top of the pile at my feet. "Ulysses." I licked the pages. "Made weak by time and fate, but strong in will to strive, to seek, to find, and not to yield." I followed Frank into the engine room.

It was an easier task to free the piston this time since we knew exactly what the trouble was and how to tackle it. When we left it ready for starting we felt that it was a good job done and that we were catching up on the work bit by bit. But we hadn't got round to the mainsail yet. It was still pretty wild though not yet the gale of the warning and we were too jelly-boned to cope with a halyard up the pendulum-swinging mast. Tomorrow, we promised ourselves, if it is fit.

By night we were coming up to the Bill, having pinched and scraped all the searoom possible. The sou'westerly wind had hardened considerably. *Reliance* under jib and mizzen was tugging away to clear the Bill, upon which the light flashed brightly. Frank took a last look round: satisfied that all was well, he turned in. It was tacitly understood that rest for him was all-important.

For a while I stayed in the wheelhouse watching the Portland light and our steady progress. We were going to have ample margin. The movement of the ship underfoot had become second nature and I did not notice it, nor hear the shrilling of the wind. But I felt the cold and I lashed the wheel and nipped below for a cup of coffee.

As one is oblivious of the noise of a well-known engine and is instantly aware of a change in the beat, so I recognized when *Reliance* changed direction. Immediately I was on deck to see what she was up to.

For no known reason she had swung off course and was belting downwind for the Bill. Knowing her reluctance to go through the wind and the amount of searoom she required jibbing, and desperately anxious not to lose all we had gained, I called Frank.

As she was coming slowly round, Charles, way up at the top of the mast, played his ace; the rope grommet parted and the jib blew over the side. *Reliance* drifted stern first.

"Engine!" cried Frank.

On the way down I slipped into the galley and turned off the stove. It was bound to be an all-night session. It always was. And I knew the situation was going to be tough by the waves of drowsiness that swept over me. A sure sign.

As the torches roared I looked out the hatch. Bright were the lights behind Chesil Bank. Bright were the lights on the Portland radio masts. The beam of the lighthouse swept brilliantly past. The tide was making six knots, or more. Taking us with it.

"We haven't much time," I said to Frank, who nodded as if I had said it was raining.

The engine started on one cylinder. I went to the wheelhouse and Frank wedged the fuel injector on the forward cylinder. There was no time to play around. We had covered an amazing distance while the heads were heating and were very near to the high cliffs of Portland Bill. But half power was not enough. With the throttle wide, *Reliance* was going astern. Stern first she passed under the light, its white beam slicing the night sky overhead.

Frank took over and put her into reverse in the hope she would steer better. I looked out the door aft. Black waves were breaking high and white on outlying pinnacles of rock. Right in our path.

"Don't think we'll make it." I felt faintly surprised and automatically unhooked the lifejackets. Each time she lifted we listened—waiting.

Ahead or reverse it made no difference. *Reliance*, fast in the grip of wind and tide, passed under the end of the Bill, missing the rocks by a matter of inches. The swift immutable current swept round the point and up the eastern side of the Bill. *Reliance* went with it, stern first round the point, then broadside, bow on to the cliffs, closing nearer and nearer in every long-drawn minute.

We dropped the mizzen, and Frank went to try and clear the atomizer on number one.

"Bring her round," he said, "if you can."

With unusual docility she turned, was coming round, was nearly round when there was a sharp bark, and the engine stopped. She swung back to face the cliffs, and plunged toward them.

I thought, I know this. I've been through it all before.

As Frank bounded up through the hatch, cursing, I switched on the decklights and together we ran up the deck. The anchor was already shackled to wire and chain but as we tore at the lashings, he looked up at the towering cliffs above us and straightened.

"No use. No time," he said. "We'll have to look to ourselves."

Quickly he got the kerosene and I handed him a bundle of garments for a flare. He hesitated, "Won't you want these again?" Then he laughed shortly and soaked them in kerosene. The flare cast an orange glow over the deck and by its weird light we unlashed the float and moved it over to the lee side, ready for launching.

We were putting on lifejackets, Frank grumbling he couldn't work in one, when she struck. Lightly at first, then harder and harder. We were in front of the wheelhouse; he shouted, "Hold tight!" and we grabbed the mainsheets. Jolting and bumping on the bottom, louder and louder she crashed. Each crash the knell for our hopes, sounding the end of all for which we had labored and endured.

And I could believe none of it.

I heard Frank saying, what a shame, what a shame, as the ship rent beneath our feet. Then the tall cliff face was upon us with a tremendous splintering crash. The bowsprit snapped like kindling.

The flare was out. The night was dark. We clung to the mainsheets in a pool of light thrown by the lamps in front of the wheelhouse. She began to roll. From side to side, rails under, with incredible speed, as if she would roll right over. A colossal jolt: the shock traveling from stem to stern. The mainmast sagged, came over, seemed to hang suspended. The boom dropped and we leapt from under. Before our horrified eyes the bows of the vessel buried into the very face of the cliff.

And above the roaring sea came the terrible noise of a dying ship.

Frank yelled, "Float!" and we heaved it over the side. It swung in the water, level with the deck, in the depths below, streaming away under the counter.

"Jacket O.K.?" he shouted. "Over you go!"

I swung over the side, facing it, and, as the ship rolled, felt out with my feet for the float, missed it, and was left hanging by my arms. He leaned over and gripped my wrists. But the ship, rolling prodigiously, flung me off. I shouted, "Let go!" and dropped into the sea.

In the float I got a leg caught in the ropeworks. Each time the ship came over the mizzen boom on the counter rail drove within a hairs-breadth of my chest. I was trapped, helpless and infuriated. Frank, not seeing this, shouted, "Right?" and without waiting for a reply, climbed onto the bulwarks and leapt overboard.

I happened to look up, got an imprint of him silhouetted on the rail high above—the ship having rolled the other way—then he jumped clear into the sea. He swam to the float, clambered aboard and handed me a paddle as, panting and angry, I wrenched free. Muttering about the dangerousness of the ropeworks in the float (incomprehensible to Frank) I dug in a paddle and sculled away to the end of the line out of reach of the boom. Frank said, "Got your knife?" and cut the painter. It struck me as an unnecessarily dramatic gesture, just as making a flare from a bundle of real clothes had seemed one to him. It was impossible to believe in our predicament.

It was too dark to see more than the faint outline of the clifftops and the white smudge of waves dashing against the face. As near as we could tell, *Reliance* was aground at the foot of a bluff round which the coast fell back a bit. There was no landing for us there, the cliffs were sheer, and the high-flung spray of the bellowing breakers warned us to keep off. We struck out along the coast in the direction of Weymouth, taking care to keep clear of the boiling turmoil at the foot of the cliffs.

Our queer little craft was a lozenge-shaped ring of cork, or some other unsubmergible substance, canvas bound, and painted red and yellow. The ring was woven about with an intricate system of lifelines, and in the center of the ring, suspended by a rope network, was a wooden box. It was in this network I had got entangled. The box was double sided, with two compartments either side with sliding lids, for the containing of provisions (a point we had not taken advantage of, unfortunately). It was immaterial which way up it floated, for both sides were the right side.

We sat on the ring and paddled, with our feet on the box and water up to our knees. Sometimes the water swept across our laps. The float swooped gamely to the top of a wave and dived down into the trough. Frank said she was a good little craft, but wet. We were very cold.

We were both wearing woolen sweaters and jackets but our clothes were soaked through of course. Frank had cast off his shoes and his feet gleamed very white in the black water. I was still wearing the light rubber-soled sneakers that had hardly left my feet since we sailed from Fleetwood. In my pockets was the "shipwreck" equipment I had carried since the night off Land's End: flashlight, four one-pound notes, watch, knife, and lucky photograph. The watch was still going in spite of its immersion. We left the ship shortly after 2:00 A.M. and it did not stop until 8:23. Then it stopped irrevocably.

As we paddled along the coast, careering up and over and down the swift waves, we saw terrific activity burst out on the clifftops. A rocket shot up with a bang, leaving a white trail against the night sky. Flashlight, bicycle, and car lights appeared and ran about in a purposeful manner. An organization was going into operation. We visualized telephonings, shouts, orders; a lifeboat launched, coastguards in action . . . because of a ship in distress. *Our* ship, we realized, still unable to rid ourselves of astonishment and incredulity. Simultaneously we looked back. A yellow pinpoint of light still burned at the foot of the bluff.

"What a shame," burst out Frank, thinking of his beloved ship. Right back to the beginning again, with four pounds and a pocketknife. No *Reliance*, no future, no hope. I made some Boy Scout remark about everything going to be all right. But apart from the overriding surprise I was beyond feeling anything but a thankfulness that Frank and I were together, and a yearning to lie down and sleep for about a week.

He said, "Aren't we getting too far out?"

It was hard to say.

"No. Yes. We are a bit."

There was a point a mile or so ahead along the coast, and we thought

if we could get round that we might find a lee and a landing, and paddled toward it for all we were worth. Yet we seemed to draw no nearer.

A steamer making for Weymouth passed on our starboard hand, not
too far away. We shouted, competing ineffectively with the roaring sea,
and shone the flashlight, but the battery was almost spent and it gave
only a feeble glow. At the same time we spotted the lights of a lifeboat
coming round the point we were trying to make for.

By now we realized that the fierce current that had wrecked *Reliance*
was turning and carrying us out to sea. Inexorably we were going back,
some distance out, but parallel to the way we had come. But the ship's
lights were consoling, and the knowledge that there was a lifeboat looking for us was comforting.

We could see the masthead light of the lifeboat rising and falling.
From the tops of waves we could see the navigation lights. Then it moved
close inshore, and passed us. We yelled at the top of our voices and
waved the flashlight. It failed and went out, and our shouts were
drowned in the tumult of wind and water.

Our puny efforts with the paddles were no match for the sea. Drawn
relentlessly away, we watched the lifeboat work up the coast to *Reliance*,
then down and back again, shining a searchlight on the cliffs.

Frank said peevishly, "What the hell do they think we are? Goats?"
And I said, "It will be dawn soon, and then they'll see us."

We passed *Reliance*—the end of Portland Bill.

When daylight came, they did not see us. Nor by then could we see
them. Only from wave crests could we see land at all. The seas were
tremendous, and very steep. From the top we looked down into impenetrable depths; from the troughs we gazed, awestruck, at huge walls of
water. The cold was intense.

Wilder and wilder came the seas. Wilder and whiter. Instead of the
float's riding over the crests, the crests rode over the float. We paddled
one-handed, holding onto the lifelines.

"I do not see," I said, finding it extraordinarily difficult to move my
frozen lips, "how anyone could pick us up in this. Even if we were seen."

Frank did not reply, but looked round and round at the awful sea as
if he did not believe what he saw.

The current took us into the very center of Portland Race. The sea was
white with insensate rage. Towering pinnacles of water rushed hither

and yon, dashing into one another to burst with a shrapnel of foam—or to merge and grow enormous. From the level of the sea itself it was as the wrath of God, terrifying to behold.

Seated on the bottomless coracle, filled with wonder and awe, we worked away with the paddles to meet the seas. Bravely the little craft tugged up the precipitous slopes and plunged into the depths. I was thinking I would rather be in her than in a dinghy when suddenly I was in the sea, underneath the float, looking up through the center where the water was bright green.

There was time to wonder—is this drowning?—and—how green the water is from this side—then I surfaced and found I was gripping a life-line.

The float was swimming uneasily at the bottom of a trough. There was no sign of Frank. Terror stricken, I shrieked for him at the very top of my voice. He came up about ten yards away. He swam strongly to the float, still holding his paddle, and only then did I realize that I had lost mine. We heaved aboard, and lay athwart the ring, gasping, clinging to the lifeline.

"What did that?" I panted.

"Don't know. This is *not* funny."

Then we saw my paddle, swung upright and set off in pursuit, chasing it uphill and down stormy dale, but it remained forever out of reach.

Suddenly we were in the water again, under the float. Green water above. This time we were slower getting aboard, took longer to recover. We looked at each other in great fear.

"What do we *do*? How do we fight this?"

The upset was so sudden, happened so quickly, we had no notion as to the cause of it. And that was the frightening part.

Dizzily the float tore up and down, swinging and swaying. Tensely we watched the advance of each white-headed mountain. Frank had lost his paddle in the last upset and we could not even make a pretense of fighting.

Then we were flung into the sea again. This time we saw how it happened. Saw with slow-motion clarity, how the float was sucked up under a great overhanging crest and thrown over backwards in the boiling tumult as the wave broke.

This time it was very hard to get back onto the float.

Frank threw an arm about my shoulders. "All right?"

"Yes."

"Good-oh."

We got right inside the float, crouching on the wooden box with water up to our armpits. There must be some way of stopping its turning over, I thought.

He shouted, "Look out!"

Instinctively I leaned forward, head down on the ring to meet what was coming. And we did not turn over, but took the full force of the wave as it exploded upon us.

I found myself shouting: "That's it. That's it. Lean forward. Head down. That foxes 'em."

Shivering violently with cold I remembered something I had once read about the mechanics of shivering and put up a great show of exaggerated shudders, partly to offset the numbing cold and partly as a manifestation of triumph. Frank smiled wanly.

But the conquest was short lived. The seas grew worse, boiled in a white lather all about us, breaking in endless succession. We hardly recovered from the onslaught of one before we were gasping under the next. The weight of water and shock of cold was stunning. Each time a wave broke over us it was with the effect of an icy plunge although we were actually crouching in water all the time.

Hours dragged out in immeasurable misery as the sea struck with a sledge hammer to kill a pair of gnats.

No longer buoyed by the slightest hope of rescue we sank into an apathy of endurance, huddled together, heads on the ring, hands grasping lifelines with a prehensile, immovable grip. Passively we fought for the lives that were a little less living after every blow.

In a comparative lull I glimpsed land from a wave top. It was Portland Bill, thin and attenuated in the distance. I pointed to it. Frank slowly stood up and called in a whisper for help. It was such a pitiful travesty of his usual stentorian bellow that I was inexpressibly shocked, and with a surge of protective energy reached up to pull him down, dreading a recurrence of the horror of the other night. Then I saw it was not that. . . . I looked wildly round for help. But there was none.

He did not speak. He put out a hand, pressed mine reassuringly, smiled at me. And gradually the smile, fixed and meaningless and terrible, faded into unconsciousness, into a slow delirium when, blank eyed, he tried to climb out of the float. I held on to him and feebly tried to rub his hands, my own unfeeling.

A monster wave rose above the rest. Fury piled on fury. Curling, foaming crest. Sweeping down on us, inescapable. I threw an arm round Frank, leaned forward. The little float drove into the wall of water and was lost within it.

When it broke free, Frank was dead.

I stared at the edge of the ring, at the ropes intertwined about it, at the froth and bubbles on the water.

Nothing mattered now. No point in trying any more. The fight was over. I laid my head on my arms and closed my eyes, engulfed in a blessed darkness.

FROM

DESPERATE
VOYAGE

BY
John Caldwell

Not all sailing stories in treacherous waters involve tragedies or near-misses. In 1946 John Caldwell didn't know anything about sailing when he decided to sail from Panama, where he was stranded after the war, to home and wife in Sydney, Australia. Only a man with forbearance and a good sense of humor—and a great spirit of adventure— would risk a voyage alone in a 20-foot sailboat rather than wait for some other form of transportation. Caldwell went to sea with two kittens and his copy of *How to Sail* and after 9,000 miles managed to preserve both his life and his sense of humor, even when his leaking boat was shipwrecked on an uninhabited island on the way to the Galápagos Islands.

Caldwell's delightful, buoyant style adds much to the enjoyment of this classic story, along with his unfailing attention to interesting detail, like the battle between the kittens and a mackerel he looses in the cockpit and the mystery of the live squid he finds in his bilges when pumping. Experienced sailors will marvel at his adventure of trying to reef his sails in a blow (when his handbook doesn't exactly explain how) and using a bag of rocks as an anchor.

///

THUS, ten days after my arrival in the Perlas, I was ready to go down to sea. From jib tack to mainsail clew my little cutter was at her fighting best. Time to weigh anchor and shove off.

But the soldiers . . . there's nothing too good for a soldier. By way of thanks for their generous assistance I proposed a trip. I admit I was reluctant to do it. I wanted to be on my way to Mary. But I had to show my appreciation to the isolated soldiers.

We sailed around Del Rey's southeastern bulge to San Miguel that day. It was the bright spot of *Pagan*'s life under my hand. We returned at dusk the next day to the little bight around from Punta de Cocos. *Pagan*'s last service as a pleasure yacht had been rendered. From now till her ill-fated demise, her work was to be serious—and finally grim and relentless.

That night found me outfitted for sea: water breakers filled and bunged, lockers stocked, and gear lashed and tied. There was even a supply of canned fish aboard for the kittens, a gift from the soldiers.

One thing I was convinced of—my boat could take it. Ten days of hard usage had proved that. She had a history that made those ten days possible, and made all that she went through out on the open sea possible.

Pagan was Norwegian designed and built. Her planking, decking, ribs, knees, and timbers were from the weather-tested far northern slopes. She had blunted the challenge of turbulent Scandinavian seas for many years as a supply boat for lonely Baltic lighthouses.

In 1934 *Pagan* arrived in Panama after an Atlantic passage from Poland. Aboard were four Poles ostensibly headed for Australia as settlers. They had outlived hair-raising escapes and a discouraging series of bruising gales, after which even tropical, rainy Panama looked better than the prospect of sunny Australia.

They promptly sold *Dwaja* (spirit), as she was then known, and there followed for the little gaff-rigged sloop twelve years of peaceful "harbor circumnavigation." Light harbor sails, bellied by soft harbor breezes, were bent to her spars. From Colón to Balboa she luxuriated in the peace and quiet of yacht club atmosphere. A yachting pennant swung from her masthead. Gay parties took place in her cabin. She became well known as the "original" *Pagan*, on both the Atlantic and the Pacific sides.

At some time during her twelve years' career as a coastwise and harbor playboat her sail plan was redesigned to the Marconi rig, and *Pagan* became a sharp, fast cutter. She was regarded as one of the fastest little vessels on the Isthmus. Rail down, there were few who could match her.

The boat I was to sail with was fast and sturdy, and after my numerous experiences aboard her I knew her, I had confidence in her, and so I had confidence in myself—what more could I ask?

I stepped out into the cockpit and flashed my light through the rigging and across the decks, and found everything as it should be. I was pleased. I went below, where I lay a long time before I slept, thinking into the low ceiling, glad the time had come to be going.

EARLY ON THE MORNING of June 7 I lashed my little pneumatic raft to the base of the mast, heaved my sea bag of rocks aboard (I had taken the tools out of the bag when they showed rust, and substituted rocks), and sailed for deep water. Under a hard easterly breeze, sharper than usual for these waters, I put her immediately on a westerly course and made for the open sea.

My destination was once again the Galápagos Islands, the lonely volcanic group lying on the doorstep of the southeast trade winds.

My first stop would be Seymour Island, where an army weather station was located. That is, it would be my first stop if the army base wasn't closed down. The last word I had received before leaving Panama, from fishing boats recently in the Galápagos, was that the Army expected to be out by July first. This gave me twenty-one days to make the transit—more than enough time; I figured I could make it in eleven days.

My plan was to haul up there for a week, check my boat for her running and standing gear, and for her hull, then shove off into the southeast trades and race nonstop across the ocean to Sydney. With the hurricane season crowding me for time, I had no alternative, unless I holed in somewhere en route for three or four months till navigable weather returned. In case of necessity I had charts and sailing directions for likely island groups along the way. If trouble came it would be easy enough to put in for repairs or send a cable.

When the Perlas had faded from green to blue, and from blue to gray, I began thinking of what course I should steer to make my destination. I was in somewhat of a quandary about what to do, but remembering that the shortest distance between two points is a straight line, I laid a ruler flat on my chart and drew a straight line connecting the Perlas and Galápagos Islands. This line was my true course. It lay southwest. All I had to do now was to sail straight down it, and after a certain time, lo, there would be land. I soon learned that in deep water sailing theory is one thing, and actuality an astoundingly different thing!

The fresh easterly breeze began to wane by late morning. But it had enabled me to make a good offing. The Perlas were low down on the horizon astern. Off to starboard the Panamanian mainland was a thin, foglike shadow.

I whiled away the morning on the deck with my feline crew. The tiller was lashed and *Pagan* swayed gently and sailed smoothly as beam seas rolled under her. My native hat toned down the sun and my comfortable rope sandals kept my soles clean. I was stripped to shorts. About midmorning I cast out the fishing line, baited with the tail of a yellowjack I had hauled aboard the day before, and in twenty minutes I heaved a throbbing Spanish mackerel over the transom for the kittens.

They were the most antic little devils I have ever seen with a flapping fish. Hardly a day passed that I did not see them in battle with something I pulled up. The act was the same every day, but it never palled. At first they approach the fish with a cat's normal curiosity. A sniff tells it is a sort of *crêpe Suzette*, cat style. They jump viciously upon the powerful fish, growling for a tooth hold. With a violent flip the fish sends them bowling across the deck, and they scatter wild-eyed, tail flying, to the foredeck. In a moment the rich smells begin to torture them anew, and they come creeping cautiously back, innocent faced, hopeful looking. They move up beside the victim, crouch low as if to eliminate themselves, and sniff distantly, then bunch up tightly for the spring. I drop a hammer behind them—and trigger-quick they fly scampering to the bow.

They wait a moment or two, then peer wonderingly around the deckhouse corner with round, bright eyes. Down the deck they descry their quivering dinner. Once more they slink slowly, belly down, along the deck, range up beside the delicacy and sniff deliciously. Throwing caution to the winds they pounce athwartships of the fish and growl wolfishly. Like a desperate cowboy they cling for a few wild jumps and again scurry away—spitting as they go, tumbling over each other.

Patience is a game that is never taught; it is learned. Much to my entertainment these goofy little cats never learned it where fish were concerned. Right up to the day that I tearfully parted company with them, they were a riot of humor.

About noon the fresh breeze of the morning waned perceptibly. This was the first weather item recorded in my log. I was using a notebook for a log. It contained ninety pages; with a page for each day's reckoning, I figured I would just be filling it when I hove in sight of Sydney Harbor. Not knowing the proper procedure for annotating a log—if there be one—I just jotted, "June 7, 11:00 to 12:00 A.M. Wind slowing up." Thus the voyage began.

For lunch I had island fare: an avocado, the butt end of a pineapple, two bananas, and coconut milk. Tied gaily to the mast were two stalks of bananas. Rolling along the decks were coconuts, avocados, mangos, papayas, pineapples, taken from the abundant jungle before I sailed. These, I figured, would be the last fresh foods before Australia.

Often a meal was nothing more than a can of beans ripped hastily open and eaten from the tin. Meals were fancy or simple in turn, depending on how I felt and a lot of other things. Sometimes I shared the cats' daily fish, and at others it was easier to lie out in the soft sun sleeping the day away than go below for the can opener.

Later in the afternoon the lagging wind veered to northwest and suddenly stiffened, kicking up the first white caps of the trip. At nearly sundown it was stronger and had hauled around to where it blew out of the west, causing a confused sea. A scud was flying in from over the horizon. *Pagan* had a considerable tilt to her decks, and I found myself wondering at what precise moment does one decide to reef, and when one does, how is it done? I had played at reefing down in calm weather, but now, with wind beating at the bow and bow beating at the sea, it was all so different.

I went below and perused my handbook on *How to Sail*. Alas, it was designed for harbor sailors and those who haunt protected waters; not one word breathed it of the reefing ritual.

I handed my way out of the sloping cabin onto the wet decks. I searched the low, louring clouds for a hint of the extent of weather; nothing I read helped me. "So this is the Pacific's stormy greeting," I thought. I looked around and saw that the lee rail was awash; *Pagan* quivered lightly, her timbers creaked. The wind was definitely higher; a welter of water was surging under her, beginning to hiss and howl in the way of mounting seas. I wasn't sure that now was the "precise" moment to reef down, but I concluded it was a darned good one to do it.

How to get the sail off? How steady the spar in such a wild setting? The Indians say the best way to do a thing is to do it. But on a boat there is a proper way. One doesn't unbend the halyard, then heedlessly allow the wind to whip it from hand . . . as I did. Such negligence is dangerous because the sail spills its wind and flails wildly at loose ends. The sail can be split right down the center, the Marconi clips ripped from the luff, and four or five seams strained and rent so quickly as to leave the sail in six shapeless parts in a matter of seconds. The reason I know is that that is just what happened.

In the brief minutes that I clutched at the wind-whipped halyard, my sail flew to spare parts. I raced to it and fought with its threshing ends. The unruly boom swung across and across with maddening persistence. I clung rashly to it as I made to put the sail in stops, and in the twenty minutes or so required to lash down the sail I must have seen each side of the deck a thousand times. When I finished there seemed to be more lightning than before, and the spray stung more.

I discovered that in dousing sail I should have eased the tiller accordingly; for now I was footing it before the wind in all haste toward where I had used the day in coming from. In a questionable maneuver I worked her around—and suffered a few heavy slops of water as she broached. But I managed to heave her to on the starboard tack, with tiller lashed slightly to windward and with headsails aback.

I watched her point hesitantly into the gathering night. Now and then a heavy sea caromed off the bow, throwing it high; a comber curled under her, dancing her about. So this was all there was to heaving to in a storm. Child's play. Just let the mainsail blow to pieces, leave the jib and staysail up, lash the tiller aweather and hit the sack! Expensive, but simple.

As I stared into the night I began to feel a flutter in my stomach and the faintest hint of lightness in the head. I flattered myself by calling it weariness and went down to my pitching bunk. *Pagan*'s cabin was having hell's merry time. There were the rattle and clank of gear gone adrift; the frantic to-and-fro race of water in the bilge; the vexing warmer temperature of the cabin; the weak whine of the wobbly cats as they fumbled about sickly. Finally the wash of angry water against the planks, gurgling suggestively as it does, became a liquid knell to whatever peace I had thought I felt.

I groped full-jowled out into the screeching night. On my knees and clinging to the shrouds, I "fed the fish."

The wind was intoning a terrifying whine to resounding crashes of thunder and sea growls, and between "feedings" I grew increasingly conscious that I was in a rising gale. More darts of lightning flashed and more wetness was in the air, smacking of heavy rain and nastier weather. The jib was bellied out to maximum. Since it was an old one I instinctively felt it would soon go. The staysail was standing the gaff; the main boom was snug in her crutch.

I stretched out in *Pagan*'s lee waist and a bilious nothingness completely enshrouded me. I could think a little, and feel a little, but beyond that I was nothing. I knew the jib was straining; that any minute it would rip out from its fittings. She was shivering by the leech, and quaking the decks beneath my stomach. I turned numbly onto my side and watched the grim, hopeless match between boundless nature and man-made trivia.

The jib shivered mightily as a man will do under a withering load. A hank parted company at the luff; there was an intensity of already frantic motion. The aged fraying boltrope snapped, followed by a stringent rip of the sort fat boys make when they bend too far. At the bat of an eye the hapless sail was in tatters and its bits were whizzing off astern with the driving seas.

I attempted to pull myself together and view more sternly what was happening. The wind was still on the upgrade; the sea, growing angrier, was swept into foaming windrows. Lightning had grown to the intensity of daylight, and flashed on and off like house lights. The air was laden with bursts of rain. With staysail aback, *Pagan* was holding her own but floundering. Now that I had pulled myself to, I was sensible enough to be scared—plenty scared.

The staysail, I could tell, had reached that "precise moment" when a reef was required to save it. I loosed the halyard—but clung tightly to it and dropped the frantic sail to where I could get at the reef points.

Reef point by point I tied in the unruly strings. Staysails are uncomfortable members to deal with. You mustn't even consider reefing one down in heavy weather unless prepared to take at least a dozen buckets of water in your teeth. Then there's the sail itself to contend with. It pounds madly about your ears. The bow rears and plunges wild-horse like. With all sail off, the boat rolls. And upon the foredeck there is nothing to which you can hold. No wonder I once heard a yachtsman refer to his imperious wife as "my staysail."

I studied the screeching night airs before going down below, and what I saw didn't improve my seasickness. *Pagan* had incorporated a wild roll in her behavior and the swelling seas were beginning to bounce her about. She was falling off before the wind; it made me wonder where land could be.

Down below, I put on my life jacket and squeezed the cats between it and me, at my chest. Such tight quarters displeased them, so I took them out. I cut open an old-type life preserver and removed its cork floats. To two of these I attached a string; and to the end of each string I tied a kitten, by the hind leg. Then I went on deck and tried to feed the fish. But I had what is called the "dry heaves." The more I strained the worse I felt. I felt so useless I looked at everything and said "So what."

Sheets of spray whipped over the weather bow. The wind screamed in the rigging. A raging sea was coursing astern. The staysail had a press of wind that set her aquiver, affecting the whole boat.

"What the devil do you do next?" I thought, and went below. The cats were in a bewildered ball of legs and corks and strings. I sorted them out and sat on my bunk with them in my lap, disturbed by the noises I could hear and by my imaginings. I remembered someone's saying, at Panama, that the best place for a storm sail was the mainmast. I didn't have a storm sail . . . but . . .

I cut a dozen small lengths of one-inch line. Dragging out my aged spare staysail, I toted it lamely up to deck. The short lines I bent loosely about the mast. To each such "ring" I attached a clip connected to the leading edge of the sail and heaved the sail aloft with the main halyard. Because of her loose foot she strained considerably, but she did the work of a storm sail, and *Pagan* reared up and about less often. I dropped and furled the staysail, and hurried below.

The cats and I had dozed off into a questionable sleep when I was disturbed by the obstreperous beat of a rent sail. I found the little storm sail split from foot to peak, her frayed ends pointing to leeward. *Pagan*, of course, was wallowing violently.

What to do? Lightning was throwing the night into brilliant confusion. A series of squalls was lording it over us. It is said first things are worst; and this was my first storm. I was beginning to fear my little boat was heading for the port of missing ships. Such moments as these, when one doesn't know what to do next, are enough to make one vow to take up harbor sailing.

Pagan was lying in the trough of the seas. Boiling water, breaking over her beam, threatened, I thought, to turn her turtle. I hastened to unfurl the staysail—as a last resort. A heavy lump of water pitched into my ear, nearly knocked me sprawling into the dark deep. On an impulse and a fear I heaved my sea bag of rocks outboard and crawled into the safety of the cockpit and wondered what the effect would be. The bag sank but at the same time it dragged, and *Pagan*'s bow swung smartly upwind.

It was deep into the hours of morning; seasickness, weariness, anxiety had chafed at my reserves. I trudged down to my bewildered kittens—and sleep.

At close on daylight it happened. Luckily the wind had abated—though the seas were running high—or it might have been worse. A sledgehammer blow smote *Pagan* on her keel. We were wrenched from sleep and flung to the floor. The cats yowled. I jumped to my feet and stumbled before I could walk. A rattle of displaced gear and rending timbers, like Satan's pitchfork pounding on the cabin.

I started for the hatchway, but I was knocked flat almost instantly. *Pagan* heeled dizzily and a dozen noises fought for supremacy as she shuddered from the shock. In a moment she righted, but another thump on the keel sent me sprawling again. I was sure we had run onto a sea-pounded shore.

The thought reeled through my head: "Wrecked!" I was glad I had my life jacket on.

I groped for my cats, for I feared I would have to make some desperate leap onto jagged rocks—and I didn't want to leave my crew to perish in the hold. In the melee they had dived for cover, but I fumbled upon the cork squares, so I ran on deck, cats a-dangling.

I had expected to see the towering shadow of land leering down upon me, and a shore of bristling rocks reaching for *Pagan*'s tender planks. But I didn't see this at all. Instead, at my very feet, was what seemed the body of a mammoth whale, its tail roiling the waters off to the right.

And on the other side another whale, only smaller, was churning about lazily. I had heard of whales attacking small craft—but the absurdity of it in a storm!

I was petrified lest the monster erase me with a sweep of that broad tail. Then the outlines of "that broad tail" took a clearer shape, and I made it out to be, not the tail of a whale, but the limbs of a drifting tree. A tree whose girth was such that its lumber would have made two or three or even five *Pagan*s.

Its bole lay beneath the surface, its limbs awash, and the whole of it rose and fell with each sea. Evidently making sternway in the storm, I had come backing off the crest of a wave and landed atop it. I shoved the yowling kittens below, and made to fend the obstruction off with the boat hook. My efforts against a limb were of little avail. *Pagan* was pivoted athwart it, reeling with side-to-side motions and thumping with rebounds that were too much to take for long.

Heavy rollers crashing onto the forest giant twisted it beneath the keel, exerting a shifting pressure against *Pagan*'s timbers. She groaned deep in her parts with the whole-souled complaint of a wounded man.

When a dozen seas had pounded us, and the keel had wallowed an inch at a time its full length across the tree, it worked away and we floated free.

I hurried below and searched by light for seepage or hint of damage. I could see none. However, I saw something flash silvery in the bilge well, under the ladder. I strained my hand through the water till it struck something slippery, fleet, full of life. I pursued it and caught it, and tossed it on the floor boards. A squid! A live squid in the bilge! Full two inches long, a half inch around.

I immediately thought of a leak somewhere in the hull, large enough for him to slip through.

I went out into the cockpit where the bilge pump jutted up from the after end of the cabin and pumped *Pagan* dry, and, observing the bilge, I watched a determined trickle of water flow rapidly into it. Another search over the ribs and planks in the cabin, and below the water line, revealed nothing. She had sprung a leak deep in her timbers, possibly somewhere along the keel and its adjoining strakes. I decided on the moment to head for the closest land. I could only think of Del Rey.

I pumped the filling bilge dry and put *Pagan* about. Unshaking the reef from the staysail, I hauled it aloft and belayed it. I pulled my sea-bag anchor aboard. In greatest haste, and perspiring in spite of the cool wet wind, I uncovered my good jib and lugged it topside and strung it. I regretted that I had been so careless as to blow out my good mainsail. I needed it badly. Under staysail and jib she ran off before the wind, pushed helpfully by stern seas.

I put her on a course of east by south, assuming that during the day and through the storm she had slipped a little north. One part of the sky was darker than the other; the sun was rousing from its bed; the headsails, higher up, were catching the faint light. I made the Perlas Islands dead ahead.

I pumped the bilges and thought I observed that they had filled a little more quickly than before. As a precaution, I started the engine and gave her full throttle ahead. Even in the short time I had engaged the engine, the bilge had filled. I worked the pump till it sucked dry—a sound dear to the heart of a seaman on a leaking vessel. But even as I finished I could look into the well and see it refilling defiantly.

Pagan was making fast time, but it wasn't fast enough. I thought of the spare mainsail in the sail locker and what it would mean to have it flying. I started below to break it out. A disturbing sight met me: the bilge had filled and overflowed; an inch of water was standing on the floor boards.

I jumped back to the pump and pumped till I tired . . . and the bilge was dry. I stared eagerly over the whitecaps at the colorless land, and it seemed a long way off.

A half hour went by. I never took my eyes off the islands except to watch the bilge fill.

Del Rey was about eight miles distant with Punta de Cocos still farther. On the port beam San José was about five or six miles off. I must have stared too long at the land for when I looked down there were at least three inches of water washing over the cabin floor. The leak was growing.

I took to the pump and worked it at an aching pace. I changed hands several times and still water gurgled in the bilge. When at last the pump hissed dryly, I sighed and peered anxiously over the long miles to Punta de Cocos. I could hear the splashing of new water in the swaying bilge, so I took to pumping again. After pumping a seemingly overlong time, I found that I hardly gained on the rising water. And in the time taken to peer below, I had lost the gain.

I jumped to the tiller, unseized its single lashing, and changed *Pagan* to a course of due east. I was now scudding her toward San José, three miles to leeward. Once more I stood by the pump. The water inboard had risen alarmingly, its slopping had wetted down the bulkheads, and my cats, curled and shivering in my bunk, eyed the rising water disdainfully. I pumped furiously to outpace the water. Ahead was an open beach. At its extreme left end stood a jagged promontory behind which was a protected shore. I had no alternative but to put *Pagan* on it. I heard that seamen under compulsion had often run their craft ashore for repairs or scraping and painting.

I altered course three points to port and stood bow-on toward shore. I worked madly at the pump, afraid to look at the distance yet to go. Suddenly the motor sputtered, coughed raucously, and fizzled off to silence. I took a quick look at the engine—it was covered by water. I leaped back to the pump and worked it fitfully. I was hoping *Pagan*'s momentum would carry her well in, because the tiny headsails barely pulled. Slowly, slowly the shore closed in. I jerked still more wildly at the pump, but *Pagan* was settling. Water lapped at the gunwales. Below, the cats were crying mournfully; I knew that they had been washed off the bunk.

I expected to see *Pagan* dip her rail under and sink at any moment. Then, ever so lightly, the keel scraped bottom and she steadied, losing her way. The kittens swam out the hatchway into the cockpit, towing their cork blocks. I tossed them atop the cabin and hurried to the work of dousing the headsails. Then I busied myself with making *Pagan* fast to the shore.

The decks were awash and the insides were afloat. I undogged the fore scuttle, dropped up to my waist in the hold, and fished out a two-inch hawser. This I clove-hitched to the bitt; the free end I fastened about my waist.

I grabbed the kittens and gave them a toss shoreward. They splashed about twenty feet from the sand. I dived from the bow and came up near them, and saw them as they attempted the impossible—trying to claw

atop the bobbing corks. I took their corks and towed them the few feet
to the beach. Leaving them to shiver beneath the cold sky, I led my line
to a mangrove stump and secured it with a round turn and double half
hitches.

My feline mariners, with "salt in their eyes"—which is to say, shipwrecked—tottered weakly up the beach, weary of the sea and its vicissi-
tudes. Suddenly they saw the towering jungle loom up blackly and glare
down over them with all its silence. With minced steps and yowling com-
plaints they swore at their seaman's lot and squatted back on their
haunches to berate their wetness and fright.

I scooped up my sea mates consolingly. Poor little sea-weary blokes.

Up till now my only name for them had been "kitty." But under present circumstances a name for each naturally evolved. The little blond
female I named Flotsam, and the darker tom, Jetsam. Unfortunately
their name day wasn't a joyous occasion. They spent it under a bucket on
the beach, out of danger, so they wouldn't stray to the jungle to become
table d'hôte for a crocodile or a boa.

I sat on the damp beach and viewed the dreary picture of my boat,
foundered to her scuppers on an uninhabited isle. Right before my eyes
she heeled over and settled to her beam on the watery bottom. Her port
rail cleared the surface, and the mast appeared about three feet away,
slanted skyward at an unseemly angle. It told the story of shipwreck. Still
drooping from it was the tattered storm sail.

FROM

DARK WIND

BY
Gordon Chaplin

The treacherous waters experienced by Gordon Chaplin at first may seem less threatening than those in other stories. After all, when the storm descends upon his heavy Dutch-built 36-foot sailboat, he is anchored—safely, he thinks—off a small atoll in the Marshall Islands of the Pacific. He can even see lights ashore, at least until the air is too thick with water to see anything at all. But bluewater sailors have always known that the safety of shore is illusory, especially when it's a lee shore, and most prefer to head for open water when heavy weather threatens. That is one of the lessons Chaplin learns from the tragedy that crashes down on his boat in the night.

Like Réanne Hemingway-Douglass and her husband Don, Chaplin has sailed off with his lover on a great adventure. But unlike Don Douglass, he is cautious, not driven to taking risks. With his new love he seeks the paradise of warm Pacific waters as they recover from their other broken marriages and rediscover passion on the high seas. They've already crossed the Pacific and cruised Hawaii, and until now their voyage has been idyllic.

Lacking good information about the coming storm, Chaplin's fatal error is his decision to remain at anchor. When the full brunt of the typhoon hits, it's too late to escape either to land or open water.

Chaplin's tragic memoir combines the skill of a master storyteller with the dark, brooding undertones of a man submerged in guilt and wrestling with the new knowledge of his own limitations.

///

I groaned. We were out of range of High Seas Radio in San Francisco and had to place our calls now through Sydney Radio in Australia. Even in the best of weather the routine was long, complicated, excruciating. "Couldn't we call them all after the storm?" I said. "Please?"

She finally agreed. We uncorked a bottle of cold California Gewürztraminer from the refrigerator, poured ourselves glasses, looked at each other, toasted, and drank. The rising wind in the shrouds made a little trilling sound every once in a while, like a songbird, and the faint but somehow reassuring smell of the garbage curled through the cabin.

"Well," I said, "I guess tomorrow we'll know what we should have done, won't we?"

We heated up two cans of extra-hot Hormel chili while the wind rose steadily and backed into the north, so we were no longer protected by the island. By 9 P.M. the sustained force seemed to be approaching 50 knots (not that easy to judge in the dark with no anemometer) with gusts over 60—stronger than anything we'd been through before. The 9:48 weather on WWVH hadn't been updated, so we assumed there hadn't been any major changes in the storm's direction or intensity.

We called the village radio and asked them what they'd heard. They said the storm was due to pass at around midnight or a little later. We drew its projected course on our chart and figured that the wind might get a little stronger, but not much. I went up on the bow to check the anchor lines, adjust the antichafe guard on the nylon one, and let a little out so that as the boat swung farther into the north the strain on both rodes would remain the same.

As soon as I got out there, it seemed, the wind picked up. It whistled in my teeth and blew a tune through my nose. Looking directly into it was difficult. My shorts flapped painfully against my legs. When I got back I checked with Susan to see if I'd imagined the change, and she said I hadn't.

At about 10 P.M. we started the big Perkins diesel, which hadn't failed us yet. The idea was to warm it up and get it ready to use later, if necessary, to take strain off the anchor rodes by motoring slowly ahead.

As usual, one touch of the starter was enough. The needles jumped in the dials and gradually settled into their accustomed places: temperature 80 degrees centigrade, oil pressure 50 psi, RPM 900, transmission pressure 140 psi, starboard alternator charging at about 20 amps. Under the floorboards, the engine was warm and purring.

When I went down in the cabin to take a leak (the wind was too strong to do it over the side anymore), there was a faint smell of decay. I assumed it was from the garbage bags back on the stern but noticed that instead of getting weaker as I moved forward toward the head, it got stronger. I realized it was coming from two gleaming black-spotted tiger cowrie shells we had found a couple of days earlier, alive, in shallow water just short of the drop-off on the barrier reef. I'd found one and, later, Susan had found the other.

At the time, I hadn't realized that shells in some cultures are considered bad talismans. But when I found my shell, glowing eerily in the darkness of its crevice, I'd felt an odd current that was not the joy of discovery. Still, I hadn't resisted taking it back to the boat and showing it to Susan. As she took its smooth, dark heaviness into her hands she had that same wide-pupiled look she had when we made landfall in Hawaii and dropped anchor here.

We let the animal in my shell gradually die and deliquesce until it could be washed out in salt water. The smell was so horrendous that we tried a different approach when she found hers, boiling it briefly to kill and harden the animal and then picking it out with a fishhook. Her way was more humane and the smell wasn't as bad, but the boiling had caused slight chipping and discoloration.

The two shells were now side by side in a sea-railed pocket on the drop-leaf teak salon table. It was too late to throw them overboard; the animals had already died. They were just beautiful skeletons now, and

Susan had always been on good terms with skeletons. She collected bones of all kinds, went out of her way to visit cemeteries, and had once put together a photographic essay on the death markers along the Transpeninsular Highway of Baja California. She'd want to keep hers, and it would be wrong to heave mine even though it was the smellier.

No, the two shells should stay together, in death as in life.

The boat was beginning to pitch uneasily in the short chop when I came back up to the wheelhouse. Susan, holding on to the grab rails with her small, strong hands, was looking out the window at the one light still visible on shore: the generator-powered electric light in the community center. All the kerosene lanterns were gone now, and the boat could have been floating in outer space. Susan's face was lit from below by the amber numerals on the depth finder, the pale green glow of the GPS, and the lamps in each of the engine dials. Neither of us spoke.

In that same illumination I could see the face of my watch; a little after 11 P.M. We'd been in darkness for five hours and had at least seven more to go before dawn.

Land people, most of them anyway, tend to sleep through the night. It's different on a boat at sea. The watches continue, no matter what time it is. You sleep a few hours at night and a few hours during the day.

In our usual voyaging schedule, the last watch of the night carried over into daylight and Susan took that, while both of mine were in darkness. On long passages I seemed to be awake at night more than during the day, becoming a creature of the night—a small, vulnerable one. I was well acquainted with the stars, the Southern Cross, the moon (in all its phases), the feel but not the look of big ocean swells. It was a fearsome beauty.

Squalls always seemed to come at night. Cold, sharp, horizontally moving raindrops would rattle against the black windows of the wheelhouse, and the sails would begin to boom like shotguns. I'd cut the automatic pilot, trim the sheets, and try to find the wind, which would be shifting wildly through all points of the compass. Confused, choppy seas would broadside the hull, break into the cockpit, and make me worry about the thin glass in the wheelhouse. The seas would be invisible as always, except for the white foam running down their fronts, but they'd sound like sliding rocks.

Ships always passed at night, too, moving at more than 20 knots, so fast they could be on us twenty-five minutes after their lights appeared on the horizon. And once again I'd marvel at how, in the middle of nowhere, two boats on two different courses originating on opposite sides of a vast ocean could pass so terrifyingly close.

I've read a lot of rhapsodies on the joys of night sailing in the trades. Personally, I was always very glad to see the sun come up, to have survived yet another twelve hours of uncertainty, punctuated by not a few of those waking nightmares, snatches of disembodied conversation, lights and huge waves that didn't exist. When dolphins streaked through that darkness like glowing comets, with unearthly breathing and startling churnings and splashes, I'd tell myself they were the spirits of my dead father enjoying themselves and wishing me well on this voyage. But I never believed it.

The sustained force of the wind now seemed over 60 knots, with occasional gusts that felt well over 80. But how could you judge? It was a dark wind, while the storm in Honduras—our only standard of comparison— had been a daytime one. Does being able to see what you're faced with make it worse or better? You'd think better, except that sometimes at sea, when the sun comes up and illuminates the waves you've been taking for granted all night, they look terrifying. All I can say for sure is that this warm, damp, heavy entity sometimes felt a little stronger than anything we'd experienced before, and sometimes quite a bit stronger.

"*Lord Jim*, how are you doing?" asked Wotho Radio. Usually it was the mayor himself who talked to us, but the mayor was away at the President's Invitational Billfishing Tournament at Kwajalein atoll about fifty miles southeast. The speaker's English was better than the acting mayor's, whom we'd met earlier in the day, so we couldn't put a face to the voice. It would have been nice to have been able to. "We're doing okay so far," I said. "Have you heard anything new?"

Nothing new. The storm center was still due sometime after midnight, it was still headed west-northwest, and the present latitude was about 11 degrees. It still should pass well to the north.

"Are you sure you don't want to come ashore?" Wotho Radio asked.

It was the voice of experience talking, and we should have listened. Maybe Susan did listen and wanted to go, but she didn't tell me. I didn't ask her. I couldn't make out her expression in the dim light. I wanted her to stay. I was confident in our technology and even more confident that as long as we stayed together everything would be all right.

We couldn't have rowed ashore, of course. The inflatable dinghy would have been blown downwind like a balloon. But swimming ashore in the warm, cozy water would have been easy. It was only 300 feet to the protected beach. I could have swum in with Susan and then swum back. Or I could have stayed ashore with her and let the *Lord Jim* fend for herself.

"We'll hang on here," I said, trying to make out Susan's face. "But your light is very helpful. It lets us know where we are."

"Okay, roger, roger. Wotho Radio standing by."

The idea of abandoning ship—our home, our career, our life—was unthinkable to me, at least at that point. We weren't in trouble, not even close. There were many things we could do if it got worse, but how much worse could it get? I was prepared to take a chance, and I assumed Susan was too.

I went forward to check the anchors again and, as before, the wind seemed to pick up immediately. I could feel the features on my face changing under it into a wind-tunnel grimace—my lips pulled back over my teeth, my eyes squeezed shut, my cheeks flapping.

I had let out all hundred feet of the nylon rode and needed more, so I tied one of the braided orlon dock lines to it with a double fisherman's bend and fitted another polyethylene chafe guard on the other side of the knot. The wind blew through my fingers and made them clumsy as I paid the line out through the bowsprit roller and snubbed it. On the other bowsprit roller the anchor chain, held with a chain hook attached to a 15-foot length of springy one-inch nylon rope to absorb the jerks, still had some belly left in it.

I was cold and breathless by the time I got back to the wheelhouse. Susan handed me a towel. "It doesn't seem to like me going out there, does it?" I joked. I was always complaining that she took things too personally, even the weather. "That last gust was a good eighty knots, didn't you think?"

She nodded without smiling back.

"Maybe we ought to try putting it in gear," I said. "Take the strain off the lines." My hand was shaking slightly as I pushed the Morse control lever forward and watched the RPMs climb to 1,000, the slowest possible motoring speed. "I'll have to go up again and see what's happening."

She put a warm hand on my arm. "Oh, wear your harness. Please!"

It was the first time she'd sounded fearful; maybe she was wishing she was safely onshore. It should have worried me. "We're at *anchor*, Susan." Grinning. "We're not out in the middle of the ocean. If I fall overboard I can climb back on. Actually, it would be really nice to be in the water." I meant it. The air was filled with cold 80-mph raindrops that stung like buckshot. The water, as I imagined it, would be comforting, almost motherly.

This time there was no question: as soon as I left the wheelhouse the wind gusted to the highest velocity yet. I could tell by the weight of it on my body. I had to crouch and shield my eyes. Through the tears, I could see that the engine had caused us to run up dangerously on the anchor rodes and at the same time fall off to port.

I let the wind carry me back to the wheelhouse and took the engine out of gear. Towel again. "Hope we didn't piss off the storm god," I said, with the old casual reassuring grin. I leaned out the wheelhouse door and shouted, "Sorry! For Christ's sake, we're *s . . . o . . . o . . . o . . . o . . . r . . . r . . . y!*"

Maybe if I'd known then what I know now, I wouldn't have shouted so cockily. Maybe. Though the WWVH weather broadcasts told us otherwise, by dusk the storm had actually turned 20 degrees to the southwest and was now headed right at us, with an intensifying wind speed of between 85 and 105 knots.

We were targeted.

The storm god hates technology. For the first time in the four years we'd owned the boat, the depth finder began to malfunction. It would register the correct depth of eighteen feet for a little while, but then the number would be replaced by a line across the screen, meaning that its range had been exceeded or that it was actually sitting on the bottom. The line would be replaced by arbitrary numbers, and then—at increasing intervals—the real ones would come on again. This was unsettling, because a change in depth would be the best way to tell if we were dragging.

Another way would be by the light onshore. But what if the light onshore went out?

A third way could be by means of the GPS, which was accurate to a quarter mile. I programmed a way point that corresponded to the spot where we were anchored so that later, if we seemed to be dragging, we could check our actual position against it.

By this time, Susan had taken up a position on the floor of the wheelhouse near the closed door leading out to the cockpit, the most protected space on board. I was on the settee next to the radio and weatherfax. The boat rolled and pitched sharply, and the noises around us had deepened in tone from a screaming to a deep thrumming vibration. Talk was difficult; there didn't seem to be much to say anyway. The wind outside blew our thoughts away, even though inside the air was calm.

I wondered idly whether the large wheelhouse windows would blow in. The big diesel pulsed. We hung on and waited for the clock to move, and it had never moved more slowly.

Sometime after midnight, I saw that the light onshore was no longer there, although I thought I could still see the loom of the island. There was a chance we could be dragging.

"I better go check the anchors again," I said.

"*Oh, God, don't go out there.*"

I grinned and said something flip, even though I understood very well what she was worried about. To go out would make the storm worse. At the time, I didn't wonder how bad things would have to get before the insouciance she hated so much gave way to tenderness and sympathy.

I tugged the wheelhouse door open. "Well, anyway, the garbage is still on board."

Susan didn't answer. I turned to see why not (in the darkness I couldn't make out her expression), almost went back, almost put my arms around her, but instead I went out and closed the door behind me.

Standing upright on deck now was impossible, so I hauled myself forward from handhold to handhold in the crouch of a man who has had too much to drink—the old Hurricane Walk.

The anchors were holding, but the nylon rode was tight as a piano string and the thick nylon spring line on the anchor chain was stretching more than a foot with every heave of the boat. As it stretched, it chafed against the sharp edge of the bulwark next to the bowsprit. The belly in the chain was gone.

I considered letting out more chain but that would have meant a complicated series of maneuvers. Susan would have to add power from the engine to take the strain off the rodes. When the strain was off, I'd have to reach down with my hand and release the steel bar that locked into the cogs of the windlass and held it immovable.

As Susan cut back the power and the chain paid out, I'd have to control it with the windlass brake while slacking the nylon rode with my other hand. When they were both out enough, I'd have to snub them (the chain with the windlass brake and the nylon with the cleat) and attach the chain hook again. If the brake slipped while I was releasing or engaging the locking bar and the strain of the boat suddenly came back on the chain, I could easily lose a finger or a hand.

I decided not to try, to wait it out and hope for the best. How much worse could it get? We had a third 45-pound CQR plow anchor to throw in an emergency. But for the first time, I began to feel a hint of passivity, a slight inclination to say to myself, "It's gone too far; it's out of my hands."

Back in the cockpit, I saw that our ten-foot inflatable dinghy, which had served us faithfully and well since we'd bought the boat, was floating upside down behind us. As I watched, the wind blew it right side up again; then for a while it left the water completely and streamed out behind us at the end of its painter like a kite. I grabbed the line and shortened it up until the dinghy was snubbed against the hull, but the chafing was worse that way. I tried to haul the whole thing into the cockpit but didn't have the strength.

Finally, I just let it go, feeling that curious passivity gain a little. And, thinking about it later, I realized that the garbage must have blown away by then or it would have been in my way.

For the first time, Susan and I didn't talk about whether the wind had picked up while I was outside. "I don't think the spring line is going to hold much longer," I said, as she handed me the towel, pushing it into my hand as she'd been trained to pass a scalpel to a surgeon in an operating theater. When I tried to check our position against the way point I'd programmed into the GPS, I noticed some unfamiliar symbols next to the numerals. The numerals didn't change when I punched the keys, they didn't respond. There was some malfunction in it, too.

Normally, I would have opened the chart table, taken out the GPS manual, and painstakingly gone through it to find out what the numerals signified. But I didn't. I just didn't seem to have it in me. I sat down on the settee to rest for a minute, and the feeling of inertia gained another notch.

Susan was back in her protected position by the wheelhouse door, staring at me. We were witnessing a performance. What next? Nothing we had been through before in our lives had prepared us for this, but we stayed calm because we had each other. Because everything was going to work out. And because at that moment there was nothing else to do.

Except jump overboard and swim for shore. It would have been easy. But even now, I was pretty sure that the wind wasn't going to get much stronger, that if the spring line broke the chain would hold, that if the chain broke, the emergency anchor on another 200-foot three-quarter-inch nylon rode could replace it. If it didn't we could beach the boat under power, make her fast to some palm trees, and repair the damage when the storm had passed. The big propeller gave so much thrust I still didn't want to put it in gear and risk overriding the rodes.

"Jesus," Susan said, as a banshee gust once again stretched the limits of what we could imagine. Her eyes looked black. There was a heavy, dense thud and the hull lurched backward off the wind for an instant and came up again. "There goes the spring line," I said, on my way out the door. Up on the bow, the anchor chain was rigid as a steel rod. The lunatic wind blew my brain clean. There was nothing to do but let the force carry me back to the cockpit.

My head stayed empty—*too empty to put the engine in gear*—as we sat in the wheelhouse and waited for the chain to break. Or not. The passive feeling gained a few more notches. Five or ten minutes later the chain did break, with the same dense thud. The hull lurched backward again but did not seem to bring up.

Blessed action. The tonic of movement, of carrying out a plan. Susan was at the wheel, applying enough power to move the boat up parallel to the anchor we were still attached to. I was out on the foredeck again, struggling with the emergency anchor. The plan was: when we got into position I'd drop it, and we'd fall back again on the two rodes. I waved my arm, motioning her forward, but the boat had turned far enough broadside to the wind for the high deckhouse to catch its full force. We were blown over at a 45-degree angle and held there, as if the 8,800 pounds of ballast in the keel didn't exist.

We had entered the realm of the storm god. The performance had turned into a demonstration. We were his, now. He set the rules. He made the plans. He wrote the script.

Up on the bow, though, I was so busy reacting that I didn't have time to think. Everything seemed as natural as anything else, as in a dream.

The heavy anchor, the coil of rode, and I slid down the steeply inclined deck to leeward and brought up against the bulwark. I worked slowly and methodically to get things cleared away; the hull now broke the wind so I felt comfortable, as if I could work there forever.

Reality now being beyond question, it didn't surprise me in the least that our little waterproof flashlight, which I'd used on all previous ventures forward, was dimming out. And neither did it come as a great shock, when I finally got the anchor over the side and began to pay out the rode, that there was no strain at the other end. It wasn't holding.

Neither was there much strain on the other rode, when I tested it. Maybe we were still drifting down on it, after having powered upwind to drop the emergency.

Anyway, the job was done. When I stood up to work my way aft, the wind caught me and for a second I was flying. I landed on my knees on our newly nonskidded deck and skidded over the sharp little nubbles, pushed by solid air, wondering how much skin and flesh would be left but, clambering into the tilted cockpit, too busy to look.

"Head her up in the wind!" I yelled at Susan. She was clinging to the wheel to stop herself from slipping down the floor. I closed the wheelhouse door and latched it, and suddenly the enveloping nightmare outside turned stagy and unreal, like a movie from the thirties. I felt her warm, dry body against me as I turned the wheel into the wind and applied power.

We couldn't hear the engine but the tachometer registered 2,200 RPM, full power. It made no difference at all. The boat stayed broadside to the wind, held by it at 45 degrees from the vertical and drifting to leeward, not moving forward or heading up. The depth finder continued to malfunction, but I knew there were coral heads near us and expected one or both of the anchors to snag and pull the bow around. We had shipped no water, and once the bow was back in the wind the boat could straighten up again.

It was as if the anchors didn't exist. We continued to drift to leeward, and now I noticed the engine temperature was into the danger zone, well over boiling. No surprise: it was all part of what was happening. I shut it down, rather than run the risk of ruining it forever; both the propeller and the cooling system intake must have been out of the water.

My watch read 1:10 A.M. I noticed the clasp had been damaged as I'd wrestled with the anchor, so I took it off and carefully put it next to my glasses on the ledge under the wheelhouse windows. It was an old Rolex Oyster diving watch my father had given me when I was eighteen, and I didn't want to lose it. "Well," I said to Susan, "you better call Wotho on the radio and tell them we're drifting"—I checked the compass—"south, out of control."

She called, but (no surprise) there was no answer. Then she said, "Do you think we better get our life jackets on?"

I shrugged and grinned, a strange reflex, but there it was. I'd done all I could. Life jackets were her area of responsibility, her decision. To me they'd always been a little like the EPIRB: a harbinger, a Jonah. An admission of defeat.

"Well, do you?" She sounded angry.

"I guess we should," I said.

The life jackets were inflatable Mae West–type U-shaped vests. You put your head through the upside-down U. The two ends of it were attached to a web belt that you fastened around your waist with a jam buckle. You inflated it by blowing into a tube past a one-way valve. We put them on and stood there on the tilted wheelhouse floor, looking at each other. If anything, seeing Susan in the jacket made things even less real than before.

"I guess we shouldn't blow them up completely right now," I said. "We need to be able to maneuver."

She put her mouth to the tube and blew hers up about two-thirds of the way. When I tried to blow mine up, nothing happened. "Do you have to twist it or something?" I asked. "No air is going in."

"No you don't have to twist it," she said impatiently. "Just blow."

I blew as hard as I could, felt the one-way valve give reluctantly and the vest inflate. I stopped when it was one-third full.

We drifted downwind in silence for a while. Inside the wheelhouse it was still warm and dry. Someone in Kwajalein was speaking English on the radio, about supplies he'd be delivering somewhere the next day. His call sign was "Mr. Bill."

"Sooner or later we're going to hit the reef," I said. "Or an island. I don't know how much time we have, but we've got to think about what we're going to need." My mind felt sluggish. We both seemed slow, in movement and thought, as if we were in a dream.

Gradually we assembled the emergency items that Susan had prepared: a grab bag of flares, another flashlight, a pocket knife, a compass, a signal mirror, a large polyethylene waterproof container with a first-aid kit and drugs, emergency rations, fishing line and hooks, ship's and personal papers, my swim fins, the EPIRB.

"You better put your watch and glasses in the waterproof container," Susan said.

It was an impressive, foresighted idea, but I never got around to implementing it. I was trying to coax my sluggish mind to think of more immediate things we'd need. *Wet suits?* We each had a three-millimeter-thick full-body surfing wet suit that would help buoy us up, protect us from the coral, and keep us warm, but they were in the forepeak locker, and the forepeak was full of stuff from on deck. I started down to get them anyway but Susan begged me not to. She was worried about a propane gas explosion, and indeed the red light of the gas sensor had been on for some time. But more than anything, anything in the world at that moment, she didn't want me to leave her alone.

Looking around the wheelhouse and the cockpit for more accessible things, I noticed the pile of dock lines formerly hidden by the bags of garbage. I selected a fifteen-foot three-quarter-inch line and tied the ends around our waists, using bowlines, a knot that doesn't slip tighter or jam. "Now you don't have to worry," I said. "I'll never leave you." I do believe I was grinning when I said it. "Is it tight enough?"

She pulled at it. "I don't think so."

I undid it and tied it again. I didn't want it too tight in case it snagged on something and she needed to get out of it. "How's that?"

She raised her eyes, looked me full in the face for a full count of five (I remember every count), and nodded.

We finally grounded with the kind of jarring lurch that usually makes a sailor's heart dive overboard, but all I felt was a strange relief. "Well, there's the reef." I nodded wisely. At last something had happened the way we'd thought it would.

The wheelhouse was still warm and cozy. Electronic equipment glowed blue, green, amber, and red. The radio crackled with snatches of talk. And the quarter-inch safety-glass windows still safely sealed us in.

Our keel bounced at shorter and shorter intervals but never completely settled, as the surf picked it up and dropped it over and over again on the coral. I turned on the roof-mounted searchlight and spun it around, looking for land. There was nothing in sight but howling, undifferentiated blackness. The light made it worse.

Eventually, we slid open the heavy teak wheelhouse door and worked our way out into the real world. We were still removed, not really with it, like newborn babies. The tilted hull rose over our heads and broke the unimaginable force of the wind. To leeward a strange white element that was a mixture of water, air, and rocks hissed and rushed. Invisible surf from the lagoon pounded the exposed bottom of the hull at our backs while unseen waves coming across the reef from the open ocean occasionally broke directly into the cockpit and threw us around. There was one thing, though, that we knew for sure. The water was warmer than the air.

Side by side, clutching the things we'd gathered together, we sat on the uptilted cockpit thwart, our feet braced on the downtilted one. All the literature said to stick with the boat until the last minute. There was no question of inflating the life raft—it would have vanished immediately. Our best chance was that the hull might work its way higher and higher onto the shallow reef until it was solid. Meanwhile, the searchlight continued to play on nothingness, unless you called that white fire-hosing element rushing at the leeward edge of the cockpit something.

The boat was already breaking up. When I went into the wheelhouse to look for the diving knife (still connected by our fifteen-foot rope) I saw the leeward windows, closest to the elements, had shattered. The teakwood components of the wheelhouse had started to split off jaggedly from the fiberglass of the hull. Down in the cabin, the red warning light of the propane gas sensor pulsed. Water, mixed no doubt with acid from our new Surrette Type D batteries, was over a corner of the floorboards and climbing up the settee toward our new blue canvas seat covers.

The knife was nowhere to be found. I reeled myself back along the rope to the small wet person alone in the cockpit, sat down next to her again, and put my arm around her. Automatically she leaned forward to clear her hair. She always did that, because she hated to have it pulled.

The last wave held us underwater for too long. It was time to go, and quite easy. We let the soft, almost blood-temperature element carry us clear of the foundering hull.

We were holding hands. The searchlight, now only a few feet up, shone away from us into blackness. The wind was easier, with only our heads in it. The noise was somewhere in the background. We were breathing the element, and it seemed breathable.

Drifting downwind from the hull, Susan's voice came more like a thought. "Where are we?"

I heard my matter-of-fact answer. "I don't know." The searchlight was extinguished, leaving us in darkness. The boat was gone. I blew on the tube to inflate my vest the rest of the way but no air would go in. A wave from the lagoon broke over us, tearing her hand out of mine, scraping my back against the reef. It was not sharp coral here, but weed-covered smooth rock. That was lucky.

Three-foot waves began breaking over us about every fifteen seconds. In the darkness we couldn't see them coming. They were big enough to roll us over and disorient us, to hold us underwater for a few seconds, to scrape us against the rocks but not to smash us. I held Susan around the waist with one arm and with the other held on to my partially inflated life vest.

Its belt had come undone and the U-shaped part had slipped off my head. In the darkness, I couldn't make out how to put it back on. The valve was still stuck. All the things we had brought with us had disappeared by this time, or I would have put on my fins. They would have made swimming twice as easy.

In some of the waves we couldn't hold on to each other. We'd catch our breath, get oriented, get a new grip. Another wave would come and go. We'd start the process over. Then I lost contact with Susan completely. I pulled on the rope. There was no resistance; finally I felt the knot at my fingertips, the empty loop. Nothing was visible.

The energy I used up in the next three or four strokes equaled all the previous energy combined. But she was there, not far away. Quite near. My arm was back around her soft waist and her voice was back inside my head, almost like a thought. "I've come out of my jacket."

She was holding on to it now, like I was holding on to mine. Her wet round head, mouth open and facing up, was in silhouette—against what? Against blackness, and yet I could see it clearly, the first thing I'd been able to see since we'd left the boat. Between waves, I tried to fit the loop back over her shoulders, under her arms. And failed.

We were in deeper water, no more rocks under our feet. Had we drifted out over the reef into the open ocean? Her voice again. "*Hold me up.*" An arm around my neck, a hug, an embrace, like so many times before.

"Not the neck, pet. Not the neck." Obediently, she took her arm away. Her back was to me, my arm was around her waist. A few more waves rolled through and I yelled, "Hold on to your jacket. Hold on to the rope. Are you all right? You have to tell me if you're not all right."

She was making an oddly reassuring noise, "*Oh, oh, oh, oh.*" I knew it well. It was the noise she made when she was scared—as we rowed our tiny inflatable dinghy closer and closer to a sleeping whale or when a car shot out in front of us on the highway without warning. When she made that noise, I knew, there wasn't any real danger. When the danger was real, when our car actually left the road on a rainy, foggy night in upstate New York and flew through the air into a ten-foot-deep culvert; when the seventy-foot shrimp boat broke loose in the last storm in Honduras and began to drift down on us; when the Cessna 172 I was trying to land began to porpoise down the runway—there had been no noise from her at all.

I knew how she hated and feared being rolled in the waves even on a good day, but as long as she made that noise there couldn't be any problem. Things would work out. We were together.

We were underwater again. I opened my eyes and saw her clearly, as if she were outlined in black fire. She was relaxed. There was a little smile on her lips and her eyes were half closed. Her long hair spread out in the water. The top of her head was about a foot under the surface, and when I put my hand under her chin and tried to push up, another wave was there.

She moved farther away from me below the surface and the black light around her was extinguished. I reached out and felt her hair—the soft, fine ends. The tips of my fingers could still feel it as the tickly bubbles and warm currents of the next wave curled around me, wrapped me up, and did what they wanted with me.

I can feel it now.

FROM

INAGUA

BY
Gilbert Klingel

In the 1920s amateur biologist
Gilbert Klingel wanted nothing more than to make
his own adventure while perhaps contributing
something to the study of the world's flora and
fauna. To that end he secured the backing of the
American Museum of Natural History, saved what
money he could, and eventually commissioned a
replica of Slocum's famous 38-foot yawl *Spray* to sail
about the Caribbean observing nature. With his
friend Wallace Coleman, who had never sailed at all,
he set out in 1930 on an 1,800-mile voyage, teach-
ing himself navigation and the finer points of seamanship along the way.

Their first night aboard bodes ill but suggests
something of the nature of their adventure. Having
left Baltimore and anchored for the night in the
Chesapeake Bay, they don pajamas, smoke their
pipes, and go to sleep—only to awake at midnight
to find their new anchor chain broken just below
the surface and the boat drifting about the Bay as a
storm hits. As the wind rips their sails, they almost
comically struggle to get the pandemonium on
deck under control, still in their pajamas.

The excerpt below encapsulates their entire
voyage from the Chesapeake to the island of Inagua

in the Bahamas where they are shipwrecked. For Klingel, the sailing story is only the start of a much longer story, as he stays on the nearly deserted island to study its plant and animal life as an amateur naturalist, a would-be Darwin.

Even during the voyage, however, Klingel is like Thoreau as he philosophizes and writes of the sea and Nature in a style rich with metaphor. The realities of a fierce winter storm scarcely dampen his romanticism. Only when their ship crashes on a coral reef does their struggle to save the ship, and then themselves, turn his prose to immediate realities when confronted by treacherous waters. . . .

///

WE who live in the heart of great cities, who lead our entire lives in deep straight canyons of brick and stone or on the peaceful meadows of farms, forget in the security of our mode of living that there is a sea, that only a short distance from our Manhattan, Philadelphia or Boston lie miles upon miles of restless water, turbulent lonely reaches that stretch away to infinity and beyond. In our complacency we forget that the sea is the greatest geographical feature of the earth and that it has endured unchanged for long ages while continents rose and fell, came into being and disappeared.

The sea is the last wild frontier. Yet here in constant changeful mood, nature reveals the entire scope of her emotions. No sunlit meadow alight with flowers and with gauze-winged insects is more peaceful than a calm ocean, nor is there a land scene more replete with life and vigor than a teeming seascape in the trades where the white caps curling from the tops of the waves hurtle forward and spend themselves in white froth against the dark blue. Then there are the times when Nature, brooding over her wastes, sends the clouds and the fog, deepens the sea tones and spreads a mournful melancholy over the depths. And yet again, the sea is a savage place, she sends the gale screaming from the four corners of the world to remind men that their proper habitat is the land. When this happens the ocean becomes the most awesome spot on earth, a turmoil of mountainous waves, of bubbly froth and swirling breakers. Only those who have lived through a great storm at sea, who have fought and battled with the ocean on its own terms, can know what this means.

We forgot all this. A deep sense of awareness, once latent but brought to the surface by the leaving behind of land ways, filled our minds as we made ready to go. In the pale gray of early dawn we raised our sails and on the wings of a gentle land breeze slipped out of Hampton Roads. It was chill that morning and very quiet save for the soft hissing of the waves at the waterline. In the dim haze near Norfolk we could make out the stark outlines of a large four-master, the schooner *Purnell T. White.* As we watched, her sails rose, one after the other, stretched taut and filled as she came about.

She was a beautiful thing in the early light, sails all pink with the newly risen sun and white hull glinting against the green water. How could we know that in the short space of eight days this ship would be a sodden helpless wreck or that, three years later, refitted and repaired and once again in service, her captain and crew would all be dead men, lost off the Carolina Capes?

Side by side we put to sea, the towering schooner and the tiny yawl. Our mast hardly reached her railing, or so it seemed, as she swept grandly past and headed for the capes and the rising sun. We watched her go with a feeling of friendly interest, for she was built by the same hand that with such care constructed our tiny ship.

Fifteen miles ahead lay the capes, barely discernible in the haze, and beyond the open sea. Thimble Shoal passed astern and then Willoughby. Gently but swiftly, the promised northwest wind died and left us wallowing. The tide, now at full ebb, began to flow again, carrying us back whence we came. It seemed we were destined to remain permanently in the Chesapeake.

Just when we had reached the point of uttermost exasperation Providence, weary of playing a game of checkmate, relented and sent aid in the form of a low-hulled Coast Guard vessel. This Coast Guard ship had seen us slowly drifting on the tide and in a spirit of comradeship had come near to inquire where we were going. We told some uniformed figures on her deck that our landfall was to be San Salvador in the Bahamas, whereupon we could hear the captain say something that sounded like "Holy smokes," could hear the engines reversed, saw him direct a sailor to pass a line with instructions to make it fast. Wondering, we did as directed, and a moment later were pleased to find ourselves being whisked along at the grand pace of eight knots straight for the open sea. Soon we passed the tall black and white lighthouse at Cape Henry, passed the land's edge and went into the blue. And I suppose those jolly Coast Guardsmen would have towed us further had not the line parted and cast us loose.

They came on board for a few minutes, examined our papers, found them in good order and wished us pleasant voyage. As they departed they gave us a salvo of whistle blasts and a chorus of good-byes. Then, as if in answer to our prayers, a gentle breeze came up and wafted us into the broad Atlantic.

Of what took place from the moment of leaving the Coast Guardsmen until about three o'clock the following morning I have little recollection. Much of the events of that afternoon and evening is blotted from my mind and has been reconstructed from Coleman's notes and from what he has told me. It seems that after leaving the Coast Guardsmen we set a course east south east into the open ocean so as to be well clear of the land should the breeze change. We watched the shore slowly fade and in time disappear altogether. And it seems the sun set in a great lowering bank of clouds that hung in dark masses on the horizon. But the northwest wind remained with us and we thought nothing of it. Night came, and the stars that gleamed with it, stars that gleamed with a brightness we had seldom seen before. That is, all save the portion of the sky that was wrapped in gloom and from whence no light came except the faint loom of the lighthouse many miles away. We stood watch on and watch off, one man on deck while the other slept in the cabin below. The first watch came and passed and the second, and all this time the patch of gloom on the horizon spread, cutting off the stars one by one, blotting out the milky way, and drawing a dark cloak over the zenith. And by the time of the third watch the entire firmament was drowned in gloom and we moved only by the pale shine of the running lights and by the faint gleam of the binnacle. All beyond the decks was blackness, though a blackness that seemed alive if one could judge by the myriad water sounds that came from off the sea's surface.

A certain heaviness seemed to lie over the ocean that night, a heaviness that oppressed though it was cold on deck and the wind was sharp. And this feeling of heaviness increased when, toward the end of the third watch, the wind slackened and hauled to another quarter. Still we did not feel alarmed but continued on our way. Coleman was on deck and he had made the necessary wheel and sheet adjustments for the change of wind. It was then about two in the morning. At three o'clock he came down in the cabin and shook me.

"You had better come on deck," he said, "there is something brewing."

And there was. Even down in the cabin we could hear a new tenor in the sounds coming off the water, a certain restlessness that stirred above the wave whisperings.

We glanced at the barometer. It was extremely low. The lowest we had ever seen. Hurriedly we struggled into oilskins and jackets and ascended to the deck. From out of the sea were coming great smooth swells, much too large for the wind that was blowing. We knew what that meant.

For a moment I stood beside Coleman at the wheel.

"I think we had better take in some sail," I muttered, "while we can."

Hardly were the words out when the thing happened. A freak wave rushing from out of the darkness caught our stern, lifted it high out of the water and, catching the bow as it passed, swung our tiny ship to one side. And as the stern rose, the great spreading mainsail with its heavy boom swept to center and then jibed with a sickening crash. Hundreds of pounds of heavy canvas, iron and wood driven by a strong wind caught me a smashing blow full in the face and dropped me senseless to the railing.

How long I lay there I do not know. Coleman groped for my inert body in the darkness and hauled me to the wheel box where he sat with one leg entwined about my waist to prevent my slipping over the low railing. Then from out of the ocean came a low moaning sound that momentarily increased in volume, a swelling chorus of wind-lashed waves combining in a wild medley that knows no description. Only those who have heard it will understand. The thing we had most feared had come.

With a surge of cold air the storm broke. Our tiny vessel, still under full sail, heeled far to the blast, heeled until the lee ports were under water, until it seemed that we must turn over. And Coleman in all the welter of spray and churning water struggled in the dark to secure my body so he would be free to shorten sail; with one hand he spun the wheel to relieve the strain. Soon huge waves from out of the darkness were washing our craft from stem to stern. The wonder of it is that the sails were not blown away or torn to ribbons. But by some miracle they held. Before leaving our native Chesapeake Bay, the oystermen and yachtsmen had laughed at our heavy sails and rigging, were amused at the canvas they said was thick enough for a three-masted schooner. But this same stoutness saved us that night and in the days to come when without our forethought we would have been lost indeed.

A full half hour passed before I regained consciousness. At first I was only dimly aware of what was going on, but as surge after surge of cold water swept over me and dribbled into the scuppers I was brought into wakefulness. My head ached excruciatingly. And I was cold. Bitterly so— drenched with water and lashed by the icy wind. I can dimly recall Coleman's leg pressed into my side, could feel it strain and flex as he struggled with the wheel. I tried to remember what had happened but could not, nor can I to this day. On one knee I rose, fell again and then painfully and slowly struggled to a sitting position. My neck and shoulder muscles seemed almost torn from their fastenings. Ten more minutes passed before I was fully awake. Then, in spite of the pain and violent headache, I began to realize the gravity of the situation.

We must get those sails in.

As soon as Coleman saw that I was able to fend for myself he threw the ship into the wind so that we might reduce canvas. Then began one of the most grueling half hours we have ever spent. Reefing sails in normal weather is a simple enough job, consuming on a ship as small as ours only fifteen or twenty minutes. But in the midst of a storm, with the ship plunging and pitching, with waves sweeping the deck from one end to the other, it is a difficult task. As though this were not enough, every jolt of the boom and shake of the canvas sent shooting pains darting up and down my head. The greatest job was getting the mainsail down. This task took the combined effort of both of us and our utmost strength. The wind would catch the sail and with the force of a titan belly out the slack canvas, jamming the jaws against the mast. Only by catching it between squalls and exerting our united weights on the downhaul were we able to get it down and reefed.

We saved our sails. The immediate danger was over. We were so exhausted by our efforts we had to sit for a few moments on the deck to recover. Our hands and fingers were torn and burned by the whipping of rope. In all the melee the jib lazy-jacks had chafed through and were flying out from the masthead like pieces of string. Reefing a jib in a storm with the lazy-jacks gone is a nasty job. You must creep out along the footropes, feeling with your heels for the next strand, and hope that the oncoming waves do not wash you from the bowsprit to which you are holding with all your strength. As the surging water sweeps up and the bowsprit dips you are plunged over your head into icy water only to come up and be buffeted by the wild flapping of the sail. Lazy-jacks hold a sail in an even bundle, but with these gone the canvas becomes a battering ram that thrashes and thunders in the grip of the wind.

Even with the sails reefed we were not out of danger. We had to continue to beat off the coast, for the wind was coming out of the northeast and we were a bare forty miles from shore. Forty miles is not much in a screaming northeaster that in a few hours could pile one on the beach. Though we would have liked to have hove-to until morning we dared not, but beat on into the dark.

The hours of the first night passed and morning came, but the storm did not abate. Instead, it increased in intensity and low clouds scudded just above the water. By the light from the east we could see that the sea was no longer green but a deep indigo, a dull blue that showed in intricate openwork between the froth patches. We were in the Gulf Stream. And, in verification, a yellow, berry-floated strand of sargassum weed drifted by and disappeared in the wake. That was a comfort. We knew then that we could heave-to and get some rest. We sorely needed it. For we were wet and cold; our fingers were fast growing numb.

With the coming of full light, even though we thought the wind could not increase in volume, it redoubled its vigor. With a sudden blast it hurled out of the north and caught our little ship in its full grip. Coleman seized a lifeline and held on to keep from being swept overboard. The sudden surge momentarily flattened the water and whipped great blinding sheets of spray from the surface. Over went the hull until the deck was at such an angle that we could not stand, but slid on our knees. A convulsive shudder shook the boat from sprit to rudder and, with lee decks completely hidden, she leaped ahead.

But this was only the beginning. In a few minutes we could barely see the bow, so dense was the spray. The din was terrific. From out of the sea came a shrieking, sighing sound unlike anything we had ever heard before. It was the sound of wind-tortured water and the bass roar of huge breakers. Only those who sail the sea in small ships, who tread decks a foot or so above the surface, can hear this. It is a sound that hangs close to the sea's surface, an indescribable medley that those who travel on large steamers do not know. After the passing of ten years, when civilization and city living has dulled much of the details of the great storm, we can still hear those gale sounds, they are so indelibly impressed on our memories. Perhaps the most awesome moment is that in which one discerns vaguely through the driving mist the form of a great wave advancing before the wind. Then the wave thins at the top, curls, and in a ferocious roar sweeps all before it. It is a deep-throated sound, sullen and powerful. And the rigging sounds—low mournful whistles rising and falling in weird crescendos with the speed of the gale. Only the wind about the house eaves in a winter blizzard approaches it in tenor. Nor is this all, for there are the ship sounds, mighty creakings of wood, the groanings of mast and boom, the twanging of taut ropes and the noisome clatter from down below where loose objects are battering back and forth.

That blast nearly finished us. But like the stout vessel she was, the *Basilisk* bore under the strain and carried on. We were growing weak from exhaustion and cold. We could not stay on deck much longer, for the waves that were spilling aboard were tremendous and bid fair to sweep us into the sea. We had prepared for this emergency, however, and loosened the sea anchor from its lashings on the cabin top. Laboriously we made it fast to a heavy hawser and eased it over the bow. Swiftly the big canvas funnel filled out as the ship drifted back. In a moment the hawser was taut and the bow in the wind. We could now go below and let the storm blow itself out.

There was not much else to do. The wind was blowing so hard that we could no longer stand on deck. Swiftly we opened the companionway slide and slipped below, slamming it shut before another wave came aboard. Our comfortable cabin! It was a shambles. Much of the cargo that we had so carefully stowed and boxed had broken loose and was strewn about. Pots and pans, a barrel of potatoes, stove lids, notebooks, charts and tin cans littered the floor in little piles. And with each lurch these piles would slither from one end of the cabin to the other. For a moment they would remain quiescent, then with the tilt of the ship gather speed and bang into the distant bulkhead. Then back again with a crash, intermingled with the tinkling of glass and the duller sounds of metal. It was inconceivable the number of articles that had come loose. Items that we had nailed tightly in boxes and bins. How they ever got away was difficult to understand. But they did.

The coal stove in the galley was a mess. The iron doors were opening and banging with a clatter that sounded like the rush of a gang of riveters working overtime and anxious to go home. With every wave that swept the deck a gush of salt water came down the stove pipe and burst from between the grates in a miniature flood. That meant another trip to the deck with rope and canvas. We tried to salvage some of the material drifting about on the cabin floor. It was useless. As soon as one object was stowed another came loose. The flat stove lids replaced on the range jumped off again when the ship suddenly plunged to one side and then back with a severe jolt. This same jolt sent the pair of us spinning the length of the cabin to pile in a sodden heap at the far end. It was impossible to stand. Progress was feasible only by clinging tightly to fast objects and waiting for a lull. The best method was crawling. Even then the lurching and pitching would hurl us reeling into the far wall and back again. After a time we gave it up and let the jumble take care of itself.

Our bunks were made of canvas stretched between metal frames. On our knees and between slitherings we slacked the canvas until it formed a deep hollow; then we piled in. Only thus were we able to keep our positions. As it was, we had to maintain a constant grip on the sides to keep from being thrown out. We could not sleep. It was difficult even to doze. Hour passed hour in monotonous succession. Every now and then we could hear something give, vague splinterings and tearings that came to us through the howling of the wind. Time and time again great waves would smash aboard. We could see them coming through the ports. We thanked the gods that we had full steamer ports of three quarter inch glass instead of the flimsy things generally used on vessels as small as ours. We could see these huge waves mount up and up, could see the

bow dip as if to plunge into the depths, could see the oncoming mountains suddenly rise and curl and then break in a dark blue welter of foam
and solid water. When they hit it was as if we had run into a stone wall.
How wood and iron could hold together under such hammerings was inconceivable. Suddenly the cabin would be darkened as the mass swept
over the deck, burying it under several feet of indigo water. Then the
ports would become luminous green holes in which danced hundreds of
bubbles. Shuddering, the ship would lift, spilling the water off the decks
in white froth.

At about two o'clock the sea anchor tore loose from the hawser with
a dull snap. In a trice the bow swung around until we were broadside to
the wind. Then, hurling out of the sea, came a tremendous wave that
caught the cabin full amidships. I was suddenly lifted and thrown out of
my bunk across the full width of the cabin on top of Coleman. On the return lurch we were both spilled on the floor. We struggled to our feet
and as soon as the water had cleared, climbed on deck, slamming the
companionway hatch hurriedly behind us.

The scene that greeted us was awesome. All that was left of the jib
lazy-jacks were half a dozen short pieces of rope, fuzzy frayed things only
one-tenth of their original length. The remainder had whipped away a
little at a time. The bowsprit shrouds, steel cables, had torn loose on one
side and the attached footropes hung in a jumble. Part of the solid oak
railing was in splinters and an iron boom-rest had been yanked from its
fastenings, carrying with it shredded pieces of wood and metal. Two
water casks lashed to wooden supports were smashed and the anchor
chain had been lifted out of its coil box and was hanging straight down
in the depths. A full ton of it. Getting this last back on board nearly
broke our backs. We had unshackled it from the anchor before leaving
Hampton Roads so as to have a perfectly clear deck, and now we could
not get it around to the winch to haul it in.

Hurriedly twirling the wheel we coaxed the ship around until we
were flying under bare poles. But we were in an ugly position. Somewhere to the west and not too many miles away was Hatteras with its
maze of shoals and streamers of thundering surf. There was no help for
it but to beat into the storm again. Swinging about we got under four
reefs and once again breasted the gale.

By this time it was getting dark. In all these hours we had eaten nothing, nor had we thought of food. Coleman crawled up into the hold and brought back a tin of canned beef which we devoured uncooked.

Captain Joshua Slocum, in telling of his voyage around the world in the original *Spray*, had claimed that for hundreds of miles his little ship had steered herself as accurately as if there had been a man at the wheel. Provided, of course, that the wind remained in the same quarter. The feat was accomplished by trimming and adjusting sail and rudder so that there was a perfect balance fore and aft. This claim has been disputed many times, but without foundation. We owe our lives to this one feature. For that evening, exhausted and weary, chilled to the marrow, unable to remain longer on deck, yet afraid to let the ship scud before the wind, we adjusted sail and rudder as Slocum had described. And in all that wild melee of storm the grand little ship plunged sturdily along, straight as an arrow, for the center of the ocean.

All through that night she sailed with not a soul on deck, tossed and beaten by the worst winter storm of 1929–30. Miles away the great schooner *Purnell T. White*, in whose company we had put to sea, was also fighting the gale and waging a losing battle. And far and wide, north and south of us that night on the broad Atlantic, sturdy steamers were sending out S.O.S. calls or limping into port with smashed houses and twisted decks. On and on we pressed, plunging through the waves, bobbing to the top and sliding down the valleys, proof that the old sea captain had not lied. A gallant little ship, the *Basilisk*. There should be more like her.

The second day passed and the third, and when the fourth dawned in a gloom of gray we did not think we would live to see the evening. We were so exhausted by then that we could scarcely crawl from the deck to the cabin and up again. The exertion of adjusting sheets was so great that we would have to lie on the wet deck for fifteen or twenty minutes to recover. The wind was blowing as hard as ever and the waves were sickening to behold. Up, up they towered, great sweeping mountains that seemed to reach to the sky. If ever we felt small and unimportant, it was then.

Once a wave broke over the top of the mast. *Forty-two feet five inches* our mast measured, and this breaking wave topped it by a *yard*. Coleman was down below when it struck and I was crouched by the wheel box so that I would avoid the full force of the wind. Suddenly, and without warning, a great wall of water seemed to rise in front of the ship, rose with terrific speed, forced up by some tremendous pressure beneath, rose and towered above the mast. For a brief second I could see pale light shining through it, could see a yellow strand of sargassum weed high above my head. Then down it came with an ear-splitting crash. With stunning force it hit the deck, threw me against the aft railing and buried the ship under tons of water. It seemed that we would never come up. All I can remember is choking and fighting to get to my feet as the mass poured over the stern.

A minute later a dazed Coleman cautiously opened the companionway slide a few inches. He looked groggy and a great bruise showed on the side of his face. He had been clinging to his bunk trying to get a few moments' rest when suddenly the wave hit. In a brief second all light was blotted out and tons of falling liquid hit the deck. Water squirted in great streams through the seams in the hatch and companionway slide, dousing the cabin with water. For an awful minute all was dark and then with a sickening lurch he had been thrown out of his bunk. He came on deck fully expecting to find me washed away.

Three similar waves boarded us that night, straining the woodwork and opening many of the deck seams. Then it was that we saw the picture of the "Gulf Stream" run water. Gulf Stream water too, the sea's turn to laugh!

And though we did not think we would last through the night, we somehow plunged on, heading ever further into the ocean. In all these hours we had taken no sights, had no idea of our whereabouts other than by dead reckoning. We felt by this time, however, that we could afford to turn tail to the storm and run before it. As Coleman put it—"If we are going to hell, we might as well go flying." Running before the wind eased the strain somewhat, but was risky business. Added to the danger of jibing was the hazard of being pooped by a following wave. But by this time we did not particularly care. Anything seemed better than hammering into the gale,—hour after hour of terrific punishment and not getting anywhere was wearing on our nerves. Due south we headed the *Basilisk* and there began one of the most thrilling portions of the entire voyage.

With the speed of an express train we tore down the massive watery hillsides, tore on and into the south. Hour after hour the miles reeled behind us and were lost in the foam. While tearing thus before the wind we witnessed one of the most magnificent sights that the sea has to offer.

We had just mounted the crest of an exceptionally large roller when from under our bows burst a great porpoise. Another came and another until the water fairly seethed with them. And at the same moment, from out of the ocean, from the depths that just before had been lifeless, from as far as we could see on the crest of that gigantic wave, burst forth other porpoises leaping and hurtling toward the ship. There must have been hundreds of them. Sleek black things that surged and dived in effortless gambol, all heading for our bows. There they collected in a heavy mus- cled swarm, gloriously graceful, active and free. Weary and tired as we were we could not help but feel a tingle of pleasure at the sight. And as mysteriously as they came they disappeared. All vanished as one, as if by given signal they slipped into the depths at the same moment and were gone. There was only the swirl of foam and bubbles where a minute be- fore was activity.

The porpoises made us feel better, helped to take away some of the lonely feeling that had come over us in our exhaustion. They were the first life that we had seen since leaving the land. Later the same day two petrels swept by, little black things hardly visible through the spray. We could hear them calling, a plaintive whistle that somehow seemed to have a certain sad timbre. How could they live in that chaos of water hundreds of miles from land,—how could they survive days of gale with only the spray-swept water to rest upon? But they do. Mother Carey's chickens! Brave little things, that fly on sickle-shaped wings close to the water's surface, feeding on floating tid-bits, stray things that the sea gives up, subsisting on tiny crustaceans, larval fishes and pelagic eggs. Storm and calm, hurricane and smooth sea, it is all the same to Mother Carey's chickens. Their niche in the scheme of things is not an easy one.

The gale lasted nearly a week and a half. Ten days of torture and mis- ery. There were hours on end when we thought that every boarding wave would be the one to split us wide open and send us to the bottom. We had taken in hundreds of gallons of water. The cabin floor boards had come up and were sloshing about, mixed with a jumble of wreckage. We were weary and tired, sick of the sea and the storm. We did not know where we were. There had been no sun to take sights from. The chronometer had stopped, beaten into somnolence by the terrific jolt- ing. But it was becoming warmer. We no longer needed coats on deck. Long ago we had discarded every bit of useless apparel. In times of stress it is common custom to be rid of all superfluous appurtenances. We had thrown our shoes aside—could keep the deck better in bare feet. Our hands were a sorry sight. Calluses, open blisters, deep red seams, raw scale covered our fingers and palms. It seemed we had been to sea for an eternity. Ten days. In ten days we had got down to elementals. We were no longer concerned with a scientific program—we would worry with that later—if we survived.

But one morning the wind dropped, the sun burst from the clouds and nature once again smiled. Hungrily we drank in the warmth, basked in the golden light that streamed from the sky. We had almost forgotten there was a sun. It cheered us immeasurably. And though from out of the north the waves still came piling they did not break, but lifted us gently and passed on as if to say, "There you are, we wouldn't hurt you."

From out of the sea came flying fish, gliding creatures that skimmed from one wave crest to another. They cheered us too. It is good to see live things around even though they are no more than fishes. With hope renewed we set about straightening ship. It was a herculean task. As if half afraid the sea was playing us tricks, we carefully opened the hatch and bailed water. Gallons and gallons of it we dumped into the sea. Even when we had it all out, the cabin was still the dampest place imaginable, so much so that in the evening, rather than sleep below with all the wreckage to remind us of what we had been through, we lay on the deck beneath the stars.

We adjust ourselves quickly to new conditions. With life no longer a struggle for existence our thoughts once again turned to the program before us. Where were we? We wished to make the island of San Salvador where Columbus first made landfall on that memorable morning in 1492. Here we were to check on certain faunal conditions before proceeding to other islands to continue our investigations. As nearly as we could estimate from dead reckoning we were about eight hundred miles off the Florida Coast. With the chronometer stopped we could not figure longitude. Latitude was an easier matter though we had to break open the cabinet drawer to get out the sextant, so swollen was the wood from the wetting it had received. Noon sights showed us to be in the latitude of Nassau. We decided to continue south until we reached the parallel of San Salvador and then make westing on the prevailing trade winds.

On and on we sailed. At first we were almost afraid to shake out full canvas, so fearful of the wind had the storm made us. But the continued sunlight brightened our outlook and we dipped gently on the wings of a mild breeze. A day passed and another, and still no sight of land. Once in the early morning, shortly after the sun had risen, a yellow-billed tropic bird had come out of the west, circled in the blue and turned back again. The following morning we saw a man-of-war bird and it, like the tropic bird, circled and disappeared westward. Land was somewhere over there. How far we did not know. The latitudes of Eleuthra and Cat Island came and passed and still no land showed up. We must be too far to the east. Noon sights gave us the figures 24 degrees 3 minutes. San Salvador was due west.

As we swung the bow toward the afternoon sun the wind shifted contrary to all rules of the trades and began blowing briskly out of the west. Soon we were having hard going. Was the sea never to be through playing with us? We held a consultation and decided to continue south again in the hope of sighting Crooked or Mariguana Islands, or, failing these, the Caicos group. At any of these we could rest, clean ship and work back to San Salvador at leisure after once establishing our location. We must investigate these anyway and were bound to no order. On we went again. Ever southwards. Still no land. The wind continued beating out of the west cutting up a choppy, but not dangerous sea. Hour after hour we sailed, straining our eyes for a glimpse of green turf. There was nothing but rolling waves, yellow patches of sargassum weed and white caps. Several times Coleman climbed to the masthead. He could see nothing. Crooked and Mariguana were nowhere visible. Caicos then. Noon showed us to be exactly on the Caicos latitude. Water, everywhere water. We had never before realized that there was so much of it in the world.

Disgusted, we busied ourselves about the ship. At least we couldn't miss Hispaniola. We would sight it at sunrise. Coleman went below to tend to some duties and I became interested in the wheel ropes that had slackened badly and needed attention. Already the sun was setting, lowering in great banks of orange and red cloud. In a few moments it would be dark and I wanted to have the rudder in good shape. Busily I worked on, tightening the line and adjusting it about the drum. Casually I looked up.

There, strewn over the horizon, was land. Little mounds of it stretching in isolated lumps far in both directions.

"Land," I yelled down the companionway.

Coleman came bounding out and swarmed up the mast. It was land all right, good solid land silhouetted by the sinking sun. We had never thought that land could look so good. With big grins we shook hands in congratulation. Coleman went below again and returned a moment later with a pencil and a piece of soggy paper to make a sketch. He said it was such a pleasant moment he wished to remember it. As for myself, I did nothing, just stood there and gazed. Now at last we could rest and begin our work.

How little we knew!

IN THE LATE AFTERNOON of the following day we slowly climbed a low sandy bluff. At the top we paused a moment and then sank wearily to the ground. Before us the sand sloped away to a wide beach on which the shadows were lengthening rapidly. Even as we watched, little breakers slipped up the damp soil, hissed and sighed as they passed over the sand grains, and slid back again. As they slid they left on the beach myriad small objects—queer-shaped things that turned and rolled in the tide. Wreckage! Flotsam and jetsam that the sea had done with and was giving up to the land. Bits of spars, rope, sodden books, tin cans, instruments, bottles, boxes—and a picture of the Gulf Stream showing a man lying on the deck of a dismasted vessel, sullenly watching a shark that was circling by. The sea's turn to laugh. Journey's end.

Journey's end, indeed. Beyond the waves that sighed on the beach, beyond a lagoon of pale green water, glistened a line of seething white surf. A white frothy line that moved and pulsed, and emitted a constant throaty roar. The sound of breakers crashing on a coral reef. Squarely in the center of that seething line lay all that remained of a stout vessel. Each wave that rolled in lifted the hull a foot or so and with a resounding crash dropped it heavily into the spreading branches of coral. A sad ending for a stout vessel that had weathered a great winter storm and had gallantly carried its crew to safety when larger and better manned ships had gone to the bottom.

Journey's end and dream's end. There would be no sailing the isles of the Indies. It was a bitter dose. The irony of the thing was that after going through so much, after living through so much misery, so much cold and wetness, after all this, after coming through a great winter storm we should meet disaster on the very last stretch. And irony on top of irony; the wind that was crashing the breakers on the reef was the usual trade that we had expected to take us westward to San Salvador. Too late now, too late to do us any good. The breeze that should have carried us to safety was tearing our vessel apart and spreading our gear on the bottom of the sea.

But worst of all was the stinging fact that we had met disaster in a near calm. There was no excuse of storm or heavy wind or great waves. The sea was like a millpond when Nemesis boarded us. As flat and calm as a sea can be, save for a long gentle swell from out of the east. Treacherous ocean! When wind and wave had failed she had still one trick up her figurative sleeve, a trick that we should have known about. The current—the smooth gliding current that, welling up from the cool depths, glides its invisible intangible way to the surface. The current had caught us unawares.

In the cool long hours before the coming of new day it had caught us, had slowly, gently pulled us from our way, had quietly without a sound dragged us to the waiting coral. Then in a sudden last surge the swells had caught us and dashed us onto the cruel coral. And the sea, in a last boisterous shout of glee, had sent the wind, the trade wind to bring the matter to conclusion. The sea had won.

After sighting land the evening before, reaction had set in and we had fallen into a deep sleep. With the sinking of the sun the wind had died, leaving us to wallow in a calming ocean. For the first time since the ending of the storm we slept below, utterly weary, confident that with hove-to sails we would wake in the same spot in the morning. We would then approach the land, establish our location and proceed to the nearest port. All this while a strong current was carrying us northward where it swept around a point of land. But just before reaching this point it set directly into a maze of coral and reefs. On and on we drifted, nearer, ever nearer until the roar of the breakers must have reached the decks. But down below we slept on, exhausted by the days just past.

With a frightening crash we hit. Both Coleman and I were thrown to the floor. Dazed and sleepy, startled by the roar that came from outside, we rushed frenziedly for the deck. As we reached it another swell came from out of the ocean, lifted the ship and with a terrific lurch threw it on one side. Coleman grasped the railing and saved himself, but the lurch threw me spinning the entire length of the deck, through the jib sheets and over the bow into the foam. For a brief second I remember hurtling through the air, could dimly see the swirling surf beneath, and then plunged into the water. As I went down I was rolled over and over by the comber and into the arms of a great coral branch that held me in a strong painful grip. For another second I lay dazed. Off in the dark I could vaguely make out the mound of another roller, black against the stars. On and on it came, rose, curled and made ready to break. With a shout of alarm I quitted my painful bed of coral and dived headlong to one side. And as I dived the stricken ship rose on the tide and came down on the coral I had just left. Had I remained I would have been ground to a bloody pulp. The wave that so nearly finished me, rolled me a few feet further and then sucked me back to the bow. Hurriedly grasping the sprit chain I hauled myself inboard and onto the deck.

We made one last effort to save the ship. If we could only get one of our small boats overboard with an anchor and drop it behind the reef, we might still by quick action on the winch pull ourselves clear. With a knife that Coleman dashed into the cabin to secure we cut the lashings of the first boat and dropped it over the rail. Even as we did so another roller caught us amidships, lifted us slightly and brought us down on the skiff. It was mashed as flat as a flounder. The other boat fared a little better but was swamped a moment later.

It was no use. We were hard and fast. Every swell that came in carried us a foot or so further. A second later the rudder snapped off and was washed into the lagoon beyond the reef where it sank to the bottom. There was but one recourse—to save as much food and equipment as possible. A wind was coming up, the trade for which we had waited in vain. If we were to get anything ashore we must do it quickly. Food and water first. Particularly water. We knew that some of these islands were barren—dry waterless places where one could soon die of thirst. Quickly as we could on the careening deck we cut the lashings of the watercasks and with mighty heaves threw them into the surf. Disregarding everything else for the moment we jumped overboard, severely cutting ourselves on the jagged coral, and between crashing rollers edged the casks over the reef and into the calm waters of the lagoon. Satisfied that they would not float out to sea or be broken by surf we battled our way back to the ship again. Our feet and legs by now were bleeding freely from coral cuts and we were scratches and bruises from head to foot. Once again on the ship, we fought our way through the foam to the cabin. It was full of water. Somewhere underneath, the planking had torn loose and the bitter salt was surging in in a torrent.

The floor boards had come up and were rushing back and forth. They had the force of battering rams. The cabin was a fright. We leaped for our prize possessions. Frantically I clawed a cabinet apart to save my camera. It had accompanied me in all my jaunts in Haiti, in South America and at home. I would rather have lost a finger than that camera. Coleman dived for his microscope and other valuables. Holding them high above our heads to spare them further wettings we made our way to the deck. It was now careened at such an angle that we could not walk on it. We slid into the water and struggled for the lagoon.

Back again. This time for the sextant, motion picture camera, ship papers, collecting equipment and choice books. Some we got ashore, some we did not. It was a herculean task. The reef was the worst of all, though swimming the eighth-mile lagoon was not easy. By the third trip the hull had heeled so far over that we could swim directly into the companionway. It was heartbreaking. All our valuable instruments and materials were being washed back and forth. Even as we tried to salvage them great rollers would dash in the open companionway, snatch them from our fingers and wash them out on the reef. The white sand bottom for yards around was strewn with glittering tins, paper and brass. The cabin was a dangerous place. Floating boards, boxes and weighty containers were being hurled about with every entering wave. Every now and then the ship would turn and roll on the opposite side. Then with a mighty rush all these floating things would charge the length of the cabin and slam into the farthest bulkhead.

Coleman had a narrow escape. He was in the cabin alone trying to retrieve a valuable item that was packed low down in one of the lockers. The missing object could not be found and he had dropped on his knees holding his breath underwater so that he could better feel with his hands. Without warning the ship lurched far to one side, rushing all the water to his part of the cabin, carrying with it loose boards and a floating bunk mattress. One of these boards and the mattress wedged above his body, pinning him tightly against the cabinet. He fought like a madman to get free but could not budge the material. Still fighting, he could feel the breath leave him in little bubbles, could feel himself growing weaker and weaker, saw everything turn black. And just when he was about to lapse into unconsciousness a roller surged into the massed wreckage and released him. He struggled to the companionway, crawled to the deck and lay there panting and coughing water.

Morning came and passed and by late afternoon we were still working. All this while the wind had grown stronger until the hour arrived when we knew it was too dangerous to return to the wreck. Wearily we swam ashore for the last time, plodded through the soft beach sand, climbed the bluff back of the beach and, there, exhausted, flung ourselves on the ground.

The sea had won.

NIGHT SAIL

BY
Jonathan Hall

As many of the selections in this collection demonstrate, sailing a small boat along a challenging shore can be dangerous, especially at night when waves and winds threaten. At such times ocean voyagers at least have the consolation that they're not about to hit a rocky ledge or lee shore, which can be just as dangerous to the boat and anyone on it as a capsize or pitchpole in open water, or more so. In this unpublished memoir Jonathan Hall describes his first night sail off coastal Maine and the terrors and doubts it raised in a boy alone in big waters. His creative responses to a situation involving a dead flashlight and invisible chart make for delightful reading.

///

IN September of 1962, I embarked on a solo night sail in a small boat on Penobscot Bay. I had not planned this sail. It came about as the result of a combination of circumstances that made it an irresistible temptation. I should have known better, for that summer I had been reading Slocum's account of his solo circumnavigation, and so was all too aware of the difficulties of solo sailing, and, in particular, the perils of solo night sailing in dangerous coastal waters. Slocum, who had had more than his share of sailing adventures, referred to the time he was lost at night off the northwest coast of the Horn as his "greatest sea adventure."

Penobscot Bay is not the Horn, but neither was I Slocum.

I had learned to sail at age ten in the waters around Castine, Maine, in upper Penobscot Bay with my grandfather, who had acquired a harbor-front cottage there in the fifties where I spent most summers. My parents had inherited his house on Water Street after his death in 1959 and, although my grandmother had sold his boat, I continued to spend summers in Castine working at local boatyards and restaurants and borrowing or renting boats to get out on the water at every opportunity, for during those years sailing was my passion.

My original plan for this sail had nothing to do with either solo or night. I planned to rent a small boat and, with two friends, cruise down to Monhegan Island, about ten miles out in the Atlantic off the mouth of Penobscot Bay, a four- or five-day round-trip cruise, depending on the weather. But last-minute family contingencies required that my friends forgo the return trip.

Although I had never done any solo cruising, I was confident that I could manage the return trip alone, and so on a bright clear day I found myself in a rented 18-foot daysailer named the *Bessie V* sailing with my two friends down Penobscot Bay before a brisk northwesterly. We stopped for the night in Tenants Harbor, and the next day we sailed the ten miles out into the open Atlantic to Monhegan Island. My friends left for the mainland on the mailboat the next morning, which was foggy and windless. Since I couldn't sail, I spent the rest of the morning exploring the island trails and reprovisioning.

The island was impressively different from anything I had ever experienced. It is ringed on its northern and eastern sides by cliffs hundreds of feet high in places. The mainland was not visible that day, so I had the sense of the island being much farther out in the ocean than it actually was, and for the first time experienced some nervousness at the prospect of sailing back alone. This feeling intensified when, exploring Lobster Cove on the southern side of the island, I came upon the scattered remains of the iron seagoing tug, *Fitzgerald*. The twisted and rusted wreckage was a dramatic reminder of the potential power and danger of the sea. I was amazed to learn from the curator of the local museum that there had been no fatalities when it went aground in fog while towing a coal barge.

By midafternoon the fog had cleared and the wind was rising from the southwest, so I prepared to sail. Looking over the chart, and considering the direction of the wind, tide (still coming in), and the time of day, I thought I would try for Port Clyde, a run of about nine nautical miles. Since I would be running with the wind and tide and sailing pretty much as the crow flies, I thought I could make it in three or four hours. If the wind dropped or changed direction and I didn't make it by sundown, it looked like there were some islands between Monhegan and Port Clyde that would make secure anchorages. I took particular note of Benner and Allen Islands, because the narrow stretch of water between them was designated "Georges Hbr," so I assumed there would be a good anchorage there.

I paused in my preparations to watch the mailboat *Laura B* dock. The passengers disembarked and walked down the pier above me, some glancing down at the float where *Bessie V* was docked. I resumed my preparations as though I were on stage. It is slightly embarrassing to recall the self-conscious thoughts that passed through my mind at the time. I felt proud to be the skipper of a small boat and sailing alone, and I wondered if the people walking by were as impressed with me as I was with myself. I speculated on their thoughts, putting into their heads the admiring (and slightly envious) thoughts I would have if I encountered someone as young as I sailing his own boat far from home.

The last person off the mailboat was the Captain, and as he passed by, I was surprised to see him looking intently down at my boat, then turn and start down the ramp to the float. I felt somewhat alarmed, thinking that, perhaps, he was going to tell me that I had to get off the float for some reason.

He approached the boat, greeted me, and, putting one foot on my deck while steadying himself with a shroud, asked what kind of boat I was sailing. It was clear that my alarm was unfounded. I reluctantly admitted that the boat was borrowed, and told him that I really didn't know what kind it was. He said it looked like one he had sailed down on Cape Cod when he was my age, and since he already had one foot on the deck, I invited him aboard to tell me more. He asked the name of the boat, perhaps thinking it was the very same boat he had sailed, and said he thought she was a Golden Eye and had been built by a famous builder down on the Cape whose name he couldn't remember. He asked me where I had come from and where I was headed. I told him, and he commented that it was a long sail in a small boat, but he knew from his own experience that she was pretty seaworthy and that these days people were crossing the Atlantic in things smaller.

I thought I should take further advantage of what I assumed to be his extensive knowledge of local waters, and asked him what he had heard about the weather. He told me that there was talk of a low-pressure front moving in Thursday, but that he hadn't seen a sign of it yet. I then asked about Georges Harbor, pointing to it on the chart. He said he thought there was good holding ground in there, though it could be pretty rolly when the seas were up and the wind from the south. He then stood up to take his leave and told me he'd look for me on his five o'clock run back to Port Clyde.

I set sail in clearing weather about half an hour later. The wind dropped long before I reached Port Clyde so I turned on the outboard and made for what I hoped was Georges Harbor. Around five I saw the mailboat passing a mile or so west of me silhouetted against the bright evening sky. I wondered if the captain recognized my boat. The sunset was very beautiful, but I noticed a mackerel pattern in the high cirrus clouds and realized that they probably indicated the approaching front of which the captain had warned me.

As I approached Allen and Benner Islands I wondered how I was going to anchor singlehanded, something I had never done before. I had lashed the anchor with excessive care to the bow deck, more concerned about its not falling off while I was underway than how I was going to unlash it quickly when the time came to drop it. The best solution, I thought, was to unlash it, bring it aft, and have it ready to throw from the cockpit. Now was the time to do this, so I lashed the tiller to keep the boat on course and went forward to make the arrangements. But the boat would not remain on course for more than 30 seconds, and I didn't feel comfortable being on the narrow bow deck with the boat wallowing beam to the swells. Almost losing my balance at one point, I also became anxious about falling overboard and having the boat continue on without me. I wondered, if I did go over, whether I would be able to grab the dinghy and haul myself aboard. It never entered my mind to tie a line to myself or even put on a life jacket.

After lashing the tiller in several different positions, and even considering rigging some lines to it which would let me steer from the bow, I discovered that I could keep the boat on course from the bow simply by standing and shifting my weight. The difficulty was that I had to be standing up to shift my weight quickly and effectively, and I could not unlash the anchor from a standing position. Finally, maintaining a high squatting position, and keeping my lateral balance by bracing my buttocks against the mast, I managed to undo my lashings and bring the anchor back to the cockpit. Holding the tiller under my arm, I arranged the chain appropriately and coiled the line so I could easily toss it from the cockpit when the time came to anchor.

It was near dark when I reached Georges Harbor, and because it is a narrow harbor consisting of a narrow north-south passage between two thickly wooded islands, it was far darker there than it had been out on the open water moments before. Mine was the only sailboat in the harbor, but there were eight or ten lobster boats and trawlers on moorings. The harbor was very quiet, although there was one trawler with its lights still on tied to a float, and I could make out someone on deck apparently unloading fish. I thought of going over and asking for suggestions about where to anchor, but self-consciousness—and a wish to appear to know more than I did—kept me from it.

I found a likely spot and threw the anchor. Almost 40 of the 75 feet of anchor line I had ran out, and when I put the engine into reverse to set the anchor it became immediately clear that it had not caught. I tried a few other places with the same result. I figured the bottom must be rock or sand since no mud had come up on the anchor, and thought of motoring over to nearby Burnt Island and anchoring in its lee. I wasn't certain I could reach Burnt Island before dark, however, and the prospect of trying to anchor in unfamiliar waters in complete darkness was even more unappealing than the thought of remaining where I was.

Not only was I uneasy about the apparent lack of holding ground, despite what the *Laura B*'s captain had told me, but I found this harbor somewhat eerie. While anchoring I had noticed out on the northwest point of Allen Island a huge white cross. It was brightly illuminated by the setting sun and was in striking contrast to the darkness of the inner harbor. I began to think that there might be some kind of a religious colony on the island, and Jesus' words to his apostles in the New Testament ("I will make you fishers of men") flashed through my mind. I did not want to be caught by the religious fanatics who I imagined inhabited this island.

Nonetheless, having decided to stay, I continued to seek good holding ground. I had just pulled up the anchor for the third time and had reluctantly decided to carry out my plan to move to Burnt Island when I heard the sound of an outboard coming from the direction of the trawler at the float. It appeared that I was going to have a visit from the fisherman I had noticed when I first entered the harbor. He came alongside and said that if I wanted to I could tie up to his trawler, though he was going to be leaving early in the morning. I thanked him for his offer but said I'd rather not, and asked him if there was any good holding ground elsewhere in the harbor. He said farther up the harbor, in the direction of the cross, I'd find holding ground in about 10 feet at low tide. I thanked him, motored over to the place he had indicated, and threw the anchor. I backed down on the anchor, keeping my eye on the light at the float. When its bearing remained steady I assumed the anchor was securely set and shut off the engine.

I sat for a moment listening to the surrounding silence and then realized that I was famished. I was also exhausted, however, so I crawled into my damp sleeping bag after eating only a slice of bread with jam. I found, however, that I was too wound up to sleep and so, by flashlight, I reread Slocum's account of rounding the Horn until I dropped off.

I awoke during the night to the sound of rain on the cuddy roof and the increased motion of the boat. I reached for my flashlight, but was alarmed to find that I had fallen asleep with it on and the batteries were dead. By feel I managed to locate my last pair of fresh ones deep in my duffel so I could replace the dead ones. I then scrambled back out into the cockpit. The wind had come up, but the harbor was completely dark so I couldn't tell whether its direction had changed or, more important, whether my anchor was holding. The rain was also increasing, so I ducked into the cuddy again to put on my slicker. Stepping out into the cockpit once more, I shined my flashlight around the harbor to see if it would reveal anything useful, but the weak beam showed nothing helpful.

I knew that I wasn't going to get any more sleep while I felt insecure about the anchor holding, but the only way I could tell if I was dragging was to create my own reference point. I employed a method I had read about earlier in the summer: I tied a piece of fishing line onto my cast-iron skillet and lowered it over the side. Then, leaving some slack, I ran the other end of the line over the boom and tied it to an aluminum pot, the only other cooking utensil I had brought. The theory was that if the boat moved significantly from its present location the string would become taut and the pot would bang around, I would wake up, and then . . .

I wasn't really sure what I would do then, but I was too tired to think about it. I crawled back into my sleeping bag and slept soundly until around 6 A.M., when I was awakened by the sounds of my pot banging around and boat engines starting up nearby.

It was still raining and blowing quite hard from the northeast, even in the shelter of this harbor. However, the fishermen were going out so I figured it couldn't be too bad. The tide was falling, and I had swung dangerously close to the rocks on the eastern shore of Benner, so I quickly disassembled my anchor alarm, gulped down breakfast, and made preparations to get underway. I briefly consulted the chart. The night before I had planned to try for Tenants Harbor or even Camden, but a northeast wind would be right in my face if I headed that way. So I decided the best thing to do would be to go to Port Clyde under power and then continue on if the wind became more favorable.

I stowed the chart, started the outboard and, leaving it in neutral, went forward to pull up the anchor. The anchor broke loose easily but was dripping with mud. There was, however, no time to wash it for I was drifting backward toward the rocks. I carried it and the snarled line back to the cockpit, dropped them to the floor, and quickly threw the engine into forward. It immediately stalled. Leaning over the stern I could see why: the prop was tangled with seaweed rising from the quickly shoaling bottom. I cleared off what I could with my hands, reengaged the engine, and fully opened the throttle. Much to my relief the engine kept going and I headed out of the harbor by the northwest entrance.

I gazed at the white cross on the point of Allen as I left and tried to make out with my binoculars if there was anything written on it. But it was too rough and the rain was falling too hard to see anything clearly.

As I left the protection of Georges Harbor the wind and seas hit me with frightening force. Between the spray and the rain seeing was difficult, and I tossed the chart into the cuddy for fear that it would blow out of my hand or become so waterlogged that it would become completely unreadable. The engine also seemed to be running roughly, perhaps still snarled with seaweed, and I was barely making headway. I worried about being driven onto the lee shores of Allen or Burnt Island where considerable surf was breaking, and I had no idea what I would do if the engine actually quit since the winds seemed almost too strong for sailing, even if I could get the sails up before being driven aground. I was also nervous because, sailing without my chart in hand, I was now depending on memory to avoid the submerged, unmarked navigational hazards in the area. At least with the seas this high the most serious unmarked hazards would be revealed by breaking waves. Still, I would have felt safer in open waters.

When I reached Marshall Point off Port Clyde harbor I had to decide whether to continue toward Tenants Harbor or run into Port Clyde for temporary shelter. The boat was holding its own, and the engine had given no signs of quitting, so continuing on into more open water even in rough conditions did not seem out of the question. To settle the matter I hailed a passing lobster boat to ask what weather was predicted. The stern man shouted something unintelligible to me and pointed to the Marshall Point Coast Guard Station where the red flag indicating small-craft warnings was flapping in the 25-knot wind already blowing. I yelled my thanks and decided that the prudent thing to do was to take shelter at Port Clyde until conditions improved.

The entrance to Port Clyde harbor was clearly marked and I easily made my way in and tied up at the float near the ferry dock. I felt a little embarrassed at the unshipshape state of the boat and began to do some housekeeping, starting with cleaning and stowing the anchor and line and ending with bailing both the boat and the dinghy, for both had taken on considerable water between Georges Harbor and Port Clyde from the combination of heavy rain and spray.

Having straightened out the boat to my satisfaction, I walked around Port Clyde to stretch my legs but found little to interest me beyond the museum, which was closed, and the Coast Guard Station at Marshall Point Light. I walked out on the white-painted catwalk to the lighthouse and gazed at the surf pounding on the rocks below and the stretch of gray, wind-whipped water to the south over which I had just sailed. The rain, which had lightened to a drizzle during my walk, became heavy again, so I returned to the boat, made a peanut butter and jelly sandwich for lunch, and settled down in the cuddy to read more of Slocum until the weather cleared. The monotonous sound of rain drumming on the cuddy roof in combination with my restless night and strenuous morning soon put me to sleep.

I awoke when the rain stopped, feeling very disoriented. I'd been dreaming heavily, but about what I couldn't recall. I stepped out into the cockpit and was dazzled by the late afternoon sunlight glittering over the harbor, and the brilliant blue sky. By the angle of the sun I estimated it was about six o'clock, and a glance at my watch confirmed my estimate. I could just make out the white tower of the Marshall Point Lighthouse from where I stood and noticed that the small-craft warning flag was still flying, though there seemed no reason for it. The red nun buoys in the harbor almost seemed to be glowing red from the inside as they caught the low light of the sun. I had rarely seen a Maine harbor look so beautiful.

The flag flying from the mailboat landing and the look of the waves in the harbor indicated that a moderate northwest wind was blowing, and the idea of the night sail was born at the moment. I felt I had to experience this gorgeous evening from a boat under sail.

I took out my charts to decide what I could do and noticed that the channel up the center of Penobscot Bay was marked by lighted buoys. One of them was right off Port Clyde. I had never before sailed at night, much less alone, but the prospect thrilled me. I knew I needed to get a quick start to take advantage of the afternoon wind, which I feared would drop, as it usually did after sunset, so I started my preparations immediately. Giving some quick thought to what I might need at hand in the cockpit, I grabbed a flashlight, my jacket and slicker, and my grandfather's fishing cap and stowed them in the cockpit cubbies.

I then plotted my course. I calculated the bearing from the bell off Mosquito Island to the nearest lighted buoy (a whistle with a 4-second flasher) and found it to be almost exactly 90 degrees. My next mark would be a gong, also due east, at a distance of four and a half miles and with a light characteristic of "1 Qk Fl," which I took to mean one quick flash. Two Bush Light House, about a mile due north of this, would be easy to recognize with its 5-second flash pattern, and I would keep it north and west of me to avoid getting tangled up in the shoals and islands of Muscle Ridge Channel northwest of it. From the quick-flasher it was 4.74 miles at a bearing of 87 degrees to "Mo (A)," a lighted whistle buoy which would flash Morse Code for the letter A (dot-dash), and from there I could sail five miles true north along a longitude line actually marked on the chart to another "Mo (A)" gong off Rockland Harbor. Finally, I would make for the lighted gong off Camden Harbor, by which time it would certainly be light. It looked easy. I raised the sails and cast off at 7 P.M.

The direction of the wind allowed me to sail easily off the dock, and this pleased me, for I had not yet figured out an easy way of holding the boat into the wind and raising the sails by myself while underway, although I knew there had to be one. As I rounded Marshall Point the treeless Gunning Islands stretched out in front of me, the seared yellow grass they were capped with glowing like green gold in the low sunlight. I easily found the passage between The Brothers and Mosquito Ledge conveniently marked by a nun to the north and a can to the south, and soon made out ahead the bell off Mosquito Island where I would turn due (magnetic) east and head for the 4-second flashing whistle buoy, the first of the line of lights I intended to follow up Penobscot Bay.

I looked over my shoulder to watch the sun sink behind the dark mass of mainland as Mosquito Island slipped behind, and was amazed to realize that the black islands silhouetted against the red sky were the same Gunning Islands that had so recently been glowing in sunlight. When I faced forward again I noticed that the whistler ahead had started flashing, and I timed the flashes to see if they were actually every 4 seconds as the chart indicated they should be. I was reassured to find they were.

Then the wind shifted a few degrees east and I could no longer hold my course. However, since I was now confident that I could keep the flasher in sight even if I wasn't headed right toward it, the thought of heading off the wind and then tacking back did not disturb me. I consulted my chart to see if there were any dangers in the more southerly direction I was now sailing and found that I was headed toward the northern point of Metinic Island. Looking up, I made it out dead ahead, looming black against the cobalt water about four miles away. Returning to the chart I noticed that there were several ledges lying in the general direction I was headed: Roaring Bull, south of my course, marked by an unlighted can; Metinic Island Ledge, also marked by an unlighted can; and Hupper Shoal and Black Rock, both unmarked. Unfortunately in the available light I could not read the depths associated with these obstacles with any certainty, and I had to be certain. At night unlighted markers were not going to be much help to me in avoiding rocks and ledges; in fact, it suddenly occurred to me that, at night, an unlighted buoy could itself be a dangerous obstacle.

Placing a beach rock I had picked up on Monhegan on my chart to keep it from blowing away, I pulled my flashlight out of the cubby where I had tucked it and shined it on the chart. It didn't help much. I was disturbed to see how weak the beam had become, and I now realized that in my hurry to set sail I had forgotten to replace the batteries I had used up when I fell asleep reading Slocum. I was, however, able to make out the depths I needed to know, and I could see that only Roaring Bull posed any danger to me. If I could hold my present course I would leave it at least two miles to the south of me, but both tide and wind were pushing me south so I did need to consider my lateral drift.

While consulting the chart I had taken my eyes off my 4-second flasher and was amazed, when I looked back up, that I could no longer find it. In the place where I expected it were some steady white and red lights quite close together and a cluster of dim white lights in what seemed a linear arrangement. I could not judge their distance from me. I checked my compass—now almost impossible to read without a flashlight—to see if the wind had changed direction significantly. Since I had been steering merely by the feel of wind while consulting the chart, a change in wind direction could have caused me inadvertently to change my heading. The compass showed there had been no change in direction, and I felt mystified and, for the first time, a little frightened.

I consulted the chart again to see if there were any lighted markers northwest of me that fit the general description of what I was seeing, but found nothing. Then, with a feeling of slight shock, I realized that I was looking at the port riding light of a large ship. The white lights would be the masthead light and ports. I remembered then that this was a shipping lane, fairly heavily traveled by tankers, which off-loaded oil at Searsport, and other heavy shipping out of Rockland. I had often seen the tankers when sailing off Castine. If this was the case, the ship must have come between me and the flasher and the flasher should reappear in a few minutes. But when I judged enough time had elapsed for the ship to pass, I still could not relocate my flasher. For one thing I could no longer see the second hand of my watch to reliably time the flashes of anything, and for another the bay suddenly seemed filled with a myriad of lights, none of which I could identify with any certainty.

The wind had also begun to rise noticeably and with it the seas. It occurred to me that even if I could read my watch, the increasing seas might intermittently obscure lighted buoys, making it impossible to rely on their flashing characteristics for identification. And in any case it was now becoming impossible to keep the boat on course, read a blowing chart by the light of my dying flashlight, and systematically sort out the many lights surrounding me. I had to admit I was lost, although I was somewhat reassured to know my position within a couple of miles.

Assuming the direction of the wind held, and its velocity did not increase beyond the sailing capacity of my boat, I felt my best strategy was to tack back and forth in the area of clear water that I knew surrounded me for two to three miles on every side. To keep in the clear I would have to take into account the southward drift of the boat due to the wind and tide until midnight when the tide was due to turn. Another alternative was to heave-to, but since the closest dangers I knew about were to the south, I felt it best to remain in sailing mode and tack slowly northward. I also entertained thoughts of using the engine, but rejected this option when I thought about trying both to douse the sails and start the engine in the dark. Also, under power it would be both more difficult to hear approaching dangers such as breaking surf or boat engines and harder to judge my direction, since I was now taking my bearings primarily from the direction of the wind.

I was comforted with the thought that I could use the stars to orient myself, but when I scanned the sky I saw that the stars had vanished behind a thickening cloud cover. And the wind and seas were still rising. Perhaps the small-craft warning flag I had noticed at the Marshall Point Coast Guard Station had not been left up in error as I had thought. The calming effect of my rational strategizing vanished when I recalled that all my thinking had been based on the assumption that the weather would hold. This now seemed doubtful.

It seemed to me that over an hour had passed since I had passed the Mosquito Island Bell, and at the three knots I estimated I was moving, I must be close to Metinic Island. It was time for my first tack. I glanced at my watch and the compass, but found I was going to need my flashlight to read either of them reliably. Holding the tiller under my arm and the mainsheet with my right hand, I reached for my flashlight with my left and then, since my watch was on my left wrist and I could only illuminate it if I had my flashlight in the opposite hand, I attempted to shift the flashlight to my right hand and the mainsheet to my left. In the midst of this awkward maneuver I dropped the flashlight and, when I managed to locate and retrieve it, I found it no longer worked when I switched it on. I suspected I had broken the bulb, but it had also gotten soaked, having fallen to the lee side of the cockpit where a considerable amount of water had collected because of the boat's steep heeling. I attempted to read my watch with the help of the small amount of luminosity emitted by the dial and the remaining light in the sky; I thought it read somewhere around nine, though I couldn't be sure. The compass seemed to show me at a heading of ten degrees south of east. I was probably less than a mile from Metinic and had better come about in short order.

Settling into my new westward tack and thinking of the hours I had ahead of me until dawn, I became aware for the first time of how cold I was. The numbness of my fingers had certainly been a factor in dropping the flashlight. Even before coming about spray had begun coming over the bow. Now it was coming over with nearly every wave and the increasing wind gusts were regularly blowing it back to the cockpit. My hands actually began to hurt with the cold as the repeated drenchings sucked the warmth out of them. I struggled into my jacket and slicker, something I should have done long before, and pulled my damp sweater sleeves over my hands to protect them from the wind. I also put on my grandfather's fishing cap with its black plastic visor to shield my face from the spray and I pulled my slicker hood over that.

Feeling a little warmer, I began to think how I could keep track of time to time my tacks since I could no longer rely on my watch. I estimated my east-west motion at 2 to 3 knots, so I figured I should be tacking every hour to keep in clear water. If I counted seconds in "chipmunks" or "Mississippis," the two methods I knew, that would translate into 3,600 chipmunks or Mississippis per hour. I began to count, but my mind drifted long before I reached even 500.

I could see nothing ahead clearly except the waves breaking immediately in front of the bow but, straining my eyes, I thought I saw dim, intermittent lights in the indefinite distance. I supposed them to be the headlights of the trucks I was hearing, for I believed (mistakenly as it turned out) that Route 1 followed the shore on this part of the mainland. I knew there was one danger spot—Hart's Ledge—on the otherwise bold coast I was approaching, and I felt relieved that I would have the audible warning of the trucks long before I was near enough to the shore to have to worry about running into it.

I came about, uncleating the jib on the lee side with some difficulty because of the pressure on the sail and my numb hands. The wind seemed to have moderated slightly but I speculated that this might be only because I was close to land and was getting some protection from the wind. I breathed deeply and thought I detected land scents in the wind, which further confirmed my supposition about where I was. Based on my assumptions about my movement north, my only worry on this new eastward tack would be the complex of reefs the charts referred to as the Northern Triangles about five miles east. I would again tack at 3,600 chipmunks, if I could remember to keep counting.

As I emerged from the lee of the shore the wind increased and a sudden hard gust of wind put the lee rail under. I released the mainsheet and pushed the tiller hard over to keep the boat from going over, and as I did I heard something give way. When I eased the boat back off the wind, the jib continued luffing violently. My first thought was that the noise was simply the jib sheet pulling loose from its cleat. If this was the case, the sheet was trailing overboard off the lee rail and, after heading up, I scrambled forward to gather it in from the jib clew and lead it back to the cleat to resecure it. I could not, however, locate the cleat, and when I reexamined the deck in the area where I thought it had been, I encountered a ragged edge of torn canvas decking and empty screw holes. The cleat had pulled out.

I crossed to the other side of the cockpit to secure the sheet to the windward cleat, but at that moment another knockdown gust of wind pushed the boat off the wind and again put the leeward rail under. The flailing boom caught the visor of my hat, dislodging it along with my slicker hood, and my hat was carried off into the darkness by the wind. I swore as I got a turn around the windward cleat and pulled my hood back up. I decided not to hitch the jib sheet because I wanted to be able to release it quickly in case of another knockdown gust.

Sailing became increasingly difficult with both hands now holding the sheets. I had also completely lost track of time and so felt very unsure of my location. Every time I saw whitecaps ahead I feared they were signs of the Northern Triangles, which I knew were somewhere out ahead of me. I calmed myself with the thought that I would probably be able to hear whitecaps produced by waves breaking on rocks, but this reassuring thought was partly inspired by the fact that I was so painfully cold and tired that I didn't want to tack any more than was absolutely necessary. The pain in my hands made me think about reefing or taking down the main altogether, but my hands were so numb and waterlogged that I doubted I would be able to tie the reef points, even if I could manage all the other logistics of reefing on a lurching boat in total darkness. Given my decision not to reef, my next best course of action, in order to spare my hands and minimize the risk of going over, was to let the main spill most of its wind and sail with the jib. I tried this, but the tremendous noise of the flapping sail obscured the sounds I was counting on hearing to know when I should next tack, so I retrimmed the main and put up with the discomfort of hanging onto the sheet.

As I continued to put off coming about, I began to imagine what it would be like being aground on a reef in the middle of Penobscot Bay on a night such as this. I saw my boat filling and breaking up and me trying to maintain a footing on jagged, slippery rocks with freezing water breaking around me. This vision gave me the energy I needed to come about and begin my second westward tack. If I was going to go aground, I would much rather be aground near the mainland than in the middle of the bay.

I now accepted that counting was not going to work for me as a way of estimating time and decided instead to sing, knowing that a typical song lasted about three minutes. If I stuck to my plan of tacking every hour, I would sing twenty songs per tack, and the time would be well spent, for I could rehearse my repertoire. I paused between each song to listen for the sounds of breaking surf or trucks on the mainland. The singing both raised my spirits and kept me alert.

Suddenly, while in the middle of "Streets of Laredo," I saw a flashing light to the north twenty or so points off my starboard bow. The brevity of the flash was such that I knew its intermittent quality was not being caused by the intervention of waves. It could be the quick-flashing gong, which was to have been one of my lighted waypoints up the bay if things had gone according to plan. I headed up as much as I could to pass as close to it as possible and strained to hear the sound of the gong, but could make out nothing definite. Either it was not the quick-flasher I thought it was or it was too far away for the sound to carry over the hiss and roar of the waves and wind. I noticed another more elevated and diffuse intermittent light in the same general direction, but I couldn't tell if it was nearer or farther away than the quick-flasher. If farther, it could be Two Bush Light, which flashed every 5 seconds; if nearer, it could possibly be the masthead light of another boat, and I kept my eye on it to see if riding lights would appear. They didn't, and I watched as the gap between the two lights closed. When the more diffuse light passed ahead of the quick-flasher I knew it was more distant and almost surely Two Bush. I deeply regretted not having my flashlight, for if the second light was indeed Two Bush I could have used the alignment of the two lights to pin down my east-west position on the chart—if I'd been able to see it.

The wind began to moderate, and according to my tally of songs sung, I should be entering the lee of the mainland and approaching the shore. I began to listen for trucks and watch for lines of surf and within fifteen minutes saw and heard what I expected. This confirmation of my speculations regarding my location relieved my anxieties considerably, and when I came about to begin another eastward tack I was virtually certain that the dim light I had seen beyond the quick-flashing gong was Two Bush Light. I timed with chipmunks its now-brighter flashes and they did seem to be at 5-second intervals. If I kept south of Two Bush— which marks the southern end of Muscle Ridge Channel—I would have ten miles of clear water to the east. The direction of the wind seemed to be holding steady at something close to north, so I felt quite confident about my direction of sailing.

I thought it must now be near midnight, when the tide would be turning. I would have to sail somewhat south of Two Bush to compensate for the north-running tidal current, and I headed off the wind accordingly to keep Two Bush safely off my port bow. I resumed my singing, starting with "Four Strong Winds," though I realized that once I had passed Two Bush I would have so much open water ahead that the timing of my tacks would no longer be a concern.

As I expected it would, the wind gradually increased as I left the lee of the mainland, but sailing a little off the wind seemed more comfortable than the beating I had been doing. After something like an hour, however, I noticed that the wind had become more gusty—I had had to head up several times to avoid going over—and had gradually shifted westward, for although my bearing relative to Two Bush had remained constant—about 20 degrees off my port bow—I was now almost on a reach. It struck me as ironic that not long before I had been singing "Four Strong Winds," whose chorus refers to the winds as things that "don't change come what may," but my literary musings were interrupted by the sound of a bell buoy.

I strained my eyes ahead, nervous about the possibility of running into it, but could see nothing although the ringing seemed to be growing louder by the minute. I also thought I heard the thundering sound of breakers upwind. Then, with shocking suddenness, the bell emerged out of the darkness no more than 20 or 30 feet off my starboard bow. I tried to decipher its markings as it slipped past (it looked like "25 B") and noticed that it was leaning toward me despite the direction of the wind. I then realized that the tidal currents at the entrance to Muscle Ridge Channel were considerably stronger than I had estimated them to be. If so, I was very likely being carried by the strong north-running tidal current up into Muscle Ridge Channel and was now in real trouble, for I knew the waters there were filled with shoals and small islands. The increased choppiness of the seas also confirmed that I was in an area where a strong tidal current and wind were in opposition.

I at once saw that this hypothesis also explained the apparent wind shift. The wind had actually remained north and the Two Bush Light had remained at a constant bearing with respect to my bow, but my track had turned increasingly south as I was pushed northward up the channel by the tide. There was nothing to do but head off and run south with the wind until Two Bush was again clearly north of me. Then I could again turn east into safe waters.

My stomach, however, tightened at the prospect of running before a strong, gusty wind in high seas. The most dangerous point of sailing for a small boat is running before the wind. Although having the wind astern decreases the angle of heel, which is desirable when the wind is more than your boat can comfortably handle, it is much more difficult to quickly spill excessive wind from the sail on this point of sail. In beating and running, wind can be spilled by the dual action of easing the sheets and heading up, but in running the first option is not available because the mainsheet is already out to its full extent. The second option is dangerous because if you head up without pulling in the boom, you expose yourself to the danger of broaching when the main dips into the water while the boat is rolling crosswise to the high seas and the boat is dragged over by pressure of water against the sail.

Despite my anxiety I felt I had no other options. I cleated the jib sheet so both hands would be free to handle the main and tiller, and headed off as much as I dared, for I feared a dismasting if I jibed in this wind. It was also difficult to judge the direction of the wind when it was coming from behind, for I lacked the feel of it on my cheek. Only the set of jib would indicate that I had not fallen off too much, for if it jibed, the main could soon follow suit.

I struggled to maintain a steady course, but it was impossible to prevent yawing in the high and confused following seas, and after nearly jibing several times, I decided I had to get the main down even if I couldn't reef. I headed into the wind and stumbled forward to uncleat the main halyard. The sail started to drop, but the boat then fell off almost immediately and the pressure of the wind on the filling sail prevented it from coming down further. I rushed back to the tiller to turn the boat back into the wind, nearly tripping as my feet caught in the invisible tangle of the halyard on the cockpit floor and the boat rolled violently. Repeating this perilous trip from mast to tiller several times, I finally managed to yank the sail down and lash it in place with the main sheet. I then turned off the wind to sail under jib alone.

No longer in the lee of the mainsail, the pressure on the jib and jib sheet, which was crossed in front of me, was tremendous. If the port cleat went the way of the starboard one, I could get hit in the head and seriously injured, so I shifted the sheet to the main cleat and felt more secure. Sailing in this way I managed to maintain control until Two Bush was safely north of me. Then I headed east under jib alone. In about twenty minutes I again made out the quick-flashing gong ahead and south of me, and this time when it was abeam of me I actually heard it.

Tremendously relieved to be reoriented and free of Muscle Ridge Channel, I continued east for what I estimated to be several hours, then came about and sailed on a westward reach again toward Two Bush and the mainland. Sailing on a reach under jib alone was far drier and more comfortable than beating and the wind appeared steady enough for me to feel comfortable leaving the jib sheet firmly cleated. This freed my hands and allowed me to warm them one at a time by blowing on them and keeping them between my thighs or pocketed whenever possible. I felt almost comfortable.

When I came about again off Two Bush, I noticed that the sky in the east was growing lighter and glancing up, I made out a few stars between gaps in the cloud cover. Two hours later as I prepared to come about for what was to be my last eastward tack, I could actually make out the dark coastline of Vinalhaven against the brightening sky to the east. The still darkened sky above me was now free of clouds and filled with stars. As I approached the mainland an hour later, it was light enough for me to clearly make out the profile of the mainland to the west, and soon I was able to see the tower of Two Bush Light and read my watch. It was 4 A.M. I located my chart where I had tossed it into the cuddy hours earlier and, holding it up to catch the eastern light, could see enough to confirm my position and begin to think about what to do next.

The wind was dropping and I was near Tenants Harbor, so exhausted that I was tempted to run into it and sleep. But I was also a day behind schedule and if I slept now I would miss the tide, which was due to turn in a few hours. I decided to motor north to Camden where I could sleep for a few hours and then continue home.

I took down the sails, lashed them, and started the outboard. As the sky turned bright yellow and pink from the refracted rays of the rising sun, I climbed to the bow deck and, arm around the mast, began to steer by shifting my weight. A full rainbow of colors spread across the sky as the sun lifted above horizon and the remains of a new moon vanished as its reflected light was eclipsed by the overpowering glare of the rising sun. This was my first sunrise at sea; it would certainly not be my last.

My gaze returned to the water in front of me, the teal and magenta afterimages of the dazzling sun dancing against the background of sea and mirrored sky. I was marveling at this phenomenon when my eye caught what seemed to be an object floating on the tossing waves just off the port bow. At first I thought it was a lobster pot or deadhead and scrambled back to the tiller to avoid hitting it. I turned in time, and as I watched the object pass close off the port rail I realized that it was a floating hat—my grandfather's fishing hat that had blown off my head a few hours earlier. Its waterproofing had kept it from becoming waterlogged and sinking. I almost laughed aloud at the coincidence of finding it again and, though I'm not a believer in the occult, it occurred to me that this was a communication from my grandfather from the "beyond." I started to turn the boat around to retrieve it but it had disappeared in the glare of the now fully risen sun, and I thought I'd rather get to Camden and get some sleep than spend the time looking for it.

I made Camden Harbor by eight, dropped anchor in the outer harbor and slept hard until noon when the wake of a large boat passing nearby rocked me awake. The weather was clear, with a good southwest breeze already up. I thought I would go into the inner harbor, replenish my gas supply, and get some lunch. If I was quick about it I could be on my way by one o'clock and back to Castine by five or six. In an hour, according to plan, I was out in western Penobscot Bay running north before a good 15-knot breeze.

During the sail home I looked at my chart to see if I could make sense of my experiences of the night before. The buoy I had almost struck was "2SB," which marks a ledge called the South Breakers just north of it. The ledge must have been the source of the surf I had heard as I passed the buoy. My theory that I had been swept up into Muscle Ridge Channel by the tide was correct, and I would almost surely have come to grief had I not realized what was happening in time.

I stepped from my dinghy onto the beach in front of my grandfather's house shortly after 4 P.M. and, with my heavily laden duffel on my shoulder, started the long trek up the decrepit wooden stairs from the beach to Water Street and my grandfather's house.

I was startled when I reached the top to see a strange car parked in front of the house and a man at the front door obviously watching me as I approached. He came down to meet me as I walked up the path to the door and introduced himself as a reporter. He explained that I had been reported a day overdue and that a sea-and-air search for me was underway because it was feared I had come to grief in the storm of the previous day. I let the reporter into the house so he could telephone the Coast Guard to call off the search. He then proceeded to interview me.

I am quoted in the resulting article as saying, "There was some sea and wind during Thursday night's sail, but I experienced no real difficulty." Clearly I was a better liar than I was a sailor.

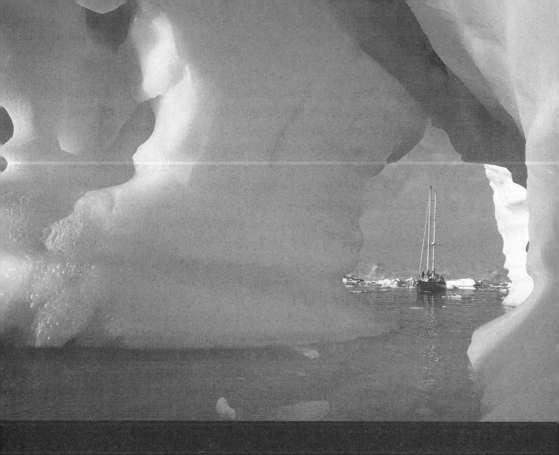

polar waters

FROM
TIME
on ICE

BY
Deborah Shapiro
and Rolf Bjelke

In the early 1980s

Deborah Shapiro, originally from Pittsburgh, and Rolf Bjelke, originally from Sweden, had made a 33,000-mile voyage that included a passage from the Arctic to the Antarctic. They fell in love with the high latitudes and the stark and lonely beauty of places small-boat cruisers seldom see. Soon afterward they began planning a three-year second voyage in *Northern Light*, their 40-foot steel-hulled ketch.

From Sweden they would pass below Iceland and around Newfoundland on their way to the United States, then past Bermuda and across the North Atlantic to the Canary Islands, then south to South America and down past the Falklands, and finally across the Drake Passage south of Cape Horn to the Antarctic Peninsula. A year later they would sail back north to Sweden.

Such a voyage requires considerable planning and training in addition to strength of character, as well as a secure personal relationship. Rolf had learned solo winter survival techniques in the Swedish Army, sleeping in snow caves and traveling on skis through bitterly cold mountains carrying everything he needed to survive. In preparation for this voyage they climbed mountains and practiced pulling their gear on sleds. By summer 1989 they were ready to go.

"There is something to be said for experiencing brand-new things as an adult," Deborah writes in the introduction to their book. "Just when you think you know the routines, have made the same yearly cycle so many times, even feel (one thinks) justifiably blasé about some things, everything one 'knows' and takes for granted is suddenly set on its ear. I think it is for that reason that so many of us from temperate or tropical zones liken our arrival in Antarctica to traveling to a new planet."

The following selection begins as they are just northeast of Cape Horn with the Chilean Navy attempting to warn them away from the Drake Passage and the Antarctic. In addition to the risks of all small-boat ocean voyaging are greater dangers south of the Horn: bitterly cold water, high winds and waves, and icebergs. They are determined, however, and proceed south to Antarctica where they will spend the next year, including a long winter frozen in the ice, totally on their own.

///

THE Japanese trawler *Casula Maru* crosses our wake just south of the Strait of Le Maire. "Shall I give them a shout on the VHF and ask if they have a weather forecast?"

"Sure, go ahead," Rolf replies. "The wind's increasing quickly. If it's a precursor of some really bad weather, we can backtrack to Staten Island and wait there for it to blow over. No reason to stick our heads out into something nasty."

My call to the trawler is answered by an onboard Argentine fisheries observer. He tells us that a new forecast is due in about ten minutes, so we should stand by and wait for their nearby base to come on the air. In due time, a military radio operator on Tierra del Fuego calls us. His conversation doesn't start with the weather, however.

Instead he asks, "What is your vessel's name and registration number?" I supply the information and then other requested descriptive particulars of the hull and rig. But I am still not rewarded with a weather report.

"What was your port of clearance?"

"Mar del Plata," I answer.

"And you are cleared to . . . ?"

"Puerto Williams, Chile."

"How many on board?"

"Two," I reply.

"When did you leave Mar del Plata?"

"The tenth of December."

"When do you expect to arrive at Puerto Williams?"

Here we go. Puerto Williams is only 70 nautical miles away. Even at a snail's pace in head wind, it couldn't take us more than a day. Today's date is December 22, 1990. "We should arrive around the fifth of February 1992," I answer.

"Could you repeat that?"

I do. A long pause follows, during which Rolf and I half smile, half shake our heads. We know exactly what conversation is transpiring in the radio room.

Then, on the voice of authority, comes our weather report. "Today: strong wind, then very strong wind from the southwest sector. Light cloud, good visibility, except in rain showers. Forecast: very strong to storm force wind from the west sector. The Navy recommends that you do not endeavor to cross Drake Passage at this time. I repeat: do not go out into Drake Passage at this time. Furthermore, do not attempt to spend the winter in Antarctica. It is not possible in such a small boat. And during the winter months, we will not be able to help you."

First things first. Rolf wants a translation of their plain language weather report. "Ask him how many knots of wind in very strong and storm-force wind." Their answer: very strong is 27 to 33 knots and storm is 33 to 40 knots. I thank the radio operator for the information and tell him that we will be happy if we can cross without getting more than 40 knots of wind and that we are able and ready to handle at least 60. I also inform him that we will rely on ourselves during the winter and have prepared to need no outside help.

Their recommendation is not unexpected, for we have heard it before. When we requested to be cleared from Chile for Antarctica in the summer of 1984, the commandante of the naval base in Puerto Williams summoned us to his office. It was a snowy, blustery day. Seating us before a roaring fire, bordered by windows through which we couldn't help but watch *Northern Light* straining her anchor chain, the commandante tried to talk us out of sailing for the Antarctic Peninsula. He minced no words. First, he didn't like that we were a crew of only two, especially since I am female. He thought we should never sail in these waters without at least a third crew member—another man—on board. In hindsight, thinking about all the anchor chain I had pumped up in deep Chilean anchorages and all the times I rowed shorelines and set and gybed sails, I wish I had asked him right there to arm wrestle.

But I do not mean to belittle his opinion or his advice. The Chileans are exemplary seamen. Given the heavy weather conditions of the channels, they have to be. During his years of service, the commandante had probably encountered his share of dangerous work involved in the rescues of yachts and yachtsmen who hadn't succeeded in the channels or in rounding Cape Horn. We appreciated that his port clearance was not simply formality.

The commandante also expressed his belief that "even if you *are* tough enough, when you get out into Drake Passage and are hit by a westerly storm—as heavy westerlies are a certainty—your boat simply will not be able to hold enough westing to make the peninsula. Next stop, in that case," he said "is Cape Town."

Rolf reiterated, "We are sailing for the peninsula." But the commandante had the last word, reminding us that the granting of clearance is an implied agreement of intent. "I will not be responsible for granting you clearance for Antarctica," he intoned. "As I write on your papers, I clear you for the High Seas. You may go where you wish." He rose from his armchair, walked to his desk, and signed our papers. We were dismissed.

Had we not felt secure in our preparation, including contingency plans, we could not have taken the responsibility of negating an authority's directive. The same holds true today. We are in no way complacent about crossing Drake Passage or about our wintering plans. In fact, we have serious concerns. We have done our very best to identify and deal with them all, long before now. We've done our homework and preparation. Among a million details, the watertight bulkhead's door is battened for this passage, as are floorboards and cupboard doors, and Rolf's waterproof ventilation system is fully functional, even upside-down. This time, as in 1984, the balance hangs on our competence and, as the commandante said, in the total energy one man and one woman can muster.

The weather information the Navy radio operator has just given us—that the approaching depression is forecast to pack 40 knots—is actually good news to us. Since Mar del Plata we've been constantly trying to take weather charts, but the Argentines make it difficult by not keeping to the schedule. What we do know is that the current slew of depressions have been mild, the upper-level isobars are evenly spread, and the lows are currently taking a track north of us. This forecast continues that pattern. And because the heaviest weather is on the northern side of the low—if we can scoot out into Drake Passage and use these 40 knots of wind to make some hundred miles before the next low—we may be lucky and have it pass north of us also.

Yes, lucky is the right word. Once you leave South America and sail into Drake Passage, the dice are rolled. Gales occur every third day here, and secondary lows can build behind any of them, usually far too quickly for any shore station to predict, and the secondary wave is the one that packs the punch. Superimpose a lightning-fast wind shift on an already high sea and you get furious cross sea and therefore an increased possibility of freak waves. Meeting one can mean turning a boat over or flipping it end over end. One Drake crossing out of ten can be a question of survival. To be properly prepared, sailors must be ready for that storm.

The worst part for us is that we are not as physically adjusted as we would like to be, like we were the last time we crossed. Then, we had come from three months in the Patagonian channels where we had sailed in strong wind, enduring rain, and steadily declining temperatures. Our bodies were used to cold, were hardened. This time, it is a mere two weeks since we enjoyed full summer in Mar del Plata. We will no doubt suffer until our bodies adjust. Our metabolism is already speeding up—a sign that our internal furnaces are dealing with cooler weather and perhaps the excitement and broken sleep—but the skin on our hands hasn't toughened yet nor have our fingers ballooned from increased blood circulation. We've been trying to speed up the acclimatization by not wearing gloves or too-warm clothing, but two weeks is simply too short for the process. The French have a saying: "You either pay for Cape Horn before, or you pay later, but you pay." My fingers and toes tell me I've already anted up.

We don't sight Cape Horn—my diamond in the rough—because all afternoon the wind continues to shift counterclockwise until it reaches southwest, gusting 40 knots plus a little. While still in the shelter of the southern tip of South America, we sheet *Northern Light* up as hard as we can. The ideal course is a little west of south, and although the compass reads exactly that, our course over ground is affected by a 1.6-knot northeast-setting current, resulting in a true heading of only south-southeast. Still, we are pleased. The current runs with the sea, dampening the waves. The mild sea state allows us to keep to 6 knots, *Northern Light*'s maximum speed close-hauled, and that transports us to the latitude of Cape Horn at midnight. We're out, into Drake Passage and the control of the West Wind Drift, so dominant a weather determinator that meteorologists refer to it as the "flywheel of the atmosphere." The concept of power is about to become tangible.

Every minute of heavy weather experience is worth its weight in gold, because for every knot of higher wind managed, there is one less to worry about. When we passed Cape Horn southbound in 1984, I was so intensely worried about the storm we were bound to get in Drake Passage that the blinding-white anxiety made me what I call "emotion sick." We indeed encountered a six-hour blow of 60 knots from the beam. It started halfway through my watch and continued all through Rolf's, and it presented him with the heaviest gusts he had ever experienced at sea. Off watch, I slept through that while *Northern Light*, flying cutter staysail only, made 7 knots toward the next waypoint. *Wow*, I thought to myself when I went back on watch and looked at the turbulent scene. *This boat can obviously withstand a lot more than its crew. Take the hint, Deborah, and steel yourself. You'll be able to think more clearly.*

Yes, with all certainty, a seaworthy boat is a good thing to have under you. A boat, designed to be in harmony with a high wind's sea, rides gently there, comparatively speaking. Seakindliness means not only that crew can rest; it also means that we can work more safely on deck. I can't imagine crossing the Drake in a boat not designed for heavy weather.

For the novice sailor, like me when I first signed on *Northern Light*, there is no other option than to take weather one step at a time. I worked on deck in higher and higher wind speeds and sea, learning and becoming accustomed to the different routines needed to match each successive state. Early in the game, Rolf taught me his heavy-weather downwind sailing maxim: Sail fast; speed creates safety. As he explained, in a gale or storm, even if a displacement boat is driven as hard as possible, its speed is very slow compared with the speed of the waves. Waves therefore continuously overtake the boat. As the top of a wave passes, the boat actually "backs" through the breaker. The more one reefs down, the slower the boat sails, and therefore the larger the impact the wave has as it hits.

Based on that, he told me that the rule for sailing with the wind in heavy weather is to always sail the boat as close to its hull speed as possible. To put it to the test, we decided we should sail *Northern Light*, a medium-heavy displacement boat, "too hard." What we wanted to find out was, with the wind aft of abeam, does driving the boat hard lead to loss of steerage and result in a broach?

In the beginning of a very strong gale in the Roaring Forties, when the average wind speed was 45 to 60 knots, we purposely carried 50 percent, 75 percent, and then 100 percent more sail than necessary to keep *Northern Light* at hull speed. The point was to press her so hard that on the back side of each wave, where speed normally decreases, the boat would maintain its theoretical maximum speed of 8.35 knots. Over twelve hours, we covered 103 nautical miles, an average of 8.58 knots. Yet even though we sailed faster than the boat's theoretical maximum speed, there was never any tendency to broach.

The only time Rolf has experienced a knockdown was on his first voyage with *Northern Light*. It happened because they had sailed too slowly. They had overreefed one night specifically to delay an arrival at an atoll until daylight. Hours before dawn, the stern was lifted by a breaking sea, and as one could expect, the boat didn't have enough speed for the rudder to have effect. The boat yawed and broached, and the mast hit the water.

What about other points of sail in heavy weather? To claw off a lee shore in storm-force winds is not exactly accomplished easily; there are tremendous forces involved. The principle to keep in mind in a heavy-weather beat is the same as when on a broad reach: drive the boat as efficiently as possible. Of course, a boat on a beat has to be reefed more than when sailing with the wind, but not so much that it doesn't sail fast.

Beam reaching should be avoided as much as possible when the sea is steep and high, however. And that concept should be kept in mind when reefing for a heavy-weather beat, too. If reefed too much on a heavy-weather beat, a boat won't have the power it needs to make it over the waves. Instead, it will get forced beam to, temporarily beam reaching, with the topsides exposed to the sea. That leads to a moment of vulnerability, and if the boat is taken by the wave, there's a big mess onboard.

For a contrast to last time's hurricane-force gusts at this latitude, I am taking advantage of today's light wind to bake chocolate chip cookies and bread. I might as well stock up. As fast as depressions fly through Drake Passage, we'll encounter at least one more blow before we get there and, regardless, we'll soon be to the Antarctic Convergence, where a new job will be added to the list of watch responsibilities.

The convergence is an ever-shifting though well-defined line that marks our zero-altitude, sea-level entrance to the Antarctic. Circumscribing a wavy circle through the southern portions of the Pacific, Atlantic, and Indian Oceans that comprise the Antarctic Ocean, the convergence is the northern border of the southernmost continent's surface cold water. The convergence is not a constant line and does not remain where the dotted line is marked on the charts; instead, it is where it is. The fun way to find it is to watch. Chances are, you will either see seabirds aplenty feeding on the poor krill and other stunned creatures that suddenly find themselves in the wrong temperature water or you will see Cape pigeons and other birds that prefer to be south of the convergence. But if there's nothing to be seen or it's too foggy to bother looking, you can do as we do: measure the water temperature. When it dips below 35.5°F (+2°C), you're at Antarctica's threshold!

The convergence also happens to be the place where we start to have twenty-four-hour light, the gift of high-latitude summer. It's a big aid now, because south of the Antarctic Convergence it's time to keep an extra sharp, constant lookout for every form of ice from little chunks to huge tabular-shaped bergs.

Even in good conditions, it is exceedingly difficult to detect "growlers" that lie at the surface and heave in the swell. A diffuse, almost invisible shadow is the only thing that betrays the presence of these old, smoothened bobbing ice chunks. As far as we are concerned, growlers are floating rocks. We are not allowed to sail into one. When the wind picks up and the sea begins to break, these polished clumps of ice are almost impossible to detect. Oh, why does it have to start snowing, just now when we can't afford bad visibility?

The first iceberg we sight is 100 nautical miles from the Antarctic land mass. It is not a large table-topped piece of the ice shelf but a piece twice as high as our mainmast and a cable in diameter, with a jagged edge and spires on top. Translucent blue, glowing from within, it's an absolutely beautiful ice castle. The biggies have to be described differently. Lacking appropriate figurative descriptors, we usually rely on numbers. Yet the enormous dimensions of icebergs that break away from the Antarctic ice shelf are still difficult to appreciate.

For example, consider one of the biggest bergs to break away from the ice shelf in the Weddell Sea recently. It is understandable that these big bergs are given a number and reported here, where they pose a considerable danger to ships, but this one is so large that its march north toward the South Atlantic is being reported on the news in the United States and Europe. Andy has related to us that iceberg number A-24, measuring 50 by 70 statute miles, is three times the area of the state of Rhode Island. But just how big is that? We take out our calculator and learn that A-24 is so big that not only could everyone on Earth stand side by side on it, but each person would have two square yards! Perhaps even more impressive is that the iceberg could provide drinking water for all 5.5 billion of us for no less than 450 years.

Toward the end of my watch, 60 nautical miles west of the peninsula, I awaken Rolf to share the moment when we sail over the edge of the continental shelf and into a 15-nautical-mile-wide band of bergs, spaced 2 to 3 nautical miles apart. Rolf climbs the mainmast to the second spreader. To the southwest, the visibility is very good and ice glitters as far as he can see. He scans the horizon and reports that a weather change is coming at us from the northeast. We are soon ringed by snow gusts and the visibility drops to near zero. We take turns keeping a lookout on the foredeck and searching for the best path through the labyrinth of ice.

The visibility never drops to the point where it would be prudent to heave to, and the northeasterly wind increases incrementally until it lifts the low cloud a little and affords us a better view. Although it's an exciting time, I am sent to bed to put some hours "in the bank." Landfall is never a certainty here, and safe anchorage are two words we won't combine again until we return to lower, lazier latitudes.

DEBORAH AND I have often discussed how we think it will feel to sight the Antarctic continent again. Last time we were so captivated by what was an unknown for us that the mere sight of it forever changed our lives.

That was seven years ago. Since then we've often wondered if the overwhelming feeling of humility would be equally strong if we ever came back. I expect so. After all, a drama plays continuously around this continent, the likes of which are to be found nowhere else on Earth.

While researching for our first visit, we came across paintings made by artists aboard the first ships to visit Antarctica. They pictured a coastline more frightening than even our imaginations could accept. The same applied to the icebergs, which were depicted as grotesque monsters about to swallow the ships. We chuckled at the painters' fantasies. They painted from their emotional impressions, rather than from reality, or so we thought. But when we arrived and looked with our own eyes, those paintings suddenly came alive. For seven weeks we lived in such breathtakingly scary surroundings that we were ashamed of our own naiveté. After all, the pilot books had warned us to not trust our charts; when the soundings were taken, icebergs could have hidden shoals. In addition, we had difficulty learning to distinguish between snow-covered islands, islets, and skerries and icebergs or find shoals and rocks because they were overrun by ice. Truly safe navigation was impossible. Spots on the chart that looked like promising anchorages turned out to be blocked by ice or rimmed by calving glacier walls and we had to press onward, no matter how cold or tired we were. Good shelter often turned bad in a wind shift or a tidal change. Ice pieces, often as beautiful as a marble sculpture on first view, turned nightmarish as they let loose their captured energy, heaving, cracking, and rolling without warning.

Last time, we made our landfall as far south on the Antarctic Peninsula as that year's ice allowed, trusting that the information on the area's pilot chart was correct. According to the wind roses, we should have had fair winds from the south when we turned around, but that wasn't the case. The prevailing winds along the peninsula proved to come from the opposite direction, resulting in a long and sometimes very demanding beat back north. Therefore, this time we have decided to make our landfall at the Melchior Islands, off the northern part of the peninsula, to be able to sail with the wind as we continue south.

So far, everything is unfolding according to plan. The northeasterly wind that developed during Deborah's watch has remained steady during mine. The sea hasn't grown, however, and is more moderate than what we are used to for this wind strength. There's a reason: cold water is denser than warm water. Therefore, waves here build more slowly and break later. In fact, not until the wind is above gale force do the near-freezing water's waves first start to break. We must always remember that cold water's breaking seas have more punch and are thus more danger-ous than their counterparts in warmer climes.

Late morning, the northeasterly wind starts to intensify, and by noon it reaches 23 knots. In response, I roll in the genoa to the second reef marker. I also take in a reef in the main but keep full mizzen for the time being. To be on the safe side, I also set the cutter staysail. Then, if there's a rapid wind increase, I can furl the genoa without losing headway.

I sincerely hope this wind increase is not the beginning of the Antarctic Bellows, a wind condition we named the last time we were here. When we met meteorologist Rubens Villela in Brazil, he explained that our bellows is actually called a low inertial jet. The phenomenon oc-curs when a cell of high pressure exists in the Weddell Sea east of the Antarctic Peninsula and a depression moves through Drake Passage. North of the high pressure, the air stream is easterly. Usually, that wind's flow is blocked by the mountainous ridge of the peninsula, and the higher altitude's layer of cold air puts a lid on it.

Without an escape valve, the pressure builds. When the approaching depression "lends" some energy, drawing the air out and around the tip of the peninsula, it joins forces with the depression's northeast air flow to rush west past King George Island. When it reaches Deception Island, it is often a hurricane-force wind. It continues to arc along the penin-sula, passing Brabant Island where it starts to diminish.

Around two o'clock in the afternoon, the atmosphere in the cockpit is like the waiting room at the dentist; although there's nothing to worry about, butterflies flutter nonetheless. I start looking for land. The visibility is at best about 10 nautical miles, and even though we have over forty miles left to landfall and I know looking is senseless, I can't resist. Were the weather clear, I would certainly see both Brabant and Anvers Islands high above the horizon. They are each well above 6,500 feet high (2,000 m), and right in between them lie the Melchior Islands, our designated landfall. Even more than for orientation, I'd like to see land to check for condensation streams trailing off the highest peaks. If so, then soon the ferocious northeasterly will descend to sea level. The tension builds as the hours pass, my feelings churning along with the low clouds and the gray sea.

When we have 30 nautical miles left, a small clearing wipes part of the cloud away. As the sun breaks through, I catch sight of a solitary cluster of high, white mountain peaks 10 degrees to starboard. They must be the highest peaks of Brabant Island. Behind them remains high gray cloud, now brilliantly banded by a light underside, which is the sunlight reflecting from a huge glacier located on the peninsula. I can't see any sign of Anvers Island yet; it must still be too far away. But that's as far as my thoughts get. Suddenly, the boat is laid on its side by a tremendous gust. To keep my balance, I instinctively grab one of the windward winches.

To ensure that we could make it in to the Melchior Islands without any forced tacks, we have gained as much height as we could the past two days, and right now I'm thankful we did. That extra easting enables me to fall off to a beam reach now, easing the genoa so the boat straightens up, and still steer the right course. Before bothering to adjust the mainsheet, I open the cupola and tell Deborah that she should dress in foul weather gear and be ready to give me a hand. "The wind is increasing very rapidly," I tell her. She smiles and looks quizzically at me from her position in the galley. By her compound expression, I understand that she also had difficulty hanging on a few seconds ago.

While the hatch is open, I take the opportunity to lean farther down into the boat and grab my tether. The timing couldn't have been worse. The boat is bashed broadside by a wave, which crests and breaks with its full power on the topsides. The hood on my foul weather gear is not up. As I close the hatch and stand up, ice-cold water pours down my neck and runs down my spine. I look to weather. In a few seconds, the sea has nearly doubled and our safety margin has been crimped. In the steep sea, it has suddenly become more difficult to see if there's any ice ahead.

We'll now be lucky to see growlers at a distance of two wavelengths. If we don't spot them until the wave crest just before, then we will only have four boat lengths to avoid them. Considering the speed that we are sailing, that gives us less than ten seconds. It's barely enough.

We can't afford to take any chances. Deborah will have to keep a continuous lookout. But instead of having her come on deck, I decide that she shall remain inside the boat and look out through the cupola. There she can concentrate on her job. On deck, where she can help me, were something not to work as it should and were she to turn her gaze away from her lookout, she could easily miss seeing ice.

As soon as Deborah is positioned on the ladder and understands her job, my mind turns to the question, How much do I dare reef? For the purpose of the lookout, I want to sail slowly, yet speed is essential for steerage in this sea condition. If our speed decreases, we will not be able to steer away from ice as easily, and the impact of breaking waves can be greater, than if we were sailing faster. I don't want to sail below 6 knots.

A swell, barely discernible earlier as a long gentle heave, has taken on enormous proportions since we entered more shallow water. When it meets the waves that the wind is pushing from the opposite direction, the sea stands on edge and explodes like two heavily loaded express trains colliding. When we happen to be in the same place, the sea roils and roars across the deck. There's no established rhythm to these waves, whose vertical breakers are 10 feet (3 m) high. Sometimes the boat is drenched from both leeward and windward simultaneously. At worst, the entire lifeline is buried under masses of water.

I have never seen anything like this in my entire life. And it's never felt so ghastly to have to go on deck. But I have no choice; the sails must be reefed. During the time it takes me to clip on my tether and move to the mainmast, the wind has increased to over 42 knots. I immediately take in the third reef in the main and then the second reef in the mizzen. But to have as much drive as possible in the sails, I don't totally furl the genoa. Instead, I have a 3-square-yard "storm fleck," the purpose of which is to steer the wind in behind the staysail. Doing so practically doubles the staysail's driving force.

I alternate reducing sail with stowing all the lines and sheets leading into the cockpit in their respective cubbyholes so they can't wash overboard and interfere with the windvane's pendulum or, even worse, tangle in the propeller. The more I work with the boat, the more my discomfort dwindles. In its place I start to appreciate the fast and exceedingly dramatic sailing. It is so exhilarating that were I younger, I probably would've wet myself.

When the work is finished, I lean out to the lee to check if the foresails are properly sheeted. I spot a stretch of brash ice a couple hundred yards ahead of the boat. To make sure that Deborah also sees it, I tap on the cupola to get her attention and point forward.

Hand signals are something that we have developed over the years; without them, it would often be impossible to coordinate our work on deck. Deborah answers me by pointing to her eye and then nodding her head. When she signals that she has already adjusted the course to sail closer to the wind and, by moving her forefinger away from her thumb shows me just how far she has pulled the control line to the windvane, I sheet the sails accordingly.

The wind continues to increase. Eventually it's above 50 knots and gusting above 65. At this stage I don't dare drive the boat harder, so I roll in the genoa completely. Then, since I know that in this wind strength *Northern Light* will make above 8 knots with just the mizzen and staysail, I decide to drop the main.

Seas break continuously over deck. When I move toward the mainmast, the water is more often than not up to my knees. As I ease the mainsail halyard, I have to brace my upper body against the mast. The work goes very slowly. Probably six or seven minutes pass before I pull down what's left above the third reef. There's a constant threat of getting my feet washed out from under me, and I maintain "one hand for me, one hand for the ship." I also have to concentrate more on the sea and how it affects the boat's movement than on the work I am trying to accomplish. Even so, I am surprised two times by heavily breaking seas.

When the mainsail is finally secured, I make sure to start back for the cockpit at the right moment. To have something to hang on to the entire way, I creep on the windward side from one stanchion to the next, the upper lifeline running under my armpit and my hand gripping the toe rail. I continuously keep my eyes on the sea, but I do not see much. The air is loaded with spray. The force of each approaching wave is therefore best judged by the speed and angle the boat moves in the valley while rising to meet the next sea.

On my journey aft, the boat takes itself up and over the first and the second waves with no problem. But when the boat is in the third valley, I hear the hissing noise that proceeds each breaker suddenly change to a deep rumble. We hit a momentary vacuum. All motion takes a pause. When I look up I see, just as I could expect, that the coming wave has built tremendously higher than the others. The breaker starts its lionish roar, and instinctively I loosen my grip around the rail and rush for higher ground. To make it up on the main boom seems to be my only possible escape. As quick as I can, I lock my arms around the boom and try to heave myself up on top of it. But halfway there I come to a dead stop. I'm yanked to the side and end up hanging by my arms.

For safety's sake, when I left the cockpit I attached my tether to the jackline, a stainless steel wire that runs on deck from bow to stern. This tether is made to be just so long that there's no way I can possibly ever be washed farther than the rail. That's great, but for the moment the short length of my tether keeps me from being able to reach safety!

I am almost completely exhausted. Pulling down the mainsail used up practically all my energy. And because it would be meaningless to attempt to make it down on deck again, free the tether, and then figure out where to rehook it before the next breaker hits, I decide on another plan. I throw one leg around the boom and heave myself up just far enough to hang underneath it. Suspended upside-down, I watch how the cockpit, cupola, and Deborah inside it disappear under churning water.

I feel like a cat that's been chased up a tree and is waiting for the appropriate moment to come down again. The entire incident has become very comical. When the wave has rolled by and I spot Deborah again, I grin and wave at her. She opens the cupola momentarily and calls out to me, but I can't make out what she says; her voice is drowned by the engulfing din. I could, however, see that her look was quite tense, which is enough to tell me that she doesn't exactly share my appreciation of the moment.

It's not always easy for other people to understand my sense of humor, but just why eludes me. But the fact that I, during difficult situations often perceive circumstances as pleasurable whereas onlookers can't see past the life-threatening elements, can be explained medically. During stress, the body produces adrenaline and endorphins. Without these chemical changes, we wouldn't manage the work that we—even with the help of these chemicals—perceive as both physically and mentally difficult. Then comes the good part: when the physical work is over, there's a very pleasurable side effect that I have felt strongly many times. So, it is not strange that I think there's a real kick to rough days. Of course, the one who is not working can't feel it. All I can say to Deborah in this instance is an American saying she taught me: tough luck!

Around six o'clock in the evening, we come in line with the northern point of Brabant Island. In its shelter the wind drops quickly, but the novelty doesn't last long enough for more than a surprised look at each other. The next second we are in the path of an enormous downdraft rushing off the glacier-covered mountainside. There is no remote possibility to parry it by steering into the eye of the wind. Were we to do so, the sails would flog and be torn to pieces. When one of us sees one of these katabatic gusts churning up the surface of the water, we simply warn the other and hang on. For a few seconds, the shriek in the rigging is painful to hear. Three times, with just a couple of minutes in between, the boat is knocked down. We wait for the fourth, but nothing happens.

Northern Light glides forward a bit on its own momentum, then slows to a stop. She doesn't even roll. The sea has died completely, and the absolute, almost stark quiet is broken only by the calls of two penguins in search of each other. The quick transformation from inferno to calm borders on the incomprehensible. Positively dumbstruck, Deborah and I look at each other. After sixteen days of strenuous sailing from Mar del Plata—and before that, years of wonder and worries—we have reached our destination.

We still have to find a place where we can anchor, though. All the reefs are released, but that doesn't help; there's no wind for the sails to catch. The airstream is totally blocked by the islands. Because it seems meaningless to just wait while the current takes us somewhere inside the island group where we *don't* want to go, we start the engine.

While dropping the mainsail, I had noticed that the antenna had snapped at its attachment point on the mainmast. So, while we motor I attach a new temporary antenna—a quarter-wave length of household electrical wire (!)—and climb the mizzen to hang it. Precisely on time, as if we had been waiting the whole day, Deborah tunes the new antenna and contacts the other amateur radio operators in the United States who are always waiting to hear from us. I take the wheel while she gives them all the good news. In this case, *all* isn't exactly a short message. While the *yackety yack yack yack* continues I'm glad to have an engine with which to power the radio!

When Deborah eventually finishes, we look at the detail charts of the Melchior Islands and see an excellent anchorage in a lagoonlike bay on the west side of Eta Island. The depth there is between 23 and 30 feet (7 to 9 m); in other words, it's ideal. At eight o'clock in the evening, we make ready to anchor. So that I know when to put the engine in reverse, Deborah sings out the readings from the depth sounder: "One hundred and sixty-five feet [50 m]. Hundred and fifty [46 m]. Hey, it's getting very deep. . . . Three hundred and twenty-seven feet [100 m]!" We turn around and circle for nearly an hour, but we never find any bottom less than 100 feet (30.5 m) deep.

It remains absolutely calm. Because there's very little ice, eyeball navigation should be easy. Besides, there's no rush. Deborah suggests that we put the charts away and use our imagination to find a place with the desirable depth. I agree. After all, exploration makes life truly exciting. "Imagine that there had been signs marking the anchoring spots. There wouldn't be much wilderness feeling left then, would there?" Deborah asks. I agree with her but wonder if I really should have. "You agree? With *me*? Again?" she asks. For the next few moments, Deborah looks very serious and stands with her hands on her hips, but then I see a spark in her eye as she points toward a cove she thinks is good and protected. "While we're on the same wavelength, let's anchor and fix the double berth," she says.

Around midnight we are still awake and our spirits are too high to consider sleeping. The only thing that doesn't fit the mood is the squeaking and grinding noise of the anchor chain. We have apparently anchored in a "rock garden" and I can only assume that there's no real holding. The thought pulls me out of bed, but when I look through the cupola I see that we're still in exactly the same spot, and there's no danger. It's perfectly bright outside and still calm. The only change since we anchored is that it has become overcast and snowed some. Because it is only a few degrees below freezing, the snow is light and the boat looks like a newly hatched gosling whose down has just dried. I feel as if I too have just been born to the life I love. As Deborah said to our friends over the radio, "What an arrival!"

FROM
ICE!

BY
Tristan Jones

The frigid waters of polar regions are treacherous in many ways. In addition to the dangers of storms and lee shores, icebergs may sink your boat or pack ice may freeze you in for the winter. Many sailors shun these areas and stay in more hospitable seas, but a few are drawn to the isolation and beauty of polar areas, or to the cold and ice itself. Compared to those tropical areas visited by so many boats, some sailors have viewed the Arctic and Antarctic as the last great wild areas, the last great adventure. This is part of why the world-sailing Tristan Jones decided to push as far north as humanly and technically possible in a small boat, and to do it alone.

Needing a suitably rugged ship, he converted an old 34-foot wooden rescue lifeboat into a yawl and provisioned and supplied her for two years, including a winter he would be frozen into the pack ice as close to the North Pole as he could get. From Ireland he sailed with his three-legged, one-eyed dog first to Iceland and then north to Greenland, and in spring 1960 he headed north. The record for a solo voyager was the high latitude of 84 degrees north, and Jones wanted to beat that if possible.

The selection here begins as he leaves Scoresby

Sund in southeast Greenland, at the latitude of 72 degrees. Only 13 degrees more to the record! he thinks as he sets sail, only 780 miles due north through the ice! And ice there is, everywhere, as he seeks a passage north through the drifting bergs and pack ice, and soon he is trapped in it and being attacked by a polar bear.

Tristan Jones is one of the most popular authors of sail, the author of nearly a dozen books about his adventures all over the globe. His boisterous style is reminiscent of classic tellers of yarns and tall stories. And indeed some claim not all his stories are true, though readers can decide for themselves how much that may matter. . . .

/ / /

MY aim, upon departing from Scoresby Sund, was to sail north as hard and fast as possible through the ice fields, along the shore lead, between the shore ice and the pack ice. My destination was Kap Bismarck, on the coast of Queen Louise Land, approximately 380 miles north, on latitude seventy-six degrees, forty-five minutes north. If I made a swift, easy passage, I should arrive within two weeks. If, on the other hand, the passage was slow because of ice obstacles and hazards, and I arrived late in the northern summer, I would winter near the Danmarks Havn wireless station, in a small bay which might or might not be ice free. Then, when the ice broke up the following summer, I would press on north up the coast of Germania Land and attempt to buck the current and the ice to a point north of latitude eighty-four, the furthest north ever reached to date by a sailing ship.

If the passage was fast, I would call briefly at Kap Bismarck, then press on further north while the ice was still fairly loose, hoping to reach the magic eighty-four-degree point that same autumn. Then, the ice would seize the boat and, on the current, carry *Cresswell* south again over the winter, back to civilization. If the drift back south was slow, I still had a good chance of weathering it out, for there was two years' supply of food onboard, and plenty of seals around.

The yearly inspector's ship was expected to arrive any day, and as I was eager to beat the coming winter in late September, I sailed out of Scoresby Sund anchorage with few regrets, apart from losing the fine company of the Danish radiomen and meteorologists, who had been hospitable and informative.

I motored out of the Sund through the loosening pack ice, dodging mountainous icebergs floating out into the Arctic Ocean. Once clear of the shore ice, which extended about forty miles, I found a wide-open lead to the north, though well dotted with isolated ice floes of all sizes. I was headed for the radio station at Myggbukta, on the coast of Hold with Hope peninsula about 160 miles north. After three days and nights of hard sailing, in a flat sea, with the south wind dead astern, I was off the island (Ø) of Bontekoe, where I moored onto an ice floe which had found its way around to the southern side of the island and gone aground. Here I slept fitfully for one "night." I was concerned in case another floe should come around the island and trap *Cresswell* against the one she was already moored to. After a few hours' sleep I decided to stay at Bontekoe Ø for one more day, carrying out the necessary chores which had been neglected during the three-day passage north, when I had been on the wheel practically the whole time.

After the work was done, I took a good look around, though I did not leave the boat. I could have climbed over the piled up ice on the southern shore, but I was wary of possible accidents and also of the boat's breaking loose from the floe, if the wind shifted. During the day, it was warm enough to wear my normal sailing clothes—jersey, sheepskin jacket, long cotton underpants, and blue jeans, with long stockings and sea boots. But at night it turned cold, and I was glad to be in the sleeping bag for the short "dark" hours.

I watched the broken-up bits of the great pack ice field as they floated by the island—long ice fields, several miles across, which took hours to pass; "ice cakes" only as big as a motor car; chunks and the slushy "brash," melting on the sides of the larger floes and sinking into the ocean. On many of the floes and fields, there were seals, sometimes in small groups, sometimes alone, and I watched them through the binoculars as they woke from their brief naps and popped their heads up for a startled look about for marauding bears.

Over to the west, as soon as the sky clouded over, a strange phenomenon appeared. A perfectly recognizable map of the terrain below was reflected on the white bases of the clouds. It tallied up quite well with the information I had on the charts. Water of the fiords and leads showed up black on the surface of the clouds, while the ice and snow was a mottled grey color, and the vegetation, lichen on the rocks ashore, reflected a yellow or brown. It was as if someone was holding a huge mirror in the sky. This is what the Danes called the "ice-blink." "Very useful," I said to Nelson. Now I knew how to find a good water lead in cloudy weather.

By this time I had taken to wearing snow goggles, because the summer sunlight, which strikes a glare through the dry, clean air, made the ice of the floes shimmer with blinding light. After suffering a headache, I soon realized that snow blindness is in fact the result of eyestrain caused by the constant, instinctive seeking of shadows which, because of the angle of the sun's rays, are almost nonexistent. Man's greatest aid to judging distance, in normal conditions, is the effect of light and shadow. If the shadow effect is changed, as it is, for example, in moonlight, or under fluorescent lighting, then our eyes search continually for the normal references, straining themselves to gauge distance. The effect of the reflection of light from the ice is also a cause of blindness, but a minor one compared to trying to find normal seeing distance in abnormal conditions.

The thought of the continual procession of bergs and ice fields across the top of the world, for thousands of square miles, was, at first, somewhat terrifying. I was relieved that there was no one else with me. Eventually I realized that the so-called Arctic hysteria, the feeling of panic which exploring parties have reported, is, in fact, only a form of mass hysteria transmitted from one nervous member of a group to the others. Being alone, I stood a much better chance of avoiding this affliction. I decided to consider only the immediate environment, and to hell with the rest of the Arctic. That could look after itself.

When I left the ice-floe off Bontekoe Ø and headed north for the radio station at Myggbukta, it was obvious that I stood no chance at all of getting to the shore. The ice was one solid frozen mass of heaped-up, stranded floes and bergs, with ledges and needlepoints jumbled up higgledy-piggledy into the sky as far as the eye could see. The nearest I could approach the shore of Gausshalv Island, where the radio station was located, was about thirty miles, and I dared not chance walking over the shore ice for that distance. I decided to carry on north.

Here I had to turn my course east, out into the ocean, towards the moving continent of pack ice floating down from the North Pole, looking like an army on the move—horsemen and gun carriages, coaches and long lines of foot soldiers marching across the rim of the world.

After heading east for forty miles offshore, I eventually found the edge of the fixed mass of shore ice and, picking my course carefully, headed again north. There was little wind on this passage, and progress was painfully slow. I did not use the engine, as I wished to conserve fuel for emergencies, in case I was trapped in thin ice. The wind was so weak that it took me almost ten days to cover the eighty miles to latitude seventy-four, away out over the ice piled up on the Home Foreland. I was still in an area where the British Liverpool expedition of 1824 had left marks, right up the coast, in the names of headlands and islands.

At latitude seventy-four progress was almost halted altogether, for the pack ice was much closer to the shore ice, and the shore lead, so-called (though it was anything up to two hundred miles out to sea), was very indistinct. Many times I headed up one lead only to find myself in the middle of a solid field of ice many times bigger than a New York City block. Then I would have to turn the boat around and motor out against the southerly breeze, running with the current to escape the mass of ice closing around the boat.

It was now the first week in August, and there was already a noticeable change in daytime temperatures. After two more weeks of struggling to find my way through this maze of icy jigsaw puzzles, the wind changed to the north and the temperature fell below freezing. I donned my fawnskin underwear, a shirt and an extra jersey, the Eskimo-made caribou-skin jerkin and trousers, and the sealskin boots.

Until the eighth of August there had been light twenty-four hours a day. After that the sun was down below the horizon for rapidly increasing periods of time, so that by the end of August, daylight and darkness each took half of every twenty-four hours, as they do below the equator. As the skies were mostly clear of cloud, I was still getting quite accurate sun sights. However, I had difficulty in finding my course through the ice, for there was rarely any ice-blink, which would have indicated water passages.

I reached Pendulum Island, at latitude seventy-four, forty-five north, on August 18, and, to my delight, found clear water running north, ahead. There were still many, many ice floes around, and after a brief rest (tied up against a floe in fairly open water), I pushed on, ever north, using the engine, as there was rarely room to beat against the wind. Progress was slow, as the engine was only ten horsepower and *Cresswell* was heavy with stores. Hammering against the strong north wind and current, I could not make more than two knots over the ground, and most of that to east or west, dodging the floes and bergs, which were becoming disturbingly frequent, especially at the end of the easterly legs.

When I reached the edge of the shore ice, off Kap Philip Broke, the southeastern cape of Shannon Island, at latitude seventy-five north, I saw my first polar bear. They are difficult to spot except when they are fairly close, say about three hundred yards. The dirty yellow color of their fur blends in perfectly with ice which is more than one season old, but I happened to be scanning the inshore side of the ice, as best I could, with the binoculars, when suddenly a slight movement in one hummock of piled-up floe caught my eye.

It is difficult to gauge distance in clear air over ice, but I reckoned he was about two hundred yards from the boat, walking on all fours. From fore to aft he was all of ten feet long, and he looked as if he weighed a ton. By this time, with the wind coming south off the ice, Nelson had picked up his scent and went rigid, sniffing the air, the classic pose of the hunting Labrador. When he sighted the bear with his one eye, he jumped and disappeared down below.

I had been warned about bears out on the ice by the Danes in Scoresby Sund. They had told me that a polar bear ashore was, like the grizzly bear out of the woods, a timid beast, who would avoid any encounter with an enemy. But once out on the floes, he was king of all he surveyed. He had only seals and wolves (possibly) to deal with, and he became a hungry, arrogant, violent, very dangerous wild beast, whose weight alone was enough to knock the life out of the strongest man. I put *Cresswell* on a broad reach, out to the east, adjusted the sails, for there was a perfectly clear stretch of water ahead on that course, then went below to make hot chocolate and warm myself.

"Thank God there's water between us and him," I said to Nelson, who was cowering under the cabin table. He bumped his tail in the floorboards. But I was disturbed by the thought that if I did not fetch Kap

Bismarck and got stuck in the southward drifting ice pack, one of these brutes, or maybe even more than one, might get wind of us and attack.

By August 30 I was on latitude seventy-five degrees fifty minutes north—only sixty miles south of Kap Bismarck and safety. But try as I would to find a clear passage, it was almost impossible. Stretched right across the northern horizon was a solid barrier of piled up shore ice, rising in hummocks up to three hundred feet above the ocean level, along with a moving mass of pack ice and bergs, some of the latter up to nine hundred feet high and three miles from bow to stern.

Choosing one seemingly promising narrow lead running slightly west of north, hardly wider than three times the beam of *Cresswell*, I pressed on. By now the tops of the ice floes were well above deck level of my boat. I was, therefore, most of the time protected from the wind to about a third of the way up the mast. The engine was pushing the boat at four knots over the ground, going flat out, while the ice floes, moving on the current, were traveling at around a knot and a half. Our combined speed, therefore, was around six and a half knots—eight land miles per hour. All day, all night, for two days, I stayed at the wheel continuously, without a break, wending my way through these never-ending walls of gleaming ice as high as a garden wall, sometimes in a narrow passage hardly wide enough for the boat, sometimes in wide stretches.

I was still cold, even though I had thrown two blankets over my Arctic clothing and rigged up a windshield of canvas, forward of the wheel, to keep off the boat's own wind, created by her speed. The rigging was frosting up. This was a great worry. Every time I reached a stretch of wide lead or clear water, I had to lash the wheel, leave the boat at the mercy of the current, climb the masts, and knock off the ice with a small ax.

Doing this became a nightmare of cold and superhuman effort, short of sleep as I was. High up the mast the north wind blew intensely cold, frosting up all my clothes, with my breath forming an inch-thick layer of solid ice over the thick scarf tied up around my head between the goggles and the collar of my jerkin.

Not to have knocked the ice off the rigging would have been to commit suicide. It formed so quickly in the wind that within three hours it could create such a weight high up on the craft that it would overcome the weight of the ballast in the keel and capsize her. *Cresswell* would sink immediately. If I did not drown right away, I would freeze to death. If I managed to clamber onto the floe, I would both freeze and starve to death anyway in a long, protracted agony over a couple of days. Getting rid of the ice was a matter of staying alive.

By the morning of September 1, I was almost falling asleep on my feet. I had reached latitude seventy-six degrees ten minutes north. Bismarck station was a mere thirty miles away. Perhaps there was just enough clear water ahead to make it to Bismarck and sleep in safety. Perhaps around this next cape of ice, perhaps around the corner of that berg, the ice would clear just enough to get me thirty miles. Thirty miles in an ocean-crossing sailing yacht was a mere six hours' normal sailing; in a motor car, half an hour on a good road. Thirty miles—the difference between safety for the duration of the bitterly cold winter, and extreme discomfort, danger, and possibly even death, a cold, lonely death, in the ice. I pressed on, more by willpower now, for my physical strength was ebbing with lack of sleep. I was about three hundred miles nearer the Pole than the northernmost tip of Alaska.

Suddenly, my fate was decided for me, though I did not realize it at the time. The lead I had followed for the past day of cold torture ended up in a perfect wall of ice. I turned a corner, and there I was, like being in a harbor. By this time my fuel stock was so low, and the engine so cold, that getting out of this impasse under power was out of the question. I decided to take a chance. I tied the boat by a bowline only from the end of the cul-de-sac and went to sleep. I slept four hours, dead to the world.

When I awoke, feeling much stronger and more confident, I climbed onto the floe. Earlier it had been difficult to mount the floe to drive the stake in, as I had to cut steps out of the side with an ax in order to get on top. I had been too weak to jump up. Now it was much easier, and the sky had lightened into a grey twilight. The wind, however, was still screaming over the floes from the north, and once on top of the floe, it was a job to remain upright.

I looked first to the north; what I saw was one of the bitterest, most disappointing sights I have ever seen in my life.

There, only forty yards from where I stood, on the other side of an isthmus joining two huge fields of jammed-up pack ice that stretched away as far as I could see east and west, northeast and southwest, was another lead heading north, and away, at the end of it, at its mouth, was a great stretch of clear water right across the north horizon!

"Goddamn it, bugger it, and blast it!" I cursed myself, the floes, the forty yards, everything. Then, more in anger than in desperation, I clambered back onboard, grabbed the big tree-felling ax, and started to hack away at the ice. But after a few minutes the foolishness of trying to carve through a forty-yard-thick wall of ice twelve feet deep became obvious. I sat down on the ice. Tears were futile in this temperature, for they would freeze as soon as they left my eyes. Then I thought of what would happen if these two fields of ice, each higher than the boat, came together.

There was only one solution, for sailing back south was out of the question. It would take days to overtake the miles and miles of ice fields, and during those days they could crush together anyway, especially if the westerly field hit the fixed shore ice. I would not stand a chance. If I stayed where I was, I was a dead man; if I tried to sail south, I was probably a dead man. The third alternative, difficult though it might be, was the only solution. I must try to get the boat up onto the ice floe, about seven feet above sea level. But how?

There was only one possible way. I must hack a slipway out of the ice, wide enough for *Cresswell*'s hull to slide up, then I must lighten her bows, get her bows onto the ice whilst the stern was still loaded and low in the water, then unload all her other gear, and drag the empty hull up the incline.

And this is what I set to doing. I hacked away with the ax and shifted tons of ice, solid hard ice, until, after nine days' steady hard labor, I had a "ramp" leading from just below water level, back through the ice floe at a steady incline of about twenty-five degrees, back almost to the other side of the ice-floe isthmus. I worked all the daylight hours, axing, throwing, shoveling, slashing, until a fairly smooth ramp was created.

On the ninth of September I unloaded all the stores, all the sails, all the tools off the boat, having made a ladder out of some spare lumber, so I could climb off the deck straight onto the "deck" of the floe.

With the forefoot now above the waterline, I turned the boat bows onto the ramp and dragged her until the keel, just an inch of it, was resting on the ice. Then, I started to unload the midship parts of the boat, lifting the forefoot even higher above the bottom edge of the ice ramp.

Then, with much labor, I dug a five-foot hole in the ice at the inner end of the ramp, and into this I dropped the eighty-pound hurricane anchor. The chain from the anchor was secured to a three-inch-diameter nylon storm running line, a hundred fathoms of it—six hundred feet. I filled the anchor hole up with salt water and had a short sleep after a hearty meal of corned beef, rice, and porridge.

When I awoke the salt water in the anchor hole had frozen solid, and I had a good "deadman" to pull the boat up against. I had no winches in *Cresswell*, so the whole thing had to be done with blocks and tackles, five of them, six-inchers, with three sheaves apiece. I dug footholds into the top of the floe, reeved the storm line through the blocks, and set to pulling four and a half tons up the twenty-five-degree incline. It took me five days to get the forefront up to the chain, a matter of twenty-eight yards or so. The bottom of the keel was then only about a foot below the top of the floe. She was out of danger. She was sitting almost on top of the ice, exposed to a bitter cold wind, covered in frost and driven ice, but she was safe. That was the main thing. Wearily I reloaded my stores onboard, except for some of the cartons of corned beef, which would take up valuable space in the cabin. These I covered with an old sail, pegged down into the ice. Then I noticed that the northern exit from the floe had jammed up solidly with ice floes.

"One good thing about this situation, old son," I said to Nelson, as I clambered below to get a long rest, "at least we don't have to worry about the rigging freezing up now." But the ice would still have to be knocked off regularly, at least twice a day, to prevent its weight snapping the masts.

I made a big pot of burgoo, so I could rest thoroughly during the next day or two, and tacked up all my mutton cloths on the inner lining of the hull around the cabin, then fixed felt pads over the portholes and the skylights, while the tiny cabin warmed up with the heat of the cooking. Then I went topsides to have a last look around.

The wind had died at last, and there was little noise except for the distant cracking and crunching of the ice. The sun had dropped over the southwest horizon, changing the sky to pale blue, deepening into turquoise, Prussian blue, then Stygian black. In the north and east the stars shone so bright, so close, that it seemed as if they hung around my shoulders. The dryness of the atmosphere made the rays of the stars diffuse into each other. The effect was like standing under a great chandelier of a billion-trillion shining candles.

I decided it was too cold to piss in the open air. I would do it in the big wine demijohn, hermetically sealed, which I used in inclement weather. I touched the mizzen shrouds with my mittened hands. Small bits of glistening ice fell off the rigging wire. I made a mental note to clean my ice goggles later. I had removed them, for the twilight was deepening. The smell of a good stew simmered up the companionway hatch.

Although I had failed to reach Nansen's latitude of eighty-four degrees north, I had got very close—within eight degrees. I had reached a point only 850 miles from the North Pole itself, and despite the potentially terrifying situation *Cresswell* had been in only two weeks previously, she was now reasonably safe, unless the ice under her broke up.

As I turned to go below, I saw the bear. Twelve feet long, padding silently, swiftly over the snow-laden ice. He was only fifty yards away, coming straight at the boat!

"JESUS CHRIST ALMIGHTY!" I said under my breath to Nelson, who was also on deck to perform his ablutions over the side. But he had gone stock rigid, his ears quivering, his eye glaring at the monster advancing towards us. Then, without thinking, I was down the companionway ladder, grabbing Nelson as I went.

For a second or two, slithering down the ladder, my mind was in a dither. Instinctively grabbing my harpoon, an eight-foot-long ash shaft with a fine, greased steel tip sharpened to a needlepoint, from its stowage on the deck head of the cabin, I turned to mount the ladder. Then my mind started to work. Fast.

"Move!" I shouted to Nelson. "Move, you silly sod. Make the bastard think you're a fox! Move!" Nelson jerked out of his stupor and jumped, then ran as fast as his three legs would carry him up the side-deck, to the fore deck, where he stood his ground, snarling.

By now the bear was hauling himself upright, with his great paws clawing at the guardrails. As his head, with its fierce fangs and glittering, menacing eyes, appeared over the gunwale, I jabbed at him with the harpoon from where I was standing in the companionway. My idea was to fight him off from there, where the lower part of my body was protected and I could duck if he made a swipe at me.

The bear jerked his head and body back in surprise, his great massive claws tearing away the upper wire of the guardrail, bending the one-inch-thick galvanized iron stanchions as if they were putty. Then I realized that this huge creature could, if he wished, literally tear the boat apart with his strength. At the same time Nelson made a gallant charge towards him aft along the side-deck, yapping, snarling, and barking. All hell broke loose. The bear recovered from his shock and rebounded back, his whole body thumping against the hull, which slid sideways, the keel jarring against the side of the ramp. I reacted fast and jabbed at his right paw, which was tearing at the canvas deck cover, the huge nails ripping into the covering clear through to the wood underneath. The harpoon struck home. It went through the bear's forefoot and stuck in the wood underneath. The bear let out a roar loud enough to shake the boat to pieces. Then he ripped his paw, harpoon and all, out of the deck and dropped down onto the ice. The harpoon went flying, clattering over the floe. I could feel his breath, hot and oily, like a cloud of steam from a locomotive. For a second or two Nelson and I stood stock-still, petrified with shock and alarm. The bear crawled on all fours around the side of the boat, bumping the hull with his shoulder. Then I remembered the Very rocket gun.

This is a device, shaped like a pistol, with a barrel eight inches long and an inch and a half bore, into which flare rockets are loaded. Fired by mariners in distress, the rocket will rise into the sky up to four hundred feet and slowly descend, its phosphorous flakes burning all the way back down to the sea's surface. When I had sighted the first bear, off Shannon Island, I had loaded the Very pistol in readiness for just such an attack as this. Now I slithered below, fumbled at the fireworks box, and grabbed the pistol, my hands shaking badly.

The bear had climbed up above the ramp on the other side of the boat and was pawing at the gunwale with one forefoot, while swiping at Nelson, who was trying to lure him forward away from me. I climbed the ladder and turned to face the bear. Holding the Very pistol in one frozen hand, I slammed down as hard as I could on the doghouse roof with the other, fist clenched.

The bear turned his jaws towards me, showing his great fangs, his hungry, wicked eyes crackling with anger. I fired, sending the rocket straight into his throat, a great stream of red light particles. With a grunt, the bear threw himself backwards onto the ice floe, rolling in agony, for the phosphorus of the flare was burning fiercely in his gorge. Then, jumping up and down with tremendous force, he beat the ice with his paws, all the while weaving his upper body from side to side, while

Nelson slithered onto the ice and snapped at his hindquarters. After a few more mighty thuds on the top of the ice floe, which actually shook the boat, the bear took off fast across the ice and dove into the water on the other side of the floe. This did not save him, however, because phosphorus burns underwater. There was a mighty splash in the distance and he disappeared.

Shivering with fright and excitement, I went below, still holding the pistol. Once below I found that my fingers were stuck to the rocket gun. Frostbite! I grabbed a flannel cloth in the galley, threw it into the still simmering stew, then fished it out again with a fork and slapped it, steaming, over my hand. I didn't feel a thing for about thirty seconds, until the circulation was restored, and then the hot stew started to scald the hand, and I knew it was safe. I checked my face, which had been exposed just below the eyes, above the icy scarf. There were two fish-belly white spots, one on each cheek. I repeated the burgoo-stew treatment, in my hurry splashing the hot, gooey liquid onto my eyelids, and in a few seconds the cure was made. The pain almost sent me through the roof.

By this time Nelson was back in the cabin, still shaking with fight-lust.

I threw him a bone and some hardtack, then, after closing the companionway door and hatch cover to try to warm the boat up again, I collapsed on the berth. "Jesus!" I thought, "I hope there's no more of *those* around!"

Wearily I stood at the galley and doled out some stew, but I couldn't eat much. I felt sick with concern and relieved at the same time.

Sleep, when it came, was fitful and full of fantasy. But before I dropped off, I made two resolutions. One was that I would not, while on the ice, sleep more than two hours at a stretch, and then would always leave Nelson on guard in a box in the cockpit to protect him from the wind. The other was that before sleeping I would always, whenever possible, search the floe, out to a perimeter of a thousand yards, for signs of bear.

The Danes had told me that bears generally haunt broken floes and areas where there are many seals, and that, usually, where there is a bear, the white fox is never far behind, eating the scraps of seal left by the bear. Not only the tracks of bear in the ice would warn me of their presence, but also the much smaller spoor of the fox.

Seals are the bears' only food. They are supposed to catch fish, but none of the Danes I met in Iceland and Scoresby Sund had ever seen a bear fishing, neither had any of the Eskimos I met later. There is a conundrum here. If, as the dieticians tell us, fat is only fuel, and protein is the bodybuilder, how is it that the bear, whose only food (evidently) is seal meat, which is practically all fat, manages to build up such a huge, strong body?

During the short days which followed, I remembered everything that the Danes told me about bears. How they stalk a seal, with their great bulky bodies splayed down on the ice, surprisingly flat and inconspicuous from nose to tail. If it's a bearded seal, a great heavy animal, weighing up to six hundred pounds, the bear will satisfy his appetite, then he will leave the rest of the carcass and amble off to sleep. After two or three days' rest, he will return to the frozen seal remains, a great mass of solid hard blubber and bones, and gnaw it, grinding the rock-hard mass between his teeth till there is nothing left. That is if the foxes have not gotten to it while the bear is sleeping.

The bears are usually followed by the fox, as the lion is followed by the hyena and the jackal. But the two ignore each other. The bear knows he cannot catch the swift fox, and the fox knows the bear is too slow for him; so as he follows the bear, the fox runs around and around, playfully teasing the great, lumbering king of the Arctic. Ashore, the white fox tends to treat man in the same way as he does the bear, running round him with not a care in the world. The fox confuses man with the bear. The bear confuses dogs sleeping or lying down on the ice with the seal. The bear also confuses a still man, sitting or lying down, with the seal. The bear confuses a standing or running dog with the white fox. How he sees an active man is not quite clear. It is either as another bear or as another type of hunting animal. Whichever, out on the ice floes the polar bear will attack, because he cannot stand competition in the fight for survival.

During the short daylight hours, I obtained fair sun sights, and it was soon evident that the drift of the floe was more or less due south, at the rate of around half a knot. That is about twelve miles a day, but as the days progressed, this seemed to be slowing down, until by the end of September, it was down to six miles a day. The great ice field was moving steadily and surely, and I was by then at around latitude seventy-three, which put me somewhere near the wireless station at Myggbukta and Ella Island. I kept the boat clear of ice and driven snow as best I could to make her show up against the whiteness of the floe, in case a plane passed overhead. One day, during the twilight, I actually saw a flying boat heading northwest, but it was far away on the southern horizon, and with the bear threat I did not dare waste my signal flares trying to attract his attention. I had only eight flares with me and no idea how many bears might show up. But fortunately none did, although on two occasions I saw them through the binoculars, walking over distant ice floes.

By the first of October my floe, which I had christened *Ark Royal*, had started to break off here and there, with loud cracks, groans, and wheezes. The lead to the north of *Cresswell* was once again widening up. *Ark Royal* was shaped something like an hourglass, with the two sand vessels pointing east and west and *Cresswell* sitting on top of the narrow stem. If the western edge hit against the solid shore ice, the two "sand vessels" would part company, which would split the floe just about where *Cresswell* was.

I made plans to get *Cresswell* back afloat. It was pointless to slide her back down the ice ramp into the southern lead, for it no longer existed. Where the lead had been was a long line of tossed-up ice cakes and chunks piled up into the air for a distance of about two miles!

The only reasonable course was to dig another ramp through the ice over into the northern lead, then slide *Cresswell* down it and try to emerge from the ice field by way of that route, which seemed to be fairly loose, being low, flat, "young" ice, newly formed. If I could get her afloat again, there was a chance I could get out.

I was out on the ice, huddled up in my Eskimo gear, with a screaming storm coming up from the south, blowing ice particles so strong that I could feel them drumming on my caribou-skin jerkin, even through the inner layer of thick hair. Nelson circled me slowly, keeping watch just within visibility range, about fifty yards. I was probing the ice with the harpoon, plotting the course of the new ramp. Ahead, through a momentary gap in the flying ice, I saw a black lump stretched out on the floe, not more than fifty yards away. A seal! I dropped down flat onto the ice.

Nelson was behind me, out of eyeshot of the seal. I lifted my head up and looked around, trying to appear like a seal, jerking my hooded head in quick, sniffing motions. Nelson sat down in the driving ice. He had sensed something was afoot, even though the wind was blowing at an oblique angle from our side to the seal's. I waved my hand down and Nelson dropped prone, his nose twitching.

There, in front of me, was a highly sensitive animal, with built-in natural alarm systems; an animal which never slept for more than three minutes at a time, which continually was on the lookout for foes, and which could move with surprising speed over the ice and into the safe water. Behind me was another animal, highly intelligent at stalking, hunting, and recovering, courageous and bold, but crippled. His missing eye did not seem to affect his sight much. The trouble was the missing forefoot, which deprived him of the hunting dog's speed, though only by a small margin. In between was me, man, intelligent enough to develop weapons capable of killing a seal from a mile away, yet reduced now to becoming a seal himself until he could get near enough to strike.

Soon I was within forty yards of the seal. He raised his smooth head up, with his shoulders supported by his flippers, and slowly looked around. Then he dropped down on the ice. I watched him for a few seconds, then inched forward again. Every five minutes or so I raised my head, just as the seal was doing, and gazed around. Nelson stayed prone, but he too was slowly slithering forward right behind me, keeping my body between him and the seal. After another hour of inching forward little by little, I was within twenty yards of the seal. After several hard stares, each lasting about a minute, he no longer looked my way. He still rose up on his fins and looked around, but only at the quarters of his vision away from my direction. Then I realized that he had made up his mind that I was another seal.

I scrabbled quietly forward, keeping as close to the ice as I could. By this time my dark goggles had started to steam, and I longed to take them off and clean them, but of course this would have warned the seal. I moved ahead again, perched up, looked around. Nelson had stopped moving with me. He was too crafty to come near enough for the seal to see him and think he was a fox following a bear. Another hour, another ten yards, then a slow nudging forward over the smooth, twilit ice. The next five yards took about twenty minutes to cover, as I moved a little faster because the seal seemed to be getting restless and I was concerned in case he should suddenly take off.

By this time I could study him at close quarters. He was about nine feet long and must have weighed a good four hundred pounds. He was a bearded seal, what the Eskimos call an *ugrug*. Every now and then he would rise up, like a huge slug, and search the area away from me. At intervals his tail flapped lazily against the ice. He looked fat and satisfied; there was enough food on him to give me energy to build ten ramps. I edged closer, trying to make the same breathing noise as he, a sort of heavy wheeze, like a person snoring in his throat.

Fifteen feet away I raised my feet and slapped the ice, just as he was doing with his tail. As he rose to look around away from me, I slowly lifted the harpoon and flung it, hard as I could, straight at his neck. It went right through and he dropped like a stone, with no twitching, no jerking, nothing. His huge carcass just collapsed on the ice.

"Come on, boy!" I jumped up and fell on the harpoon handle, twisting it out. Nelson was up in a flash, snapping and snarling, standing just clear of the seal's head and throat, his back teeth bared, ready to bite. I plunged the harpoon again into the shoulder, as deep as I could. There was a slight resistance as the steel barb entered the tough skin, then it slid right in like a dart into a slab of lard.

Satisfied the seal was truly dead, I looked around for bear and then trudged back to the boat for a bucket and a box. In another two hours I had enough blubber laying alongside the boat to feed a small ship's crew for a fortnight and more.

After a meal and a reconnoiter around our perimeter, I had a sleep, with Nelson on guard, gnawing at a huge chunk of raw seal blubber.

Once awake, I started to dig the new ramp. A weary, backbreaking job. On the first one I had great difficulty shifting the huge slabs of ice with mittened hands. I made a "longshoreman's hook" out of a great shark-fishing barb by fixing a wooden handle on it, and so I could now grab onto the ice and drag it clear. It took until October 15 to complete the ramp. For two days I was immobile, taking refuge from a raging blizzard. The next task was to start moving the boat.

The first thing was to dig out the hurricane anchor, then plant it again into another hole astern of the boat. Then the fifty-pound fisherman anchor had to be dug into yet another five-foot-deep hole just over the top of the ramp, about ten yards down. The idea was to use the fisherman to slide the boat forward, until she was sitting, bows forward, on top of the ramp, then brake the slide down into the water with the storm line secured to the hurricane hook.

Much easier said than done, but on October 16 all was ready and I started pulling the boat, using the great blocks, or pulleys, as landsmen call them, to inch the boat along the ice, after unloading two and a half tons of removable gear and food onboard. On the seventeenth, after many hours of hard labor in the freezing cold, interspersed with heavy meals of boiled curried seal blubber, biscuits, and porridge, with great dollops of strawberry jam smeared over the lot, the boat was teetering on the top of the ramp. I married up the brake line to the hurricane hook, gave the stern a mighty heave, grabbed the brake line to control it, and she was away, just like a ship being launched, only *Cresswell* went bows first. I had left a good amount of weight in the stern, and as she hit the water, the empty bows danced up into the air, the stern swung around sideways, and she was afloat, checked by the heavy line from colliding with the small ice floes in the water.

Then, using the ladder with a plank lashed along its length, I reloaded the boat, dragging the stores over the ice on a species of sled which I had knocked together during the comparatively idle day-nights on the floe. With me pulling on one rope and Nelson grasping the other in his teeth, we soon made a quick job of shifting and restowing all the gear. It was not easy, as it was very dark in the boat, with just two small kerosene lamps flickering.

After a short sleep and another meal, I went out to try the engine. It was frozen solid, despite all the attempts I had made to keep it warm. I had even constructed a chimney from the galley to the engine compartment to conduct warm air, but to no avail. The blowtorch onboard refused to operate despite an hour's fumbling with frozen fingers. There was only one solution. I laboriously dismantled the cabin stove and chimney and, in a matter of hours, had it fitted up in the engine compartment, with the fumes going through the engine exhaust outlet. This did the trick, and early on the eighteenth I had the engine running and was moving slowly out, through thin new ice, to the northwest. As I was on the lee side of the *Ark Royal* ice floe, the sea was flat calm, and by running the engine flat out, I shoved my way between the thin cakes floating like shining water lilies on the surface of the freezing sea.

Sunrise on the eighteenth of October was around eleven in the morning, and there was daylight until around one in the afternoon, then twilight until about four. I made good time, for *Cresswell*'s hull was tough as an ox and I rammed my way through thin ice. Gradually the lead widened. Once I broke out of the pack ice field into comparatively open water, I intended to head south, and so out to a point where I could turn east for Iceland, or perhaps even make my way into one of the Greenland fiords, to winter there.

Suddenly, again, my fate was decided for me. There, on the western horizon, was a smudge of smoke, coming closer. I fired off one of my emergency signal flares. As I gazed at the ship's hull, which by now was plainly visible, with the lights shining from her cabins, I saw a brighter light flashing away from where I imagined the bridge was. They had seen my flares!

I patted Nelson on the back of his head. "Now behave yourself, mate, we've got company coming!"

The ship was soon very close, having broken a wide swath right through the thin ice. She was wearing the Danish flag and her name was *Gustav Holm,* her port of registry Copenhagen. Seeing my tattered, barely recognizable red ensign, one of her officers sang out in English over his megaphone.

"Where are you coming from?"

"Reykjavík—I was trying to make for Jan Mayen Island, only I got stuck."

"We can see—how was your trip?"

"Up and down, up and down."

He laughed. As the ship edged closer, I distinctly heard him say to the others crowded on the bridge deck, "Bloody Englishmen. Bloody crazy fools!"

"Hey, up there!" I hollered, between cupped mittens. "Hello, up there!"

"*Ja?*" he replied, bending down low over the bulwark, his gloved hand around his ear. I could plainly see his cleanshaven face under the clean parka hood.

"*Ja?*" he shouted again.

"*Welshman, if* you don't mind!"

FROM
the BRENDAN VOYAGE

BY
Tim Severin

In the mid-1970s Irishman
Tim Severin set out to prove that the legend of
St. Brendan's voyage could be true; that a sixth-
century Irish monk might actually have sailed a
small leather boat from Ireland across the Atlantic.
With a team of craftsmen and researchers, he built
an oxhide-covered curragh, a narrow two-masted,
square-rigged boat, using only materials and
methods that would have been available at the
time, including ancient tanning methods and the
use of wool grease to waterproof the hand-stitched
leather. In 1976 he set out with a small crew and
sailed first to Iceland. The next summer they continued the voyage from Iceland, past the southern
tip of Greenland, and finally reached Newfoundland.

I hough they carried a sextant and radio for
safety's sake, they made the voyage on their own
under sail as St. Brendan himself might have done,
carrying all the water and supplies necessary for
the voyage. The *Brendan* was a mostly open boat,
with only a small tentlike shelter to sleep under.
Even at the height of summer they encountered ice
and freezing weather that tested their survival
skills, and all in a tiny craft with a leather hull only

a quarter-inch thick over wood strips fastened together with leather thongs.

The following selection occurs as they cross the notorious Davis Strait between Greenland and Newfoundland and encounter, after surviving gales and near-capsizes, the more serious threats of pack ice.

///

THAT

evening George finally gave up the unequal contest of trying to compete with Arthur's flailing knees and elbows inside the confines of the main shelter, and he moved his berth forward to a spot under the bow canvas. We slept with the tent flaps open because the weather was so still, and it was a surprise to find a rind of ice covering *Brendan* in the morning. We were now some 1,600 miles along our route from Iceland, and across the ice-field lay Labrador, only 200 miles away. Moreover our encounter with *Mirfak* and *Svanur* had put *Brendan* back on the map for the outside world. The Canadian Coast Guard radio stations now arranged a special listening watch for us; and on the afternoon of June 15 a small plane flew over the boat for five minutes and took pictures. By radio the plane warned that large areas of pack ice lay to the south and west of *Brendan*. But there was little to be done. *Brendan* was still becalmed.

At quarter past three the next morning, however, I was awakened by the sound of water sliding past the leather hull. That's odd, I thought to myself, *Brendan* is not heeling to the wind. Nor can I hear the sound of waves. On my last watch the weather had been very settled, and there had been a flat calm and no sign of wind.

Then I heard Trondur and George speaking softly, and some sort of commotion, punctuated by light thuds and the flapping of a sail, and several splashes. What on earth were they doing? Was George helping Trondur restow some of the stores? But that was ridiculous; it was dark, and George was off-watch, and should be asleep. Finally, I could contain my curiosity no longer, and called "What's going on? Do you need any help?"

No answer. Then abruptly, the thuds and splashes stopped. I heard the others moving back down the boat.

"What's up?" I asked again.

"Oh, Trondur just lost a pilot whale he had harpooned," came back George's casual reply. I pulled on a sweater, and listened to their story.

Trondur had been on watch by himself when a large school of pilot whales surfaced around *Brendan*, splashing and puffing. Although it was dark, this was the opportunity Trondur the Hunter had been waiting for. Without bothering to wake up anyone, he clambered forward to his cabin, unshipped his harpoon, and scrambled up onto the very bows of the boat where he could get a clear throw. George was awakened by the sound of Trondur clambering across the thin tarpaulins just over his head. George got up, and emerged just as Trondur saw his chance—a pilot whale of the right size swimming near the boat.

Chunk! From a kneeling position on the bow Trondur tossed his harpoon three or four yards to starboard, and made a clean hit. It was a classic shot.

Immediately the harpooned animal dived. There was a tremendous flurry among its closely packed companion whales. The water churned as the animals thrashed in panic. The shaft of the harpoon snapped under the press of bodies, and then all the whales were gone, leaving the stricken animal to its fate.

Fascinated, George watched as Trondur began to play the whale like a fisherman with a salmon on the end of a line. At first the thirty-foot harpoon line was pulled out taut to its fullest extent. Trondur had tied the free end of the line to the foremast as a strong point, and the harpooned whale began towing *Brendan* briskly along. If the whale had been any larger, this could have been dangerous, but Trondur knew what he was doing. He had selected a whale of the right size, about fifteen feet long, small enough to handle from *Brendan*. As the whale grew tired, Trondur began to haul in on the line. The animal darted back and forth underneath the bows, trying to rid itself of the clinging harpoon. Flashes of foam and phosphorescence rolled up off its body and fins as it fought to escape. Inexorably Trondur continued to haul in. As the line shortened, the pilot whale began to weave up and down; its tail scooped dollops of water aboard *Brendan* as it fought to resist. Trondur's strategy was to pull the animal high enough to the surface so that it could get less grip on the water. At the crucial moment, however, when the whale was right alongside the boat, the harpoon head pulled free. A second later, the animal was gone.

"Harpoon too far back in whale," said Trondur, sadly shaking his head. "More forward and it would have been good."

I wondered to myself what on earth we would have done with a fifteen-foot pilot whale on *Brendan*. We didn't have that much extra space. But Trondur the Hunter had done remarkably well to harpoon the animal in the dark. "Never mind," I said, "you picked a good whale. It was towing us in the right direction at a good two to three knots."

Our adventures and misadventures all seemed to be happening in the dark, or at best, in the last hour of daylight. On June 18 the barometer began to fall rapidly. So did the temperature. Then the wind backed into the northwest and blew strongly, bringing driving rain. In short, it was a thoroughly villainous evening, and it was lucky, in view of what was to follow, that Trondur and Arthur unlashed and stowed the bonnet from the mainsail before they ended their watch at dusk. George and I took over on a foul, black night, rigged an awning over the cooker, lit the kerosene lamp, and huddled over it for warmth, taking an hour each at the helm. Our only consolation was that *Brendan* was thrusting briskly through the murk, sailing at a good pace. At 3:00 A.M. it was my turn to seek the shelter of the cabin, and I crawled in thankfully. I had just pulled off my wet sea-boot socks when suddenly there was a high-pitched crackling sound, rather like stiff calico tearing. "What on earth was that?" I exclaimed, poking my head out of the cabin. George was already standing up, flashing a torch on the sails. "I don't know," he replied. "Everything looks okay. The sails seem all right." "Perhaps a bird was flung into the sail by the high wind, and was thrashing to get out," I suggested. "No," said George, "I thought the sound came from the hull— still, there's nothing we can do about it in the dark," and he settled back down on the thwart.

Crack . . . crack . . . crack. There it came again, something weird was happening, a strange snapping noise, this time much louder. George was right. The noise was coming from the hull. George was back on his feet, peering into the darkness, trying to see a few yards in the pitch black. Hastily I began to put on my outer clothes again, knowing by instinct that we had a crisis on our hands.

"It's ice!" George suddenly shouted. "We're running into ice! I can see lumps of it all around." Crack . . . crack . . . crack, we heard the sound again and realized without looking what it was. *Brendan* was hitting lumps of ice at speed, and they were swirling and bumping along her flanks so hard that they rattled and crackled along the oxhide skin.

"Drop the sails," I yelled. "If we collide with heavy ice at this speed, we'll knock her to pieces. Our only chance is to stop and wait for daylight."

George moved into action. By the time I had struggled into my oilskins, he had lowered the mainsail and scampered forward over the icy tarpaulins, and already had the headsail halfway down. I went forward to help him secure the sodden canvas. It was perishingly cold. In an instant our bare fingers were numb as we secured the lashings on the sails. Neither George nor I said a word as we worked frantically. We could glimpse indistinct shapes in the water, and felt under our feet that *Brendan*'s hull juddered softly against unseen obstacles. We hurried back to the helm and took out the two most powerful hand torches. They were the only spotlights we had. We switched them on, one each side of *Brendan*, and shone them over the water. Their beams penetrated only fifty yards through the spray and sleet which hissed down in white streaks through the shafts of light. But fifty yards was far enough to reveal a sight which brought the adrenalin racing. All around us floated chunks and lumps and jagged monsters of ice. This was not the same ice we had seen a few days ago. In place of the well-defined ice edge, there was now a nightmare jumble of ice floes of every size and description, with channels of clear water opening and closing between them as the floes moved with the wind. But this ice should not be here, I told myself. I knew the ice chart by heart. That same day I had painstakingly marked in the ice boundaries according to the latest information radioed by the ice information service. *Brendan* should be at least sixty miles clear of the nearest ice. Yet here it was; and with a morbid feeling of satisfaction I knew exactly what had happened. The same northwest gale which had been spinning *Brendan* so happily on her way had swept over the main ice sheet and burst it open. The compact ice raft we had seen two days ago was now sprayed like shrapnel right into *Brendan*'s path. Later I learned that the entire pack-ice front had advanced across a broad front so that the Straits of Belle Isle, well to the south of *Brendan*, were nearly closed to merchant shipping.

Our torch beams showed us that *Brendan* had blundered into a type of sea ice known as Very Open Pack, and that most of the ice was rotten. Very Open Pack would have presented no problems to a large ship, which would have been able to shoulder forward, driven by powerful engines. But it was a totally different matter for *Brendan*. How much of a battering would her leather hull withstand, I wondered, and what would happen if a couple of ice floes bumped together, and *Brendan* was caught in the middle? Would she burst open like an overripe banana? And just how much sailing water was there among the ice floes which lay ahead? The devil of our situation was that there was no way to plan a strategy. We might only be in a small zone of ice, a temporary obstacle which we would soon clear. Common sense said that it was far more likely that we were in a major area of ice and that sooner or later we would find massive rafts of consolidated ice still frozen together. We had already seen the grinding action of the giant ice floes on a relatively calm day. I shuddered to think of what would happen to *Brendan* if she was blown into that sort of obstacle in the dark. She would be fed in like mincemeat. For about an hour George and I tried to keep the boat out of trouble. Without her sails, *Brendan* was still moving through the pack ice at one or two knots, driven by the pressure of the wind on the masts and hull. But sail-less, *Brendan* was at her worst—slow to maneuver and only able to turn through a very small arc. If too much helm was applied, she merely drifted sideways, out of control.

Everywhere the torch beams probed, white lumps of ice winked back out of the dark. Painfully, we wallowed past them, heaving on the tiller, and silently hoping that *Brendan* would respond in time. Smaller floes bumped and muttered on her leather skin; and out of the darkness we heard the continuous swishing sound of the waves breaking on ice beyond our vision.

George hoisted himself on the steering frame to get a clearer view. "There's a big floe dead ahead," he warned. "Try to get round to port." I pulled over the tiller as far as it would go. But it was not enough. I could see that we were not going to make it. "Get the foresail up," I shouted. "We've got to have more steerage way." George clipped on his lifeline and crawled forward along the gunwale. Reaching the foremast, he heaved on the halliard to raise the sail. It jammed. A loose thong had caught in the collar that slid up and down the mast. "Trondur!" shouted

George. "Quick, pass me up a knife." Trondur's berth was right beside the foremast, and he began to emerge like a bear from hibernation. But it was too late. With a shudder from the top of her mast to the skid under her, *Brendan* ran her bow into the great lump of sea ice. It was like hitting a lump of concrete. The shock of the impact made me stagger. "That will test medieval leather—and our stitching," I thought. Thump! We struck again. Thump! Once more the swell casually tossed *Brendan* onto the ice. Then ungracefully and slowly, *Brendan* began to pivot on her bow, wheeling away from the ice floe like a car crash filmed in slow motion. Thump! The boat shivered again. We had a feeling of total helplessness. There was nothing we could do to assist *Brendan*. Only the wind would blow her clear. Thump! This time the shock was not so fierce. *Brendan* was shifting. Scrape. She was clear. "Is she taking water?" George called back anxiously. I glanced down at the floorboards. "No, not as far as I can see back here," I replied. "Try to clear the jammed headsail. I'll get Boots up as well. This is getting dodgy."

Scarcely had I spoken than a truly awesome sight loomed up out of the dark just downwind of us—the white and serrated edge of a massive floe, perhaps the dying shard of an iceberg, twice the size of *Brendan*, and glinting with malice. This apparition was rolling and wallowing like some enormous log. Its powerful, squat shape had one great bluff end which was pointing like a battering ram straight at *Brendan*, and it was rocking backward and forward with ponderous certainty to deliver a blow of perhaps a hundred tons or so at the fragile leather.

George took one look at this monster and leapt up the foremast to try to clear the jammed sail and give us steerage way. It was a slim hope. "Hang on tight!" I bellowed at him as the swell gathered up *Brendan* and pushed her at the great ice lump which heaved up ponderously to greet her. Crack! Thump! The whole boat shook as if she had struck a reef, which indeed she had, but a reef of ice. The impact flung George backward from the mast. "Christ, he's going to fall between *Brendan* and the ice floe, he'll be crushed," I thought, horrified. But George still had the jammed halliard in his hand, and clutched at it desperately. The rope brought him up short, and for a heart-stopping moment he dangled backward over the gap like a puppet on a string. Now the wind was pinning *Brendan* against the great block of ice so that she was nuzzling up to it in a deadly embrace. The next impact was different. This time the ice floe rocked away from *Brendan* as the swell passed beneath us. *Brendan* swung over a broad spur of a wave-cut ledge projecting from the floe. The spur rose under us, caught *Brendan* with a grating sound, and began to lift and tip the boat. "We're going to be flipped over like a fried egg," I thought, as *Brendan* heeled and heeled. Then, with another grating sound of leather on ice, *Brendan* slid sideways off the ice spur and dropped back into the water.

Crash. The next collision was broadside, halfway down the boat's length. The leeboard took the impact with the sound of tortured wood.

This can't go on much longer, I wondered. Either *Brendan* will be blown clear of the floe, or she will be smashed to smithereens. As I watched, *Brendan* jostled forward another six feet on the next wave, and there was a chance to gauge the rhythm of destruction. It was obvious that the next blow would strike the steering paddle and snap its shaft. That would be the final problem: to be adrift in the pack ice with our steering gear smashed. Now the great floe was level with me where I stood at the tiller bar. The face of the floe stood taller than I did and in the light cast by my torch, the ice gleamed and glowed deep within itself with an unearthly mixture of frost white, crystal, and emerald. From the water-line a fierce blue-white reflected up through the sea from the underwater ice ledge. And all the time, like some devouring beast, the floe never ceased its constant roar and grumble as the ocean swell boomed within its submarine hollows and beat against its sides.

Here comes the last blow, I thought, the final shock in *Brendan*'s ordeal. I felt a wave lift the leather hull, saw the bleak edge of glistening ice swing heavily toward me and—feeling slightly foolish—could think of nothing else to do but lean out with one arm, brace against the steering frame, and putting my hand on the ice floe I pushed with all my strength. To my astonishment, *Brendan* responded. The stern wagged away and forward from the ice wall, and instead of a full-blooded sideswipe, we received a glancing ice blow that sent a shiver down the hull, but left the steering paddle intact. One wave later, the great floe was rolling and grumbling in our wake. It had been a very close call.

Trondur and Arthur were soon up and dressed in sweaters and oilskins ready to help. I should have called them earlier, but their off-watch rest had seemed too precious. Now their assistance was needed, because I planned to try to get *Brendan* through the ice by increasing speed,

which in turn meant that we might be blundering into the main consolidated pack ice and wreck the boat. But it was a risk we had to take. It was
better than gyrating into loose floes and being broken up. "Boots!
Trondur! Go forward by the foremast and stand by. We'll raise and lower
the foresail as we need it, and trim the sail to port or starboard, depending on the position of the bigger ice floes. We're going to run through
this ice. George, could you act as look-out, and sing out the bearings on
the larger floes?"

George climbed up on to the shelter roof, wrapped an arm round
the mainmast for support, and from his vantage point spotted the approaching dangers.

"Big one dead ahead! Two floes on the port bow, and another on the
starboard side! I think there's a gap between them."

As he called the position of each floe, he aimed the beam of his
torch at it to identify the hazard for me at the helm. In turn I called out
instructions to Boots and Trondur to raise and trim, or lower, the headsail to catch the wind and pick a route through the ice. "Up foresail . . .
down!" We slipped past a white shape of ice, ghostly in the dark. "Up
foresail . . . sheet to starboard," and I hauled over the tiller bar so that
Brendan slid past the next floe. It was a crazy scene, an icy toboggan run
in the dark, with a minimum of control, no way of stopping, no knowing
what lay fifty yards ahead. From where I stood, I could see the shape of
George's body clinging to the mast, the gale plastering his oilskin to his
back; then the line of the midships tarpaulin running forward to where
Arthur and Trondur stood, one by each gunwale. They had opened a
gap in the tarpaulin, and the upper halves of their bodies poked out like
the crew in an open airplane of First World War vintage. Only the hoods
of their oilskin jackets now made them look more like monks in cowls,
and the impression was heightened by the red-ringed cross on the foresail, which raised and lowered and bellied out with a thundering clap
above their heads. Beyond them, still farther, was the blackness of the
night out of which loomed the eerie white shapes of the ice floes, occasionally illuminated by George's torch beam through which still flicked
the streaks of rain and spray.

After three hours of this surrealist scene, the gloom began to lift.
George switched off his torch, and found he could detect the white
flashes of the ice floes without help. Dawn lightened the horizon, and we

started to identify ice patterns beyond our immediate orbit. We were surrounded by pack ice. Off to one side was floating a huge, picture-postcard iceberg, a sleek monster of ice sloping spectacularly to the ocean with virgin white flanks. But the berg was no danger, for it was at least a mile away. Our real troubles lay ahead and around us in the contorted shapes of the floes which had ambushed us in the night. Now we could identify them by type. There were "bergy bits" broken from the dead icebergs, ice pans of assorted sizes, and "growlers," the unstable chunks of hard ice which twisted and turned in the water and threatened to do most damage to *Brendan*'s quarter-inch-thick leather hull. Now with enough light we could see to avoid these obstacles. Surely the way ahead must be clear, I thought to myself. *Brendan* had shown her worth yet again. Her leather skin and hand-lashed frame had survived a battering. No more could be expected of her. "Is there any water in her yet?" George asked again.

"No," I replied. "She came through like a warrior."

But my hopes were soon dashed. Ahead we began to discover mile upon mile of ice, floe after floe, oscillating and edging southward under the combined effects of gale and the current. *Brendan* could neither hold her position nor retreat. Her only course was forward and sideways, hoping to move faster than the pack ice until we eventually outran it and emerged somewhere from its leading edge.

All that day we labored on, trying to work our way diagonally across the pack ice and find its limits. It was a nerve-wracking business, trying to pick our way from one gap to the next. Planning ahead was impossible, because the ice floes changed their position, and our horizon was very limited. From time to time fog banks gathered over the ice and visibility was often less than a mile. Our only advantage was that the water was very calm within the pack ice. As we penetrated deeper, the wave action died away even though half a gale was still blowing. The great carpet of ice muffled the waves like an enormous floating breakwater, leaving only a powerful swell which rocked and spun the floes. Sometimes we came across patches of open water, dotted with only a few lumps of rotting ice. Here we sailed without hindrance for a few minutes. Sometimes ice barriers and ice ridges rose ahead of *Brendan* where the floes stretched right across her path, forming an impenetrable wall which had to be avoided at all costs. Once or twice there loomed out of the mists the magnificent shape of the great icebergs, one hundred feet high and more; and as we drew closer to them we could discern ominous cracks riven through the ice blocks where the bergs would split and calve. Such bergs had to be avoided because downwind of each one lay its attendant cluster of broken ice. Even more awkward were the patches of consolidated pack ice, the larger relics of the old ice sheet. This consolidated ice floated in broad jumbled rafts, heaped and contorted where one floe had piled upon another, and then frozen into one mass, like a breaker's yard where every block weighed a score of tons or more.

Brendan's ability to maneuver past these dangers was so limited that virtually every floe had to be skirted on its leeward side. This meant sailing directly at the floe, putting over the helm at the last moment, and skidding around the lee of the ice where the scud and foam sucked and spread as the floe rocked in an endless see-saw motion to the swell. Our advance was a cross between bumper cars at a fairground and a country square dance, except that our dancing partners were leviathans of ice as they dipped, circled, and curtsied. Again and again we slithered past floes, listening to the bump and crunch as ice brushed the leather hull, the sharper tremor and rattle as we ran over scraps of small ice, the shudder as ice fragments the size of table tops and weighing a couple of hundred pounds ricocheted off the blade of the steering paddle.

"Well, you wanted to see ice on this trip, George," I said. "You can't say you've been disappointed."

"It's fantastic," he replied ruefully, "I'm glad I've seen it. But I don't think I ever want it again."

The strain on the crew was terrific. When daylight came, we tried to revert to our normal watch-keeping system and get some rest. But it was impossible to relax with the clatter of the ice reverberating through the little thin hull so close to one's head. And time after time every man had to be called into action—raising and lowering the sail to vary our speed, hauling and readjusting the sheets to alter the slant of our course; and, when the worst befell, leaning out to poke and prod with boat hooks to fend off the boat, or, once or twice, even sitting out on the gunwale, putting feet on the floe, and kicking off with all one's might. Once again I was reminded of the early voyages—this time of a famous picture of

Elizabethan sailors fending off the heavy ice from their ship with just the same simple technique. But I had to confess to myself that I had not expected to find *Brendan* in quite the same predicament.

All that day, June 18, we were kept so busy in the pack ice that there was no time for proper meals. At noon Trondur cooked up a hot mush which we spooned down between emergencies, and there was just enough time for two cups of coffee later in the day. But breakfast was a failure—I found my pannikin of cold cereal at tea time. It was still sitting untouched, in a safe place under the thwart.

It had to be admitted that the ice had a certain lure and majesty. The ice was rotting and disintegrating into thousands upon thousands of weird shapes and sizes, odd corners and pillars, which floated low in the water and speckled the surface as far as the eye could see. The colors were entrancing—opaque whites, deep greens of undersea ledges, transparent flecks the size of cabin trunks, vivid blue glacier ice, dirty ice coated with ancient dust and grime. Once George reached out and broke off a morsel of blue ice from a passing floe, and popped it in his mouth. "Delicious," he quipped. "Please pass the whiskey."

But each color signaled its own danger. The least worrying was the transparent dead ice in the last stage of melting. This ice was riddled with myriads of tiny air pockets so that the outer layer crushed on impact with *Brendan*'s hull and cushioned the shock. Its only disadvantage was that this type of ice floated so low in the water that it was hard to spot in time to avoid. Most of the big heavy growlers were equally difficult to see because they revealed only a small portion of their bulk above the surface, usually a sleek, round lump of opaque white dipping innocently below the swells. But under the water the growlers could be massive— great blocks of menace that heaved and churned in the current. They could deal a tremendous blow to a small boat. The snow-white surface floes, though thinner and lighter, were awkward because they tended to form up in strips and block our path. Our only chance was to bear down on the line, hoping to pick out a gap at the last second, and slither through. It required judgement, skill, and a lot of pure luck that a gap would open at the right moment. Usually *Brendan* bumped and weaved her way through safely, but occasionally she would run her bows right onto the floe. Then for a moment or two, we would ride on top of the ice, waiting for the wind to catch *Brendan*'s stern and lever her back into the water, pirouetting away in her strange ice dance. "It's easy to follow our path through the ice," Arthur remarked, "just follow the line of wool grease marks on the edges of the floes in our wake."

The two colors we treated most warily were the deep green of the underwater ledges, which threatened to gouge upward into *Brendan*'s hull as she glided over them, and the stark diamond-white and blue of the floes made of very old ice. The latter had been born many years earlier as snowfalls in interior Greenland and Baffin Land, compacted, and squeezed out as glaciers and finally spawned into the ocean as icebergs. This ice had scarcely begun to melt at all. Its floes were sharp and hard and utterly uncompromising.

Bump, slither, swing sideways, charge at the gap, don't think about the quarter inch of leather between yourself and the icy sea, ignore the rows of stitching offered up to the constant rubbing of ice along *Brendan*'s flanks; fend off with the boat hook. Helm up, helm down, search for the space between ice floes ahead; calculate, calculate. Wind, leeway, current, ice movement. For hour after the hour the ordeal continued, until by dusk, with the wind still blowing half a gale, the ice seemed to be thinning out. And this time we really did seem to be nearing the edge of the pack.

Then Brendan Luck finally ran out.

We were in sight of relatively open water and passing through a necklace of ice floes when two large floes swung together, closing a gap *Brendan* had already entered. The boat gave a peculiar shudder as the floes pinched her, a vaguely uncomfortable sensation which was soon forgotten in the problem of extricating her from the jaws of the vise. Luckily the two floes eased apart enough for *Brendan* to over-ride one ice spur, and slip free. Five minutes later, I heard water lapping next to the cooker and glanced down. Sea water was swirling over the floorboards. She was leaking. *Brendan* had been holed.

There was no time to attend directly to the leak. The first priority was still to get clear of the pack ice while there was enough daylight to see a path. Otherwise we would find ourselves in the same predicament as the previous evening, blundering into ice floes in the darkness. "One man on the bilge pump, one at the helm; one forward controlling the headsails; and the fourth at rest," I ordered, and for two more hours we worked *Brendan* clear of the pack until there was enough open water to run a fairly easy course between the ice floes, and set the mainsail, double reefed. The helmsman still needed to be vigilant, but the man at the headsail could at last be spared; and after twenty-four hours of sustained effort, we could revert to our normal two-man watch-keeping system. The risk, it seemed to me, was as much a question of human exhaustion as of the frailty of our damaged boat.

"We can't tackle the leak tonight," I said. "There's not enough light to trace it, and then to try to make a repair. Besides, we are all too tired. But it's vital to learn more about the leak. I want each watch to work the bilge pump at regular intervals and record the number of strokes needed to empty the bilge and the time it takes to do so. Then at least we will know if the leak is getting worse and gaining on us. If we've torn the stitching somewhere, then more stitches may open as the thread works itself loose, and the rate of leakage will go up."

Trondur tapped the leather at the gunwale. "I think stitching is broken by ice," he said calmly.

"It's very possible," I replied, "but we can't be sure. We've simply got to find out all we can."

"Ah well," said Arthur cheerily, "that's what the right arm is for—pumping. It's our watch. Trondur, I'd better get to work." And he crawled forward to get to the bilge pump. It was none too soon. Even as we had been talking. the water level on the floor by the cooker had risen noticeably. The water slopped back and forth around our boots, and would soon be lapping into the lee side of the shelter.

Pump, pump, pump. It took thirty-five minutes of non-stop pumping to empty the bilge. *Brendan*'s bilge, though shallow, was broad and relatively flat in profile and so held a great deal of water. Just fifteen minutes after being pumped out, the water level was as bad as ever, and threatening to get worse. Pump, pump, pump. "How many strokes to empty her?" I asked. "Two thousand," Arthur grunted as he collapsed, exhausted. I did a rapid sum. Two thousand strokes every hour was within our physical limit, but only temporarily. One man could steer, while his partner pumped and kept *Brendan* afloat. But this system would work only while our strength lasted, or, more likely, we ran into bad weather, and waves began once again to break into the boat. Then we would no longer have the capacity to keep emptying *Brendan* fast enough. It was a tricky situation: In slanting out of the pack ice and clawing to seaward, I had brought *Brendan* out a full two hundred miles from land, and even then the nearest land was the thinly inhabited coast of Labrador, from which little help could be expected. We were running before half a gale, and now the damping effect of the pack ice was gone, the waves were beginning once again to break and tumble around us. Nor were we entirely free of ice danger. Here and there we could see in the darkness the occasional white shape of a large growler, stubbornly refusing to melt. "We've got six hours before daylight," I said. "There's nothing for it but to husband our strength until dawn and then tackle the leak. It's best if one man in each watch keeps pumping continuously, turn and turn about. If we can keep the bilge empty, *Brendan* will ride lighter and take fewer waves on board."

That night was the most physically tiring of the entire voyage. It was difficult to rest or sleep properly. On watch one stood for half an hour on the helm, then went forward to take over the pump, scarcely having time to nod to one's partner as he struggled wearily back, to go to the helm. There, peering through the murk, one tried to decide whether the white flashes ahead were the manes of breaking waves or the telltale sign of a growler lying in *Brendan*'s path.

As soon as the first watch ended, I called the Canadian Coast Guard radio station at St. Anthony in Newfoundland. "This is the sailing vessel *Brendan*," I reported. "We have been in open pack ice for the last twenty-four hours but now seem to be clearing the ice. We have suffered hull damage and the vessel is leaking. In the next twelve hours we will attempt to trace and repair the leak, but it is important to note our estimated position, which is 53° 10′ N., 51° 20′ W. I repeat, this position is only an estimate, as we have lost our log line sheered off by the ice, and due to poor visibility have had no sight of the sun for two days. We are not in immediate danger. But could you please investigate the possibility of airdropping to us a small motor pump, with fuel, in case we cannot contain the leak. I will call again at 14.15 hours GMT to report progress. If no contact is made at 14.15 hours or 16.15 hours, we may have activated an emergency locator transmitter on 121.5 and 243 megacycles. Over."

"Roger, Roger," replied the calm voice of the radio operator at St. Anthony, and he confirmed the details I had given. Then he advised me that he would inform the Rescue Coordination Center at Halifax, and listen out for *Brendan* on the next schedule. Later I learned that the Canadian Coast Guard responded unstintingly to our request for standby help. An aircraft was readied at Halifax, and the Operations Room at St. John's calculated that a Canadian Coast Guard icebreaker could reach us from Goose Bay in twenty-one hours. "But to be honest," said an officer who was on duty that night in the Operations Room, "we didn't know how our ship would be able to locate you in time. And after the loss of the *Carson*, which sank in the same ice not many days before, when we heard that a leather boat was in trouble in the ice, we rated your chances of getting out as nil. How could a leather boat survive when a steel icebreaker went down?"

Nevertheless, at the time of our ordeal, it was very comforting to know that someone, somewhere, was informed of our plight and, if worst came to worst, we could call for help. Partially relieved by this thought, I sat hunched in my sleeping bag and tried to concentrate my mind. *Brendan* was leaking at the rate of two thousand pump strokes an hour. This represented a sizeable leak, and obviously we had to track it down without delay at first light. But how on earth would we find the leak? It could be almost anywhere in *Brendan*'s hull below the water already filling up the boat. We would have to shift all our gear, section by section, along the vessel; lift up floorboards, remove the fresh-water storage tubes from the bilges—and where would we store the drinking water temporarily?—and then try to trace the leak by following any current or bubbles in the bilge. All this would have to be done in a rough sea.

And if we were lucky enough to trace the leak, what then? Suppose we had cracked the skid keel under the boat when *Brendan* rode upon an ice floe, or pulled its fastenings through the leather hull? At sea we could neither refasten nor mend the skid. And what if we had gashed the leather skin or ripped the flax stitching? Then, I feared, we would be in an even worse way. I could not imagine how we would ever stitch on a patch under water, it would be impossible to reach far below the hull, and equally impossible to work on the inside because there was not enough space between the wooden frames and stringers to put in a row of stitches. The more I thought about our straits, the gloomier I felt. It seemed so futile if *Brendan* were to sink so close to the end of her mission. She had already proved to her crew that an early medieval Irish skin boat could sail across the Atlantic. But how could people be expected to believe that fact if *Brendan* sank two hundred miles off Canada? It would be no good to say that there was less pack ice off Canada and Greenland in early Christian times, and that the Irish monks would probably not have faced the same problems. To prove the point about the early Irish voyages, *Brendan* had to sail to the New World.

To clear my mind, I took up a pen and made a summary of our position:

1. *Brendan* is leaking fast. We can keep her afloat for two days, or less, in bad weather; indefinitely in fair weather but at great physical cost.
2. First priority is find the leak—skid fastening? Burst stitches? Hull gash?
3. If we cannot trace and mend a leak, the Coast Guard may get a motor pump to us. Do they have a suitable pump? Can their plane find us? This will depend on visibility and sea state.
4. No pump—we MAYDAY and abandon ship.

It was a grim scenario and the situation did not become any more cheerful during that night. Driving rain reduced visibility to a few yards, and with an increase in wind strength, the helmsman no longer had the option to dodge potential growlers in the water. *Brendan* could only flee directly downwind, and we trusted to luck that we did not hit isolated pieces of ice, or worse yet an iceberg recently set free from the pack.

All of us were desperately tired. The constant strain of bilge pumping was a stultifying chore, which battered mind and muscle. First there was the awkward slippery climb along the gunwale to go from the steering position to the midship's lashing in the tarpaulin. There you had to open the lashing with half-frozen fingers, drop into the dark slit, turn around to unclip your lifeline, duck under the tarpaulin, and tug the tarpaulin shut. If you did not, the next breaking wave would cascade into the midship's section and drop even more water into the bilge. Once under the tarpaulin, you had to strip off your oilskin jacket or wriggle half out of your immersion suit. Otherwise the next half hour's work would drench your clothes in sweat. Now it was time to squirm down the tunnel under the tarpaulin to reach the handle of the bilge pump. Grasp the handle with the right hand, lie on one's left side on top of the thwart, and pump four hundred to five hundred strokes. By then the muscles of the right arm and shoulder would be screaming for relief; and so you reversed position laboriously, lay on the other ribs, and pumped for as long as possible with the left arm. Then reverse the procedure, and begin all over again, pumping and pumping, until at last came the welcome sucking sound of the intake pipe, and you could begin the laborious return journey to the helm, put on oilskin top, unfasten and fasten the tarpaulin, clamber back to reach the helm, and arrive just in time to find that the water level had risen to exactly the same place as when you had started the whole operation. Only now it was the turn of your watch companion to empty the bilge.

Rocking the pump handle in the dark tunnel of the tarpaulin had an almost hypnotic quality. The steady rhythm of the pump, the dark wet tunnel, and aching tiredness combined to produce a sense of detachment from one's surroundings. The feeling was heightened by the incongruously pretty little flashes of phosphorescence which slid aboard with every second or third wave crest, and dripped brilliantly down the inside of the leather skin of the boat in random patterns that confused one's weary eyes and created illusions of depth and motion. The motion of arm and torso, rocking back and forth relentlessly at the pump handle, was matched visually by a strange phosphorescent glow in the translucent bilge pipes. This strange glow varied in intensity with each wave, sometimes soaring to bright sparks of luminescence, but usually a somber green pulse like a ghostly heartbeat. Under the dark tarpaulin, eyes tricked, shoulders aching, head drooping down onto the thwart with exhaustion, it was desperately tempting to drop off to sleep while still mechanically rocking back and forth. Only to be jerked awake by the rattling crash of yet another wave breaking onto the tarpaulin just above one's head.

At 6:00 A.M. dawn came, and I looked at the crew. They were haggard with exhaustion, but no one had the slightest thought of giving up. In the night watch I had surreptitiously stolen five minutes to lever up the stern floorboards and check the aft section of the bilge to try to find the mysterious leak. It was a job that really should have been left until morning, but I could not restrain my curiosity. When I told George what I had done, he confessed that he had made exactly the same investigation in his forward berth and already examined the bow section without finding the leak. It seemed there was no holding back *Brendan*'s crew.

"Well, here's the battle plan," I explained. "Each man has a cup of coffee and a bite to eat. Then Trondur and Boots work on both pumps amidships to get the water level as low as possible, and keep it there. This will allow George and me to work down the length of the boat, shifting the cargo area by area, and checking the bilge for leaks. We already know that the leak must be somewhere in the main central section of the hull."

The others looked very tough and confident, and utterly unperturbed. We had just eight hours, I reminded myself, to find and repair the leak before I should be in touch with the Canadian Coast Guard.

Three of us had coffee and then I went forward to relieve George at the bilge pump.

As I sat by the pump, waiting for George to drink his coffee so that we could begin our search, I wondered where we should commence our hunt—aft, under the shelter? But this meant shifting all our personal gear. By the foremast? But this was where we had put the heavy stores like the anchors and water cans. Then, quite unconnected, a thought occurred to me. Last night, while pumping in the dark, the flashes of phosphorescence over the gunwale had been repeated almost simultaneously *inside* the boat and in the bilge pump tube. I knew nothing of the physical properties of phosphorescence, but imagined some sort of electrical connection was required. If so, then the phosphorescence had traveled directly from outside the hull to inside the hull, apparently by a direct link—the leak.

With a faint stir of interest I abandoned pumping and traced the line of the bilge pipe to its intake amidships on the port side. At that point I peeled back the tarpaulin and hung head first over the gunwale. There, just on the water line, was the most encouraging sight of the day—a sizeable dent in the leather hull. The dent was about the area and shape of a large grapefruit, an abrupt pock-mark in the curve of the leather. With growing excitement I scrambled back inside the hull and began shifting away the food packs which had been stored there. As soon as I had uncovered the hull, I saw the grapefruit-shaped pocket and the cause of our trouble: Under tremendous pressure from outside, the leather had buckled inward into the gap between two wooden ribs, and opened a tear about four inches long. The force of the pressure had been so great that it had literally split the leather. The skin had not been cut or gashed. Despite a tensile strength of two tons per square inch, the leather had simply burst. Now, whenever *Brendan* wallowed, a great gush of seawater spurted through the tear and into the bilge. Jubilant, I poked my head up over the tarpaulin and called "Great news! I found the leak. And it's in a place where we can mend it." The others glanced up. There was relief on all their faces. "Finish your breakfast," I went on, "while I check that there are no other leaks." Then I went round the boat, hanging over the gunwale to see if there was any more damage. In fact, apart from that single puncture the leather was still in excellent condition. Indeed it was scarcely scratched by the ice. The other floes had simply glanced off the curve of the hull or skidded on the wool grease.

Except that one puncture. There, a combination of the curve of the hull, the wider gap between the ribs at that point, and the nipping between the two floes had driven a knob or sharp corner of ice through *Brendan*'s hull. By the same token, however, we also had room to wield a needle between the ribs and could sew a spare patch of leather over the gash. George and Trondur came forward. "The patch had better go on from the outside," I told them, "where the water pressure will help squeeze it against the hull. First we'll make a pattern, then cut the patch, and stitch it in place."

"We must cut away some wood," suggested Trondur, examining the ash ribs.

"Yes, whatever's needed to get at the work properly."

"I'm going to put on an immersion suit," George announced. "This is going to be a cold job."

He was right. George and Trondur in their immersion suits now had three hours of bone-chilling work. First they cut a patch of spare leather to size, then George hung down over the gunwale, his face a few inches above the water, and held the patch into position. Trondur poked an awl through the hull and the patch, followed by a long nine-inch needle and flax thread. George reached for the needle with a pair of pliers, gripped, tugged and pulled, and eventually hauled it through. Then he took over the awl, stabbed from the outside of the hull, groped around until he could poke in the tip of the needle, and Trondur gathered it up from the inside.

It was a miserable chore. The top row of stitching was difficult enough, because it lay just above water level, so that each time the boat rolled on a wave, George was lucky if he went into the water only up to his elbows. With the heaviest waves, his head went right under, and he emerged spluttering and gasping. Each large wave then went on to break against the hull, and drenched Trondur who was crouching in the bilge, stitching on the inside. All this was done in a sea temperature of about zero degrees Centigrade, with occasional ice floes and icebergs in the immediate vicinity, and after nearly two days without proper rest. Inch by inch the stitching progressed, and a pancake of wool grease and fiber was stuffed between the hull and the patch to serve as a seal. Then the last row of stitches went in. This last row was completely under water, and George had to use the handle of a hammer to press in the needle.

Finally it was done. The two men straightened up, shivering with cold. George wiped the last of his protective wool grease from his hands and they had a well-earned tot of whiskey in their coffee. Even Trondur was so exhausted that he went off to curl up in his sleeping bag. Arthur pumped the bilge dry, and scarcely a trickle was coming in through the mend. I inspected the patch. "It's almost as neat and tidy as if you had put it on in Crosshaven Boatyard and not in the Labrador Sea—John O'Connell would be proud of you," I congratulated George.

"Well, that's a job I would not like to have to do again," he replied with quiet understatement.

tragedy

FROM
survive the
SAVAGE
SEA

BY
Dougal Robertson

In 1968 the Robertson family, Scottish dairy farmers, spontaneously decided to cruise the world. Dougal had twelve years of sea experience and held a Master Mariner certificate, and Lyn was a registered nurse, so they were confident they could cope with whatever might happen. Their children were excited to go. Two years later they'd sold the farm and bought *Lucette*, a fifty-year-old wooden schooner.

Between January 1971 and June 1972 they crossed the Atlantic, cruised the Caribbean, and transited the Panama Canal into the Pacific, where their first stop was the Galápagos. They loved the sea and all its life, but ironically their problems began with an encounter with a pod of fast-moving killer whales. Almost as spontaneously as their initial decision to sail, they found themselves sinking and had to abandon ship with no time to radio for help or collect gear and provisions necessary for survival a thousand miles from land.

The following selection is the beginning of their book, a story that would continue for another thirty-seven days. Satellite rescue beacons were very rare only three decades ago, and castaway sailors were on their own. Survival for an individual was a test of character, intelligence, and will to live, but for a family with children it also required spirit, self-sacrifice, and the strong bonds of love. Even in this brief excerpt you can see those qualities in the Robertsons.

///

THE black volcanic mountain of Fernandina, the most westerly of the Galapagos Islands, towered high above the tall masts of the schooner *Lucette* as she lay at anchor, rolling gently in the remnants of the long Pacific swell which surged around the rocky headland of Cape Espinosa, and sent searching fingers of white surf curling into the sheltered waters of the anchorage.

We had spent a pleasant morning sailing across the strait from Tagus cove on Isabela Island, where Douglas, now eighteen, accompanied by the twins Neil and Sandy, now twelve, had carefully recorded *Lucette*'s name and registry among the impressive array of names of yachts and fishing vessels which had visited the cove over the past fifty years. The names, painted on the cliff sides of the cove in two-foot-high letters, gave the anchorage an atmosphere of gaiety and companionship which lingered on after we had left the sun-sparkled waters of the cove, and seemed reflected in the joyous antics of the seals and dolphins as they escorted us into the strait. Now, however, as gathering clouds obscured the sun, we shivered in the slightly sinister atmosphere of Espinosa, where we hoped to see the Galapagos penguins and the flightless cormorants disporting themselves in factual support of Darwin's *Origin of Species*.

The black volcanic sand of the beaches, the jagged fangs of black rock jutting out from the headland, the rather scruffy appearance of the birds, so sleek and beautiful on the other islands, all lent this air of depression to Espinosa, so that it was without our usual feelings of interest and wonder that we saw half a dozen penguins grouped at the water's edge ready to take to the water at our near approach. Robin peered anxiously through his glasses at the lens of his camera to take a rather distant photograph of the penguins, then muttered darkly as he moved closer to a better vantage point, causing the penguins to plop neatly one by one into the sea and disappear. I walked with him, past the loathsome piles of black marine iguanas and the scarlet shells of the rock crabs to where my wife Lyn searched the rock pools for additions to her shell collection; a white-crested crane walked with dignified gait on the nearby rocks quietly ignoring us as it scanned the small pools, while pelicans flapped their ungainly wings overhead, suddenly changing shape to streamlined projectiles as they hunted their prey in the cloudy waters of the bay.

We had passed the bloated body of a dead seal on our way in, with the sinister triangular-shaped fin of a white-tipped shark near by, so I told the lads to keep close in-shore if they wanted to swim. As it was, only Douglas had ventured into the water and even he, intrepid reef explorer that he was, had come ashore when a seal, covered with boils, had poked a belligerent snout at him.

As we rowed back to *Lucette* in our small fiberglass dinghy we felt rather disappointed at this anticlimax to our journey around these wonderful equatorial islands, with their strange anachronisms of wildlife.

We were on the eve of our departure for the Marquesas Islands, three thousand miles to the west, and now, as the wind swung to the east under a gray mantle of rain cloud, I felt anxious to be gone, for if we left now we would be out from under the lee of the island by morning. Lyn protested vehemently at the thought of starting our journey on June the thirteenth, even when I pointed out that the most superstitious of seafarers didn't mind so long as it wasn't a Friday as well, but Douglas and Robin both now joined with my feelings of anxiety to be gone, and after a short spell of intense activity, we stowed and lashed the dinghy and secured all movables on deck and below.

By five o'clock in the afternoon we were ready for sea, and with mainsail and jibs set we heaved the anchor home, reached past the headland into the strait, then altering course to the west ran free toward the Pacific, a thousand square feet of sail billowing above *Lucette* as she moved easily along the ragged black coastline of Fernandina toward the largest stretch of ocean in the world.

Lucette had no self-steering device, and so with night watches arranged, we sailed quietly through the darkness, crossing the sheltered stretch of water in the lee of the massive bulk of the extinct volcano, until at three-thirty in the morning, booms were swung over, stays and sheets hauled taut and secured as the schooner heeled, gently at first, then with steeply inclined decks as she reached across the increasing force of the southerly trade winds at a steady seven knots. By the morning of the fourteenth, the Galapagos Islands were receding into the distance astern, merging with the clouds of the overcast sky above as *Lucette*, now rolling and pitching in the heavy swell and rough seas of the Pacific trades, made steady progress west by south toward the Marquesas Islands.

In spite of the fact that we had been sailing for over a year, our stomachs still took a little time to adjust from the quietness of sheltered waters to the lively movement of the yacht in the open sea and so throughout the day those of us not actively engaged in steering and sailing *Lucette* rested as best we could in the bunks below, supplied at intervals with hot soup or coffee from Lyn's indomitable labors at the stove. Unused to the sea, Robin had been sick most of the way from Panama to the Galapagos, but he now seemed better adjusted to the physical discomfort of the constant heave of the hull. He was able to steer a fairly accurate course by compass, and although the principles of sailing were still something of a closed book to him, he could help Douglas and me with the night watches while Lyn and the twins helped with the watches during the day.

The wind moderated a little during the following night and breaks in the clouds enabled us to catch glimpses of stars in the pre-dawn sky; on the morning of the fifteenth we had our first glimpse of the sun since leaving the Galapagos and with the slackening of wind and speed *Lucette* settled to a more comfortable movement in the diminishing seas.

The morning sun shone fitfully from the thinning cloud, and as I balanced myself against the surge of *Lucette*'s deck, sextant glued to my eye, I watched for the right moment when the image of the sun's rim would tip the true horizon, no easy combination when both deck and horizon are in constant motion. Douglas and Sandy were in the cockpit, one steering and the other tending the fishing line, while Robin, finding it difficult to sleep in his own bunk on the port side of the main cabin, had nipped quietly into Sandy's bunk on the starboard side of the fo'c'sle to rest after his spell on the four to eight morning watch. Neil was reading a book in his own bunk on the port side of the fo'c'sle, and Lyn had just started to clean up the usual chaos which results from a rough stretch of sailing. At last the sun, the horizon and the deck cooperated to give me a fairly accurate reading, and noting thc local timc by my watch at 09ʰ 54ᵐ 45ˢ, I collected my logarithm tables and Nautical Almanac from the chart table and retired below to the relative comfort of the after cabin to work out our longitude; it was my first position sight since leaving the islands.

With my sextant carefully replaced in its box I had turned to my books to work up a reasonably accurate dead-reckoning position when sledgehammer blows of incredible force struck the hull beneath my feet, hurling me against the bunk, the noise of the impact almost deafening my ears to the roar of inrushing water. I heard Lyn call out, and almost at the same time heard the cry of "Whales!" from the cockpit. My senses still reeled as I dropped to my knees and tore up the floorboards to gaze in horror at the blue Pacific through the large splintered hole punched up through the hull planking between two of the grown oak frames. Water was pouring up through the hole with torrential force and although Lyn called out that it was no use, that the water was pouring in from another hole under the w.c. flooring as well, I jammed my foot on the broken strakes and shouted to her to give me large cloths, anything to stem the flood. She threw me a pillow and I jammed it down on top of the broken planking, rammed the floorboard on top and stood on it; the roar of the incoming water scarccly diminishcd, it was alrcady abovc thc level of the floorboards as I heard Douglas cry from the deck "Are we sinking, Dad?" "Yes! Abandon ship!"; my voice felt remote as numbly I watched the water rise rapidly up the engine casing; it was lapping my knees as I turned to follow Lyn, already urging Neil and Robin on deck.

Wading past the galley stove, my eye glimpsed the sharp vegetable knife, and grabbing it in passing I leaped for the companionway; the water, now up to my thighs, was already lapping the top of the batteries in the engine room; it was my last glimpse of *Lucette's* interior, our home for nearly eighteen months. Lyn was tying the twins' lifejackets on with rapid efficiency as I slashed at the lashings holding the bow of the dinghy to the mainmast; Douglas struggled to free the self-inflatable raft from under the dinghy and I ran forward to cut the remaining lashings holding the stern of the dinghy to the foremast, lifting the dinghy and freeing the raft at the same time. Lyn shouted for the knife to free the water containers and I threw it toward her; Douglas again shouted to me if he should throw the raft over, disbelieving that we were really sinking. "Yes, get on with it!" I yelled, indicating to Robin, who now had his lifejacket on, to help him. Grasping the handles at the stern of the dinghy, I twisted it over from its inverted stowed position and slid it toward the rail, noting that the water was now nearly level with *Lucette*'s deck as she wallowed sluggishly in the seaway. Douglas ran from the afterdeck with the oars and thrust them under the thwarts as I slid the dinghy seawards across the coach roof, then he took hold of the stern from me and slid the dinghy the rest of the way into the sea, Robin holding on to the painter to keep it from floating away. The raft, to our relief, our great and lasting relief, had gone off with a bang and was already half-inflated, and Lyn, having severed the lashings on the water containers and flares, was carrying them to the dinghy. I caught up the knife and again shouted "Abandon ship!" for I feared *Lucette*'s rigging might catch one of us as she went down, then cut the lashings on a bag of onions, which I gave to Sandy, instructing him to make for the raft, a bag of oranges which I threw into the dinghy and a small bag of lemons to follow. It was now too dangerous to stay aboard, and noting that Douglas, Robin and Sandy had already gone and that Neil was still sitting in the dinghy which was three-quarters full of water, I shouted that he also should make for the raft. He jumped back on *Lucette*, clutching his teddy bears, then plunged into the sea, swimming strongly for the raft. Lyn struggled through the rails into the water, still without a lifejacket, and I walked into the sea, first throwing the knife into the dinghy, the water closing over *Lucette*'s scuppers as we left her.

I feared that the whales would now attack us and urged everyone into the raft, which was fully inflated and exhausting surplus gas noisily. After helping Lyn into the raft I swam back to the dinghy, now completely swamped, with oranges floating around it from the bag which had burst, and standing inside it to protect myself from attack, threw all the oranges and lemons within reach into the raft. The water containers had already floated away or had sunk, as had the box of flares, and since the dinghy was now three feet under the water, having only enough flotation to support itself, I made my way back to the raft again, grabbing a floating tin of gas as I went. On leaving the dinghy I caught a last glimpse of *Lucette*, the water level with her spreaders and only the tops of her sails showing. Slowly she curtsied below the waves, a lady to the last; she was gone when I looked again.

I climbed wearily into the yellow inflatable, a sense of unreality flooding through me, feeling sure that soon I would waken and find the dream gone. I looked at my watch; it was one minute to ten. "Killer whales," said Douglas. "All sizes, about twenty of them. Sandy saw one with a big V in its head. I think three of them hit us at once." My mind refused to take in the implications of the attack; I gazed at the huge Genoa sail lying on the raft floor where Lyn was sitting with the twins. "How the hell did that get there?" I asked stupidly. Douglas grinned. "I saw the fishing-line spool floating on the surface unwinding itself," he said, "so I grabbed it and pulled it in; the sail was hooked in the other end!"

Three killer whales; I remembered the ones in captivity in the Miami Seaquarium weighed three tons and that they swam at about thirty knots into an attack; no wonder the holes in *Lucette*! The others had probably eaten the injured one with the V in its head, which must have split its skull when it hit *Lucette*'s three-ton lead keel. She had served us well to the very end, and now she was gone.

Lyn gazed numbly at me, quietly reassuring the twins who had started crying, and, apart from the noise of the sea around us, we gazed in silent disbelief at our strange surroundings.

WE SAT ON the salvaged pieces of flotsam lying on the raft floor, our faces a pale bilious color under the bright yellow canopy, and stared at each other, the shock of the last few minutes gradually seeping through to our consciousness. Neil, his teddy bears gone, sobbed in accompaniment to Sandy's hiccup cry, while Lyn repeated the Lord's Prayer, then, comforting them, sang the hymn "For Those in Peril on the Sea." Douglas and Robin watched at the doors of the canopy to retrieve any useful pieces of debris which might float within reach and gazed with dumb longing at the distant five-gallon water container, bobbing its polystyrene lightness ever further away from us in the steady trade wind. The dinghy *Ednamair* wallowed, swamped, nearby with a line attached to it from the raft, and our eyes traveled over and beyond to the heaving undulations of the horizon, already searching for a rescue ship even while knowing there would not be one. Our eyes traveled fruitlessly across the limitless waste of sea and sky, then once more ranged over the scattering debris. Of the killer whales which had so recently shattered our very existence, there was no sign. Lyn's sewing basket floated close and it was brought aboard followed by a couple of empty boxes, the canvas raft cover, and a plastic cup.

I leaned across to Neil and put my arm round him, "It's all right now, son, we're safe and the whales have gone." He looked at me reproachfully. "We're not crying cos we're frightened," he sobbed, "we're crying cos Lucy's gone." Lyn gazed at me over their heads, her eyes filling with tears. "Me too," she said, and after a moment added, "I suppose we'd better find out how we stand."

This was the question I had been dreading; feelings of guilt, that our present predicament was not only due to my unorthodox ideas on educating our children (there had been plenty of critics to object that I was needlessly jeopardizing the children's lives) but also that I had failed to foresee this type of disaster, now engulfed me, and this, added to the fact that we had lost almost everything we possessed as well as *Lucette*, depressed me to the depths of despair. How could I have been so foolish as to trust our lives to such an old schooner! Then I saw, once again, in my mind's eye that damage under the floorboards of *Lucette*. Not only had the frames withstood the impact of the blow, but the new garboard strake of inch-and-a-half pitchpine, fitted in Malta at the surveyor's recommendation, had been one of the hull planks which had been smashed inward. Her hull had taken a full minute to sink below the waves, but a modern boat, constructed with less regard to brute strength than *Lucette*, would have sustained much heavier damage and sunk even more quickly, with more terrible results.

I looked at Douglas; he had grown to manhood in our eighteen months at sea together; the twins, previously shy, introspective farm lads, had become interested in the different peoples we had met and their various ways of life, and were now keen to learn more; I tried to ease my conscience with the thought that they had derived much benefit from their voyage and that our sinking was as unforeseeable as an earthquake, or an airplane crash, or anything to ease my conscience.

We cleared a space on the floor and opened the survival kit, which was part of the raft's equipment, and was contained in a three-foot-long polythene cylinder; slowly we took stock:

Vitamin fortified bread and glucose for ten men for two days.

Eighteen pints of water, eight flares (two parachute, six hand).

One bailer, two large fish-hooks, two small, one spinner and trace and a twenty-five-pound breaking strain fishing line.

A patent knife which would not puncture the raft (or anything else for that matter), a signal mirror, torch, first-aid box, two sea anchors, instruction book, bellows, and three paddles.

In addition to this there was the bag of a dozen onions which I had given to Sandy, to which Lyn had added a one-pound tin of biscuits and a bottle containing about half a pound of glucose sweets, ten oranges and six lemons. How long would this have to last us? As I looked around our meager stores my heart sank and it must have shown on my face for Lyn put her hand on mine; "We must get these boys to land," she said quietly. "If we do nothing else with our lives, we must get them to land!" I looked at her and nodded, "Of course, we'll make it!" The answer came from my heart but my head was telling me a different story. We were over two hundred miles downwind and -current from the Galapagos Islands. To try to row the small dinghy into two hundred miles of rough ocean weather was an impossible journey even if it was tried by only two of us in an attempt to seek help for the others left behind in the raft. The fact that the current was against us as well only put the seal of hopelessness on the idea. There was no way back.

The Marquesas Islands lay two thousand eight hundred miles to the west but we had no compass or means of finding our position; if, by some miraculous feat of endurance, one of us made the distance the chances of striking an island were remote.

FROM
AFTER
the STORM

BY
John Rousmaniere

John Rousmaniere, an acknowledged master of modern seamanship and sailing, is the author of *Fastnet, Force 10* and *The Annapolis Book of Seamanship*, among other books. His *After the Storm: True Stories of Disaster and Recovery at Sea* has been called "a thinking man's *Perfect Storm*." In it he explores famous sea storms and their effects on the sailors involved, from Percy Bysshe Shelley to John Guzzwell and the Smeetons (who appear elsewhere in these selections) with a perspective born of both history and personal understanding: his own experience in the disastrous Fastnet race storm that sank so many boats.

What follows is a selection from his story and analysis of the tragic deaths of Robert Russell Ames and his sons in the North Atlantic in 1935. At the time, Rousmaniere reminds us, races of amateur sailors in small boats across oceans were still a new sport that "struck old-time mariners as heretical if not crazy." Still, thirty-eight ocean races had been held between 1866 and 1934, with a total of only ten fatalities among two thousand sailors. This was, of course, long before the advent of modern boats complete with electronic navigation, radar, inflatable life rafts, EPIRBs and myriad other safety gear.

Ames was a Boston real estate developer, and his crew were five young Harvard men, among them his two sons. They believed in the code of "the strenuous life," following the rugged independence of the heroes of the time such as Joshua Slocum, Teddy Roosevelt, Charles Lindbergh, and Amelia Earhart. The hardships of the sea represented a way to build character, and Ames's 54-foot two-masted sailboat *Hamrah*, launched in Castine, Maine, in 1932, was the perfect mode for family rusticating. In 1934 they raced twenty-eight other boats from Connecticut to Bermuda, arriving in four days but losing to all but two of the fleet. The experience convinced them to enter *Hamrah* in the 1935 transatlantic race to Norway.

Six sailboats prepared for the 3,200-mile race. George Roosevelt, commodore of the Cruising Club of America, which was sponsoring the race, tried to convince Ames that his boat and crew were not ready. The route would involve icebergs, freezing air and water temperatures, fog, and frequent gales. "Sometimes a good crew can save a poor boat," he said, "but an inexperienced crew is liable to lose any boat." Ames was not convinced. His enthusiasm marked the spirit of the times.

The other five boats reached Norway. The *Hamrah* made it through the treacherous waters off Cape Sable and almost halfway across the North Atlantic before tragedy struck.

///

THE favorite in the race to Norway was a fifty-four-foot yawl, *Stormy Weather*, an evolution of *Dorade*. Commanded by Rod Stephens Jr., she was sailed by her crew of seven young amateurs with a band-of-brothers exuberance and discipline that would have pleased Theodore Roosevelt or Henry Richards. When they were not sailing, sleeping, eating, or keeping a watch for ice, they often assembled the ship's orchestra—two accordions, a guitar, a clarinet, and three harmonicas—and played exuberantly, with varying degrees of skill. The sailing aboard *Stormy Weather* was far more adept than the musicianship. When one of her crew, Kenneth Davidson, went home after the race, he inscribed a sailor's supreme compliment in the log: "It has been a great privilege to sail in *Stormy Weather* and to share, very humbly, the spirit of seamanship which has always prevailed." She finished at Bergen on June 27 after little more than nineteen days, or just five hours slower than the much larger seventy-two-foot ketch *Vamarie*. When the handicaps were figured she was presented the trophy put up by King Haakon of Norway. After George Roosevelt's *Mistress* came in a day later, Roosevelt admitted that he had been so "scared pink" that he had averaged only three hours of sleep a day as he kept a constant watch on his navigation and a lookout for ice. The Germans took thirty-five days, ten more than the Yale students on the *Vagabond* who, when they crossed the finish line, sent up distress flares; they needed a doctor to attend to a crew member who had recently broken his arm.

That was not the only accident or close call. Early on, two of the boats were almost run down by a passing ocean liner coming at them out of the fog. *Vamarie*, owned by a colorful Russian named Vadim S. Makaroff (who was known as "the caviar king" for his success as a specialty foods importer), lost her professional skipper, Alexander Troonin, overboard one day while he was on the bow setting the spinnaker. After the boat sailed right over him, the thoroughly keelhauled Troonin somehow managed to grab the logline—the spinning line dragging astern that measured speed—but it snapped, leaving him in a big ocean of 40-degree water watching the stern of his vessel rapidly shrink as she sailed on toward Norway. The helmsman was Sherman Hoyt, a legendary old seaman whose adroit steering had helped win the America's Cup in 1934. He spun *Vamarie* 180 degrees, leaving her stopped dead with her bow in the wind and her sails useless. Like *Hamrah*, *Stormy Weather*, and George Roosevelt's *Mistress*, she did not have an engine, which meant she had to make her way back to Troonin under sail. As the crew cleared away the mess, Hoyt got her moving again, and only eight minutes after Troonin went over the side, he was back on board.

Hamrah, alas, was not so fortunate. Her accident can be reconstructed from survivors' accounts:

After the starting gun, the green ketch beats slowly into the fog with no hope of keeping up with *Vamarie*, *Stormy Weather*, or *Mistress*. (Margaret Ames will not even board a liner for Norway until June 24, more than two weeks after the start.) The captain is fifty-two-year-old Robert Ames. Dick Ames, twenty-three and recently accepted by Harvard Business School, is navigator and self-appointed safety officer, daily reminding his shipmates to move around carefully and hook on their life belts (although he cannot make a dent in his father). Harry Ames—as like his short, stocky father as his brother is like their tall, lean mother—is twenty now, with that sunny, kindly, energetic Ames disposition. Harry recently completed his first year at Harvard and captained the freshman wrestling team. With them are three young men who have much in common with the Ames boys; all have been with them at Harvard, and all but one have also been at Milton Academy. Roger Weed was in Dick's class, and Sheldon Ware is Harry's Harvard roommate. The single outsider is only marginally so: Charles F. Tillinghast Jr., son of the winner of Tom Day's pioneer race in 1904, was raised in Providence and attended another boarding school before Harvard. The most experienced offshore sailor of the six, Tillinghast at twenty-one has already sailed in two Bermuda races.

The breeze freshens and, unluckily for *Hamrah*, goes into the east—on the nose, exactly where the bluff-bowed ketch does not want it as she slowly pounds into the sloppy seas. After three days of this Dick announces that they are off Cape Sable, Nova Scotia. The breeze pulls aft, allowing them to finally reach directly toward Europe under full sail. Low-pressure systems come and go, with small gales and shifting winds.

After a week of this, at the change of watch at eight o'clock on the morning of June 19, *Hamrah* reaches on the port tack at nine knots. There is a hard nor'easter—a gale of wind blowing against the prevailing westerly swell—and through this rough sea the ketch plugs along, deeply reefed and with mizzen furled. Alone on deck and at the helm, Charlie Tillinghast looks around and estimates that the seas are as high as *Hamrah*'s fifty-foot mast. Tillinghast's watchmate, Robert Ames, has finished his breakfast below and is pulling on layers of wool sweaters and socks, topped by his heavy oilskins and sea boots. He swings up the ladder through the companionway and, under Tillinghast's watchful eye, crawls across the swaying, wet deck to the port side, where he throws himself down on the bottom of the upturned dinghy near the cockpit.

The two men sit in this wild setting with its big white-capped sea, all gray and white in the confusion between the old westerly swell and the new gale's easterly swing. The younger man is more energetic as, eyes glued on the compass, he wrestles the long-spoked wooden steering wheel to muscle twenty tons of boat on course. She surges, rolls, yaws, and dives across and through the tumultuous sea. The sounds of the rigging's whine and the bow's roar are often broken by a wave's whack against the vessel's side or onto her deck—the *thump!* of Leviathan's tail, the ancients might have said—and then the loud, heavy sluice of water across the deck.

After an hour the two men are almost accustomed to *Hamrah's* jumpy motion when, with startling, surprising velocity, the bow drops and the stern rises. Out of the corner of his eye Robert Ames spies a white wall advancing from astern. He cries out—too late. Six feet of water sweep forward from stern to bow, filling the whole surroundings with white water. Barely hanging onto the wheel's spokes, stinging salt filling his eyes, Charlie Tillinghast looks around to find the boat whole, her rigging standing, her cockpit full but draining—and Robert Ames no longer on the dinghy but in the ocean astern. The wave has thrown him the full width of the boat and over the leeward lifelines and into the ocean, where he is now barely afloat as *Hamrah* sails away.

Tillinghast yells as he turns the wheel hard to starboard to bring the boat off the wind and jibe back toward the struggling man. As the bow swings down, Dick Ames, in his underwear, leaps up the companionway, spots his father, and with hardly a pause grabs the emergency line tied to the boat and dives overboard. He is only a few feet from his father when the boat jerks the rope from his grasp. He swims on and embraces his father as *Hamrah* jibes and comes toward them. Robert Ames is so passive that Roger Weed, following Dick up the hatch, is convinced he does not know how to swim.

Tillinghast brings the bow to within fifteen feet of the two men. The others toss a life preserver and a small life raft just as a breaking wave separates the rescuers from the victims. Although the raft is blown away, the swimmers have the life preserver, which offers enough buoyancy to support them as Dick holds his father's head up. Harry is frantic to dive in after them. The others persuade him to stay: without an engine, they need him to help sail the boat.

Tillinghast jibes again, and as the reefed mainsail bangs across in the second jibe, the boom and gaff break, leaving the sail billowing uselessly. Now many yards downwind of the Ameses with only a small jib set, Tillinghast, Ware, and Weed pause to clear away the damage with a hatchet and hacksaw and then set the mizzen. Harry, meanwhile, is untying the dinghy and sliding it into the water. Charlie Tillinghast again begs him to stay with *Hamrah*. They need sailors to handle the boat to get to his father and brother. Harry pushes the boat over the side and leaps in and applies his wrestler's arms to the oars.

Days later, when Charlie Tillinghast describes these dreadful moments in an article in a Providence newspaper, his Yankee self-discipline holds his bitter frustration in check:

> *While we were putting the mizzen on her, Henry, the younger son, launched the small rowboat and reached his brother, whom he got aboard. His father was by this time possibly drowned; at any rate I did not see him. The rowboat was to windward, so we jibed again and sailed as close to the wind as possible, hoping that the small boat would be able to back downwind to a point where we would get it. Unfortunately, it was swamped at this point. It was then clear that we were going to leeward more quickly than was the swamped small boat.*

Heaving the mess of the broken boom and torn mainsail overboard, they finally can try to beat toward the Ameses, who by now are barely visible five or six big waves upwind. The last they see of the Ameses, Dick and Harry sit side by side on the bottom of the upturned dinghy, waving. A wave breaks. They vanish.

Hamrah and the three survivors circled until nightfall, finding nothing more. The gale increased, and they had to heave-to for two days in the same area where their friends and shipmates had drowned. Perhaps they welcomed those two days as an opportunity for quiet reflection. Charlie Tillinghast, who had gone through the Naval Reserve Officer Training Corps program at Harvard, took command. They decided to sail west to America. Although St. John's, Newfoundland, was closer, they chose the nine-hundred-mile route to Sydney, Nova Scotia, to avoid ice and because they had better charts for that area. They sailed into shipping lanes in hopes of finding a vessel to take a message, perhaps even the liner that was carrying Margaret Ames to Europe, but the report had to wait until after a long beat to windward in moderate wind. The ubiquitous fog thickened near land, and there was little sleep over the last few days as *Hamrah* felt her way, entering Sydney on the night of June 30.

We know almost nothing of that ten-day passage, but judging from the thoughtful statements that Tillinghast and Weed provided newspapers after they arrived, the young men seemed in firm command of their emotions. On their arrival in Nova Scotia, the only outward signs of strain were their exhausted faces. Weed and Tillinghast later said they were satisfied that they had done the best they could. It may have helped them that, as sailors, they were used to dealing with risk, chance, and an environment that is beyond human control and often hostile. But even more important may have been the phenomenon that even when rescue efforts are futile, rescuers who are closest to the scene may feel rewarded for their efforts.

FROM
red SKY in MOURNING

BY
Tami Oldham Ashcraft
with Susea McGearhart

In some ways Tami Oldham Ashcraft's story is the flip side of Gordon Chaplin's (see earlier selection); here, the male skipper is lost overboard in a storm, and the woman must carry on. In the fall of 1983, Tami and Richard are sailing in *Hazana*, a 44-foot yawl, on a delivery cruise from romantic Tahiti to San Diego. They'd left their own smaller sailboat behind to take the delivery job and they knew they were taking a calculated risk making the crossing during hurricane season. Yet the first part of the voyage is a pleasant sail through manageable seas crisscrossed by whales and dolphins. Then twenty days into the cruise they hear on the weather radio that a hurricane is heading right for them. They are halfway between Hawaii and Mexico with nowhere to hide. They prepare the boat for heavy weather as best they can and brace for the battle to come. . . .

///

SUNDAY, October 2, Day Eleven on *Hazana*, was special for

Richard and me. At dusk, phosphorescence sparkled in the turquoise sea. We opened a bottle of wine and toasted our crossing the equator that day and entering the northern hemisphere.

Ahead of us shot a geyser of silver and translucent green spray: A large pod of pilot whales was coming to play with *Hazana*. We connected the self-steering vane and went to the bow to watch them leap and sing their high-pitched greeting. Grasping the stainless steel pulpit, Richard leaned against my back, his bearded cheek next to mine as the whales created beautiful crisscrossing streamers of chartreuse in front of us.

"Aren't the whales magical, love?" He asked, fascinated.

"Look how they surface and dive," he said as he slowly started undulating against my backside. As *Hazana* rose over the next swell, he whispered in my ear, "Surface . . ." And as the bow plunged into the trough, he said, "Dive."

"You could be a whale, Richard," I teased.

"I am a whale, love. See, I'm surfacing"—he nudged me forward, the rhythm of the whales sparking something amorous in him—"and now I'm going to dive."

As *Hazana* glided down into the trough, Richard reached around and untied my pareu as he clung onto me with his knees. He knotted the material onto the pulpit with a ring knot and cupped my breasts with his warm hands. I let go of the bow pulpit and stretched my arms out wide, *Hazana*'s fair figurehead.

"Ummm," I hummed.

"I want to dive with you, Tami," Richard murmured in my ear. "I want to surface and dive as these wild mammals do." I reached back and undid his shorts. They fell onto the teak deck.

With growing momentum we surfaced and dived, surfaced and dived, wild and free like the whales, before God, and heaven, and sky. *Hazana*, the queen whale, set the rolling rhythm we matched. "Bliss" I later wrote in the logbook.

Day Twelve, we hoisted the multi-purpose sail, the MPS, a very lightweight sail, and made four knots with the southeast trades finally catching us. The trades stayed with us for a number of days, pushing us to the east. We often saw whales, and now dolphins were showing their cheerful faces.

Dawn of October 8 broke gray, rainy and miserable. The winds were unpredictable. They gusted from southeast to southwest and back around from the north. We were up near the bow checking the rig when a small land-bird crashed onto the foredeck. The poor thing panted, unsteady on its short toothpick legs. Richard got a towel and dropped it over the bird. Scooping it up, he brought the bird to the cockpit, out of the rain and wind. Behind the windscreen, on top of the roof of the cabin, it squatted low, ruffling its wet feathers to warm its tired body. I crumbled a piece of bread, but the bird appeared too afraid to eat. The absurd winds must have blown the tiny bird far offshore. Richard later scribbled, "Cyclonic?" in the logbook.

The next day the weather channel WWV informed us the storm they had been tracking off the coast of Central America was now being classified as Tropical Depression Sonia. They said it was centered at 13° N by 136° W and traveling west at seven knots. That put her over a hundred miles west of us.

WWV also warned of a different tropical storm brewing off the coast of Central America. They were referring to it as "Raymond." In comparing our course, 11° N and 129° W heading north-northeast, to the course Raymond was traveling, 12° N and 107° W and heading west at twelve knots, Richard wrote: "WATCH THIS ONE!"

Near midnight the wind dropped. Then it came around to the east-northeast, which fueled Raymond's fury. We got hit with squalls and rain.

Monday, October 10, the wind veered to the north. At five in the morning, we changed our heading to north-northwest to gain speed. Our goal was to get as far north of Raymond's track as possible.

The wind died down to one to two knots, and we ended up motoring for four hours. But by noon we had two reefs in the main, the staysail up and a reefed genny, and we were plowing away at five knots to the north-northwest. Tropical Storm Raymond was now at 12° N and 111° W heading due west. The bird was gone; it had flown the coop.

We decided to fly more sail in an attempt to run north of the on-coming storm. Taut lines, also known as jack lines, ran along each side of the boat from the bow to the stern. This allowed us to clip on the tether of our safety harness while working on the deck. We pushed *Hazana* to her max. There was no choice—we had to get out of the path of the storm.

Richard and I got busy clearing the decks just in case it really got bad; we didn't need heavy objects flying around. We hauled the extra five-gallon jury-jugs of diesel down below and secured them in the head. They were heavy, and it was difficult to move them in the rough seas.

At 0100 the next morning, the genny blew out. It thrashed violently in the wind, its staccato cracks and snaps were deafening. Turning on the engine and engaging the auto-pilot, Richard and I cautiously worked our way up to the mainmast, clipping our safety harness tethers onto the jack line as we went forward. "You slack the . . ."

"WHAT?" I yelled over the wailing wind.

"YOU SLACK THE HALYARD WHEN I GET UP THERE, AND I'LL PULL HER DOWN."

"OKAY," I shouted back.

Richard fought his way to the bow. I was terrified watching him slither forward. Gallons of cold water exploded over the bow on top of him, drenching me too. *Hazana* reared over the rising swells. The ruined sail whipped violently and dangerously in the wind.

Richard couldn't get the sail down. Finally he came back to me.

"SHE WON'T BUDGE. CLEAT OFF THE END OF THE HALYARD, AND COME UP AND HELP ME PULL HER DOWN."

I did as he said and slowly worked myself forward on all fours, ducking my head with each dousing of saltwater. We tugged and pulled on the sail as it volleyed madly in the wind. Finally, after my fingers were blistered from trying to grip the wet sailcloth, the sail came down with a thud, half burying us. We gathered it up quickly and sloppily lashed it down. We then slid the number one jib into the foil, and I tied the sheet—the line—onto the sail's clew. I made my way back to the cockpit making sure the line was not fouled.

Richard went to the mainmast, wrapped the halyard around the winch and raised as much of the sail as he could by hand. I crawled back to the mainmast and pulled in the excess line while he cranked on the winch, raising the sail the rest of the way. It flogged furiously, like laundry left on a line in a sudden summer squall. We were afraid this sail would rip too. Once the sail was almost completely hoisted, I slithered as fast as I could back to the cockpit while Richard secured the halyard. I cranked like hell on the winch to bring the sail in. Richard came back to the cockpit and gave me a hand getting the sail trimmed. This sail change took us almost two hours. Richard and I were spent and wet, and we needed to eat. In between sets of swells, I slid open the hatch and hurriedly went down into the cabin.

It was hot inside *Hazana* with all the hatches shut. She was moving like a raft in rapids. What would be simple to prepare, I questioned myself, instant chicken soup? As I set the pot of water on the propane stove to boil, I peeled off my dripping foul weather gear and sat down exhausted on the quarter berth.

Seven hours later, after the horrendous sail change, Raymond was still traveling west at latitude 12° N. Richard scribbled in the logbook: "We're okay." We continued north.

All through the rest of the day, the wind and the size of the swells steadily increased. White water blew off the crests of the waves, creating a constant shower of saltwater spray. The ocean was powdered like white feathers bursting out of a down pillow. Tropical Storm Raymond was now being classified as a hurricane—Hurricane Raymond.

At 0930 October 11, the forecast put Hurricane Raymond at 12° N and spinning along a west-northwest course. Richard recorded: "WE'RE ON THE FIRING LINE." We packed on all sail. I silently lamented over the useless torn genny; it was a sail we could have really used now because it was larger than the number one jib. Richard told me to alter course to the southwest. If we couldn't situate ourselves above Raymond, maybe we could sneak below it and reach the navigable semicircle of the hurricane in the next twenty-four hours.

At three o'clock that afternoon the updated weather report told us Raymond had altered its direction to west from west-northwest with gusts to 140 knots. The afternoon sunsight gave us a second line of position. This told us we would collide with Raymond if we continued on our southwest heading. We immediately came about and headed northeast, trying to get as far away from Raymond as possible. With a shaky hand Richard inscribed: "ALL WE CAN DO IS PRAY."

Later that night, the spinnaker pole's top fitting broke loose from the mainmast and the pole came crashing down, trailing sideways in the water. Richard and I scrambled to the mainmast trying to save the spinnaker pole. He grabbed it before the force of the water could break the bottom fitting and suck the pole overboard. It took both of us to lash its fifteen feet down on the deck. Creeping back to the cockpit we saw that a portion of the mizzen sail had escaped from its slides and was now whipping frantically in the wind.

"JESUS CHRIST, WHAT'S NEXT?" Richard roared. He stepped out of the cockpit, clipped his safety harness onto the mizzen mast, and released the mizzen halyard. Once the mizzen was down, he lashed it onto the mizzen boom.

As he came back to me at the wheel, I noticed how dark the shadows were under his eyes. He tried not to sound sarcastic as he said, "Not much else can go wrong."

Where the ocean was once black at night, it was now highlighted with thick white caps of foam. The barometer dropped way down the scale as the wind's wail steadily increased, the seas becoming even steeper, angrier, more aggressive. We were terrified Raymond was catching us, but there wasn't a damn thing we could do about it but sail and motor as fast and as hard as possible.

We stayed on watch, taking turns going below to get whatever rest we could. Our muscles ached from fighting the wheel while trying to negotiate the pounding, erratic seas. Night had never lasted so long.

The next morning broke cinder gray with spotty sunlight shedding an overcast hue on brothy seas. Ocean spray slapped us constantly in the face. Wind was a steady forty knots. We were forced to take all sail down and gallop with bare poles.

About 0900 the seas arched into skyscrapers looming over our tiny boat. The anemometer now read a steady fifty knots. The churning spray was ceaseless. Richard came topside and handed me the EPIRB (emergency position-indicating radio device), as he took the wheel. "HERE, I WANT YOU TO PUT THIS ON."

"WHAT ABOUT YOU?"

"TAMI, IF WE HAD TWO I'D PUT ONE ON. JUST MAKE ME FEEL BETTER, AND PUT THE BLOODY THING ON."

So, I did. I fastened my safety harness tether to the binnacle and steered while Richard went below to try to figure out our location now and get an updated position of the hurricane. All he could hear between the pounding and screech of the wind was static. There was no way he could risk bringing the radio outside with the sea constantly cascading over the boat.

Richard came topside, fastened his safety harness and took the wheel, I sat huddled against the cockpit coaming, holding on with all my strength to the cleat where my tether was fastened. We were helpless while staring at the raging scene around us. The sound of the screaming wind was unnerving. The hull raised to dizzying heights and dove into chasms. Could the seas swallow us? The ascent of the boat over the monstrous waves sent the hull airborne into a free fall that smashed down with a shudder. I was horrified *Hazana* would split wide open. Finally I shouted to Richard, "IS THIS IT? CAN IT GET ANY WORSE?"

"NO. HANG ON, LOVE; BE MY BRAVE GIRL. SOMEDAY WE'LL TELL OUR GRANDCHILDREN HOW WE SURVIVED HURRICANE RAYMOND."

"IF WE SURVIVE," I hollered back.

"WE WILL. GO BELOW AND TRY TO REST."

"WHAT HAPPENS IF WE ROLL OVER? I DON'T WANT TO LEAVE YOU ALONE."

"THE BOAT WOULD RIGHT ITSELF. LOOK, I'M SECURE," he said, giving a sharp tug on his tether. "I'D COME RIGHT BACK UP WITH IT."

I looked at his tether secured to the cleat on the cockpit coaming.

"GO BELOW," he urged. "KEEP YOUR EYE ON THE BAROMETER. LET ME KNOW THE MINUTE IT STARTS RISING."

Reluctantly I got up, leaned out and squeezed the back of Richard's hand. The wind sounded like jet engines being thrown in reverse.

"HOLD ON," he yelled and cranked the wheel. I tumbled sideways as the hull was knocked down. I fell against the cockpit coaming. An avalanche of white water hit us. The boat shuddered.

Richard anxiously glanced at me, water dripping down his face. Fear jumped out of his intense blue eyes. Behind him rose sheer cliffs of white water, the tops blown into clouds of spray by the ferocious wind. My eyes questioned his—I couldn't hide my terror. He faltered, and then winked at me, thrusting his chin up, a signal for me to go below. His forced grin and lingering eye contact disappeared as I slammed the hatch shut.

I clung to the grab rail of the companionway ladder as I made my way down to the cabin below. The frenzied cadence of *Hazana*'s motion prevented me from doing anything but collapsing into the settee's hammock. I automatically secured the tether of my safety harness around the table's post. I looked up at the ship's clock: It was 1240 hours. My eyes dropped to the barometer: It was terrifyingly low—below twenty-eight inches. Dread engulfed me. I hugged the musty blanket to my chest as I was flung side to side in the hammock. No sooner had I closed my eyes, when all motion stopped. Something felt very wrong, it became too quiet—this trough too deep.

"OHMIGOD," I heard Richard scream.

My eyes popped open. *WHOMP!* I covered my head as I sailed into oblivion.

I OPENED MY EYES. The thought, "I could have died and gone to heaven," hazily lingered in my mind. My head throbbed. I went to touch it, but things, I didn't know what, lay on top of me, smothering me, crushing me. What was going on here? I couldn't think, I couldn't remember. Where was I? My hammock hung cockeyed. I dangled near the floor. A can of WD-40 clanged against the table post. I moved, and a book splashed into the water sloshing about the cabin sole.

I struggled to free myself. Dead weight pinned me down. Cans of food, books, pillows, clothes, and panels of the main saloon's overhead liner spilled off of me. Covered in blood, I could feel a horrendous cut on my left shin.

Where was I? What had happened? I was confused. I couldn't orient myself. My tether, still clipped onto the table post, confined me. I was obviously on a boat—what boat? My weakened hands frantically tried to unclip the tether.

Once unclipped, I strained to see around me. My vision was blurry; the pain in my head, excruciating. Putting hand to brow, I flinched, "Ouch!" I looked at my hand and saw crimson. Uncontrollable shivers engulfed me.

Laboriously, I crawled out of the labyrinth of wreckage and stared. The interior of the boat was chaotic. My God, what had happened? Books, charts, pillows, spoons, floorboards, cups, clothing, cans of food, spare parts, beans, flour, oatmeal—everything was either floating or stuck to the overhead, or to the bulkheads, or to the hull. What boat is this? Where am I?

The oven had been ripped from the starboard side of the boat and was now wedged into the nav station bookshelf on the port side. I gazed intently at the ship's clock, but I couldn't bring the numbers into focus.

Unsteadily, I stood up, my knees wobbling. I felt faint. Slowly, one careful step at a time, I negotiated my way through the obstacles floating in the three feet of water that lapped above the floorboards. I got to the ship's clock and watched its second hand jump: one thousand one, one thousand two. It read 1600 hours, 4 P.M. Wait. Hadn't it just been about 1 P.M. . . . ?

I headed for the V-berth. "Hello?" I called out. My voice sounded strange. I gaped at the turmoil in every nook and cranny. Cautiously moving toward the bow, I peeked in the head. There, in the mirror, stood a frazzled image, its face covered in blood, the forehead cut wide open. Long strands of hair, wild and matted with blood, shot out from its skull. In fear, my hands flew to my mouth. I screamed. Then I screamed again. The ungodly sight was me.

"No!" I shouted and crashed into the bulkhead as I tried to escape.

I stumbled into the V-berth. Everything there too was jumbled—topsy-turvy. The storage hammocks that hung on each side of the berth were overturned; spilled clothes lay every which way. Paperback books were off their shelves. The long mattress for the bunk was kinked, out of its place. Cans of food and even broken dishes lay strewn about.

I shook my head and wondered how the food and dishes got in the V-berth. In disbelief I backed into the main saloon.

"Ray?" I apprehensively called.

Ray? I wondered where that had come from. It's not Ray. Ray's the hurricane. Hurricane? Hurricane Ray—Raymond. Where's Richard? Richard . . . "Oh my God . . ." But that's what he said . . .

Fear dropped me to my knees. I retched. Bilge water splashed against my cheek. Richard had not come below with me.

"RICHARD?" I screamed. "RICHAAARRRD."

I pulled myself to my feet, but had barely taken a step when the heel of my foul weather boot slid. I fell against the saloon table. I threw up again.

"RICHAAARRRD?" I screamed as I crawled toward the companionway ladder, my hands splashing water in every direction as I knocked food, tools, books, whatever, out of my way.

"RICHARD? RICHARD?" I screamed over and over, choking on my words.

The companionway ladder had broken off its latches, and it lay sideways against the nav station seat. I pushed it to the floor, out of my way, and climbed up on the back of the settee, screaming Richard's name. I hoisted myself up into the cockpit. It was difficult. I had no strength.

The boom blocked the companionway. "Goddamn it!" I wailed and then painfully climbed over it.

Desperately I looked in every direction. Richard was nowhere to be seen.

"MY GOD . . . RICHARD? RICHARD?" I howled.

I looked all around. "Richard? Richard?"

Hazana was ravaged. The main mast was gone except for a four foot piece still attached to the main boom. The tabernacle, a metal housing used to raise and lower the main mast, lay on its side, a huge four-foot-piece of torn deck attached to it. The large two-inch clevis pin that had been holding the foot of the mast into the tabernacle lay on the deck, sheered in half. "Oh my God," I wailed as I looked down through the gaping hole on deck into the main cabin. The mizzen mast was in the water only holding on by the starboard shroud. Stainless steel rigging hung overboard, with the roller-furling jib and staysail trailing in the water. Only a couple of stainless steel one-inch stanchions were left standing, tweaked like pop cans. The rest of the stanchions, and their lifelines, were gone. The propane-locker hatch was missing, and the propane tanks were gone.

Oh please, God, please. My legs gave way—I hung onto the boom and retched again.

He couldn't be gone. The dry heaves choked me. In total fear, I grabbed the boom and lay dazed, my cheek against the cold aluminum.

"*Get up. Move.*" An inner voice slammed into my thoughts.

Bawling, I crept over the broken-down boom, reached into the companionway and groped for the binoculars. Miraculously, they were still strapped in their place.

After slithering back over the boom, I stood bracing myself, thinking, "I can save him, I can save him," as I scanned the ocean around me with the binoculars. I could not stop trembling: The eye holes of the magnifying glasses pressed hard against my skull—drumming against my eyebrows.

I peered in every direction. All I saw was a vast desolate sea, with rolling four-foot swells. Nothing, not one goddamned thing, was out there.

"*Try the engine!*" the inner voice barked.

I pulled out the choke, adjusted the throttle and pushed the engine's start button. Nothing. Not even a grunt or grind.

I looked toward the wheel. There I saw Richard's safety line secured to the cleat on the cockpit coaming. The tether hung over the side of the hull. My God, could he be on the other end?

I lunged for the safety line, grabbed it tight and yanked hard. It flew into the cockpit, the metal making a sharp, cracking sound against the fiberglass. There lay the bitter end—the D-ring—parted.

I became a lunatic. Forcing the seat lockers open, I threw cushions, anything that would float, overboard. He's out there somewhere. Maybe he's alive. Oh God, please . . .

"Take this. And this. And this . . . Hold on Richard, I'll find you."

I clambered below and grabbed more cushions, pushing them up through the main hatch. Crawling back topside, I heaved it all overboard. The debris undulated in the otherwise empty sea. Adrenaline raced through my body causing my heart to pound furiously.

Spotting the man-overboard pole attached to the mangled stern rail, I raced to the stern and struggled desperately to get the pole untied. I threw it as far out in the sea as I could. The orange flag bobbed in the swells.

He could be alive, it's only been three hours.

His last words, "Ohmigod," roared in my brain. It must have been a huge wave. Larger than those forty-five-foot monsters. A rogue wave. We rolled, and Richard . . . Oh, my love . . . God, you wouldn't—you couldn't . . .

I started dry heaving all over again. I hugged my convulsing stomach and felt the EPIRB still attached to my waist. I fumbled to unbuckle it. I couldn't center my mind. How does this thing work?

Remove the guard. Press the switch. Nothing. I stood up and held the radio device in the air. Nothing. I turned it in circles. Nothing. I sat down and started over.

I put the guard back on and then took it off. I pressed the switch and held the EPIRB up. Fumbling, I pulled out the batteries. With trembling fingers I wiped off the connectors and then put everything back together. Nothing. Damn it!

Water. The EPIRB needs water. Yanking open the seat locker I could see the bucket lying deep in the hole. It was the bucket Richard and I had used to pour saltwater over each other to cool off. Stretching, I grabbed the line on the bucket.

Holding the stern rail I threw the bucket into the water, scooped up as much saltwater as I could lift and heaved the bucket into the cockpit. I dropped the EPIRB in it. Bubbles rose, but nothing else happened. No lights or beeps. I yanked the EPIRB out of the water and shook it. Nothing. Disgusted, I threw it back in the bucket. Saltwater splashed all over, burning the deep cut on my shin.

I couldn't think clearly. My head throbbed and my body ached with every movement. There was nothing else I could think to do, short of jumping overboard and ending this nightmare. If Richard had beckoned, I would have jumped.

"Don't, he could be alive."

"How in the hell can he be alive?" I shouted to no one.

Defeat and exhaustion engulfed me. I couldn't bear to look at the reality of the situation any longer. I crawled below.

I STEPPED DOWN into a deep puddle. A good three feet of water covered the cabin sole. I gasped and thought, my God the boat's sinking, I've gotta get out of here. I went to the companionway and hoisted myself out. Frantically I struggled to move the heavy life raft to the side deck where I secured it to the cabin-top handrail. Instinctively I grabbed the rigging knife I kept on my belt and slid the sharp blade under a strap that held the raft shut and started cutting upward. It was too tough—I was too weak. So, I resorted to hacking away at the straps.

As the last strap split, the life raft inflated as it flung open. Inside I found fishing gear, hand flares, a miniature medical kit and cans of water. Something was wrong, something was missing. I tried to think, fishing gear, flares, medical kit, food and water. Food? There's no food. There's cans of water but no opener for the cans. How can a life raft have no food and no way to open the water? I flashed in disbelief.

Going back over the boom, I banged the deep gash on my left shin. It started bleeding again. I ignored it. It was nothing compared to . . .

I went below to get food. Wading through the river, kicking everything in my way aside, I picked up a duffel bag. Grabbing biscuits, cans of beans, tuna and peaches, I threw them into the bag. I took hold of the portable world band radio receiver and a can opener, and threw them in too. I pushed a blanket and a pillow out the companionway into the cockpit.

Water. I must have more water.

I looked around and saw the solar shower bag dangling from a shelf. It could hold two and a half gallons of water. "Richard will be thirsty when I find him," I said out loud. Grabbing the bag I took it to the galley and began to fill it using the pressurized fresh water system. As the bag was filling, the stream of water started slowing down. It became a sputter, then a spit. "My God, I don't have any water!" Wait—the water filter's canister; there's bound to be at least a half gallon of water in it.

I pushed in the solar bag's stopper and struggled to get the heavy bag out the companionway. Slipping back down to the cabin sole, I took hold of the now-full duffel bag and fought to get it topside. It weighed a ton, it tapped every ounce of strength I had.

I loaded the duffel bag into the life raft and then the bedding. As I was grabbing the solar bag, a swell hit *Hazana* broadside, causing her to roll. Everything in the life raft tumbled overboard.

"NOT THE RADIO!" I screamed, as I watched the duffel bag sink and the bedding float away.

I couldn't stand it. I became a raving lunatic, stomping on the cabin sole and kicking at the life raft. "THAT WAS STUPID, STUPID. I'M SO STUPID. RICHARD, WHERE ARE YOU? YOU COME AND GET ME. DO YOU HEAR ME? YOU COME AND GET ME! GOD, YOU'VE GOT TO HELP ME!"

Wailing with utter frustration, I grabbed the solar bag and crawled inside the life raft, shaking with fear and futility—babbling: "I can't take it, Richard, I just can't take it. Why didn't you take me with you? You said, 'The Captain goes down with the ship.' Remember? You said that! You lied to me. The ship did not go down. Where are you? How can I go on without you? What am I supposed to do? I don't know what to do. God, what should I do?"

"*You never leave the ship,*" came Richard's soothing voice. He said it over and over, softly in my head. Hugging the water bag to my chest, I shut my eyes and sobbed, "But you left the ship, you left the ship." I cried myself to sleep in the rubber raft, not caring if the ship and I did sink.

FROM
LET ME
SURVIVE

BY
Louise Longo

It was just going to be a simple three-week cruise off the Atlantic coast of France, and a reunion for Louise Longo and her husband Bernard, who had been separated for two years. Their five-year-old daughter, Gaëlla, is happy to see her father again and thrilled to be aboard his 36-foot ketch. She'd lived on their previous sailboat for the first two and half years of her life, a happy time for them all. Louise too is happy again through the perfect beginning of their voyage in September 1994. "I love this day where we do as we feel, thinking, playing, tidying, dreaming," she writes of their first day at sea. "Each of us is happy. A sacred happiness, on a day like today."

The following section begins on their fifth day at sea in the Bay of Biscay, notorious for unpredictable severe storms. They are only some forty miles offshore when the events leading to their terrible tragedy begin.

///

WEDNESDAY October 5, in the morning, the wind is howling. It has begun to rain. Bernard decides to tack out to sea to avoid the coast. We should reach Vigo on the 6th, in the morning. We still have a ways to go, but the boat is handling perfectly. We've switched the engine off, the sails are fine, and the *Jan Van Gent* does not heel too much. Gaëlla is not even seasick.

I sleep when it is time to sleep; our watches are an hour long. Normally people have four-hour watches but I think that's madness. I can rest and recuperate much better in an hour than in four hours. That's the way Bernard and I have always done it.

In the evening we begin to pitch and bang around in earnest. Bernard has put a reef in. It was a struggle, with the mainsail. Impossible to head into the wind so we had to work with the wind abeam. A real exploit. I don't like this sudden change, however. We've seen this before, but without Gaëlla. When we set off we both slept in the forward cabin, for safety. This evening we change everything. Neither Bernard nor I are hungry, but Gaëlla is. The stove is on gimbals, and we have to secure the pot in order to heat up the raviolis she's so fond of. The apples roll back and forth constantly and this makes her laugh.

Ten o'clock at night. Bernard looks worried; there are hollows beneath his eyes. This squall has come upon us so quickly, in a few minutes everything has changed. He comes down to the saloon, pale, soaked.

"It doesn't look good, Louise. I'm trying to get someone on the radio to find someplace closer than Vigo, an inlet, but I can't get through to anyone. It's impossible to find out the direction of the bad weather."

"How far off are we?"

"Fifty miles, roughly . . . I just don't get it. There are plenty of calls on channel 16 as usual but no one is picking up."

This portable VHF radio does not carry as far as the regular ones, but it worked fine with another sailboat we passed just before the storm. Besides, we've been trying it regularly every day. We've spoken to trawlers, freighters, only quickly of course, since channel 16 is an emergency band and you can't talk too long, so you don't tie it up.

"There's nothing, Louise, no one's answering."

He wasn't expecting a cruise like you'd get in the West Indies, but he wanted to try out the sails, have a good time, and give us, too, a lovely trip; and instead, he's going to have to fight. Gaëlla. He's thinking of her, above all. We've been through stuff, the two of us. We've been through worse.

"Go get some rest, Bernard. You won't hold up, otherwise. I can handle the boat, I'll take your watch."

"No, it's up to me to be at the wheel, we'll head for La Coruña. That way we'll have the waves from the quarter."

I am worried, but still not too much. The boat is behaving well. Without the mainsail she has settled down, with a tiny bit of jib and the engine at midthrottle.

"Bernard, you've got to get some rest. Be reasonable. I can take the wheel, you know that. Gaëlla's asleep, why don't you do the same."

He can't take it anymore. We have had to block the door of the wheelhouse, it was constantly banging. The hook doesn't hold. So each time he wants to go out on deck in a hurry he has had to climb through the port window. An irritating exercise. He rages against this stupid door lock.

"Things like this are dangerous . . ."

"Try to sleep, and if there's the slightest problem, I'll call you."

He finally agrees. I get up quietly, without waking Gaëlla, who has been asleep in my arms, and we go up to the wheelhouse. Bernard decides to lie down on the cabin sole, moving the folding seat to starboard.

I take the helm at 10:35 P.M. The boat rears up, the waves thunder by. With all this noise Bernard hardly sleeps. He opens his eyes and closes them again regularly; he's anxious. He listens to his boat, trying to figure out the struggle going on with the hull. He sees that it is hard for me to steer. Not that it is tiring, we have hydraulic steering, it's flexible, but because of the height of the seat I have to rest my feet on a heavy tool chest. In calm weather that's no problem, but in this tumult I lose my balance most of the time, my legs slipping out before me.

But still I manage, I can feel the waves unfurling, port broadside, I can sense them coming. The *Jan Van Gent* toils forward, slowly. I am exhausted by every wave we encounter, but I'm still in control. The boat is sturdy, the wave crashes down, sweeps the deck, the windshield wipers make their little back and forth motion, I hold on, my legs swing, then I start all over.

The moon has become enormous, the light on the mast is very

bright and I say to myself, Louise, this is just one battle. In reality, it is war. I barely have the time to shout: "Bernard!"

It's not a wave, it's a wall. Ten stories of wave, a tidal wave. And the thousandth of a second where I say to myself, "Oh no, have mercy, not that one . . ."

It has risen to port, and the boat is in the trough. I've seen it in nightmares, that wave, in my childhood, after hours spent reading stories of sailors and buried treasure, adventurers of the South Seas. Often I would wake up with a start, terrified by the watery giant about to sweep me away. I have been haunted by it.

"Bernard!"

The wall crashes down, the boat lies over, all the way to starboard, like a leaf. I am thrown from my seat with such violence that I picture myself already going through the wheelhouse. The sea is going to gulp me down, swallow me, bury me beneath tons of water. The sudden vision of this liquid wall in the halo of fire of the masthead light is so violent, at that moment, so powerful, that my brain spins, breaks away. My lungs are filled, ready to explode. Impossible to describe such terror, the way one's entire body is crushed. Not even time enough for simple fear. It is well beyond fear. I see myself drowned, I feel drowned, I have already died.

I want to breathe, I don't want to die like that. It's madness. I see myself doing a breast-stroke. I can hear something cracking; from what height have I fallen?

(Even today I cannot describe that wave. Words fail me. A wall. That is the only one I can find. To describe the height, the enormous size, the power. Nobody has been able to understand this wave, and every time I have tried to describe it there has been this frustration, and I can see that other people cannot see it as I did. It was a liquid, dark wall, topped by another white wave at its crown. As high as the mast. A rolling, breaking wave; a killer.)

And then the enormous noise. Everything that was to port went flying at the same time, the cupboards opening, the supplies, cans striking the ceiling, water, water. The boat lies glued to the sea, and torrents of water pour into the wheelhouse, and the windows shatter. There is a boiling, a shrieking; something overwhelming, flying, exploding. I am afraid of being torn from the wheelhouse, and that is when I begin to panic.

The boat rights herself with a terrible slowness.

Chaos all around me. Food everywhere, jam, tomato sauce, peas, on every wall and bulkhead of the cabin.

And Bernard is getting up with difficulty; the heavy toolbox hit him right in the chest.

"Are you okay? Are you okay?"

"Okay . . ."

He does not seem to be hurt, but the blow must have been very painful. He looks at me: something like a nightmare in his eyes, a terrible distress. It hurts to see him like this. Am I the same? The same madness in my eyes?

Immediately I think of Gaëlla. She is still lying on the bunk in the saloon, brutally woken by the shock, but she saw nothing and does not know what is going on. She is soaking. The comforter took the shock, she's all right. I take her in my arms to reassure her, there is water up to the bunks, I can hear the noise of my boots in the cabin where toys are floating. Bernard joins me, holding his stomach, bent over.

"The engine's had it, the batteries too."

At that point I notice that he is, like me, covered with tiny scratches. The glass of the wheelhouse windows exploded, the way old windshields do, into a thousand microscopic fragments. One of my buttocks is hurting, I must have struck something when the wall of water came down on us.

Bernard doesn't know what hit him. If he had been at the wheel he would have understood, but stretched out on the floor as he was, dozing, he did not see what I saw.

The boat's a shambles now, a real nightmare. A strange chaos where everything is floating upside down. Gaëlla is crying.

The conversation between Bernard and me at this point is made up of short, hacked-off sentences, circling around our daughter. Rapid questions, rapid answers. The engine has stalled. The deck light is still working, the cabin lights too. The brand new inflatable, solidly lashed on deck, has exploded. It is half past midnight. The engine refuses to start.

We have to take stock: we are roughly forty miles offshore.

I don't know how much time we had before the second rogue wave. So strong it lay the boat on her side again and caused her to spin 180 degrees. Like a top.

Instinctively I put my head down, holding tight to Gaëlla. I don't know what I expected—another liquid wall. But we went down quickly, then rose again just as quickly.

This is definitely a sturdy boat.

Bernard is concerned about the liferaft. If a wave tears it off, we'll have nothing left. And there is always a third wave.

The seconds, the minutes trickle by to the clamor of the sea, with infernal slowness. I try to find a flashlight in the surrounding chaos, but we can't find a thing anymore. Bernard is looking too. We talk without shouting, in order not to frighten Gaëlla.

"Louise, we cannot risk a third wave. It would be impossible to get out at the last minute. If we were alone we could do it, but not with Gaëlla. I cannot take that risk."

"I don't want to leave the boat. You should never leave the boat."

I remember *Fastnet* 1979, that race off the coast of England where some of the sailboats were found deserted. Some sailors had died of cold in their foul weather gear; others had disappeared. Boats can hold out a long time, not men.

I don't want to leave.

"I sent out an SOS, Louise, they must have heard! We're near the coast. If we were on the open ocean, we wouldn't stand a chance, but here, they'll find us!"

My entire body, instinctively, rejects this solution. I feel myself splitting in two: one part of me is listening to Bernard saying, over and over, "There will be a third wave, it will be too late . . ." The other Louise sees, parading through her mind, empty sailboats, their skippers gone forever. It's madness! We mustn't! Yes, but that wave, that monster, if it comes back it will be to kill us. The third wave, the famous one, is always the worst, or so they say.

Some of the floorboards in the wheelhouse have lifted, you can see the drowned engine. I refuse to panic. Bernard is not really panicking, but he is tense, in shock, and the decision to be taken at this fateful moment belongs to him alone. He is responsible for both of us.

"I cannot even steer, we must have something caught in the propeller!"

"And if we put a line out to the liferaft? We could wait for the storm to grow calmer, and if the boat doesn't sink we could come back on board . . ."

"And if the wave throws us against the boat? If we lose the raft and the boat? What do we do then? Can you picture us in the ocean, the three of us?"

Still I resist. But the liferaft lashed to the roof of the wheelhouse is moving, the lines have loosened. If the next wave carries it off, we'll have no choice left at all. I am shivering, and so is Gaëlla. Bernard decides to climb on the wheelhouse to examine the lines.

"Put your harness on!"

Bernard puts his lifejacket on and fastens his harness. He has to wriggle to get out on deck through a port window, struggling with it for a moment before he is able to make it slide open.

God forbid that he falls in the water!

"Don't fall! I won't be able to get you out of there!"

It was silly but that's what I shouted. He didn't even hear me.

Noise above my head. He's taking care of the liferaft. I am holding the wheel, trying to bring her into the wind, but she hardly responds.

Long minutes go by, I can hear Bernard tramping around above us, then he finally comes back the way he went out, streaming with water, so pale.

"Get your things ready, let's go! I've tied the raft to the port stern!"

I look at him, stupefied, my eyes wide open. He has decided. Now it's too late. Once the liferaft is inflated, we have no more choice. We have to get into it.

"It's madness! You shouldn't have! Have you any idea how many people have been lost at sea because they did just that? Bernard, I did not agree . . ."

"Listen, Louise, we have to go. There were some lights, earlier, you saw them too! There are surely some fishermen nearby, we'll send off a flare from the liferaft, they'll see it!"

"Wait a bit longer . . . perhaps it will get calmer . . ."

"Wait for what? For the third wave to get us? It will be too late . . . the boat won't be able to take it, Louise . . . It can't take it . . . Think of Gaëlla! We can't get on board if all hell breaks loose. We've got to go now!"

It's all over. I've given in. I'm not pleased with myself, but in moments like this, it is the more convincing argument which wins. And above all, it is Gaëlla's eyes. Her fear. With a child on board you don't reason in the same way. All Bernard's arguments parade through my head at the same time. The coast is not far, there were lights from the fishermen, we sent our SOS, our flare. A bad moment to go through and then we'll be picked up. He's right. He must be right.

I dress Gaëlla in a track suit and some socks, her boots and lifejacket, explaining to her as calmly as possible what we are going to do. She is no longer crying, and she listens as I talk.

As for Bernard, he says he will take care of the food supplies. I see him fiddling in the open cupboards, lifting up soaked cardboard boxes.

"Where is the money?"

"Wherever you put it. In the Nescafé jar!"

"It's not there! Did you take it?"

"Of course I didn't! You'll find it!"

As for me, I hastily gather up a few papers and our passports, and I stuff a duffle bag with towels, warm clothes, gloves, bonnets, scarves. My daughter is calm, because we are calm.

"Mommy, are you taking some orange juice?"

I grab a bottle of orange juice. At the same time I fill an empty bottle with fresh water.

"Mommy! Are you taking cookies?"

I stuff a package on top of the clothing. I don't take care of the rest. Bernard said:

"I'll take the food and the cigarettes!"

The sacrosanct cigarettes. He's getting irritated, he hasn't found the money, and in this shambles there's nothing surprising about that. I get angry in turn.

"Forget it! You must have put it somewhere else!"

"I'm not going to forget twenty-five-thousand francs! Louise, we'll need it! Are you sure you didn't put it somewhere else? You didn't take it?"

"I told you I didn't!"

There's something surrealistic about this argument, amidst the pounding waves and the urgency of getting ready to abandon ship. He's wasting valuable time, valuable calmness. I know the money is important, but if it went overboard, through the wheelhouse . . .

He gives up, despairing.

I see him pick up a plastic bucket; he's filling it, rapidly, while the boat pitches and rolls, and we find it so difficult to hold on in the chaos of the saloon, in this water swishing a mass of objects from one side to the other. I'm too busy with Gaëlla to look at what he is doing.

"We'll go out this way . . . you see . . . Mommy will go out first, then Daddy will help you . . . don't be scared . . ."

But I make one last attempt with Bernard to try and delay the moment when we will have to climb into the liferaft and be lost to the storm.

"We could connect the raft to the boat with lines tied one to the other, we'd have a good length, four or five hundred feet, don't you think?"

He has his back to me, wedging a bottle of rum in the plastic bucket. He grumbles:

"If it got really bad, we wouldn't have time to cut the mooring lines, they are too thick . . . Hurry up, Louise . . ."

The image of the *Jan Van Gent* sinking inexorably into the sea, dragging us along with it like a parcel . . . I shiver.

In my mind I also rage against the wheelhouse, as high as a watchtower. If it weren't for the wheelhouse the waves would have passed over the boat without causing any damage, like a simple sailboat for example. Damned wheelhouse—all these shards of glass, everywhere, the feeling of drowning that seized me earlier when the boat lay over on her side, it was so horrible. I am soaked. Neither my boots nor my lifejacket can prevent my teeth from chattering. I've given up the idea of putting my foul weather gear on top of everything, I wouldn't be able to move.

"Hurry up, Louise."

"The fishing lines! We must take them!"

"There will be some in the raft! Hurry up!"

The raft is tied to the hull. We have to go out through the sliding window to port, move along the deck to reach the raft. I have never seen a liferaft inflated. I'm suddenly terrified of the thing. Six feet across. We're going to close ourselves inside that thing, and then what? Have we made the right choice?

He has persuaded me, I obey, but in some corner of my mind I am still thinking, "This is a bad thing . . ."

And in another corner: "Gaëlla. He's right, for Gaëlla. We cannot risk Gaëlla's life . . ."

The raft is not tied on in the right direction; the usual opening, through which one is supposed to enter, is facing out to the sea. In front of me is the hole for catching fresh water. A sort of cone-shaped tunnel in the canvas. It is not meant to let a body through easily.

Bernard says to me, very quickly:

"Go ahead, I'll pass Gaëlla over to you first and then the bags!"

My daughter's black eyes are wide with terror and she begins to scream: "Help! Help!"

"Gaëlla, sweetie, don't shout, no one can hear you!"

"I don't want to go! I don't want to go in there! I want to go in the dinghy!"

The dinghy is the inflatable which was lashed on the coach house and which exploded with the wave. She's used to the dinghy, she went out for rides with her father before we set off.

I climb over the lifelines, holding with one hand, and twist myself around to dive through the tunnel. I force my way through with difficulty, legs first, my head outside, while the damned raft never stops moving in every direction.

Once I'm in there, closed inside this tiny, round dome, I hear Bernard's voice, stifled by the clamor of the waves:

"Take Gaëlla, Louise! Hurry up!"

I pull my daughter over, forcefully, by her legs; I make her slide through as I did, and she continues to cry.

"I don't want to . . ."

Her lifejacket gets stuck, and it takes all my strength to pull her towards me.

"Easy . . . easy, sweetheart. You'll be okay . . ."

I can barely see her little round face, her wide, frightened black eyes; I can sense her trembling mouth, her chin wrinkled in sorrow.

Am I thinking of anything in particular at this moment? No. I don't think so. I act, I settle my daughter into the corner of the raft, under the little orange light. Rapid, precise gestures. I realize that Bernard will not be able to squeeze through that stupid hole. And the opening is on the other side. I call out to him:

"Pass me the bags and turn the raft around! You tied it on in the wrong direction!"

In fact, the opening of the raft had been put in the wrong place to begin with.

He struggles for a moment before he manages to swing it around. In the meanwhile great masses of seawater cause him to waver; he hangs on, growing exhausted. Finally he is able to slide through the opening; I see him take his knife from his boot.

"What are you doing!"

"I'm cutting the line before we crash against the hull."

The blade slices through the rope, and he throws the knife overboard.

"Why did you do that? Why did you throw it overboard?"

"The blade could puncture the raft!"

No time to reply; in a few seconds we are thrown far from the sailboat. I can make out the masthead light, flashing to the rhythm of the waves; then it grows distant and disappears, taking life with it. I could cry. The *Jan Van Gent* gave birth to this round bubble, so light that we feel every furious splash of water beneath our buttocks. The boat cut the cord, the umbilical cord; the boat is abandoning us.

Five seconds. It's so quick; we have left her behind so quickly.

I feel that we are so small, three tiny larvae thrown onto the ocean. I say nothing. It smells like rubber and sea water; the little lamp throws a faint light onto our tiny dwelling space. At times, through the opening, I can see lights in the distance, so far away, so faint.

Bernard sets off a flare. We wait for a moment, our necks stretched in the direction of those hopeful lights.

Nothing. Now the lights have disappeared, the rubber bubble is turning on itself, in the stormy night.

Where is the boat? Will she reappear suddenly above us? Crush us? We look at each other in silence.

A wave wakes us brutally from this short, strange apathy. It penetrates, swishing, through the opening, soaking all our things in one second.

We have to close the opening to the raft, tie the flap to its three fasteners. One in the middle and two on the sides. I struggle with the thing until I realize that the flap which is supposed to be the door has a strap which must first of all be passed through the buttons on the outside of the raft. Nothing is practical in this raft. There are no nets to stow the bags and nothing to hold onto.

We are tossed around incessantly. Bernard settles Gaëlla down in the middle, and we sit on either side of her to stabilize the raft. I look through my bag. The cookies are a sodden mush and I throw them overboard so it won't make a mess on the bottom. Even in a state of panic I cannot stop myself from tidying house. Then I locate a leak in the cone-shaped rainwater intake.

I busy myself with fixing it as best I can and tying it up. The wave soaked us, and there is a small lake splashing in the bottom of the raft.

I caress Gaëlla's face; she is no longer crying and looks at both of us with her serious air. I smile to her; smiling is my weapon, my defense, my way of struggling against adversity. I give her a kiss. I always need to touch her, to cuddle her, to caress this little bit of woman I brought into the world.

"You are not grumpy, sweetheart, are you?"

Bernard looks very pale to me, but the light in here does not make us look our best. We look like corpses. We can't stand up. We have to watch every move we make. And it's horrible not to be able to see the sky, to be shut inside this thing, hunched over like toads.

"Are you all right?"

"I've got a bruise in the stomach, but I'm all right . . . don't worry . . . And you?"

"My bum . . . I don't know where I hit myself, but otherwise I'm okay . . ."

All night we try to sleep, but the waves leave us no time. The bubble threatens to capsize at any moment, to turn us upside down. We have to keep everything balanced on the wobbly floor, curve ourselves against the rubber rings, spread our arms out, let the wave pass under us and get ready for the next one. Most of the time the wave pushes against us, throwing us onto each other or making us spin like a top. Another mistake: we did not take time to set up the sea anchor to stabilize us. The cold is beginning to numb us quite severely, and water is getting in. There must be a leak somewhere. The bottom of the raft is splashing, we are sitting in sea water all the time. We must try to sleep. I manage to drift off for ten minutes and wake up when necessary. Which is often the case, every time Bernard says,

"Watch out, here comes another one!"

Our cadaverous faces, this unreal light, this enclosed space, the incessant dance of the waves, our efforts to keep the raft stable . . . At one point I thought, ridiculously, "It's like Disneyland."

Did we do the right thing? Shouldn't I have persuaded Bernard to stay on the boat, instead of letting him convince me to leave? I think about it all night long, while the sea plays with us in this rubber bubble as if we were a floating insect. While I watch my daughter curl her body up in the middle of the raft, and we lie like puppets pulling against our invisible strings.

I think too about the SOS. Someone must have heard us; in the morning, a freighter will find us.

The *Jan Van Gent* has surely sunk by now. Why did this happen to us? Why this brutal storm? I certainly did not expect a sea of glass, everyone knows this region is one of westerly winds, sudden squalls.

I think, then I sleep a few minutes, I cling onto the rings, and it starts all over.

Dawn. Thursday October 6, a pitiful sun was trying in vain to get past the layer of low gray clouds just above us. I lifted the flap to look outside, with the hopes of seeing in the distance the massive form of a freighter. We went past so many, even just yesterday.

Nothing. A leaden desert. We are drifting westward, a bad sign. The sea is still rough. Bernard is exhausted, his hands are pale with cold, the skin shriveled like mine, but he tries to sound cheerful.

"Let's get warm."

We are tossed around a bit less. He gets out the bottle of rum. Gulps some down and passes me the bottle, and I too swallow the equivalent of a capful. It heats me up, momentarily, my throat at any rate.

"Are you asleep, Gaëlla? Are you asleep, honey? Do you want some orange juice?"

I rub her little hands to get the circulation going.

"Do you want some water?"

She mumbles that she's sleepy. I insist for a bit with no result. I don't know if she really wants to sleep or if she's sulking. She is in shock, in any case.

I am beginning to feel all the painful effects of last night's thrashing. I check by moving my leg in every direction; nothing is broken. But I must have a tremendous bruise on my bum.

Bernard watches me, also making faces. He is holding his stomach, gently rubbing his chest from time to time.

"It was the toolbox, I got a direct hit. It's nothing, it'll get better."

It is then, in the early morning hours, that we go through what we've got. First of all I check the clothes in the duffle bag, and our papers. The towels are soaked, I wring them out; the sweaters too. It takes me a while before I turn to the rest.

I reach for the plastic bucket that Bernard said he would fill. A carton of cigarettes, completely soaked, some matches in the same state, the bottle of rum, and nothing else.

"Bernard!"

I remember him telling me, "I'll take care of the food and the cigarettes." It was while I was getting Gaëlla dressed. I see him, rummaging in lockers, everything thrown about by the wave, the lockers where our supplies were.

"Bernard! There is nothing here!"

He looks at me, dumbfounded. He makes a face. As if he were shrugging his shoulders, helpless.

I am completely flabbergasted. I want to scream something, but nothing comes from my mouth. Scream, but what? This is not the moment to start an argument. We'll have all the time we need back on land to tell each other off. But still, I'm really pissed off.

"You thought about your cigarettes! Your godawful cigarettes!"

They are so thoroughly soaked that I would be surprised if he could smoke one.

So we hunt through the orange bags which contain the survival kit.

A pair of scissors, a dull-bladed knife, some gauze strips, lots of gauze strips. Two sponges, a plastic bailer, a tube of antiseptic cream, some packets of fresh water—the equivalent of two liters—a sea anchor, two flares and some smoke devices.

"The flares are wet."

"The smoke devices too."

The last things are the rope and hoop which let you right the raft when it capsizes.

This bubble is supposed to be unsinkable, provided the raft is properly inflated, but it does capsize.

The rest is discouraging. Sea-sickness tablets, all in a pulp. A light which is supposed to be an SOS signal, but it doesn't work. Two wooden paddles, a repair kit with a tube of glue, "to be used only when the raft is dry."

I have no idea how the raft itself is to be used, the instruction manual is written in Flemish, in tiny letters, as is the Flemish dictionary that comes with it.

The only important thing is the pump, in good shape, fortunately, to keep the pressure in the rubber rings. No survival rations.

"Is that it, Bernard? Nothing to eat?"

"No."

"A mirror?"

"No."

"Fishing line?"

"There isn't any . . ."

I am overcome by rage at that point.

"I wanted to take them! You told me to forget it! You told me . . ."

"Normally there should be some."

"Normally? You know what you should have done, normally? Normally you were supposed to take care of the food! Normally you should have checked the liferaft! You could still have done it when it was tied to the boat!"

This "normally" is Bernard all over. With his sad eyes, like a dog who's been beaten. Punished, unhappy. He has a way at times of getting himself into the craziest situations and making me feel sorry for him to boot.

"They were right there, within reach, the fishing lines, in the fridge. We put them there on purpose."

"We won't even need them, Louise. They'll find us."

I am one of those people whose anger explodes and then subsides immediately. It's like sleep, a quick shot, and then I wake up. But even if I am calm on the outside, that does not stop my brain from racing at a hundred miles an hour. I try to get a grip on the information coming at me from all sides. Bernard is, morally, in very bad shape, and physically he's having a hard time coping. I think I know why. He has hardly eaten a thing since we left. Smoked, yes, swallowed a bit of coffee too, but that is not what you need in your stomach to be able to make it through. Fortunately Gaëlla ate well last night, and I managed to get enough down to not feel hungry right away. So . . .

My only comfort is that we have the orange juice, and the extra bottle of water which I brought. And there's the rum. On the paper which says "survival," attesting to our disaster I can just make out the words of advice: "Do not drink sea water. Do not drink urine." Okay. The inventory's over. We have to get organized. We'll tidy up, we'll take our boots off so we can free our feet from this damp, icy prison. We check the amount of water, to ration it. And finally we stream the sea anchor which gives us more stability. It feels good.

"Two or three days. I say that two or three days is the maximum we'll wait to be picked up."

The sky is so overcast that no plane could see us. There are counter-currents, the waves are very close together and still bounce us around. The sea is so gray, so empty. I refuse to be overwhelmed by this grayness. I complain, just to keep going.

"This light is driving me mad, you can't even switch it off during the day! I wonder how it works."

"With batteries, I think, it lights automatically when the raft inflates."

"Are you in pain?"

He stretches out as best he can, his arms hugging his chest, his foulies over him.

"A bit. It'll pass."

I watch him struggle over a cigarette that he is trying to dry out, hopelessly. The entire carton wasted, no hope. But he continues to insist, "The coast isn't far, I bet that tomorrow night we'll be sleeping in a bed."

I will never forget that wave that knocked us flat as a pancake. I'll never forget the moment when the *Jan Van Gent* disappeared, with her mast light, taking away all the food, the fresh water, life itself.

I am angry with Bernard. I bury this feeling deep inside for the moment. I try not to tell him. Under normal conditions I would talk about it, I would argue for as long as it takes. But all alone, the three of us in this orange bubble which will decide our fate, I keep quiet.

For the first time in my life the words, "It's too late," take on such significance. The sea is merciless in its revelations. It knows how to punish human error.

///

Sadly, this is still only the beginning of the story. When
help finally arrives two weeks later, Louise is the only survivor.
Bernard did make errors in his mad rush to the life raft, and these
undoubtedly contributed to his death. The greatest tragedy, as
they struggled without food or water, was Gaëlla's suffering. Louise
buries her at sea and in a final rage prepares to kill herself: "It's
what you want, wretched ocean. I won't fight anymore. There's no
reason to fight, you've won, you've won." But this is the moment of
her rescue. Later she will think, "It is probably my anger which
made me the sole survivor. That is probably what people could not
forgive."

///

FROM
the SHIP
and the STORM

BY
Jim Carrier

In the fall of 1998 Hurricane Mitch swept erratically into the western Caribbean. It would become the most destructive hurricane in the history of the Western Hemisphere. When it was all over, more than 18,000 people were dead or missing, among them the thirty-one sailors aboard the tall ship *Fantome*.

The *Fantome* was a 282-foot, four-masted, steel-hulled cruise ship originally built for the Duke of Westminster in the 1920s. In 1971 Windjammer Barefoot Cruises bought the ship from Aristotle Onassis and outfitted her for Caribbean cruising. She had just taken on a new group of ninety-seven passengers in Honduras when forecasts showed Hurricane Mitch increasing in strength and heading west from the eastern Caribbean. The decision was made to debark the passengers in Belize, where a charter flight out could be more easily arranged, but that left the ship in an area with no protection from the coming hurricane. The $20 million ship was uninsured.

Although he was only thirty-two, Captain Guyan March of the *Fantome* was a seasoned sailor who knew the Caribbean well, knew his ship well, and had outrun hurricanes before. He checked forecasts religiously and took no chances. In the eastern Caribbean he was used to sea room where a ship could run and hurricane holes—protected harbors—where it could hide, but the western Caribbean offered no such protections. Even Columbus in his last voyage to the New World had been terrified when caught in a gale on this lee coast full of reefs and shoals. From Belize, March and his crew headed for the Bay Islands off Honduras, which offered only a little protection but seemed better than nothing. Michael Burke, Windjammer owner, monitoring forecasts in Miami, agreed. As Hurricane Mitch built to a Category 5 hurricane with winds over 135 miles per hour and continued moving west, the *Fantome* sailed southeast for the islands, hoping to gain Mitch's navigable semicircle.

Jim Carrier, a journalist and author of seven books, is also a liveaboard sailor who has survived six hurricanes. His account of the *Fantome* and Hurricane Mitch is based on exhaustive research and hundreds of interviews.

///

ROATÁN Bay Islands, October 27, 1998,

Dawn–Early afternoon. Captain Guyan March spotted the long spiny island of Roatán at about 5 A.M. on Tuesday, October 27. A short time later his boss, Michael D. Burke, called from his home in Miami.

"How was it?"

"A little lumpy."

Burke's memory of that conversation, colored by the cool British countenance of Guyan March, filtered out the crescendo of a storm's edge. The waves in the open sea at the time were "probably 20 foot," according to Kevin Brewer, the dive master at Anthony's Key Resort, who was up at dawn checking boats. "One gust blew me across the boat."

"There was a lot of stress," said Burke. "There had not been a lot of concern in the evening. But this is still blowing at 170 miles an hour. It's a huge weather system. He's boxed in a corner. I'm sure he got some sleep, but not a whole lot. Guyan never raised his voice. If anything, there was maybe a bit more hesitation, an edge, not exactly a comfortable tone."

When Annie Bleasdale called March on the bridge, he was more to the point.

"Beam me up, Scottie," March told her.

"He said conditions were pretty bad, Force 10, huge waves. The sails they had left up had been blown out and were now stowed. He still planned to shelter from the huge swell. He told me not to worry, that he loved me and would call in a couple of days."

"Force 10," in sea parlance, is a level on the Beaufort scale used by sailors to estimate wind speeds and sea conditions and their effects on ships. Force 10 conditions mean winds of 48 to 55 knots and waves of 20 to 40 feet, with overhanging crests. The sea takes on a white appearance as foam is blown in dense streaks. Visibility is reduced, though not drastically. On the Beaufort scale Force 10 is just two steps below a hurricane, which starts at 64 knots. At Force 10, ships begin to roll heavily, and control becomes tougher. Overnight, the *Fantome* had gone from the calm behind Belize's reef, 300 miles from the storm's eye, to storm conditions 140 miles from the eye. Based on Bowditch's calculations of an approaching storm, *Fantome*'s barometer would have fallen 25 millibars.

At dawn, Mitch was again moving directly west at 7 knots. A Hurricane Hunter flight during the night had measured the eye pressure at 917 millibars, up considerably from the day before. But wind speeds were still as high as 164 knots. Mexico and Guatemala had raised hurricane warnings. The 4 A.M. forecast bent Mitch's track toward the Bay Islands by just a hair for twelve hours, "with a gradual slowing in forward speed and a bend toward the west-northwest then northwest thereafter." Plotted on a map, the forecast placed Mitch 60 miles due north of Guanaja by 1 P.M. that afternoon, 40 miles closer than predicted on Monday. Three days away it would be approaching Cozumel, Mexico.

Rounding Roatán's West Point, a spot he knew well, Captain March reported that big waves were "boiling" over the sandbar, curling around the island and following the south coast into Coxen Hole, the cruise ship port. His strategy, following standard Windjammer procedure in the eastern Caribbean, would be to stand off the island by one or two miles and steam back and forth, east and west, in the lee of the island. He would not anchor but would stay free to run or even move to the opposite side of the island when the storm passed to the west. Once he reached the south side of the island, behind its 200- to 600-foot-high ridgeline, seas dropped dramatically, to under 12 feet. March estimated the wind at 40 knots from the west-northwest and, according to Burke, put two staysails up again to steady her rolling. At 8:30 A.M. March sent an e-mail to Miami: "Good morning. We will require fuel this weekend because of our side trip we are on. Can we get 10,000 gallons on Friday or Saturday and then we'll top up the following weekend when we get the supplies. Please let the agent know which day so he can get pilots, etc. Capt. Guyan." The ship's tanks held 25,000 gallons of diesel fuel.

At 9 A.M. Hurricane Mitch began pounding the north coast of Guanaja. The sea began to rise, almost as if someone had flushed a plugged toilet. It was that fast: 1, 4, 6, 10 feet. Pushed from the eye wall of the storm like snow in front of a snowplow, the water climbed over Doug Solomon's dock on the northeast end of the island, setting boards adrift. It flooded the sand and flowers, surrounded the concrete block generator room, and began climbing the telephone poles on which his house was perched. A mile to the west, at Mangrove Bight, where scores of homes were built out over the water on pilings, the sea began churning underneath. Boats were tossed about, banging into each other, the docks, and the houses. As the waters reached floor level, people fled out on the rickety wooden walkways suspended between the shore and the maze of homes.

Harriet Ebanks' house was the first to go, at 9:45 A.M. Eyewitnesses said it looked as if a giant sea monster had just lifted it off its stilts. Heavy, wind-blown breakers, nearly 12 feet high, smashed her house as if with a fist, creating a scattered, floating woodpile. "Everything went under— the land stayed underwater," said Kerston Moore, a lobster diver. From the northernmost seawall of Mangrove Bight, townspeople on higher ground watched with horror as the sea popped, floated, and smashed houses one after another. Floating, they banged into each other like loose boats. Then they fell apart. Piles of shattered lumber—former houses—began washing ashore in a great splintered chaos. Panicked people ran pell-mell across the woodpiles, holding their babies, helping their mothers, stepping on nails, cutting their hands. Down the waterfront the surge and smashing came. The waves became waves of lumber, filling the space beneath Moore's house, surrounding the concrete block stilts. Every fifteen minutes or so a larger than usual wave would push the lumber higher. Hundreds of people ran to a church that lay at the center of the village, not 25 feet from the seawall. But lumber and water began wedging around the church, rocking it. "It's time to pray," someone cried. Just then the wind gave a shriek and someone howled, "It's time to run!" The church exploded soon after. People gathered in homes farther up the hill and huddled together in groups of twenty below granite cliffs and in canyons behind the village.

At the Bayman Bay Club, facing north from its cliffside perch, Don Pearly watched his 300-foot dock disappear. The sea rose and the water simply lifted the dock away from its moorings. "It didn't blow up. It just lifted, loosened, and floated off." Pearly and his guests were in a rein-forced-concrete basement with a windowed front that looked out to the sea. He had screwed plywood over the windows, so light inside was mini-mal. They had mattresses and a bathroom. As gusts became stronger, they would speculate on what was going on outside: "There went such-and-such a cabin." The gusts got longer. "It would get scarier and scarier and longer lasting, until finally it was constant. Shortly after that, the noise disappeared from your mind. It was more like a feeling."

Pearly and his assistant manager, Chris Norris, struggled out to check on thirty-three employees and their families in an adjacent base-ment. It was 53 feet between shelters, but the trip back and forth was tor-ture. "We'd fight to hold on to trees and beams under the cabins. The cabins were creaking and moving." Ten minutes later, coming back, it looked like a different route. New trees had fallen on the path. The noise was constant. The air was filled with salt water—"like a bucket, hor-izontally. You couldn't stand up. The hillside became a waterfall." Several cabins disappeared. Those that remained were badly damaged, with whole roofs missing.

At 10 A.M. Miles Lawrence reported that Mitch had moved only 10 miles in the previous six hours, and was 40 miles shy of where the last forecast said it would be. His fix, in fact, showed a 6-mile jog to the southeast from the previous fix. This "jog" involved two successive forecasters' best estimates of the storm's central point, a fix based on a jerky satellite loop with a stated margin of error of 23 miles. A 6-mile shift was "noise" statistically, particularly in a circle of hurricane-force winds 120 miles across. A re-enactment of the storm's track months later showed Mitch did not jog southeast but was making a slow left-hand turn to the south.

Based on his real-time analysis of the models, Lawrence wrote in his discussion: "The GFDL is almost stationary for 72 hours and the NOGAPS shows a slow, mostly northward drift." His official forecast was a "blend" of the models: a bit south of west (260 degrees) for a while, then a slow west to northwestward drift for 72 hours to near the Yucatán Peninsula. Lawrence warned in the discussion, "It would only take a 5-knot error in the forecast speed of motion for the hurricane to make landfall in 24 to 36 hours anywhere in the warning area from Honduras to the Yucatán."

Mitch's winds had declined by 10 knots to 145 knots, still a Category 5 storm. From space, the eye was a perfect hole inside a boiling white vortex. Drawn onto the satellite photo, the Bay Islands appeared as mites, insignificant, the eye itself as wide as Roatán's length.

Plotted on his chart, Mitch's reported 6-mile "jog" to the southeast shocked Michael D. Burke, who was hanging on every word and hoping for the best from the National Hurricane Center. Clutching at straws, the thought occurred to him that if the storm was going southeast, it was "going away. That's good. OK. We'll wait and see."

Aboard the *Fantome*, in the roiled wake of Roatán, March did not have the satellite photo, the weather fax, or the full array of "products" from the National Hurricane Center that were available in Miami. He was, in a very real sense, sailing blind—aided by men far away who could not hear the wind or feel the ship shudder, or sense the mounting fatigue of the helmsman at the wheel on the exposed bridge deck a few stairsteps and a couple of paces away. March himself was tired and stressed. Never very good at mathematics or at estimating time and distance, his keenness wore as he listened to the static-filled single sideband radio or talked on the satellite telephone and plotted Mitch's location on a chart table that heaved and pitched.

"Most of our discussion was about heavy weather preparation," said MDB, who, along with Paul Maskell, called the bridge periodically to check on ship conditions and boost morale. March confirmed that he had taken all possible heavy-weather precautions. Everything on deck had been removed and stored in cabins. The deck boxes had been drilled shut and duct-taped, as had the doors to the Admiralty suites on the main deck. Rope was strung across Decks A and B for safety lines. Watertight doors belowdecks were closed and dogged down, as were the lower bulkhead doors. Two empty fuel tanks had been flooded with sea-water to lower the ship's center of gravity. Burke was worried about sea-water splashing into the engine air intake, behind louvers near the entrance to the saloon. Water could damage or stop the diesels. March said he had put plywood over them and caulked the cracks with rags and rope. Burke also asked March to secure the heavy saloon doors with plywood. March said that one of the doors had been screwed down, but the other was left open. Burke interpreted that to mean that the crew was in the saloon and needed one door for possible escape. Open to the lobby, which ran with shipped water even in fresh winds, these doors were an obvious point of vulnerability. March reported that the ship was rolling somewhat but handling well, especially on the eastward tack with the wind on its port quarter.

As the morning passed, the ship's barometer dropped intermittently. Squalls washed over the deck. The wind was rising. Daylight was turning dark. It was clear that things were getting worse. When Annie Bleasdale called the bridge again, Guyan March "mentioned that MDB had said they could cut free the launches from the sides if they were rolling too heavily."

Burke, who had worried all morning about the ship being blown into the mainland of Honduras 25 miles away, asked March about other possible strategies, including tying up or anchoring at the cruise ship port at Coxen Hole. March said it was "very rough" at the entrance to the harbor. "Whitecaps were running perpendicular to the harbor. He said he couldn't get in."

"Why not anchor on the south side of Roatán?" Burke asked.

"It is too damn rough."

In his 1991 *Cruising Guide to the Northwest Caribbean*, a book written for small yachts, most of which draw 7 feet or less of water, author Nigel Calder described the southern shore of Roatán as "punctuated by a number of fjord-like inlets cutting back into the encircling hills, each one guarded by a shallow reef with a narrow opening and offering superlative protection." Calder sounded each of the inlets and found water at least 40 feet deep in Dixon Cove Bay, Brick Bay, French Harbor,

Caribbean Bight, Bodden Bight, Port Royal, and Old Port Royal. In a second publication, *Honduras and Its Bay Islands—A Mariner's Guide*, another sailor-author, Rick Rhodes, cited Dixon Cove on the west and Port Royal on the east as "viable" options for a ship with the *Fantome*'s 19-foot draft.

At the time of the *Fantome*'s dawn landfall on Roatán, the west end was already roiling with seas. March did not report conditions for the other inlets to the east. They could have been navigable early in the morning, but he had never been in them, they were not marked with navigation aids, and no one had published GPS bearings to enter in bad weather. As time passed, as the winds picked up and waves refracted around Roatán, these narrow entrances—200 yards in most cases—were most likely covered with breakers, according to Calder. In those conditions there was no way to distinguish the deep water from the reefs. March could not eyeball the ship in as he did in fair weather. "In heavy, breaking seas they'd all be extremely intimidating," said Calder. "You'd basically be doing it on trust, knowing if you were wrong, you would lose the boat. Even Port Royal, with 80-foot depths, I'm not sure I'd take a 280-foot, 19-foot draft ship and put it in the hands of somebody else's cruising guide." Terry Evans, whose family runs Coco View resort and a boat chartering business on French Harbor, said it would have been "absolutely impossible to find a way in. I put my own sailboat on a reef coming in at night in just 3- or 4-foot seas."

At no point in the morning, according to Michael D. Burke, did he and Captain March discuss a scenario to anchor the ship and get the men off.

As it was, dozens of boats were rocking but otherwise snug in Roatán's harbors Tuesday morning. Numerous shrimp boats were tucked into French Harbor and Oak Ridge. Port Royal harbored several boats. In Jonesville Bight, sixty to seventy shrimp and lobster boats and a dozen yachts cowered. "I had Jack Daniels under my pillow," said one yachtie. Most were tuned to VHF or single sideband radio. "It was kinda fun," said another. "It was like a big party. When you're sitting here, you want to have somebody tell you what is going on—even if it's wrong. You turn to all the channels."

J.C. García, who ran a dry dock used by shrimp boats, was at home in Oak Ridge watching CNN and boarding up his house, which faced

Honduras. Sometime late that morning, he noticed a four-masted schooner heading east. "Why," he asked himself, "are they going that way?"

Twenty years before satellite photos were available to mariners, a typhoon overran a U.S. Navy convoy en route to the Philippines to support General MacArthur's invasion. The storm of December 17, 1944, came to be called "Halsey's Typhoon" after Admiral William "Bull" Halsey, the convoy's commander who ignored a precipitously dropping barometer. Three destroyers capsized and sank, several ships were seriously damaged, and 790 men were lost. "It was the greatest loss that we have taken in the Pacific without compensatory return since the First Battle of Savo," Admiral C.W. Nimitz, the navy's Pacific fleet chief, wrote two months later.

Nimitz concluded in a postmortem that there had been too much reliance on weather analysis from Fleet Weather Center in Pearl Harbor and a general failure by the commanders to give up the mission and refocus attention on saving their ships. In a letter that would be codified in navy policy, Nimitz wrote:

"A hundred years ago, a ship's survival depended almost solely on the competence of her master and on his constant alertness to every hint of change in the weather. . . . There was no radio. . . . There was no one to tell him that the time had now come to strike his light sails. His own barometer, the force and direction of the wind and the appearance of sea and sky were all that he had for information. Ceaseless vigilance in watching and interpreting signs, plus a philosophy of taking no risk in which there was little to gain and much to be lost, was what enabled him to survive. . . .

"In bad weather, as in most other situations, safety and fatal hazard are not separated by any sharp boundary line, but shade gradually from one into the other. There is no little red light which is going to flash on and inform commanding officers or higher commanders that from then on there is extreme danger from the weather. . . . Ships that keep on going as long as the severity of wind and sea has not yet come close to capsizing them or breaking them in two, may nevertheless become helpless to avoid these catastrophes later if things get worse. By then they may be unable to steer any heading but in the trough of the sea, or may have their steering control, lighting, communications and main propulsion disabled, or may be helpless to secure things on deck or to jettison top-side weights. The time for taking all measures for a ship's safety is while still able to do so. Nothing is more dangerous than for a seaman to be grudging in taking precautions lest they turn out to have been unneces-sary. Safety at sea for a thousand years has depended on exactly the op-posite philosophy." . . .

Bay Islands, October 27, 1998, Afternoon. A lesser sailor might have panicked by now. A Category 4 hurricane was bearing down on him. The ship he'd been able to handle so well would no longer track and go west. The waves and wind around him were the worst he'd seen. But Guyan March was not given to panic. On the bridge of a ship he wore a look, born of ability, seasoned with success, of calm and assurance. "Never in his life did he lose control of a situation, certainly not at sea," said his brother Paul. "Calm and controlled was the way he managed and thought things through. He was very methodical and calculating."

So successful had March been as a young sailor that problems almost surprised him. Those who knew him saw this aspect occasionally—a pass-ing, stunned look. "He would never actually express it verbally, mainly because there were people around who would pick up on it," said Jeremy Linn, his old sailing instructor. In 1986, while still in sailing school, March was motoring the 72-foot *Hoshi* into a lock in Scotland when the engine failed. He was doing 4 knots. If he had kept going and popped the gate, the ship would have dropped 30 feet. "A look of total horror ap-peared—only momentarily," said Linn. "He was very quick thinking. We both dove into the engine room and turned the key. The old diesel had been running too slow and stopped. I saw the same thing in handling sails when things weren't quite right. There would be a look of just com-plete horror. He would take a moment to think about it, and come up with the right solution ninety-nine times out of one hundred. He was calm and collected. He wouldn't shout or scream."

March also impressed his shipmates from the start of his Wind-jammer career. As a mate on the *Fantome* in the late 1980s, he took con-trol of the bridge when the ship went aground in Antigua. When the cap-tain seemed powerless, Guyan "was all business," said Sharon Patterson, the purser. He was "so self-assured and confident about all things per-taining to sailing that no one ever doubted his suggestions. He could weigh the large and the small, the crew, passengers, weather, ship, responsibility, business, fun, girlfriend, life, love, and laughter and keep them all orbiting in pretty much a well-balanced scheme. Like juggling a dozen balls at once. There were times when you could see rings under Guyan's eyes and knew he needed rest badly, but he never complained about it. I don't understand how he did it, but the man never showed a grouchy side."

Ed Snowdon, who served as mate under March aboard the *Yankee Clipper*, recalled, "I have never met a man, and I've been around a lot of circles, who had more of a sixth sense and innate ability to make the right decision and know the right thing to do. It was uncanny. He didn't have to stop and scratch his head. He was not at all daredevil. He was always making the most prudent decision. When I was sailing down a coastline, he might say, 'Ed, you're 2 miles off a lee shore. What happens if you lose an engine and a squall comes up? You're going to be set down. If you're another mile off, you're in better standing.' He taught me that kind of thing. He would always err on the safe side."

March had tasted rough weather. He'd crossed the English Channel in small boats with winds of 40 to 50 knots. "At home, in the dinghies, we would be the first ones out and the last ones in," said brother Paul. "In marginal, rough seas, everyone waited. If we started in, they knew it was time to head in. Everyone gauged it on us. It went to ability. If we thought it was marginal, it really was time to go in." At Windjammer, Guyan had seen waves sweep the top of the *Fantome* and felt its heeling in big waves. He'd known the edges of several hurricanes. March, like most sailors, had a fascination with sea storms and disasters and an encyclopedic knowledge of them, according to Patterson. "He told me about rogue waves: massive waves that appeared unexpectedly and took ships and crew by surprise. We talked at length about disasters at sea, ships that encountered storms and lost crew."

March must also have known that a career at sea sometimes requires periods outside the comfort zone. That's how sailors grow, through longer crossings and bigger waves. If they survive, the bold ones revel in newfound confidence. "Every time you go out there is a risk," Windjammer owner Mike Burke believed. "That's part of the beauty of it. When you've got a bone in your teeth? And you wonder. That element of danger. It's a good feeling—if it holds together." But the wise ones recognize that their survival sometimes has as much to do with good luck, or a guardian angel, as with their own ability. On Tuesday afternoon, October 27, Guyan March, full of pride and trim, was in the hands of the gods.

"I started to feel fear from him," said Michael D. Burke. "He wasn't too forthcoming with his acceptance that we needed to run to the east. I think he was afraid. Look at his circumstances. He is leaving a lee. He is heading out. It's going to get dark in a few hours, if it's not dark already. He's in hell. He's already facing pretty horrendous conditions. His circumstances will get worse, right at dark. There wasn't a whole lot to say."

Almost immediately, Roatán's protection disappeared. From the high point of a 700-foot peak, the one used to find Port Royal, the land sloped off rapidly into the sea to the northeast. Two low islands, Morat and Barbareta, stood offshore with no lee. Then came a 14-mile stretch of deep water before the ochre bluff of Guanaja, invisible beyond the dark squalls and veils of spume, rose abruptly from the depths. Running under bare poles, the *Fantome* was making 7 knots on a compass bearing of 90 degrees. As Roatán passed by the port beam, the wind on deck increased gradually, from a "garden variety" hurricane to something above 80 knots. Sea conditions worsened dramatically and rapidly. Within an hour, waves jumped from the 10- to 15-foot range to 20 to 40 feet. The waves generated by Mitch's outer winds were still piling in from the west-northwest around Roatán's south side, more or less behind the ship. But in the open channel these waves encountered others refracting around both islands, as well as monster seas surging directly south through the channel from Mitch's eye wall, which was now just 30 miles to the north. The highest sustained winds in the eye wall were 133 knots. Gusts could have reached 198 knots. Mitch was right on the border between a Category 4 and Category 5 hurricane. The 282-foot steel *Fantome* plunged on, unprotected from the most powerful force on earth.

"Confused seas," the term used by March to describe the colliding wave trains, could not come close to describing the steep, irregular boiling that now surrounded the ship and its crew. The water leaped and sank, built mounds and cut cliffs. There was no rhyme or logic. According to wave theory, when 20-foot seas from one direction meet 15-foot seas from another, the coincident crests rear up an average of 25 feet, with periodic peaks of 37 feet and an occasional 50-foot giant. Around the *Fantome*, steep waves appeared from nowhere, then broke into cascading faces that crashed like breakers and hissed over a sea surface already white with wind-blown spume.

The rolling of the boat increased violently—30 to 45 degrees to port and then to starboard—March reported to Michael D. Burke. Waves struck the hull and poured water into the A-deck "lobby," forward of the dining saloon, and over the sidedecks between the bulwarks and the Admiralty suites. The top party deck was 20 feet above the water. B deck was a mere 12 feet. "He had gotten hit by a bow wave, a big wave, with lots of water on deck," said Burke. MDB was worried about broaching, a loss of control in which a ship heels wildly to windward, exposing its broad side to wind and sea. He questioned March about ways to prevent broaching, using a launch as a drogue trailed astern, or sails—jibs or staysails—tied to a mooring line as a sea anchor deployed over the bow. But the ship was rolling so much it would not have been safe for crewmen to be out rigging lines or wrestling a 3,000-pound boat over the ship's stern. Plus, March said he didn't think it was necessary. "The bow of the ship is broad and deep, so it is not squirrelly. So when it surfed, the ship would ride straight. It didn't turn off," said Burke.

At some point, Guyan March apparently left the deckhouse—when Burke telephoned, Brasso answered and said the skipper wasn't there—which would have required him to open the sliding hatch and struggle out onto the bridge. Grasping ropes and railing, or clipping a harness into one of the jacklines the crew had rigged, he would have pushed or perhaps crawled through wind and spray capable of etching a bloody tattoo on his face. The 20 feet across the exposed party deck to the closest stairway at the muster station would have seemed like traversing an earthquake. "He must have been blind as a bat," said Neil Carmichael, captain of the Windjammer ship *Polynesia.* "I don't think people appreciate what it's like when you start getting 50, 60, 70 knots and rains as torrential as that. I've been in 50 to 60 with a snorkel mask on. You can't see 10 feet." Having descended the forward stairs, March could have staggered aft along the port or starboard sidedeck between the Admiralty suites and bulwarks, crossed the "lobby," and pulled open the unsecured wooden door to the dining saloon in an interval between periodic deluges of solid seawater. Or, making his way forward 20 feet, he could have opened a watertight hatch and descended a ladder to Deck B, and from there reached both the engine room and the saloon. He might even have braved the length of the top deck and descended the duke's original stairway into the lobby.

Guyan March and Michael D. Burke never talked about where the men were, but Burke assumed that engineers Constantin Bucur and Pope Layne were in the engine room, perhaps with other engineers, sealed off by waterproof hatches. They would have kept busy, monitoring engines and hydraulic pressure, watching the water level in the bilge beneath them, thinking about sediment in the fuel. Routine work would have been impossible as they grasped pipes and worried. Pope Layne had been through Hurricane Marilyn in 1995 aboard Windjammer's *Flying Cloud*, the company's smallest ship, which was too slow to outrun hurricanes and was tied to a mooring ball off Peter Island in the British Virgin Islands when storms threatened. Pope and other crew stayed aboard to run the engines against the force of the wind. "He was scared to death. He said he had to crawl, literally crawl, on deck," recalled Rhonda Epperson. "You couldn't hear anything. The wind and rain were just so intense. The wooden covers to the benches were flying off. He couldn't communicate over the radio because of the noise. So people were sending messages back and forth by crawling on the deck."

By Tuesday afternoon, the rest of the *Fantome*'s men were presumed to be in the saloon. "That's where I'd be," Burke said later. That would have put twenty to twenty-six men in a room that had once been filled with rum and laughter and the twinkling brass lights of a cruise. Now grunting, nauseous men, trussed into bulky life jackets, strained to stay in their seats and hang on to the macramé-covered posts. The burnished brass lamps, if not dismounted and stowed, would have described crazy arcs, as would the gold chains on the crew's necks. The men would have been suffering great fatigue. Their muscles had been tense for twenty-four hours as they moved or hung on in the rolling ship, fighting to stay in a bunk or not be tossed about. Their last good sleep had been Saturday night, three days before. Ever since, they had been in a flight-or-fight mode. They were scared. Several of the men couldn't swim.

Deckhands and the more experienced crew, including bosun Cyrus Phillips and bosun's mate Jerry King, probably would have walked through escape routes in their minds. From where they were, they would have to climb an exposed stairway and make a suicidal dash to the top-deck muster station and life rafts. The hotel department heads, chief steward Chrispin Saunders and chef Eon Maxwell, and their staffs most likely were petrified. Without normal duties to occupy them, their minds were free to roam, to their wives and kids, to plans for the future, to beautiful women, to random promises, prayers, and regrets. The scene outside the saloon's windows encouraged their worst fears.

Phillips, at forty the "old man" of the *Fantome*, Bequia-born and with twelve years with Windjammer, was the closest any of the West Indian crew came to being a sailor from birth. He "wanted to get money together and have his own boat for freighting through the islands," said his brother, Julian Peterson, who crewed on Windjammer's *Yankee Clipper*. "It was supposed to come time in 2005."

Jerry King, in his last call home, had told his sister how homesick he was. He hadn't been home since January. When the ship next docked in Trinidad, he told her, "I'm going to roll in all that mud."

Friday, three days away, was electrician Vernon Brusch's twenty-seventh birthday, and he had promised his mother he would be home to celebrate. In his last phone call from Omoa, Brusch had laughed and said that he would be the one bearing gifts. "Oh God, Mommy, my cabin is full." Piled on his bunk before the storm were a VCR, more CDs, and a plastic tricycle for Otaphia, his pretty child who liked to wear red and white beads in her hair. "He had no room on the bed to lie down," said Athelene Brusch, who set her mind to a birthday cake, a homecoming meal, "and those kinds of things."

Kevin Logie of Trinidad, who had followed his brother to Windjammer, was due to leave the *Fantome* in a week to become lead chef on another Windjammer ship. He still dreamed of saving money to open his own tailor shop. On his last trip through Miami, Logie had twenty minutes to spend with brother Neville. "He had footage on his camcorder of my three-month-old baby. I told him I would look at it another time. He was coming back to Miami with the camcorder, CDs, a TV, VCRs—everything was in that little cabin."

Jesús Hernández, deckhand, the Honduran dock hire without a visa, was 25 miles from his estranged wife and two children, who were soon to be in the hurricane themselves. When he was ten months old in 1974, Hurricane Fifi barreled through the strait between the Honduran mainland and the Bay Islands and devastated the country. A small stream running through the village of San Marcos became a roaring torrent through Jesús' mother's house. "I couldn't hold all the children," she said later. "The river was taking Jesús away. But a neighbor came and grabbed him by the hand."

Alvin and Alan George, the Spice Brothers from Grenada, men taught to cook by their grandmother, were chefs at heart. Alvin, the neat one, had two kids at home. Alan, the good-looking brother, the life of the party, was saving his money to open a restaurant in Grenada. "I'll see you in November," he had said in his last phone call to their mother, Margaite. When she protested again about his life at sea, he had said offhandedly, "If I have to die at sea, I'll die there, instead of on land."

Francis Morain, deckhand and father of six in private school in Grenada, had turned thirty-seven on October 10. After enduring a $350-a-month job, he had the letter he'd worked for, the letter from Windjammer recommending a visa to the United States. He had told his wife, Elizabeth, to join him in Trinidad for Christmas shopping.

Carl "cool and deadly" James, engineer, was looking forward to Christmas, when he could take his sister's children downtown in New Amsterdam for ice cream.

Deonauth "Django" Ramsudh, refrigerator mechanic, had been an acolyte in the Lutheran church as a child. If he was to meet his Maker, at least he'd taken care of his three children with the $69,000 won at the casino.

Colin August, the launch driver, no doubt wished he'd taken some leave, like brother Chuckie, who was safe ashore.

Rhon Austin, deckhand, was experiencing his first tour at sea.

Maxwell Bhikham—Blinky, they called him—was a Muslim deckhand who never missed prayer time with Mohamed Farouk Roberts, another Muslim and first-year engineer. They were from Guyana, too.

Steadbert Burke and Vanil Fender were Jamaicans, a first-year carpenter and a cook. They had wives at home.

O'Ryan Hardware, the ladies' man, had followed his brother to Windjammer and become an engineer. Brother Orville had reached his dream—enough money to marry and get off the boat.

Deodatt Jallim, another first-year carpenter, had followed his brother Harry to sea. He had called his wife from Belize and told her to expect him in two weeks.

Carlisle Mason, deckhand from St. Vincent, and Wilbert Morris, the quiet, muscled welder from Guyana who helped keep the ship together, huddled with the others. Aníbal Olivas, the Nicaraguan dock hire, two weeks on the ship as steward, was there. Pedro Prince, the Honduran galley aide stuck without a visa, was thrown together by circumstance with Rohan Williams—Dr. Stone, they called him—another deckhand. Bobby Pierre from St. Lucia—so helpful and joyous as Chrispin's assistant steward and such a good dancer—was there too. He looked remarkably like a smaller version of Horace Grant, the basketball star, and lately had been dating Chrispin's sister, Beverly McKenzie, who had gotten off the ship in Belize. Whatever these men were thinking was shoved aside with each bang and howl that brought the storm back like a question from Saint Peter. At some point, they became too seasick to care.

When a storm is violent enough, even experienced mariners will eventually begin to suffer from a type of motion sickness, not the nausea most think of, but an enveloping fatigue—the "feeling that we want to close our eyes whenever we get the chance," according to Carlos Comperatore of the Coast Guard's research branch. By itself, that might not be a problem. But when it combines with sleep loss, stress, and desynchronosis—the maladjustment of the body clock—endurance drops significantly. Even the most durable mariners begin to retreat into a personal shell, walled in and enervated by the motion of the ship, lack of sleep, the physical exertion of staying upright or in a bunk, and worry. It is the first sign of deteriorated performance that sooner or later overcomes any sailor. First, the man gets quiet. As conditions worsen, he becomes forgetful. It becomes tougher to do mental arithmetic. He is apathetic and slow to respond. He might forget to check critical information, or he might act when what is called for is no action.

When he reached his men, Guyan March would likely have told them the truth about their plight, about the loss of Roatán's lee and his hope for the run east. He would likely have reviewed safety matters, especially the use of life jackets and life rafts. His presence may have had a calming effect on the crew, who would have been praying and pushing back moments of panic. These would have been held back only by the rational thought that of all the Windjammer officers they knew, Guyan March, Brasso Frederick, and Onassis Reyes were the best. "He would have gone through every single scenario in his head," said crewman Julian Peterson, brother of bosun Cyrus Phillips. "If there was one person I would want to be with, it would have been March because of his control over himself and his ability to handle the vessel."

At some point, March rejoined Brasso and Onassis in the deckhouse. Knowing what they knew, the minds of these three men likely would have raced with all the things that could go wrong. How far would she roll before the ship no longer cared whether she came upright or kept going? At what angle of roll would water downflood, and from where? Would watertight doors hold? Would the square portlights on B deck shatter and flood? If the *Fantome* was laid over, would the large, rectangular saloon windows surrounding the crew stand up to wave crests? Could the ship's most vulnerable spot—their deckhouse—stay together? The highest, forwardmost, and flimsiest shelter on the ship—25 feet above the water on calm days—must have been hell, the rolling and pitching exaggerated, the noise debilitating. In one grunted exchange with Miami, March described a chair flying.

Their conversation limited to brief shouts, the officers, too, likely withdrew inside, to that private space forced open by the knowledge that they could die. When the weather was rough, Brasso liked to sleep below the saloon, in a C-deck cabin near the center of the keel, where motion was dampened. Now, in the worst possible place on the ship, he could well have imagined time at home in his big new house on Antigua. Built from scratch on his Windjammer earnings, it was probably worth $400,000. So big in body and spirit, a rock in the midst of crisis, even Brasso could have legitimately concluded that if the ship came to grief, it would be impossible to get anyone into a life raft.

Onassis, full of vigor and promise, could have flashed on the crewmen he knew who couldn't swim, his girlfriend Glenn and their Christmas plans, or the feeling of being trapped underwater that he had experienced when a launch had flipped and he'd been snared in the canvas top. It had scared the hell out of him, Parkinson said later. "It was a realization of the reality, a random fluke. He knew how dangerous it was." He must have considered the irony that failed love had put him there to replace a heartsick mate. Or maybe he recalled his last e-mail to his mother, sent Friday night for her birthday. "Remember that you finish a new year every time you begin a new day. So it's never too late to start something new. Like doing more exercises or writing a new diary, etc. . . . My time in these waters will end soon because I finish on

December 26. . . . I'm very healthy. Running 30 miles a week (in the mud) and lifting weights. I have to buy some vitamins. Take care of yourself, Mama, and you will be hearing from me soon. Your son loves you. Onassis." . . .

At 4 P.M. the *Fantome* was approaching Mitch's longitude. Michael D. Burke thought that was good news.

"Soon," Burke assured Guyan. Soon, the ship would be east of the center. It would be in the "navigable quarter." Wind would be blowing the ship away.

Shortly after, Captain March reported that, in fact, the wind was clocking more westerly. It was coming over the stern. Burke was elated. Things were working out. Things couldn't get worse. "I asked Guyan to bear a bit south of east, to get as far away as possible." March toggled the ship's big rudder to 93 degrees.

But aboard the *Fantome*, the suffering only increased. The ship was surrounded by chaos. The sky overhead was turning a charcoal gray-black. The rain beating on the deckhouse was horizontal and as heavy as a fire hose. If he could have opened his copy of Bowditch, Captain Guyan would have seen the book's classic description of the view now outside his ship:

"As the center of the storm comes closer, the ever-stronger wind shrieks through the rigging and about the superstructure of the vessel. As the center approaches, rain falls in torrents. The wind fury increases. The seas become mountainous. The tops of huge waves are blown off to mingle with the rain and fill the air with water. Objects at a short distance are not visible."

In good times the *Fantome* creaked comfortably. Now she would have brayed. The hull, rising and falling, would have shuddered, slammed, and struck water as if it were stone. Rolling through a 90-degree arc, the beefy masts waved like willows. Even well-stored items would have come loose. Cans on shelves, glass in the refrigerator, spilled milk, rum bottles, books, CDs, toys for kids, and VCRs for their mothers would have mixed in a great, cacophonous salad. Standing water sloshed around. Doors, windows, and seams would have leaked water.

If they could see anything, March, Brasso, and Reyes in the deck-house and the men in the saloon would have watched the slate-gray, white, and turquoise mountains rise above them. Then, as if riding an elevator, they would have risen to look out on a frightful battlefield where wind and spume raged. Down again they would go, into a trough, the seas hissing around them before cascading seawater covered everything. "The radar, if working, would be giving a dubious picture," said Neil Carmichael, captain of the Windjammer ship *Polynesia*. "They're inside the bridge, with limited visibility, three or four small windows. The bridge wasn't set up to be used on the inside." Maneuvering to avoid the worst breaking seas would have been impossible, even if visibility had permitted it.

Michael D. Burke remembered the captain's description: "It was terrible, squalling, dark and dirty, yet it was not like he was about to die," said Burke later. "He was not out of control. We didn't have far to go. It was a race. If we could get to the east, with the winds southwest, we'd have the Honduran mainland to protect us from heavy seas. It was a matter of time before we and the storm got further apart. We never discussed getting into rafts or the lifeboats. We weren't of the opinion that all was lost."

In *Typhoon: The Other Enemy*, retired navy captain C. Raymond Calhoun sketched the domino effect of a hurricane (called a *typhoon* in the Pacific) on his destroyer, *Dewey*. Halsey's Typhoon, which struck the Third Fleet in the Pacific on December 18, 1944, was similar in strength to Hurricane Mitch. When the typhoon's center was 50 miles away, the aircraft carrier *Monterey* reported rolls so heavy that airplanes on its deck broke loose, caught fire, and rolled into the sea. Steering systems on light carriers failed. Two men went overboard on the *Independence*. The carrier *Cowpens* had a fire on deck. The *Langley* began rolling 35 degrees to both sides.

"At 0911 our voice radio went out. . . . electrical failures now became a recurring problem. Everything was being short-circuited by the driving rain and spray. Our helmsman was having to use from 20 to 25 degrees of right rudder to maintain a heading. At 0928 with the ship rolling 40 degrees to starboard the *Dewey* lost suction on the port main lubricating oil pump. We had to stop the port engine in order to prevent wiping the main bearings. . . . the *Dewey* was corkscrewing and writhing like a wounded animal. The inclinometer registered 55-56-57, then 60 degrees. I tried to recall the stability curves . . . my recollection was they had shown that the *Dewey* could recover from a roll of 70 degrees."

The wind "drove spray and spume with the force of a sand blaster. Capillary bleeding was etched on any face exposed directly to it." The doctor reported several men injured by falling, some with fractured ribs.

The navy ship was "tossed, shoved, beaten." Metal covers ripped away, despite heavy screw-down hasps. In two hours, despite "watertight" hatches, a foot of water filled every living space. "The pounding and rolling grew worse. We were now going over consistently to 68 and 70 degrees. Each roll I would dispatch a silent prayer, 'Dear God, please make her come back.' Engineers reported that on each starboard roll, the blower intakes, on main deck, were submerged and 500 to 1,000 gallons of water gushed into the fire rooms. Water tenders grabbed fittings and hung like monkeys. Sometimes they fell into the starboard bulkhead, shoulder deep into sloshing water, striking machinery and pumps. During one roll, a starboard hatch sprang open. Seawater poured on switchboards. There were flashes, short circuits, fires. The power went out. Steering went out. The wheel required 6 to 8 men.

"Many times I found myself hanging by my hands, with feet completely clear of the deck, in such a position that if I released my hold, I would drop straight down, through the starboard pilot house window into the sea. Several times I looked down past my dangling feet and saw the angry sea through the open window, directly below them," Calhoun wrote. The men prayed aloud: "Don't let us down, now, dear Lord, bring it back, oh God, bring it back." Each time it did, they shouted, "Thanks, dear Lord."

Outside, guy wires on exhaust stacks slackened and snapped taut with each gust. One broke with a noise like a cannon. The stack collapsed. The steam line broke. A whistle and siren and roar went off. When a fireman burned his pants, he told Calhoun: "It didn't really matter, Cap'n, I'd probably have had to burn 'em anyway."

At 4:20 P.M., Glenn Parkinson called Windjammer's headquarters and learned that Onassis Reyes had relayed a message to her. "He loves you," said a voice in Miami.

"Tell him I love him, too," she answered. Later she said, "I don't know if he ever got the message. I went home and watched the storm on TV."

For moral support as much as anything, Michael D. Burke asked Captain March to stay on the phone, to keep the satellite line open. "Me and Captain Paul [Maskell], we were not doing a lot of talking. He's in a battle for his life."

Captain March reported waves of 30 to 35 feet, "right on the stern—except for confusion. He was saying the sea was terrible. Rough. He indicated it was getting worse. He was starting to lose the lee, which was all the more scary to me. I fully realized what he was going into over the next few hours."

"Don't worry about the lifeboats," Burke repeated to March. "Even if you lose a mast, don't worry. The debris on deck—it's not an issue. Get through it. We'll fix the ship later." He asked March if the water pouring on deck was falling off.

"It's discharging," March said.

The seas were terrible. "Confused," March yelled. The ship was making 7 knots. March reported a GPS fix of 16° 15′ N, 85° 51′ W, about 10 miles south-southeast of Guanaja.

"You could feel the grimace," Burke later recalled. "The ship was rolling heavily. And that's pretty scary in itself. He would have to hold on. You'd hear sounds of exertion. I heard him groan. I heard him say, 'That was a big one.'"

"Is it falling off? Is it shedding?"

"Yes, that's not a prob . . ."

At 4:30 P.M., the satellite telephone went dead.

///

Defying all predictions, Hurricane Mitch had drifted southwest and then south—directly toward the *Fantome*. Then it stalled for thirty hours. Search-and-rescue missions began Thursday morning but found no sign of the ship. Six days later a destroyed life raft was found washed ashore on Guanaja. For weeks small bits of wreckage washed up, but what exactly happened to the *Fantome* was never known. It was presumed that she broached in high waves and quickly sank.

///

bibliography

Following is a comprehensive list of editions of the books excerpted in this volume.

Ashcraft, Tami Oldham, with Susea McGearhart. *Red Sky in Mourning: A True Story of Love, Loss, and Survival at Sea.* First U.S. paperback edition (as *Red Sky in Mourning: The True Story of a Woman's Courage and Survival at Sea*), Friday Harbor, Washington: Bright Works Publishing, 1988. First U.K. hardcover edition (as *Red Sky in Mourning: The True Story of a Woman's Courage and Survival at Sea*), London: Simon & Schuster, 2002. First U.S. hardcover edition, New York: Hyperion, 2002. First U.S. paperback edition, New York: Hyperion, 2003.

Bree, Marlin. *Wake of the Green Storm: A Survivor's Tale.* St. Paul, Minnesota: Marlor Press, 2001.

Caldwell, John. *Desperate Voyage.* First U.S. hardcover edition, Boston: Little, Brown, 1949. First U.K. hardcover edition, London: Gollancz, 1950. U.K. reissue with an introduction by Negley Farson, London: Gollancz, 1952. First U.K. paperback edition, London: Transworld Publishers, 1957. U.K. large print edition, Glenfield, U.K.: F. A. Thorpe, 1967. U.K. paperback reissue, London: Granada, 1985. U.K. paperback reissue, London: Adlard Coles Nautical, 1991. First U.S. paperback edition, Dobbs Ferry, New York: Sheridan House, 1991.

Carrier, Jim. *The Ship and the Storm: Hurricane Mitch and the Loss of the Fantome.* U.S. and U.K. hardcover edition, Camden, Maine, and London: International Marine, 2001. U.S. paperback edition, San Diego: Harcourt, 2002.

Chaplin, Gordon. *Dark Wind: A Survivor's Tale of Love and Loss.* U.S. hardcover edition, New York: Atlantic Monthly Press, 1999. U.K. paperback edition, London: Pan, 2000. U.S. paperback edition, New York: Plume, 2000.

Chiles, Webb. *The Open Boat: Across the Pacific.* New York: Norton, 1982.

Clayton, Lisa. *At the Mercy of the Sea: Her Single-Handed Non-Stop Journey Around the World.* U.K. hardcover edition, London: Orion, 1996. U.K. paperback edition, London: Orion, 1997.

Davison, Ann. *Last Voyage: An Autobiographical Account of All That Led Up to an Illicit Voyage and the Outcome Thereof.* First U.K. hardcover edition, London: Peter Davies, 1951. First U.S. hardcover edition, New York: Sloane, 1952. U.K. reissue, London: Heinemann, 1953. U.K. paperback reissue, London: Peter Davies, 1956. U.K. paperback reissue, London: Pan, 1956. U.K. paperback reissue, London: Grafton, 1988.

Guzzwell, John. *Trekka Round the World.* First U.K. hardcover edition, London: Adlard Coles, 1963. First U.S. hardcover edition, New York: de Graff, 1964. First U.S. paperback edition, New York: McKay, 1979. U.S. paperback edition with a foreword by Hal Roth, Bishop, California: Fine Edge Productions, 1999.

Hall, Jonathan. "Night Sail," unpublished, 2003.

Hemingway-Douglass, Réanne. *Cape Horn: One Man's Dream, One Woman's Nightmare.* First edition, Bishop, California: Fine Edge Productions, 1994. Second edition, Anacortes, Washington: Fine Edge.com, 2003.

Jones, Tristan. *Ice!* First U.S. hardcover edition, Kansas City: Sheed, Andrews & McMeel, 1978. First U.K. hardcover edition, London: Bodley Head, 1979. First U.K. paperback edition, London: Macdonald Futura, 1981. U.K. large-print edition, Leicester, U.K.: Charnwood, 1983. First U.S. paperback edition, Dobbs Ferry, New York: Sheridan House, 1995.

Klingel, Gilbert C. *Inagua: Which Is the Name of a Very Lonely and Nearly Forgotten Island.* First U.S. hardcover edition, New York: Dodd, Mead, 1940. First U.K. hardcover edition, London: R. Hale, 1942. First U.K. paperback edition (as *Inagua: A Very Lonely and Nearly Forgotten Island*), London: Readers Union, 1944. First U.S. paperback edition, New York: Lyons & Burford, 1997.

Leighton, Kim. *A Hard Chance: The Sydney-Hobart Race Disaster.* Minocqua, Wisconsin: Willow Creek Press, 1999.

Longo, Louise, with Marie-Thérèse Cuny. *Let Me Survive: A True Story.* Originally published as *Elle dort dans la mer* (Paris: Fixot, 1996). Translated into English by Alison Anderson. U.S. hardcover edition, Dobbs Ferry, New York: Sheridan House, 1996. U.S. mass market paperback, I Books, 2002.

Maury, Richard. *The Saga of Cimba.* First U.K. hardcover edition, London, Harrap & Co., 1939. First U.S. hardcover edition, New York: Harcourt,

Brace, 1939. U.K. reissue, London: Coles, 1971. U.S. reissue, Tuckahoe, New York: de Graff, 1973. U.S. hardcover reissue with an introduction by Jonathan Raban, Camden, Maine: International Marine, 2001. U.S. paperback reissue of 2001 International Marine edition, Camden, Maine: International Marine, 2003.

Robertson, Dougal. *Survive the Savage Sea.* First U.K. hardcover edition, London: Elek, 1973. First U.S. hardcover edition, New York: Praeger, 1973. U.S. large-print edition, Boston: G. K. Hall, 1974. First U.K. paperback edition, Harmondsworth, U.K.: Penguin, 1975. U.K. paperback reissue, London: Granada, 1984. First U.S. paperback edition, Dobbs Ferry, New York: Sheridan House, 1994.

Rousmaniere, John. *After the Storm: True Stories of Disaster and Recovery at Sea.* U.S. and U.K. hardcover edition, Camden, Maine, and London: International Marine, 2002. U.S. paperback edition, Camden, Maine: International Marine, 2004.

Severin, Tim. *The Brendan Voyage.* First U.K. hardcover edition, London: Hutchinson, 1978. First U.S. hardcover edition, New York: McGraw-Hill, 1978. First U.K. paperback edition, London: Arrow, 1979. First U.S. paperback edition, New York: Avon, 1979. U.K. paperback reissue, London: Arena, 1983. U.S. collector's edition, Norwalk, Connecticut: Easton Press, 1989. U.S. paperback reissue with an introduction by Malachy McCourt, New York: Modern Library, 2000.

Shapiro, Deborah, and Rolf Bjelke. *Time on Ice: A Winter Voyage to Antarctica [Vinterskepp].* First U.K. hardcover edition, Shrewsbury, U.K.: Waterline, 1997. First U.S. hardcover edition, Camden, Maine: International Marine, 1998. First U.S. paperback edition, Camden, Maine: International Marine, 2000.

sources

Many thanks to all the authors who allowed their work to be included here. I had the pleasure of hearing personally from many and getting to know some of them. Webb Chiles has gone back to sea, but eventually I reached him and heard back via e-mail during a stopover in South Africa. I learned from Marlin Bree about his continuing sailing adventures on the Great Lakes (for his other writings, see his Web site www.marlinbree.com). I met Jonathan Hall on a foggy beach in Maine when both our boats were on the hard; he's still writing the memoir from which his story here is taken and can be found sailing the coast of Maine or in a Castine pub. I met Réanne Hemingway-Douglass and Don Douglass while they were cruising through the lobstering harbor of Corea, Maine. Now in their seventies, they primarily cruise the Northwest and Alaska, areas about which they've written and published several cruising guides along with other sailing narratives (see their Web site www.fineedge.com). What a delightful and gracious couple! We drank blueberry wine and swapped sailing stories late into the day. In person Réanne is all we would expect from her Cape Horn narrative— self-aware, warmly emotional, reflective, and thoroughly human. Meeting her in person was the greatest validation of the authenticity of the woman we come to know so well in *Cape Horn: One Man's Dream, One Woman's Nightmare.*

I gratefully acknowledge the following authors and publishers who gave their permission to reprint excerpts from their works.

For a comprehensive list of editions of the books excerpted in this volume, see the bibliography.

Ashcraft, Tami Oldham, with Susea McGearhart. *Red Sky in Mourning: The True Story of a Woman's Courage and Survival at Sea.* Bright Works, 1988. From RED SKY IN MOURNING: A True Story of Love, Loss and Survival at Sea. Copyright © 2002 by Tami Oldham Ashcraft. Published by Hyperion.

Bree, Marlin. *Wake of the Green Storm: A Survivor's Tale.* Marlor Press, 2001. Reprinted with the permission of the author.

Caldwell, John. *Desperate Voyage.* Sheridan House, 1991. Reprinted with the permission of Sheridan House, Inc.

Carrier, Jim. *The Ship and the Storm: Hurricane Mitch and the Loss of the Fantome.* International Marine, 2001. Reprinted with the permission of International Marine and the author.

Chaplin, Gordon. *Dark Wind: A Survivor's Tale of Love and Loss.* Atlantic Monthly Press, 1999. From DARK WIND by Gordon Chaplin. Copyright © 1999 by Gordon Chaplin. Used by permission of Grove/Atlantic, Inc.

Chiles, Webb. *The Open Boat: Across the Pacific.* Norton, 1982. Reprinted with the permission of the author.

Clayton, Lisa. *At the Mercy of the Sea: Her Single-Handed Non-Stop Journey Around the World.* Orion, 1996. From AT THE MERCY OF THE SEA by Lisa Clayton. Reprinted with the permission of Orion Publishing Group Ltd.

Davison, Ann. *Last Voyage: An Autobiographical Account of All That Led Up to an Illicit Voyage and the Outcome Thereof.* Praeger, 1951. Reprinted with the permission of A. M. Heath & Co. Ltd.

Guzzwell, John. *Trekka Round the World.* Fine Edge Productions, 1999. Reprinted with the permission of Fine Edge Productions, LLC.

Hall, Jonathan. "Night Sail," unpublished, 2003. Used with the permission of the author.

Hemingway-Douglass, Réanne. *Cape Horn: One Man's Dream, One Woman's Nightmare.* Fine Edge Productions, 1994. Reprinted with the permission of the author.

Jones, Tristan. *Ice!* Sheridan House, 1995. Reprinted with the permission of Sheridan House, Inc.

Klingel, Gilbert C. *Inagua: Which Is the Name of a Very Lonely and Nearly Forgotten Island.* Lyons & Burford, 1997. Reprinted with the permission of The Lyons Press.

Leighton, Kim. *A Hard Chance: The Sydney-Hobart Race Disaster.* Willow Creek Press, 1999. Reprinted with the permission of Willow Creek Press.

Longo, Louise, with Marie-Thérèse Cuny. *Let Me Survive: A True Story.* Sheridan House, 1996. Excerpt from "Let Me Survive" by Louise Longo. Translation copyright 1996 by Sheridan House. Reprinted by permission of Sheridan House, Inc.

Maury, Richard. *The Saga of Cimba.* International Marine, 2001. Reprinted with the permission of Huntly Maury.

Robertson, Dougal. *Survive the Savage Sea.* Sheridan House, 1994. Reprinted with the permission of Sheridan House, Inc.

Rousmaniere, John. *After the Storm: True Stories of Disaster and Recovery at Sea.* International Marine, 2002. Reprinted with the permission of International Marine and the author.

Severin, Tim. *The Brendan Voyage.* McGraw-Hill, 1978. Reprinted with the permission of A. M. Heath & Co. Ltd. (London) and the Henry Dunow Literary Agency (New York).

Shapiro, Deborah, and Rolf Bjelke. *Time on Ice: A Winter Voyage to Antarctica.* International Marine, 1998. Reprinted with the permission of International Marine and the authors.